Hang on and Fly

Hang on and Fly

A Post-War Story of Plane Crash Tragedies, Heroism, and Survival.

TIM LAKE

LAKE PUBLISHING

Hang on and Fly
2015 Lake Publishing
Copyright 2015 by Timothy W. Lake
All rights reserved

Published in the United States by Lake Publishing

LIBRARY OF CONGRESS CATALOGING-IN-PUBLICATION DATA
Lake, Tim
Hang on and Fly: A Post-War Story of Plane Crash Tragedies, Heroism, and Survival/Tim Lake

Hardcover ISBN 978-0-9967360-2-2
Softcover ISBN 978-0-9967360-0-8
E-Book ISBN 978-0-9967360-1-5

1. United States Aviation, 1938 – 1952. 2. World War, 1939 – 1945 – C-46 Airplane – The Hump – Korean War, 1950-1953 - Pilots and Surplus Airplanes. 3. Nonscheduled Airlines - Continental Charters, 1946 – 1952 – Civil Aeronautics Board – Civil Aeronautics Authority – Passenger Plane Crashes – United States 1945 – 1952. 4. Curtiss-Wright Corporation – C-46 Commando– Buffalo – Pittsburgh – Miami - Newark Airport – Cattaraugus County, New York. 5. Harry S. Truman – Donald W. Nyrop. 6. Aircraft Accident Investigations - Aviation Safety Regulations - United States.

Cover design by Renee Barratt
Book design by Maureen Cutajar

For more information or bulk orders:
www.TimLakeBooks.com

*For my late grandfather, David G. Shenefiel,
and Randall G. Shenefiel, without whose tip I would not
have known about this incredible story.*

**Lt. Col. Thomas Budrejko,
United States Marine Corps**

In memory of: Lt. Col. Thomas Budrejko. 1974 – 2012.
Executive Officer, Marine Light Attack Helicopter Squadron 469,
United States Marine Corps.

Lt. Col. Budrejko was one of seven Marines killed when two helicopters collided during a training exercise on February 22, 2012, near Yuma, Arizona.

A loving father, husband, brother, and son, Lt. Col. Budrejko was a veteran combat pilot of Cobra helicopters with three tours in Iraq and one each in Afghanistan and Kosovo. During the Iraq War, when his chopper was hit by enemy gunfire on March 23, 2003, a special fuel safety control system designed for the Cobra saved his life. Lt. Budrejko's father, Commander Donald Budrejko, a retired U.S. Navy aviator, served as project manager for the Cobra's JFC-78 Fuel Control Safety System at Hamilton Standard, a division of United Technologies.

CDR Donald Budrejko USNR (Ret.), served as a researcher and consultant for this book.

TABLE OF CONTENTS

	Preface	1
1	Pearl and Ruby	10
2	"Get That Plane in the Air"	34
3	George Albert	47
4	Cursing at the Cockpit Door	57
5	Silent Night, Silent Crash	65
6	Searching and Waiting	69
7	"They're Never Going to Find Us"	81
8	Thief	98
9	Trust the Pilots	100
10	"Go Down, Never Up"	136
11	Diagnosis Interrupted	148
12	"Christmas Is Over, Huh, Lady"	155
13	Ride Down the Mountain	166
14	Big Story	187
15	Deadly Nonskeds	208
16	First Cab Chief on the Scene	226

17	Elizabeth	239
18	Whitecaps on the Water	254
19	Truman and Safer Planes	270
20	Elizabeth II	284
21	Hollywood	328
22	Souvenirs and Broken Families	333
	Epilogue	349
	Notes	360
	Acknowledgments	392
	Bibliography	401
	Illustration Credits	403

"Now you've made your very last flight. Your plane vanished on a cold, dark night. But, wherever you are tonight, my own, you'll know that in memories, I'm not alone."

—Evelyn Harris, wife of C-46 pilot,
Victor Harris. January 17, 1952

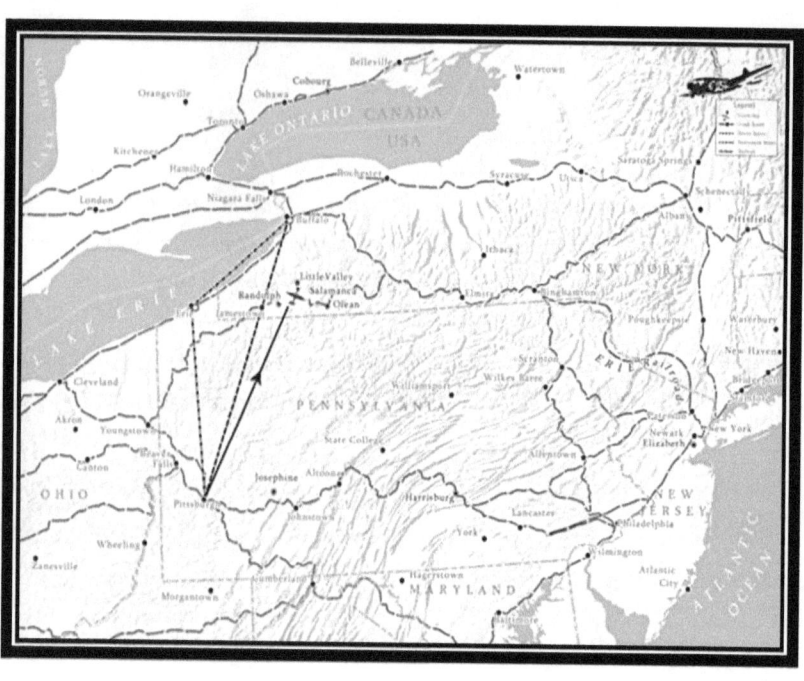

PREFACE

FINALLY, THERE IT WAS. The gleaming wreckage of one of the largest passenger planes in the world, whose disappearance had confounded searchers and the chairman of the Civil Aeronautics Board (CAB) for three days and two nights. It lay sprawled over nearly a thousand feet in the snow-covered hills of the Allegheny Plateau in western New York State. The bright aluminum fuselage sparkled among the leafless brown trees in the morning sun, the first rays to pierce the fog and clouds that hid the wreck from searchers for more than 40 hours. The crash meant a crushing death for 26 people, and it was a miracle of survival for 14 others. For miles around the crash site, there were mountains, snow and forest, and, fortunately, a farmhouse. The wreckage was nearly at the top of a long flat ridge with steep slopes on each side. From the path of splintered branches, it looked like the plane simply flew into the side of the mountain. Pushing his cheek up close against the window of the CAB's DC-3 while his pilots banked the plane for a better view of the wreckage below, the nation's top airplane crash investigator could see a dark and muddy path leading from the main wreckage to what appeared to be a campsite in the woods. So that's where they huddled, CAB Chairman Donald Nyrop and his assistants in the plane would have thought to themselves, injured, alone and desperate until one of the crash survivors bravely walked from the ridge to find help. From hundreds of feet in the air, Nyrop and the CAB crash experts could verify that one direction down the ridge into a narrow valley led to civilization while the other was a forest as far as their eyes could see. How fortunate that the survivor had walked in the right direction.

The DC-3 from Washington circled the wreck a few more times and then headed back southeast to land at the nearest airport. Soon, Nyrop would be among the many officials and local volunteers crawling around the crash scene trying to remove the last few bodies still in the plane, pilots whose critical mistakes forever changed civilian passenger aviation in America. This single monumental crash would further echo through future decades of airline passenger safety rules and regulations and shape beliefs and behavior among skittish passengers for years to come. And yet, despite its precedent-setting events, this dramatic crash and the lost wreckage with American survivors trapped on the mountain has been nearly forgotten in modern aviation history.

On New Year's Day, 1952, following the most devastating and deadly year for plane crashes in North America, the CAB investigators on board the DC-3 were taking their leader to his first plane crash scene. At no other time in the history of aviation had America's top plane crash investigator personally visited the scene of a commercial passenger plane crash. Re-appointed to his position by the President only five days earlier, he was the whip in a political clash between existing and emerging modes of public transportation in the United States. And, the new method of travel wasn't going so well. In the closing hours of 1951, Americans justifiably feared for their lives in passenger airplanes as the large twin and four engine propeller airplanes rapidly began replacing trains for long distance travel.[1] A CAB chairman's first visit to a crash scene would be a public demonstration of support for the fledgling American passenger airlines industry. Acting upon implied orders from the White House to stop the crash carnage and restore public confidence in air travel, it was also designed to calm fears. This precedent-setting visit was about to change the course of American aviation, to make everyone who stepped aboard an airplane, safer.

While the CAB plane glided into a small Pennsylvania airport nearest

---

[1] 1951 was the most significant year in passenger aviation history in the United States. For the first time, in 1951, air passenger-miles (10.6 million) had overtaken train passenger-miles (10.2 million). Part of this changeover in travel habits was caused by the instant popularity of the cheap fares on the non-scheduled airlines, the first budget airlines of North America.

the crash scene, Stewardess Pearl Ruth Moon lay on her back in a hospital bed in the small but renowned railroad city of Salamanca, New York. She looked pathetic. Cuts and contusions on her face had turned to black and blue with one of them curving downward from the corner of her right eye to resemble a large teardrop. Her head and back ached every time she shifted in her bed. But, she was alive, one of only 14 survivors out of 40 people on the plane. The others were crushed, impaled, or decapitated to their deaths. Pearl was also overcome with sadness like she had never felt before. After the crash, she held a baby girl in her arms until she died. Pearl cried tears of pain, sorrow, and failure. It was the worst time of her young professional life.

Like all but one of the survivors, Pearl had been sitting in the back of the plane. Their fortunate circumstance was the origin of a perception that is still popular today. Their survival led Americans always to believe that passengers are safest in the back of the plane. Already, their story was flashed around the world as the mysterious disappearance of a nearly full passenger plane that couldn't be found. The massive plane was lost, despite an aerial, land, and water search by hundreds of American and Canadian military forces, police officers, and volunteers covering an area from Cleveland to Syracuse and Pittsburgh to Toronto. It was an epic story that captivated flight-eager Americans, and the front page headlines would continue for several more days.

Moving away from their wrecked plane until they could no longer hear the crying and helpless passengers trapped inside, Pearl and the other survivors managed to build a smoky and ineffective campfire, and lift their spirits with Bible verses and Christmas carols for more than 40 hours. During their wait, one of them committed a criminal and despicable act upon the dead. It was the only reprehensible deed among so many acts of valor and heroism. Finally, at the end of their desperation, and giving up hope of rescue, they heard a train whistle in the valley below. Pearl wrapped a passenger's feet with strips of clothing from the dead and sent him walking off down the snow-covered mountain to find help. Their story would shock the nation, already numb from plane after plane, crash after crash, killing hundreds of travelers and innocent people on the ground all through 1951.

The wreckage, that Donald Nyrop had come to see killed four pilots, one stewardess, and 21 passengers. Pearl and the other lucky ones were the largest group of airplane crash survivors to be stranded for an extended period of time in North America without rescue and remained as such in 2015. In fact, it was the most spectacular stranding of a large group of passenger plane crash survivors until it was eclipsed by the Uruguayan rugby team crash survivors in the Andes Mountains 20 years later. Similar to the rugby players' famous story, *Alive*, from 1972, it took a brave passenger hero with help from a simple farm housewife guarding her own deadly secret to tell the world they were still alive. Their plight reached all the way to the White House.

The disappearance of the passenger converted C-46 cargo airplane also ended an embarrassing year for the CAB, the federal agency that later became the National Transportation Safety Board (NTSB). Twenty-nine passenger planes crashed in 1951, killing 367 people, right up to the final day, December 31. Imagine that happening today?[2] The causes of these horrific disasters, especially among the cut-rate, upstart non-scheduled airlines, the first budget airlines of North America, were everything from poor pilot training and foolish navigation decisions, to engine failure, bad weather, poor maintenance, running out of fuel and lax enforcement of air safety regulations by federal agencies. Now, as the 39-year-old CAB chairman prepared for landing in his DC-3, Donald Nyrop knew that his next task, ordered straight from the President, was to clean up the sloppy, irreverent, and deadly airline industry in America. With his boots and warm parka beside him in the plane, Nyrop was about to make history too. Within an hour of landing and then driving and hiking the small mountain ridge through mud and snow, Nyrop would become celebrated as the first CAB chairman to visit the scene of a commercial airliner crash. Afterward, without the standard public hearings and input from the airline owners, he would set the wheels in motion to impose sweeping new federal safety guidelines for the airline

---

[2] Passenger planes of 1951 typically held no more than 50 passengers and often carried far fewer. The events of 1951 would be the equivalent of two to three 737s, each filled with more than 100 passengers, crashing every month in 2015.

industry that we all take for granted today. But, they wouldn't be soon enough.

Within weeks of this most dramatic airplane disappearance, crash, and rescue of passengers in the mountains of western New York State, more loaded passenger planes would fall from the sky killing both ordinary Americans and a VIP with close ties to the President. Shock and then outrage from these crashes would lead to the four-month-long closing of one of the nation's busiest airports and inspire new airport designs and regulations still used today.

In *Hang on and Fly*, there are graphic details about the victims and survivors of this astounding repetition of crashes, sometimes three and four per month.³ Some of them are derived from extremely graphic newspaper articles and photographs, and federal documents while others are from long hidden and unpublished photographs entrusted to me as a veteran journalist with a close family connection to the community where the most astounding crash occurred. While these grisly descriptions may not be for the squeamish, they help explain why there was so much panic and fear among many Americans in 1951, most of whom had never flown in an airplane because of the enormous cost, but who were eager to try this relatively new and exciting mode of public transportation. Before 1951, most people were traveling domestically for business and pleasure by trains. While the incredible crashes of 1951 scared them, it didn't stop the dramatic changeover in travel habits. It was the pivotal year when the majority of travelers switched over from trains to airplanes. In 2015, U.S. airlines were carrying a record 848.1 million passengers.⁴ Most didn't give safety a second thought but if you asked them, they would say they believed they were safest in the back of the plane. In this book, I advance the theory that the public perception that passengers are safest in the back

---

³ *Hang on and Fly* is taken from a line in the 1954 John Wayne movie, *The High and the Mighty*, with permission. A slightly different phrase is included in the novel of the same name, by the author, Ernest K. Gann, whose estate also approved the use of the phrase.
⁴ 2014 Department of Transportation, Bureau of Transportation U.S.-Based Airline Traffic Data, March 26, 2015. By 2027, the number is expected to reach One Billion.

of a plane began with the incredible disaster in the remote hills of Napoli, New York on December 29, 1951.

Additionally, this book describes the coming-of-age for modern airplane crash investigations which we follow closely today through instant Tweets and Instagram postings from witnesses, survivors, and investigators. When Donald Nyrop, the young and energetic chairman of the CAB, walked up Napoli's Bucktooth Ridge to see the wreckage of Flight 44-2 on New Year's Day 1952, the pilots' bodies were still in the crushed cockpit. Today, the NTSB chairperson doesn't appear on the scene of a major commercial airplane crash quite so rapidly, but he or she is usually there within a few days, and the visit typically has a calming effect on flyer's nerves. Additionally, after the dramatic crashes of 1951 and early 1952, no longer would local residents be allowed to traipse through the wreckage, hauling victims and survivors on toboggans and homemade trailers, gawking at bloodied and mangled bodies and body parts, or collecting souvenirs from the dead and the wreckage. From 1952 on, all crash scenes would be more carefully secured, protected, and investigated only by special teams of the CAB (and later, NTSB) professionals.

My initial interest in researching this forgotten story began in 2008 when I learned that my deceased grandfather, David G. Shenefiel, had been called by the sheriff of Cattaraugus County, New York to help cut a path up Bucktooth Ridge to rescue the survivors and carry out the dead. My grandfather was the superintendent of highways for the sparse farm family-populated Town of Napoli in 1951. He organized his small crew to plow and sand the only road near the crash scene so rescuers could get through and to use a front-end loader to clear a path through the woods. From his small contribution to the rescue, the story grew from my naturally inquisitive nature developed and honed over 30 years as a news reporter covering a few plane crashes.

The first airplane crash I covered was on December 6, 1984, near Charleston, South Carolina when State Senator Paul Cantrell, Jr. flew his twin-engine Beechcraft prop plane into a wooded plantation near the Charleston Executive Airport on Johns Island. Arriving at the scene for WCSC-TV with a photographer soon after the wreckage was found, it was so foggy we couldn't see a hundred feet in front of our news vehicle.

We couldn't even get close to the scene of the crash. Senator Cantrell made four attempts to land in the fog at the Charleston International Airport that morning before his fifth attempt to land at the much smaller Johns Island Executive Airport. The crash and fire in the plane killed him instantly. It was a rude awakening for me, at 24 and a reporter for only a few years, to realize how quickly a pilot could get into trouble when encountering fog.

Another plane accident that I covered as a reporter was the crash of Delta Airlines Flight 1141 on takeoff from Dallas-Fort Worth International Airport on August 31, 1988. In the crash of the Boeing 727, caused by the pilots' failure to set the wing flaps and slats, and a malfunctioning warning system, 12 passengers, and two crew members were killed. Standing in the designated news media position on the airport perimeter along with my KPRC-TV satellite technical crew of Billy Carter and Johnny Ottea, and renowned NBC News aviation correspondent Robert Hager and several other journalists, we got to experience, at close proximity, the take-off of a supersonic Concorde jet nearly above our heads. It was one of the most amazing thrills of my life. Having seen that event so closely, it's difficult to imagine the sight of another Concorde lift-off in 2000 that ended in disaster when the world's fastest passenger jet caught fire and crashed near Charles de Gaulle International Airport in Paris, France. That crash killed everyone on board, four on the ground, and contributed to the end of supersonic passenger flight with the Concorde.

A very unusual crash I covered happened on September 13, 1991, when a Continental Express twin-engine turboprop plane fell burning from the sky into a soybean field about 75 miles south of Houston, near Eagle Lake, Texas. Speeding at more than 100 miles per hour to the scene in a news vehicle with photographer John Steiger driving, we were pulled over by a Texas Highway Patrol officer. When told where we were going at illegal speed, the officer promptly got in front of us, with lights flashing and escorted us to the crash. Upon arrival, with only a few local firefighters on the scene, one of the first things we noticed was a large piece of the plane in the soybean field about 200 yards away from the main wreckage of the Embraer 120 Brasilia turboprop. In my live report that evening for KPRC about the crash that killed all 14 people on board, I detailed the widely separated pieces of wreckage. It was unusual and provided evidence of possible break-up of the plane while in flight. It was difficult to focus because five helicopters were circling in the air above me, including one piloted by my close friend, Rod Hooks, feeding the live TV signal back to Houston in a microwave bounce from his chopper.[5] Called within hours of the crash, the theory of in-flight break-up proved to be correct when investigators later determined that a maintenance inspector failed to reinstall 11 screws in the leading edge assembly of the left horizontal stabilizer before sending the commuter plane back into service. The leading edge ripped off, and the stabilizer broke off when the plane reached 260 knots while descending. It caused complete loss of control and fire. All the passengers were found without their seat belts fastened indicating they fled their seats to escape the fire. The incredible negative G-forces probably knocked them unconscious before the plane slammed into the ground.[6] Inadequate federal regulations to monitor the activities of airplane maintenance workers during shift changes were also cited as a contributing cause of the crash. What I didn't know and was not able to report at the time was that $500,000 worth of diamonds was in a passenger's briefcase in the charred wreckage. The diamonds easily withstood the heat. They were recovered by the FBI.

These three crashes left an indelible imprint on my mind because my reporter credentials allowed me to get so close to the wreckage of each one. They were all examples of the primary causes of airplane crashes in 1951 and through all the decades up to today; bad weather, pilot error, and poor judgment, poor or improper maintenance of airplanes, and lax or inadequate oversight by federal regulators.

Today, when a plane crashes in North America we know about it within seconds and, except for rare occasions, modern technology can

---

[5] Rodney J. Hooks was a helicopter pilot for KPRC-TV for many years. He was one of the most safety-conscious pilots with whom I ever flew. A Vietnam War Veteran Huey chopper pilot known during the war in 1969-70 as "Gunslinger 30," Hooks was also an avid show horseman in Texas. He died in a tragic carbon monoxide poisoning accident while sleeping in a horse trailer-camper at the Houston Livestock Show and Rodeo in 2001.

[6] These findings and the theory are from the official NTSB crash investigation report.

find it within minutes. The crash of Asiana Airlines Flight 214 at San Francisco International Airport on July 6, 2013, proved that with instantaneous Tweets from Twitter accounts. And, the Germanwings Airbus 320 flight that crashed into the French Alps on March 24, 2015, was monitored live on the Internet until it simply disappeared, the exact location known immediately. Of the small, rural community there, a Germanwings official said it was changed forever. He's correct. In January 1952, thousands of people trekked to the top of Bucktooth Ridge as a mob just to see the most infamous passenger plane crash in American history. They looted the wreckage and reaped financial rewards from dead passengers. Generations of local families have passed down the dramatic stories of fear, death and destruction, heroism and survival, and the worst of human nature in a tragic calamity. More than 60 years after the C-46 loaded with passengers crashed into the small, rural mountainous community of Napoli, people still drive up the narrow hollow at Sawmill Run and traipse through the woods searching for the crash scene. Yes, the community was changed forever.

Imagine if a loaded passenger plane flying today between two major cities in the United States simply disappeared and nobody could find it? It happened, after a devastating year and a deadly month of plane crashes, in the final hours of December 1951.

CHAPTER 1

PEARL AND RUBY

BEFORE TAKING OFF THE pilots made a critical mistake. Their error flashed into the cockpit of their C-46 passenger plane every few seconds as a constant reminder. Small mountains of the Allegheny Plateau rose up in front of them where they believed there were none. Pulling the yoke to rise over each crest returned them to thicker fog aloft, so they were forced to descend rapidly to where their aviation lights reflected off the ground and lit up their cockpit like a war-time synchronized searchlight. That's where they could see. They were in trouble, flying too low in what was billed just a few years earlier as the largest airplane in the world. Together, they struggled with split-second decisions. Up for clearance; down to see. It went on for minutes; precious minutes as the pilots, no doubt, were thinking about their even more precious passengers, the men, women, and children they had quickly hustled aboard in an attempt to make up for lost time. They were flying only a short trip from Pittsburgh to Buffalo in the final days of 1951, but a series of miscalculations and poor judgment piled up before their most critical mistake. Now, there was too little time or fuel to make corrections. With just 18 nautical miles remaining in their flight, soon they had to find the airport for landing.

HANG ON AND FLY

In the cabin, stewardess Pearl Ruth Moon sensed their predicament. She bent down to look through the window of their jouncing airplane and saw the reflection of blinking lights on the hilly, snow-covered forest below. It meant only one thing. They were extremely low. Expertly planting her feet and gripping the curved handles on the backs of the passenger seats, Pearl's lean body stiffened with a flood of anxiety while she steadied herself for a moment in the cabin's wide aisle, and then she quickly smiled, masking her fear. However, it was too late. Some of the passengers noticed. Fear and stiffening crept into their bodies too. In another few minutes, their routine flight, hurtling through winter rain and fog at the end of a long year of many catastrophic plane crashes, would simply disappear and become the most sensational missing airplane passenger mystery in North America.

It was approaching midnight on December 29, 1951, over northwestern Pennsylvania, as Pearl tried to hide her distress. The passengers scrutinized her every move, fully aware that several crashing planes that month alone had littered wreckage and bodies and produced banner headlines. Crashing planes so plagued the first budget airlines of America all through 1951 that only the daring, frugal, or uninformed got on board. Perhaps they were flying too low, Pearl thought. It felt like the plane was much lower than she ever remembered flying on a night-time run from the Pittsburgh airport. The huge twin-engine C-46 propeller plane, nearly filled with 33 passengers and a reserve crew, was running bumpy, but otherwise in level flight, so Pearl shrugged off her worries and continued her duties. She didn't know their airplane was the only one that departed Pittsburgh that night on a visual flight plan. Because of poor weather, including heavy fog, all others had chosen to fly using instruments. It was the pilots' critical mistake.

The newest plane in her company's small fleet, with its vast main cabin formerly used to carry cargo and troops during World War II, was lined with three rows of seats separated by the aisle.[7] Seventeen men and 21 women and children were scattered about the cabin, with several

---

[7] The plane was new to Pearl's airline but it was a used C-46 cargo and transport plane left over from World War II.

seats remaining empty. The aluminum ribs of the fuselage were exposed to the passengers and without the luxuriously insulated interior of a Pan Am or American Airlines plane, the cabin noise from the two giant engines was deafening but melodious and soothing. Some of the passengers had removed their shoes, cuddled into pillows and blankets, and had fallen asleep to the thrumming engines, but others appeared to notice angst in Pearl's expression. She knew they had also seen the reflection of their lights on the ground. She sensed their fear, but she knew she could not show hers. She tried to maintain composure in her comfortable work shoes and her form-fitting gray and blue stewardess dress uniform. She padded on down the aisle. Like the passengers, Pearl placed her confidence in the pilots.

Then, the plane began heaving. Sleeping passengers burst awake. Stomachs churned. The children slid out of their straps and stood in their seats. Panic-stricken faces turned to Pearl in near unison. She could almost feel the passengers' eyes fixed on her for a signal. What was wrong, they were demanding without uttering the words. Seeing the expressionless mask on Pearl's face, the passengers turned to look for an answer from outside their windows. Flying through the night at more than 150 miles per hour, they saw nothing but darkness.

At 24, Pearl was already a veteran stewardess. Bouncing planes were nothing new to her. But, this time it felt different. The plane kept scooping down and then back up as if on a roller coaster track. Pearl knew the passengers recognized that something was wrong, but she tried to maintain a calm demeanor. If she appeared scared, the passengers would get scared too. She remembered from her training; passengers weren't supposed to get scared.

Pearl was home-based in Miami Springs, a modern residential development of small ranch homes and apartments built by Glenn Curtiss, the famous aviator whose company also built the C-46 airplanes in which she often worked. Her home was among clusters of Florida style houses that were part of emerging modern America following World War II. Her airline was also part of this modernity, as airplanes gradually began overtaking trains for passenger travel. Pearl was living a progressive lifestyle near Miami International Airport, taking regular trips throughout the Caribbean, Central and South America and, more recently, to Pennsylvania and New York State for her airline, Continental Charters.[8] Pearl jumped at the chance to become a stewardess on the upstart airline that was given birth by the abundant supply of cheap war surplus airplanes and pilots, and lax federal regulations on passenger air travel. It was also an exciting time to be working in aviation. To Pearl, it seemed like every other man she knew was a war veteran pilot and they all wanted to be captains. Like many of the other single stewardesses, Pearl was dating a few pilots. She knew that many of them were flying with hefty distractions from turmoil in their personal lives at home. Initially chosen for her attractive appearance, including her perfectly-coiffed hair, slender, athletic body, wide toothy smile, flirtatious personal style, and waitressing abilities, she excelled at her new job and quickly proved her value to Continental Charters, a small, nonscheduled airline with a few airplanes, based in Miami.[9] Pearl knew how to get passengers moving rapidly from the airport terminals into the planes and settled into their seats which helped get the planes into the air faster. Her exciting career in rapidly sprawling and cosmopolitan Miami was a drastic change from her rural childhood in tiny Franklinville, North Carolina. Born on February 25, 1927, parents Walter and Ina Moon raised Pearl with four sisters. Growing up with all-sister siblings gave Pearl confidence that women could do anything. In the airplane cabin, she was in charge. The pilots were the commanders while flying the plane, but the passengers' lives were in her hands too, and she felt a heavy responsibility to keep them safe. Up and down they went in a nauseating teeter-totter motion. Pearl could take it, but some of the passengers felt sick.

Working for a nonsked, as the budget airlines were recently nicknamed, meant that Pearl didn't have a schedule either. The nonskeds were the first low-cost, no-frills airlines of passenger aviation in North America. They catered to long distance traveling customers who couldn't afford the major airlines and who didn't have time or patience

---

[8] Continental Charters was not connected to Continental Airlines.
[9] Nonscheduled and irregular were used interchangeably to describe the first budget airlines of North America.

for the train. Because nonskeds didn't publish a regular flight schedule and flew only when full, they didn't have to follow many of the intricate rules and regulations imposed upon the majors. It was believed that nonskeds hired pilots and maintenance crews who didn't have the experience or training of those who worked for the majors. Additionally, nonskeds typically flew cheap used cargo airplanes such as the Curtiss C-46. In 1951, this had developed into a serious problem. Passenger planes, many of them nonskeds were crashing several times a month, and it made travelers jittery. Pearl quickly learned how to hide her fear on a scary ride and to be her airline's safety ambassador.

Only 13 days earlier, the most catastrophic crash of the year claimed 56 lives when a Miami Airlines nonsked C-46 crashed into a river in Elizabeth, New Jersey. It had taken off from Newark Airport for Tampa and Miami and was trying to get back to Newark after losing power in one engine. Pearl and her crew were shaken by the crash. They often saw the Miami Airlines planes and crew members at the airport as they shuttled to and from work. Then, days later, on December 20, a Robin Airlines nonsked C-46 got lost in a snowstorm while hopscotching from California to New Jersey. Low on fuel, the pilot dropped out of the clouds to find Newark Airport. Seeing whitecaps on the water and believing he was over the Atlantic Ocean, the pilot performed a miracle crash-landing when the C-46 ran out of gas. The huge plane full of passengers plowed into a farmer's snow-filled pasture – on the Canadian side of Lake Ontario. It was 200 miles off course and 300 miles from Newark. To some it was comical – a photograph showed a trail of Southern California passengers stomping through the snow on the Canadian dairy farm. Nobody was hurt, but it further jarred North Americans into a panic over the mere thought of flying on a deadly nonsked.

Pearl was reminded of the many crashes of 1951 as she arrived for work in Miami and saw the nonsked C-46's lined up with their tails at the terminal doors waiting to board passengers. The blazing headlines in newspapers she brought along for passengers were inescapable even as she climbed the ladder to board her airplane on the morning of December 29. It was a nonsked, a war surplus C-46, and both the inexperienced pilots were severely distracted by marital infidelity. Unknown to Pearl and the passengers, they had lost their heading in the winter darkness over Pennsylvania while cruising onward toward Buffalo, just a few hundred feet above the ground. They were miles off course and headed for disaster.

Pearl joined Continental Charters in August 1950 following a job as a hotel lounge waitress when the airline had an office in Greensboro. Pleased with her work performance, the airline elevated Pearl to senior stewardess in July 1951. She enjoyed her head stewardess job but when things went wrong, like on this much-delayed trip into the cold northern climate, it made her eager to get back to the warmth of South Florida. On her final run of a long shift in the waning days of the year, after the next stop when she went off-duty, Pearl hoped to relax in a passenger seat and perhaps catch some sleep during the overnight flight home to Miami. The crew change would happen soon. They were minutes away from Buffalo.

Several hours late taking off from Pittsburgh's Allegheny County Airport for the second leg of their flight, Pearl recounted the dramatic and confusing events of the day. Continental Charters Flight 44-2 departed Miami for the round-trip to Pittsburgh and Buffalo more than five hours late because of mechanical problems that she didn't understand. The pilot didn't give her many details, either. The plane was so late that passengers waiting to board in Pittsburgh for the return flight to Miami believed the plane had already completed its northern-most stop in Buffalo. It hadn't. Some of them weren't even told. With the image of warm, sunny Florida in their minds, they were heading to cold, snowy Buffalo.

As senior stewardess and one of seven crew members aboard, Pearl was given terse instructions from the captain while at the terminal to "load all the passengers on the plane now." They would skip their scheduled stop in Pittsburgh on their southbound run back to Miami. She rounded up all the passengers and got them on the plane. Pearl tried to explain to as many of them as she could that they would stop in Buffalo before heading south. She missed more than a few. Pearl's co-stewardess, 22-year-old Delores Harvey, on the job for Continental Charters only a few weeks, followed her lead and helped get the passengers buckled into their seats. Moments later, Pearl and one of the two reserve pilots on the flight swung the cabin door closed on the tail of the plane and with the sharp four-bladed props twirling, the C-46 swiveled away from the Art Deco terminal and taxied to the runway.[10] The passengers were pushed back into their seats as the nose of the plane pointed upward like a carnival ride. Only when they developed speed along the runway would the plane have enough thrust to lift its tail and level off.

In Pittsburgh on the night of December 29, the air was cold, there was snow on the ground, and it was misty at the airport, even raining north of the city in small Pennsylvania communities such as Butler, Sarver, and Kittanning. Despite a low ceiling, the pilots had more than adequate visibility to see well ahead of the runway when taking off. Unknown to passengers, the pilots were in a hurry. Although warned against it, they decided to fly visually into some of the worst weather in northwestern Pennsylvania and western New York State in the final days of the year. In the forest and farmlands along their route near Lake Erie, up to four feet of snow lay on the ground, mostly in the deep, narrow mountain hollows. The thick white blanket reflected even the smallest amount of light.

Flight time from Pittsburgh to Buffalo in the C-46 was just under an hour. At departure time, Pearl decided to hold off on cabin service for the passengers because it appeared that most of them were preparing to sleep. As she poured fresh coffee for the pilots, she noticed that a few passengers were trading seats. Passenger George Albert, a 30-year-old Miami restaurant owner, gave up his seat in the front of the plane to his 46-year-old mother, Elizabeth, because she was cold. George wanted her to be comfortable, warm, and to enjoy the view when they arrived in Miami early the next morning. Pointing to his assigned seat, George said, "Sit here, mom, it's a good seat." He then moved to the back of the plane where he found an empty seat.[11] Reserve co-pilot, Gus Athas, who

---

[10] The classic West Mifflin, Pa terminal is still in use although passenger aviation was moved to Greater Pittsburgh Airport (Pittsburgh International) in 1952.
[11] This is from George Albert's first person account of how they boarded the plane. It's presumed the seat was in the single row of seats on the right side of the front of the plane. George took a seat in the rear of the double row aisle on the left side of the plane and near the main passenger loading door.

at 25 was the youngest among the pilots, gave up his seat in the rear of the plane to Eva Woodward, 62, traveling with her bull terrier dog. Athas moved to the front and took Woodward's seat next to his reserve pilot partner, CJ Webber, affectionately nicknamed by the crew as "the old man." Webber had gray at his temples, but he was only 38. Athas and Webber had little toddlers at home in Florida.

Two of three young children on board had their own seats, so Pearl took a few extra moments to make sure they were secured in their seat belts. As the C-46 bumped along the taxiway to the head of the runway, Pearl finally strapped into her own seat in the tail of the plane next to reserve stewardess Dolores Jean Beshears, 21, on the job just four months. Beshears was scheduled to take Pearl's place as the lead stewardess on the next and final run to Miami. Pearl enjoyed takeoffs. It gave her a moment to relax.[12]

Sitting directly in front of them were George Albert, a former World War II Army sergeant who spent Christmas at his family's home in Josephine, Pennsylvania, and Navy Lt. William W. Bischof, a Johnstown, Pennsylvania man returning to his base at the U.S. Naval Air Station in Key West, Florida. Lt. Bischof spent the holidays at home visiting his wife and new baby boy. Both military veterans displayed gentlemanly gestures and comments while boarding and they gave Pearl extra confidence that this would be a comfortable and routine flight. They settled into their seats with a view of the entire cabin in front of them.

In another minute the powerful piston engines of the C-46 were pulling it gently into the rainy night air, westerly into the wind from the airport's longest runway. Checking her watch, Pearl noted that it was 9:47 pm. There was a chill on board because air speed and pressure were needed for the cabin heaters to circulate their warmth fully. It made Pearl think again about home. She realized by the time on her watch that they should have been nearly arriving in tropical Miami by now. Instead, they were headed into more cold and snow.

Continental Charters Flight 44-2 flowed first into the western night

---

[12] Despite Beshears' off-duty status, she still helped out with the passengers before taking her seat and during the bumpy flight.

sky away from Allegheny County Airport, south of the Pittsburgh skyline. Because of the weather there were only a few moments to view the dim lights of the skyscrapers and the brighter lights and flare stack fires from the region's oil refineries and many steel mills. The 44-story Gulf Tower was visible along with the new William Penn Place, slightly shorter but so modern. Forbes Field, home of the Steelers and the Pirates, in Pittsburgh's Oakland neighborhood, was probably not visible. The city's mighty bridges, including the newly built Rankin Bridge over the Monongahela River, and the Three Sisters bridges over the Allegheny River would have been easily seen by passengers looking through the few windows of the plane. A trained eye might have been able to see the new Greater Pittsburgh Airport as the plane flew nearly over it. The new airfield was still under construction and opening in a few months with a larger and more elaborate weather service, flight planning facility, and control center for pilots than what was offered at Allegheny County Airport. Banking right, Flight 44-2 began its visual heading for the northeast. Their view didn't last. Clouds were aloft. They would force the pilots to fly low to the ground.

The gleaming C-46 military surplus cargo plane floated through the sky appearing as a long silvery cigar with flat paddles on each side and a large rounded tail. It was so newly-fitted for passengers that it hadn't been painted and didn't have any markings or logo for Continental Charters. The plane's only identifier throughout the shiny mass of aluminum was a small tail number in black paint, printed with *Praxis Bold* font, *N3944C*. The digits partially covered its previous tail number like those of a used fishing boat with a new registration.

Soon after leaving the runway with the plane, the co-pilot reached to the control pedestal and switched off the retractable, take-off and landing lights. The plane's broad wings and thick fuselage were then hidden in darkness, except for the flashing position lights on each wingtip and the tail, and the white, red, green, and amber recognition lights on the top and bottom of the fuselage. These were the lights that reflected from the snow during low flight. The pilots made their final call on the radio to the Pittsburgh control tower five minutes after departure. Everything was OK, they said. The tower replied with a customary "Good Night." Most likely from the co-pilot, "44-Charlie," were the last words controllers heard from the cockpit.[13] With a visual flight, the pilots were on their own.

Normally, in such weather conditions for an 189-mile instrument controlled flight to Buffalo, the pilots would climb to about 5,000 feet heading due north to the shore of Lake Erie. Then, they would turn northeast flying over the large blocks of Labrusca grape vineyards of Pennsylvania and New York State spilling from the plateau down to the lake's shoreline. Approaching the northeastern-most corner of the lake, whose waters generated their dangerous weather flying conditions, they would descend toward the lights of the sprawling Bethlehem Steel mill in Lackawanna, the tall General Mills grain elevators of Buffalo, and then into Buffalo Municipal Airport in neighboring Cheektowaga. However, this was not a normal flight.

Each flight into Buffalo was a homecoming for C-46 airplanes, manufactured for the war in a large factory next to the airport. The C-46 was designed by the Curtiss-Wright Corporation in 1936 as CW-20, a luxury passenger plane to compete with the popular Douglas DC-2 and DC-3 passenger planes. However, with the approaching war the C-46 prototype languished.[14] Curtiss-Wright was consumed with building fighter planes in Buffalo with scores of orders from the U.S. Army, most notably for the P-40 Warhawk, which would be distinguished fighting the Germans in North Africa and the Japanese at Pearl Harbor. A speculative venture, the giant CW-20 was designed to hold more than 36 passengers, and with a 108-foot wingspan, was imposing to say the least. It was the largest plane in the world. Sitting in the back of the Buffalo factory one day in September 1940, the lone CW-20 was spied by Army Air Corps Major-General Henry H. "Hap" Arnold while he was on a nationwide tour of aircraft factories. "I want that airplane," he

---

[13] "44-Charlie" was a verbal abbreviation for the plane's tail number using the last numbers, 44, and letter, C.

[14] CW-20 and C-46 were the different names for the same plane. C-46 was its name as a military cargo plane and this name continued after the war when it became a civilian passenger plane too. Except for the prototype, the name CW-20 was not utilized for the plane for either military or civilian use.

reportedly growled, realizing he would soon be required to ship tens of thousands of troops and thousands of tons of supplies to Europe for the impending war. Hap Arnold soon got his wish.

The C-46 was the plane made infamous for vaulting The Hump during the war.[15] Unable to receive enough supplies of aviation fuel, ammunition, weapons, and vehicle and tank parts for his troops trapped in the interior of China by Japanese forces controlling the coastline, Chinese Nationalist Party General Chiang Kai-Shek sent his wife to Washington to lobby President Franklin Roosevelt for more cargo planes. The President answered by sending C-46s. Its payload nearly doubled the capacity of the C-47 cargo plane, and its powerful engines could get the heavy loads over the Himalaya Mountains more easily than the smaller and less powerful C-47s.[16] From 1943 through 1945, the C-46 pushed the limits in a massive airlift over The Hump to more than 70-thousand tons of materials a month into China. However, it was not without cost. Many of these planes and crew were lost along what pilots nicknamed the "aluminum highway," a trail of wreckage through the mountains. When the war ended, Army pilots flew the C-46s home where the federal government was determined to recoup its investment by leasing the surplus planes to the nonskeds. It was also an effort to promote flying and to get passenger planes to serve smaller cities across America. The planes were great cargo haulers as they proved for Hump duty and during the Berlin Air Lift following the war. However, the government-led initiative to turn the hundreds of surplus C-46s into passenger planes proved to be a disaster.

FLYING THE NEWEST CONTINENTAL Charters C-46 from Pittsburgh to Buffalo on the night of December 29, the pilots were desperately trying to make up for lost time. Instead of navigating by instruments as all other pilots from Pittsburgh were doing that night, they ignored the weather report, company policy, and federal flight safety recommendations, and

---

[15] The Hump was the nickname given to the Himalaya Mountains over which cargo planes were required to fly to reach the interior of China.
[16] The C-47 was the military version of the popular Douglas DC-3 passenger plane.

opted for the straightest and quickest route. Their ill-considered flight plan was to keep their elevation of a few thousand feet so they could see the ground and follow their compass on an 18 degree heading for Buffalo. They would fly by sight, and when they got close to the airport, just east of upstate New York's largest city, they planned to call the Buffalo air traffic controllers on their radio and be guided in for their landing. After refueling in Buffalo, the reserve crew was scheduled to fly the plane back to Miami, arriving just before dawn on December 30, getting Pearl, and her passengers, home in time for New Year's Eve celebrations. Many of the passengers had big plans.

When one of the largest planes in the world flies low overhead with two bellowing piston-powered engines at nearly full throttle, it generates a lot of noises. In some conditions, it's so loud that people on the ground can't hear anything else for a few moments. It's also a bit of a rough ride. Prop planes of the 1940s and '50s did not provide the smooth, effortless cruise that modern jetliners would many years later. Flying in these planes sometimes felt like riding in a rowboat in rough seas. Additionally, a low elevation visual flight required frequent changes in altitude for hills and valleys. Some of the passengers were feeling a bit nauseous by the undulating flight, even George Albert and Lt. Bischof, who were used to riding in military transport planes from their South Pacific postings in World War II. To ward off nausea, they tried to go to sleep.

Because of their weight and gas-guzzling large engines, Pearl realized that the cheap-to-lease Continental Charters C-46 planes weren't lavish or comfortable as those of the majors, but she was mostly satisfied with her job. The nonsked flights were cheap, and most travelers treated her with respect. Hours late taking off, she could tell by the quiet and subdued atmosphere in the cabin that the passengers were tired. They had waited for hours for the flight to begin and they had hours ahead of them before landing in warm, exotic Miami, they thought.

First observed by ground witnesses some 28 miles out of Pittsburgh at Sarver, Pennsylvania on its "very low" elevation flight, Continental Charters Flight 44-2 was so low to the ground its blinking recognition lights were already reflecting off the snow. By the time the loud, unmistakable roar passed low over Cowansville and Rimersburg, however, no one could see the plane because of fog, they only heard it. By then, 52 miles out of Pittsburgh, Flight 44-2 was eight miles east of its intended straight-line course for Buffalo. Witnesses further north in Sheffield first heard the roar of the plane's engines and then briefly saw it flying into a thick cloud bank where it was about 15 miles east of its intended path. How and why it got so far off its intended flight path is one of the mysteries of the flight which will never be known. It was about this time that some of the passengers and Pearl were looking through their windows at the lights of the small towns below. Peering through a window from his seat in the back of the plane, Lt. Bischof said that he thought the lights looked awfully close, and it made him uneasy. He had done some flying during his Navy career, and he believed they should have had more altitude. He felt better when he sensed the plane climbing again. It was just the beginning of their roller coaster ride.

Having made a slight heading correction just south of the New York State line, perhaps the initial preparation for arrival, the pilots were navigating 11 miles east of their intended true course for Buffalo and were rapidly approaching the tall ridges of the western foothills of the Allegheny Plateau in Cattaraugus County, New York. The pilots had gone over their route before takeoff, but nothing in their sheaf of charts provided by the airline indicated mountains along the way. Inside the cockpit of the C-46, the two pilots, who had only recently begun flying together, were at the controls of Continental Charters' newest plane, making only its second commercial passenger flight. It had been in the airline's lineup for only five days since costly and extensive renovations from its previous use as a cargo plane. There was room in the cockpit for two more people, typically a radio operator and a flight engineer, from the days when the C-46 was used for the war, but for these civilian passenger flights only two pilots were necessary. Pilot Victor A. Harris, 28, had been flying as a passenger plane pilot-in-command for Continental Charters since March, and co-pilot Hans E. Rutzebeck, 33, had become certified for twin-engine planes over the summer. Harris and Rutzebeck only recently got to know each other, since Rutz, as he was nicknamed, joined the company on July 25. This was their first flight in the new plane.

The pilots, however, had a lot in common. Both were entangled with serious marital problems. The day before their flight, Harris visited his wife in a Miami hospital where she checked in on December 27 for a personal surgical procedure. The 27th was also their son's first birthday, and there was no party or celebration of any kind. The marriage was on the rocks and Harris had been spending time with a mistress since September.

Rutz was an accomplished pilot of small bush planes and cargo haulers, but he had abruptly left his wife and two small children in Alaska earlier in the year without even a goodbye, and driven to Florida with a girlfriend to get his twin-engine pilot's license. Both men had plenty to occupy their minds that night as they sat inches apart in the dark cockpit. Broken marriages and thoughts of new girlfriends interfered with pilots' skills. In the early 1950s, the psychology of pilot errors was often overlooked.

From the cabin, it was difficult for everyone to see outside the plane. There were only five windows on each side – standard configuration for the Army C-46 cargo planes. Most of the passengers felt like they were riding in a cocoon with blinders. They could see nothing. Pearl nervously peered through each window as she pulled up and down the aisle. Sometimes she could see lights, other times there was nothing but darkness.

Flying by the seat of their pants, each pilot had nearly identical controls with a half-round yoke-wheel that was mounted on what looked like a parking meter post. They had a large display of dials, switches, wheels, levers and gauges (some that required a flashlight) surrounding them, and a wide expanse of windows, even below them, in the cockpit. The wrap-a-round windows were a unique feature of the C-46, similar to those on a bomber, providing the pilots with a nearly 240-degree view. The only problem was, on this night between Pittsburgh and Buffalo, they couldn't see very much because of poor visibility in the clouds and fog.

Flying visually meant that Harris and Rutz had their hands on the control yokes and their feet pushing pedals to control the plane. They were also frequently boosting the throttles for the engines as they flowed over the hills and into the valleys like a small ship in ocean swells. The yokes and their foot pedals were connected by cables to the ailerons and elevators in the tail of the plane to control pitch and roll, and elevation. The hydraulic assist for these controls was provided by the left engine. If it conked out, the yokes and pedals required about twice the force to control the plane. It often took muscle from both pilots to do it. Engines frequently conked out on the C-46.

Now, having covered more than two-thirds of the distance into their night-time visual flight from Pittsburgh to Buffalo, with fog or clouds obscuring the view through their surround windows, pilots Harris and Rutz were facing critical decisions. It was approaching 10:25 pm and they had less than 15 minutes of flight before their scheduled landing. Increasing elevation and calling controllers on their radio for a change to an instrument flight plan would consume valuable time and even more valuable fuel as they detoured to a prescribed radio beam flight path. Or, should they continue their low elevation flight and hope the fog would dissipate when they got closer to Buffalo for a visual approach and guidance from the controllers.[17] The weather was now causing severe turbulence, making matters worse.

In the passenger cabin, with its newly installed seats but without the padded fabric and faux wood-grain fuselage insulation materials found in the lavishly outfitted planes of the major airlines, Pearl, and the passengers were startled by the sound of a horn from a small speaker embedded in the exposed aluminum ribs above them.[18] It was 10:20 pm and they also saw a small red light illuminate with the blurting horn. They recognized the warning to stay in their seats and tighten their seat belts. Pearl knew she had just a few moments to pass the word around the cabin and double-check the children's seat belts. Scanning back and forth with her well-trained stewardess eye, she grabbed the

---

[17] Because the Buffalo weather was reported to be suitable for a visual landing, this may have inspired the pilots to continue with their visual flight hoping to break out of the fog as they got closer to Buffalo.

[18] Lt. Bischof described it as "a beautiful plane" but he may have been referring to the new seating, galley, and cabin fixtures that were installed only days earlier. In reality, the aircraft interior was crude in contrast to the elegant furnishings of a Pan Am plane of the same era. Unpainted, it gleamed, bright silver from the aluminum sheets that formed the exterior of the fuselage.

small rounded handles on the top corner of each seat. The turbulence made it difficult to walk up the aisle toward the front of the plane where the two reserve pilots, Webber, and Athas, were sitting together near the cockpit door. Then, turning around and wobbly retracing her steps, she bent over to cinch up the lap belts on the two children in their own seats and made a motion to a woman holding a toddler boy in her lap to grasp the child tightly. Stewardess Delores Harvey was also doing some last second tending to passengers in the front of the plane, and Stewardess Dolores Beshears helped Moon in the midsection of the plane. "I checked on the passengers, woke up some, to make certain their safety belts were fastened," Beshears wrote a first-person account of the crash for her hometown newspaper in Missouri. "Then I hurried back to my seat in the rear of the plane and fastened my seat belt – waited for the landing." Both stewardesses believed they were approaching the Buffalo airport. As they stumbled along toward their seats, the plane was pitching and rolling in the night air. Except for the children, the passengers were remarkably quiet. They were scared and afraid to show it.

Pearl knew the see-saw feeling of low altitude flight. She recognized that by flying so low in turbulence they could easily get into trouble, and the image of the navigation lights reflecting off the snow flashed in her mind. To Pearl, who had flown on C-46s while working for Continental Charters all through 1951, the engines sounded as if they were roaring louder. Passengers continued probing her face in a search for what might be wrong, but they remained surprisingly calm, she reasoned. She reassured them they were OK because the plane, after all, was still flying mostly level, despite the low altitude and bouncing turbulence.

As Pearl completed her final passenger check along the aisle and returned to her seat in the rear of the plane, the C-46 was flying over the state line between Pennsylvania and western New York State. Below, from his gas station-store and home in Quaker Bridge, Seneca Indian Eli Jimerson, who lived on the Allegany Indian Reservation, lay in his bed and heard a low-flying plane overhead.[19] He recognized the sound

---

[19] In a sign of the times of racial bigotry, as Jimerson reported for two days that he heard the plane, no one believed him because he was a Seneca Indian. Later,

of the engines as a large passenger plane that he had heard and seen before on the Pittsburgh to Buffalo run. Minutes later, when Jimerson got out of bed to stoke the fire in his wood burning stove, he noticed thick fog hanging in the Allegheny River valley outside his window.[20]

Farther up the valley, near Steamburg, John and Florence Jackson had not yet gone to bed. They noticed a plane flying so low overhead they could see the lighted windows of the cabin where Pearl had just completed her final passenger check. John Jackson stretched to look through the window of their house. He declared to his wife, "That plane is no more than 300 feet off the ground."[21] Within a minute it would be over Napoli where Jackson knew there were tall hills and long ridges. Some considered them mountains.

AS FLIGHT 44-2 PASSED OVER the river valley just east of Steamburg; there was a flurry of activity inside the cabin and cockpit. The ground rapidly swept up toward the plane as the first hills of the Allegheny Plateau in New York State reached up to it, and then, just as quickly, dropped off again into the narrow hollow of Sawmill Run.[22] In another split second, the shade of darkness around the cockpit windows changed as the pilots instinctively pulled up over what appeared to be ahead of them. It was the top of heavily forested Bucktooth Ridge. Whether they saw something or sensed, an obstacle isn't known. Their vision, staring at patches of fog illuminated by their landing lights, produced a vortex that could play tricks on a pilot's mind.[23] They must have believed they needed more power because they pushed the throttles forward and pulled back on the yoke. The engines roared. The passengers were pushed back in their seats. Those in the front were in the final seconds of their lives.

---

his full report was accepted by the CAB during its investigation.
[20] The airport, county, mountains, national forest, plateau, and river are spelled with an E. The Indian Reservation, state park, and the Town of Allegany are spelled with an A and without an H.
[21] The Jacksons gave their story to the CAB investigators who entered it into evidence for the crash investigation hearing.
[22] Sawmill Run is a creek that flows through a hollow and into the Allegheny River. Both the creek and the hollow are referred to as Sawmill Run.
[23] Witnesses reported seeing "headlights" on the plane.

Pearl noticed from her position in the back of the plane that Webber and Athas jumped out of their front row seats and threw open the cockpit door. It alarmed her because things like that just didn't happen during flight. The pilot was never to be interrupted in such a manner, even by other pilots riding in the passenger cabin, she recounted many years later. Pearl clearly heard loud voices, even cursing from inside the cockpit as she swung herself into her seat and snapped shut her seat belt. Looking toward a window, she heard what sounded like the right engine stuttering then roaring back to life even louder than before. Suddenly, the cabin lights went out, and the passengers heard the pilot gunning the engines in an apparent effort to gain altitude. The C-46 tilted, there was a terrible grinding noise, and then Pearl felt the plane jerk. She heard loud snapping and popping as if hailstones were pelting the plane. She instinctively looked toward the window again to see what caused it, but there was nothing, except darkness. She heard shouting and screaming, but she couldn't make out what the passengers were saying, except for one. It was a woman's voice that hollered, "take care of my baby." Pearl gasped, "Oh, my god what is this?" And then, she blacked out. She didn't feel a thing.

TWO MILES BELOW THE long flat top of Bucktooth Ridge that night, in a narrow hollow created by the plunging waters of Sawmill Run Creek, a middle-aged woman tossed in her bed. She couldn't get comfortable. Sharp pain from her armpit extended across her chest to her left breast. She grew content for a time, on her back, and then tried shifting to her side again, but the pain returned. She first noticed discomfort just over a month ago, but she put off going to see the doctor in the nearest town, Salamanca because it was a somewhat difficult and time-consuming journey down the valley from her remote farmhouse. The past few weeks had also been especially difficult in the near record-setting snow that buried western New York State between December 10 and Christmas. All month long she focused on the needs of her family and did not go to the doctor for what she feared might bring the worst news ever.

Ruby Jewel Bowles Bryant was only 45 but, after nearly 24 years of marriage, 5 children and a recent miscarriage, she knew when her body was telling her something was wrong. A plain and simple country housewife and mother of all boys, Ruby was religious, she frowned on booze, worked hard on the Bryant family's small market vegetable farm, and managed their schedules and meager finances. In her voice, she still had a bit of a twang from her childhood West Virginia accent, especially when she sang her favorite Country and Western songs at home or hymns in church.

December 1951 presented a milestone for Ruby's family living in the old Bryant farmhouse on Sawmill Run.[24] They included five boys, Ruby and her husband, Charlie, and Charlie's brother, Uncle Rollin. Their oldest boy had gone off to the Army at the height of the Korean War. When he recently came home to visit, they enjoyed Thanksgiving together because when he returned to his Army base, the family was incomplete at Christmas. This was one of the reasons, despite the pain in her breast that Ruby chose to remain home on their small farm and not take the time to go to the doctor. It may also have been a tendency to procrastinate when she didn't want to hear bad news.

The pain was there almost from the beginning when Ruby first noticed a tiny lump in her breast in mid to late November. It felt like it was under her arm at times and that made it difficult to reach up to grab something with her left hand. Worse yet, the pain had spread to her ribs with a silver dollar-sized sore spot. She didn't see a bruise there; it was just sore to the touch and when she drew a deep breath. Then, there was redness, and it kept moving around her breast.

While undressing one day in mid-December, following the advice she had read in the latest *Reader's Digest*, Ruby again felt her breast and noticed a hard, lumpy spot, like a small bunch of wild grapes. She was afraid it might be cancer that one thing or another came up until December was nearly over, and still she had not gone to the doctor. Finally, after Christmas, she called the hospital.

Turning in early on December 29 because her boys went to see a movie in Salamanca Ruby lay awake in her bed in the darkness and foggy silence of the mountain hollow, counting the few remaining days of the year until her doctor's appointment on January 4. Would it be soon enough? She worried about getting out of the hollow in the deep snow.

---

[24] Run is another name for a fast-flowing creek.

Sometimes their gravel country road wasn't plowed all the way through and already this season the heavy snow had socked them in more than once. Some areas of Sawmill Run already had nearly four feet of snow. Late that night in her bedroom, cool now because of the dying embers in their wood-burning stove, and with only two days left in the year, she worried about what it might be. Then she worried about what she knew it just had to be. She had told no one. She could barely utter the word. Few in her circle of friends and family ever said it: cancer.

Who would take care of the boys? What about little Otis, her youngest? He was only five. Could her husband get along without her? Who would fix their lunches as they headed off to work? Who would make sure the bills were paid on time? All the worst thoughts crept into her mind as she pushed the pain aside and slowly drifted toward sleep. At night, Ruby's small home was peacefully quiet. It was 10:25 pm. Despite rising temperatures into the 40's, and rain, all up and down Sawmill Run the ground in the deep hollow remained cold, covered with wet snow and ice. The air was dense and dripped with fog. Gurgling percolated from holes in the ice in the creek. Water from the rain flowed along the thickly painted galvanized steel gutters and into the corrugated downspouts above her bedroom walls in the front of the house, the rippling noise drowning out nearly all others. Suddenly, Ruby was roused by the unusual but unmistakable droning hum of a low-flying airplane. She thought to herself that it also sounded like the muffled moans of a train pulling through the Allegheny River valley below their farm. Was it a plane or a train? She couldn't be sure. Then, she heard a peculiar thump. She muttered to herself, "Now, what was that?" Snuggled in her bed for warmth, she listened for more distant noises in the night air but there was nothing. It was too cold to get out of bed to check on the mysterious sound that was probably nothing, she concluded.

Quiet minutes ticked by. The methodical gurgling in the rain gutters helped settle her head even deeper into her pillow. Everything else was quiet again. Ruby floated to sleep.[25]

---

[25] Ruby Bryant expressed her personal thoughts about discovering she had breast cancer in a 92-page diary in which she wrote daily.

BEFORE DAWN ON DECEMBER 30, David Shenefiel walked an icy path from his Cattaraugus County farmhouse to the cow barn for his morning milking chores. Thick fog smothered the sound of his boots on the ice. Inside the warm and dimly lit barn, David's Holstein cows stood patiently for their milking machine suction cups. Their heads all turned to greet him as he slid open the heavy wooden door. The squeak from the door's steel rollers announced the beginning of another routine day for the black and white cows – eat, milking, rest. The combined body heat of several 15 hundred pound cows raised the temperature inside the barn to a comfortable working temperature of 55 degrees. The cows munched on grain laced with molasses. Years of licking the sweet molasses with their powerful tongues revealed bumpy aggregate from the cement mixture used to form the feed trough. It poked through the smooth concrete as tiny pebbles. The cows' rhythmic movements rattled the chains that held them in their stanchions, and it sounded like soft melodic music. Outside the old wood barn, muffled by a thick bed of snow, and fog flowing across the farmlands, there was only stillness. Any sounds created were immediately mollified by the thick night air.

Dairy farming was a tedious job with the same chores day after day. David's routine would soon be broken. When the morning milking duties were completed, David maneuvered his late '40s Ford sedan out of the farm driveway and onto Hoxie Hill Road in the sparsely populated Town of Napoli. David headed up to the crest of Hoxie Hill on the short drive to his father-in-law's farm on the other side. No one else was on the narrow gravel and dirt road, which David maintained himself as Superintendent of Highways for the town. It was Sunday, but that didn't matter, few people traveled this road even on weekdays. Even though it was nearly daylight, his car headlights formed a line through the fog. David's habit while driving over the hill was to slow down or pause to enjoy the view created when his wife's ancestors cleared all the trees from the hill for farmland in the mid-1800s. But, this morning, there was no view because of the fog. David spent a lot of time on this hill, picking up hay or gathering sweet apples from a small orchard. On a clear, starlit night he could see the glow from the lights of Buffalo about 50 miles off to the north. All night and through the morning there was no glow. Nothing could be seen in the fog.

The name Hoxie Hill came from some of the earliest settlers in this part of Cattaraugus County, the Hoxie family, and David's in-laws. City people might have called Hoxie Hill a mountain but locals called it what it was. From the top elevation of 1,860 feet, there was a 360-degree view of the other high points around. Most of them were also called hills, or lookouts or marks, except for Oyer Mountain at 2,149 feet. Whatever who called what there was no doubt that this part of Cattaraugus County was hilly.

The best view from the top of Hoxie Hill was off to the east, through the left side of David's car window as he drove south for a short distance along the flat summit. That's where the mountains began. On most mornings, there was a beautiful unobstructed view across the Cold Spring Creek Valley, where he had been raised on his own family's farm, to the heavily forested Bucktooth Ridge on the other side. He knew the ridge well because that's where his mother-in-law was born and raised on another small farm, near where he spent many years in his youth running maple sugar sap buckets to a boiling shed, hunting whitetail deer, and cutting timber and firewood from his family's woodlot. He knew the ridge was difficult terrain and in winters such as the one they were in, it was buried in snow. The snow was so deep on the ridge that few dared walk to the top in the winter.

As he did on most mornings, David listened to the news on his car radio. The top story from Buffalo that morning was alarming. It was the disappearance of a big Continental Charters C-46 passenger plane with 40 people on board. It was a big enough story in itself, but since two other C-46 passenger planes had crashed earlier in the month, the disappearance of another generated bulletins that were broadcast in deep, serious tones by the announcers. It piqued David's interest because the radio report said the plane was flying from Pittsburgh to Buffalo just hours earlier on a route that he knew would have put it nearly over Hoxie Hill. David and his wife, Rosa, hadn't heard a thing all night. He never imagined that the missing plane could be up in the woods on Bucktooth Ridge just a mile or so across the valley.

IN THE COLD AND icy hollow of Sawmill Run that morning, Ruby Bryant got up and out of bed to warm the house. She loaded firewood into the kitchen cook stove, stoked it until the fire was roaring, and then started the coffee percolating for breakfast. Since it was Sunday the boys were sleeping in and because of the constant pain in Ruby's breast, she was starting the morning a little more slowly than usual. Part of the Bryant's morning routine was to listen to the radio news on Uncle Rollin's battery operated farm radio. It helped keep them up to date on the world events outside of their remote farmhouse. Because their son, Benton, had just returned to his post in the Army, Ruby had been paying extra attention to the war news from Korea. On December 30, however, the batteries in the radio hadn't been charged, and it was not the type she could plug into a wall outlet because the old radio ran on a different electrical current. As a result, Ruby and her family started their day without the morning news and unaware of the missing airplane. On their farm, less than two miles from the top of Bucktooth Ridge, the Bryant's were oblivious to the shocking news which Americans all over the country heard when they woke up.

THE DISAPPEARANCE OF 40 people on board a C-46 passenger plane between Pittsburgh and Buffalo became the biggest national news story of the end of the year, and it bewildered Americans. There was scant information in the morning newspapers because they all had gone to press before dawn on the East Coast just as news of the missing plane was coming out. A few of them managed to get a headline and a couple of paragraphs, but that was it. Therefore, most people heard about the missing plane over the radio, especially on the big stations like KDKA in Pittsburgh, WBEN in Buffalo, WIOD in Miami, and the CBS, NBC and Mutual Broadcasting networks in New York. The *Associated Press* and *United Press* picked up the story for their newswires, and those headlines were broadcast by smaller radio stations around the nation.

The missing plane news also grabbed the attention of officials in Washington. There was a serious problem with passenger airplanes crashing all through 1951, especially among the nonskeds. It needed to be solved before it stymied the growth of aviation into which the federal government had begun pouring money for bigger and better airports. Americans were plane crash jumpy. In the waning days of 1951 some were demanding that airports with death-delivering runways be shut down. Others demanded more safety regulations be imposed before more people got killed. And now a large passenger plane with 40 people on board had disappeared. It only added to the national trauma and panic. Continental Charters Flight 44-2, loaded with vacationing couples and businessmen, children, GI's, and a crew of seven, was missing and couldn't be found.

CHAPTER 2

"GET THAT PLANE IN THE AIR"

ON THE WEEKEND OF December 29 and 30, 1951 some of the original crew for Continental Charters' round trip Flight 44-2 from Miami to Pittsburgh and Buffalo were planning to go to a baseball game in Miami. They asked to be off work, so they were certain to make it to the ballpark on time. With dozens of employees, Continental Charters was accustomed to juggling schedules. The company crew coordinator telephoned senior stewardess, Pearl Ruth Moon, and her coworkers, Dolores Beshears, and Delores Harvey, to work in place of the cabin crew going to the ballgame. The three stewardesses agreed to work for the flight because they understood they would return to Miami late that night or very early the next morning. Some of the pilots were also planning to go to the baseball game on Sunday, December 30, but a long day in the cockpit didn't seem to bother them. Four Continental Charters pilots signed onto the Saturday flight.[26]

---

[26] It's never been determined which pilots planned to go to the ballgame. Pearl Moon said the group intending to go included both the original cabin crew and some pilots. Extra pilots were needed for the return flight because the round trip exceeded the time allowed for one crew to fly without rest.

Captain Victor Harris would pilot the first leg of the flight to Pittsburgh and Buffalo with co-pilot Hans Rutzebeck beside him. Captain CJ Webber would pilot the return trip from Buffalo to Pittsburgh and then back to Miami with Gus Athas as his co-pilot. They would be flying Continental Charters' newest plane, a re-fitted C-46 delivered to the company only days earlier, on December 24. It wasn't a new plane, but since being refurbished from its previous use as a cargo hauler, the C-46 appeared new. "It was a big beautiful plane," commented Pittsburgh passenger Robert Geyer. With a soapy bath just before delivery, it appeared to be just off the production line.

As a nonscheduled or large irregular carrier, Continental Charters wasn't allowed to publish or advertise a regular schedule of flights. It simply sold low-fare tickets through an agency and waited until seats filled up. Holidays were always a busy time for the airlines, so it didn't take long for passengers to buy the cut-rate fares in Miami, Pittsburgh, and Buffalo. Prices for this trip were typically as low as $27.50, less than half the cost of a ticket on a major airline. Take-off time for Flight 44-2 was set for 10 am from Miami International Airport. It immediately ran into trouble.[27]

CONTINENTAL CHARTERS WAS ORGANIZED in Miami in June 1947 when it was licensed by the CAB as a common carrier for passengers and cargo. Company president, former Navy and commercial pilot, John A. Belding, was the type of war veteran the federal government encouraged to get into the airlines business. Originally flying throughout the Caribbean and other points south of Florida, and to select cities between Greensboro, North Carolina, and Miami, it began moving into northern markets by 1951. Belding described his small nonsked as one that "flies according to the traffic." It contracted with ticket agencies which advertised the cut-rate fares, sold the tickets and pocketed a fee. The ticket buyers provided their telephone numbers, and when the

---

[27] The fare for Flight 44-2 has never been established. $27.50 is the lowest fare found published for a nonsked flight between Miami and Buffalo in 1951. Fares on the majors over the same route were more than $60.

flight was nearly filled, they were called and advised of the date and time for departure. This was how it was supposed to work for the nonskeds, but owners like Belding quickly discovered they could flout the rules, especially with promoting schedules, and operate almost as if they were a major airline. Many of them, such as Continental Charters, Miami Airlines, and Robin Airlines began direct competition with the majors, who were still operating on a first-class passenger structure with few low-cost coach services available on lucrative routes.

Continental Charters had been flying C-46s since 1948, having purchased or leased these aircraft, when the federal government offered attractive prices for war surplus planes to the nonskeds. It freed the surplus planes from costly mothballing. By 1951, Continental Charters had five planes, 66 full-time employees who were mostly pilots and stewardesses, and 12 mechanics.[28]

By December 29, 35 passengers had purchased tickets in Miami for the flight to Pittsburgh where 31 of them were to get off. The remaining four passengers paid to continue on to Buffalo. Twenty-eight passengers had reserved seats on the flight from Pittsburgh to Miami.[29] It's unknown how many tickets were purchased in Buffalo since they were never tendered. On the tarmac at Miami International, the C-46 being readied for the flight was pointed away from the terminal where passengers would walk about a dozen steps from the exit door to the tail of the plane. With its nose high in the air because of its sheer size and rear tail gear configuration, the C-46 was lined up with planes from the majors such as National, Eastern, and Pan Am, and along with other nonsked C-46s.

Continental Charters' newest plane was declared to be in "excellent condition" and had flown only one trip for the company before December 29; the same route to Pittsburgh and Buffalo and back to Miami. Unlike the other C-46s in the Continental Charters fleet, however, this one appeared to be a mystery plane. There were no markings, red stripes,

---

[28] Some of the mechanics were also pilots, such as Athas and Harris. Although most employees were full-time, they worked an on-call schedule.
[29] One more passenger was an infant riding on his grandmother's lap for a total of 29.

American flag, or lettering of any kind to designate the company name and logo. It simply displayed the tail number.[30] Flying a no-name plane was typical for the nonskeds.

As the passengers mingled at the terminal in Miami, the C-46 was loaded with their baggage, 1,200 gallons of high octane fuel was pumped into the large wing tanks, and 64 gallons of oil was pumped into the tanks that lubricated and helped cool the engines.[31] Its final load weight came in at 40,263 pounds, 4,737 pounds under the plane's certificated gross maximum weight limit of 45,000 pounds. This weight limit applied to Continental Charters' new plane because it had been leased and placed in service after weight regulations for the C-46 were proposed for a reduction from 48,000 pounds.

The aircraft was a Curtiss C-46A Commando ordered by the federal government from the Curtiss-Wright Company in Buffalo on October 7, 1942. It was the second among a group of ten identical C-46s released at a cost of $313,429 each to the U.S. Army Air Forces on September 25, 1944.[32] Upon completion, the plane was immediately positioned with the Central African Division of the Air Transport Command (ATC) based in Khartoum, Sudan. It would have been flown from the Curtiss-Wright manufacturing plant near the Buffalo Airport to Homestead Army Airfield south of Miami, then to South America, across the Atlantic to Africa, and into the ATC base in Khartoum with arrival sometime around October 13, 1944.[33]

One key responsibility of the Central African Division of the ATC was for C-46s to fly into Leopoldville (now Kinshasa) in the Belgian Congo to pick up uranium from the famed Shinkolobwe mine for delivery to the United States. This rich uranium was used in the Manhattan Project, the secret development of the Atomic Bomb. Based

---

[30] The other planes in the company fleet displayed a logo and phrase, *"Fly Continental."*
[31] This is a large amount of oil to be added to a plane. It may have been required because the mechanics spent hours examining the engines for whatever problem was reported by the pilots.
[32] According to *The Curtiss C-46 Commando* by John M. Davis, Harold G. Martin, and John A. Whittle, 1978.
[33] Histories of planes can be traced by their tail registration numbers.

in Khartoum for nearly a year, it's certainly possible this C-46 was one of the carriers of the precious uranium to African seaports for shipment to the United States, but there are no manifest documents available to prove it.

The plane was returned to the United States at Gore Army Airfield, Great Falls, Montana on July 22, 1945, following the Allies' war victory in Europe. The plane was transferred to the Reconstruction Finance Corporation (RFC), the agency tasked with selling surplus war materials in the U.S. From Gore, it was flown to a war plane boneyard at Cal-Aero Airfield in Ontario, California and there it sat on the mud field with thousands of other planes for four long years. When the RFC was renamed the War Assets Administration (WAA), it arranged for the former cargo planes in the boneyards to be sold or leased. Many of them were C-46s and C-47s, and sale prices were as low as five thousand dollars. The WAA Office of Aircraft and Electronics Disposal had hundreds of these planes at Cal-Aero and at similar boneyards in Walnut Ridge, Arkansas, and Augusta, Georgia. The abundance of surplus cargo planes available caused Curtiss-Wright to abandon plans for production of the CW-20, the civilian version of the C-46, as a passenger plane.

Not until December 1949 was the plane plucked from the Cal-Aero boneyard for reconditioning and use by the Civil Air Transport (CAT), the Claire Chennault and Whiting Willauer organized Chinese relief airline that ferried supplies to General Chiang Kai-Shek during the Chinese civil war. By late 1949, however, the CAT was being subsidized by the CIA and was operated through a Delaware-based corporation. By the summer of 1950, the CAT had been sold outright to the Airdale Corporation, a front for the CIA, and the Agency began using the surplus C-46s to fly civilian passengers on scheduled flights as a cover for its covert operations during the Korean War, specifically in China and Japan. It was probably the first time the plane was used exclusively to fly passengers.

Sometime late in 1950, registration records show, the plane was transferred to Lineas Aereas Nacionales (LANSA Airlines) of Honduras where on January 1, 1951, it was seriously damaged in an accident in Madrid, Colombia. Repaired and transferred again to Lineas Aereas del Caribe (LIDCA Airlines) in Colombia, the plane was finally returned to the United States and reissued tail number *N3944C* on December 5, 1951, when it was purchased by Carmas Supply, a Washington D.C. airplane leasing company. It was flown to Dallas, outfitted with three rows of forward facing passenger seats, renovated and inspected, given test flights and then leased to Continental Charters. It apparently was a rush job because no one considered removing certain military items stashed away on the airplane. An Army parachute used to jettison flares, and Army flashlights were left onboard.[34] They would prove invaluable after the plane crashed in Napoli. Because he was also an airplane mechanic, Gus Athas was one of the Continental Charters pilots sent to Dallas to fly the plane to Miami where it was placed in service for the nonsked on the day before Christmas, 1951. The large airplane of the once dominant Curtiss-Wright Company had just days to perform the service for which it was originally designed: haul citizen passengers of the United States.

THE NEW CONTINENTAL CHARTERS plane joined three other C-46s in the company's fleet, all manufactured in Buffalo, and one DC-3 that the company obtained from Eastern Airlines. Company president Belding liked these surplus military planes because they were inexpensive to lease and, although lacking interior luxury, they were sufficient for his working class, low fare-paying passengers.

The one time pride of Belding's small Florida nonsked, however, was a luxurious Boeing 307 Stratoliner, a four-engine, 45-passenger pressurized cabin plane whose design was initially based on the popular wartime heavy bomber, the B-17. Continental Charters apparently flew this Stratoliner through the latter part of 1951 but the exact time it gave up on this plane is unknown.[35] With four Wright Cyclone GR-1820 engines that had been upgraded after the war, it likely was

---

[34] The Army C-46 manual indicates three flashlights were standard equipment, but Stewardess Dolores Beshears said that six flashlights may have been on board.
[35] The Stratoliner was originally Pan Am *NC19903* and was sold to Airline Training, Inc. of Homestead, Florida in 1948, which may have leased it to Continental Charters. The Aero Transport Data Bank shows it in Continental Charters' fleet from 1948-51.

frequently flown by Captain CJ Webber because of his expertise with multi-engine planes. The extravagant Continental Charters Stratoliner was one of only ten manufactured by Boeing, and it was rolled out from the company's Seattle manufacturing plant in February 1940 for delivery to Pan American Airways in Miami the following month.[36] Boeing's Stratoliner had the wings, engines, and tail of the B-17 and was comfortable, with a 12-foot-wide deck, sleeping berths, and seats that reclined. Wood paneling lined the cabin, even the lavatory, and the Pan Am logo was sewn into the fabric on the walls. For a four engine prop plane, the luxurious insulation made it relatively quiet inside. Three Stratoliners were delivered to Pan Am, five to Trans World Airlines, and one to eccentric oil field tool and aviation multi-millionaire Howard Hughes, owner of TWA.[37] Pan Am flew this now infamous plane in the Caribbean for two years as *Clipper Flying Cloud* until it, along with the other Stratoliners, was commandeered by the Army Air Forces and renamed as C-75s to fly VIPs across the Atlantic during World War II. In 1946, this Stratoliner was returned to Pan Am where it flew the Bermuda to New York route until 1948 when Pan Am gave up on Stratoliners and transferred ownership of *Clipper Flying Cloud*, where it ended up hauling passengers for Continental Charters until late in 1951. Who flew it during 1952 and '53 could not be determined. It may have been parked, or it may have been used to train pilots. In December 1953, records show, the Stratoliner was sold to Compagnie Haitienne de Transports Aeriens, (COHATA) the transport plane division of the Haitian Air Force. It served as the personal plane for Haitian dictator Francois "Papa Doc" Duvalier until 1957. After being returned to the U.S., it was parked and neglected in an Arizona boneyard in 1969, later rescued, and eventually restored to its Pan Am splendor by Boeing with the *Clipper Flying Cloud* name.

The Stratoliner was significant in the history of aviation. Developed in 1938, it was the first passenger airliner with a pressurized fuselage to

---

[36] Pan American Airways changed its name to Pan American World Airways in 1950.

[37] The prototype Stratoliner was lost in an accident, according to the Smithsonian Air and Space Museum.

allow high elevation flight and, therefore, more comfort for passengers. After restoration and a ditching mishap in the bay around Seattle, in 2003 *Clipper Flying Cloud* was flown to and placed on public display at the Smithsonian's National Air and Space Museum, Boeing Aviation Hangar, Steven F. Udvar-Hazy Center next to Dulles International Airport in Chantilly, Virginia.

Why Continental Charters gave up its Stratoliner is subject to speculation but it required an expert pilot, was costly to lease, fuel, and maintain, and with only 45 seats, the small nonsked may have had difficulty making a profit with it. Though not quite as big as the C-46, the Stratoliner was far more luxurious than the larger Commando. The luxury travel market, however, was not Continental Charters' customer. Considering cost factors and the timing, the more expensive *Clipper Flying Cloud* was relinquished in late 1951, possibly to reduce costs so Continental Charters could lease another cheaper C-46, the company's newest plane brought home to Miami by pilot Gus Athas on December 24, 1951. Athas certainly didn't know it at the time, but he was flying home in his coffin.

EARLY ON THE MORNING of December 29, Joan Harrison Athas drove her husband Gus to Miami International Airport, from their apartment at 25 NE 55th Street in Miami. Joan was to drop off Gus and return late that night to pick him up after his flight to Pittsburgh and Buffalo was completed. Instead, they learned the departure flight had been delayed due to mechanical problems with the plane. Because Gus was not the on-duty pilot for the flight, they waited out the delay at Gus's aunt's home near the airport. Their apartment was some distance away on the north side of Miami. Gus complained of a headache during the wait, and Joan tried to talk him out of taking the flight; to go home and rest instead. He refused and told Joan he felt an obligation to go to work since he had already reported to the airport. After Joan had returned Gus to Miami International to board the flight as reserve co-pilot, he called her at home to report that the flight had been postponed a second time. It was the last time Joan heard her husband's voice.

Captain Victor Harris' wife, Evelyn, also remembers a second delay for Flight 44-2, despite the fact that it was never reported for the official

CAB crash investigation.[38] A pilot friend who also worked for Continental Charters came by Evelyn's Miami home one day, after the tragedy. He told her that Harris and co-pilot Hans Rutzebeck had started preparations for the flight with the company's new C-46 early that morning but returned to the hangar and reported a problem with the plane (it may have been a parking brake malfunction).[39] The mechanics on duty apparently found nothing wrong or they fixed a problem, and they sent the plane back into formation. After loading the passengers and taking off from Miami International, Harris and Rutz apparently detected some kind of problem with an engine, circled the airport a few times and then brought the plane back into the hangar a second time to be checked out. The mechanics found nothing. Evelyn Harris' pilot friend told her that Continental Charters' managers chastised Harris and Rutz, and they said, "get that plane in the air and don't come back in again."[40] Both the passengers and the CAB accident investigation report detail a single five-hour, 40-minute flight delay from the plane's original departure time. It's quite possible that no one reported the first delay to the investigating crew, and it was not included in the final crash investigation report because it didn't involve the passengers.[41] Said Evelyn Harris Ross many years later of her source for this information, "I have no reason to believe that (he) told anyone else of this, I just know it happened."[42]

Flight 44-2 was supposed to leave Miami at 10 am on December 29, but its first departure wasn't until 10:30 am, according to Pittsburgh-bound passenger, Mrs. Jack Schwartz.[43] This extra 30 minutes may account for the

---

[38] The 1951 married last names for Joan and Evelyn have been used for clarity.
[39] Everyone called Hans Rutzebeck, "Rutz."
[40] Both accounts of two flight delays were provided separately by Joan Athas and Evelyn Harris. They hadn't been in contact with each other for 60 years when they made these independent and similar statements.
[41] A parking brake problem would have been inconsequential after the plane had already taken off. To return to the departure airport once aloft indicates some kind of propulsion/navigation problem.
[42] Evelyn Harris provided the name of her source for this information but I have omitted it because he is deceased.
[43] Schwartz's first name could not be determined. Her recollection appeared in a few newspapers.

first delay. Traveling with her 9-year-old son, Schwartz was quoted in newspapers as saying "we made a good takeoff about 10:30 am but then the plane circled and circled for about 25 minutes." Schwartz said they landed to fix a mechanical problem and all the passengers waited in the airport until 3:30 in the afternoon when they were re-boarded, and the plane took off again at about 3:40 pm. This time, the C-46 stayed aloft and continued to Pittsburgh.

However, the plane was so late departing Miami it should have already been in Pittsburgh. And it burned valuable fuel circling in Miami and waiting for the pilots and mechanics to troubleshoot the unknown problems. Another passenger, believed to be Audrey Thomas Malcom, 24, of Lockport, New York, told Schwartz she was very concerned about the delay because she had no way to reach her parents waiting for her at the Buffalo airport.[44] Malcom was returning home from her job at a Miami restaurant to celebrate the New Year with her family. Malcom's parents ended up waiting at the airport until the early hours of the next morning.

Harris and Rutz performed the uneventful flight from Miami to Pittsburgh using instruments. Because the fuselage of the C-46 was not pressurized, the pilots guided the plane no higher than 9,000 feet and activated automatic pilot. Auto-pilot on the C-46 was controlled by flipping on a lever switch in front of the pilot's seat that activated hydraulic pressure to the system for controlling the attitude of the plane. While flying on auto-pilot, Captain Harris was to monitor his gauges and be sure to maintain no more than 140-160 pounds of hydraulic pressure. But, the pressure gauge was located in front of the co-pilot, so it was Rutz who watched it. Even without flipping off the lever switch, Captain Harris could overpower the autopilot by using about two times the force that he would normally use on his yoke and foot pedals to control the elevator and rudder. There was heavy speculation that Harris may also have been using auto-pilot on the second leg of the flight, just before the crash.

---

[44] Audrey Malcom was the only woman on the flight who had both her parents in Buffalo.

Upon leaving Miami, Flight 44-2 traveled northward the length of Florida, skirting the coastline of North Florida and then along the coast of Georgia and South Carolina. They would have maintained their maximum 9,000-foot elevation as they flew over the Appalachian Mountains. Instrument flight required them to stay at least 2,000 feet above the highest elevation on the ground.[45] The *"double Wasp"* engines of the C-46 spewed a ferociously loud groan that was inescapable for passengers no matter where their seats.[46] The ride was also bone-jarring bumpy, especially when propeller planes like the C-46 entered a storm. They could not fly higher, over storms, without pressurization and it consumed too much fuel to fly around them.

Not long into the flight they encountered nightfall so the majority of the trip was in darkness. Passengers could easily see the twinkling lights of the rapidly developing cities of North Carolina, Virginia, and West Virginia as they proceeded north into the coal region of southwestern Pennsylvania. Since it was winter and they were flying in cold air aloft, warmth in the plane was provided by two Janitrol surface combustion heaters of 100-thousand BTUs each in the cabin and one 40-thousand BTU heater in the cockpit. The three heaters were supplied with fuel from the plane's main fuel tanks, and when the plane achieved 120 mph in flight, there was sufficient air pressure to operate blowers to distribute the heat and provide defrosting for the cockpit windshield. When on the ground, it was typically very cold inside the cabin. Aside from simple lights provided by the C-46's 24-volt DC electrical system and a small (very small) lavatory in the tail, there were few passenger comforts for the long trip. Stewardesses Moon and Harvey handed out blankets and small pillows for the passengers who couldn't get warm or who tried to sleep with the constant noise and vibration, pitching and yawing of the plane. The one comfort was the seats, which

---

[45] At 6,683 feet, Mount Mitchell in North Carolina was the highest elevation but it was far west of Flight 44-2's path. Of more concern would have been Spruce Knob, West Virginia. The highest point in the Allegheny Mountains at 4,863 feet, it was near along the direct flight path to Pittsburgh.

[46] *Wasp* was the name given to a group of air-cooled aircraft engines developed by Pratt and Whitney. Another engine group was called Hornet.

were new and rather large, in contrast to compact seats of later airplanes.

At 9:15 pm, Flight 44-2 arrived at Allegheny County Airport in West Mifflin, Pennsylvania, a few miles southeast of downtown Pittsburgh. It landed on the main strip, 5,500 foot-long Runway 10-28, and taxied to the two-story terminal with the airport control tower on top. Allegheny County Airport had been opened as Pittsburgh's main commercial airport in 1931 with an Art Deco terminal building designed by architect Stanley L. Roush. The airport was already too small and too busy for heavily industrial Pittsburgh in 1951 and its rapidly growing suburbs, and within a few months it would be replaced by the new Greater Pittsburgh Airport in Moon Township, west of the city.

Flight 44-2 was originally scheduled to unload most of its Miami passengers in Pittsburgh, continue on to Buffalo, where it would discharge and then load more passengers, change crew, and return to Pittsburgh where it would load the majority of its passengers for the return flight to Miami. Because it was so late arriving on its first scheduled stop in Pittsburgh, the crew was presented with a dilemma that required a critical decision. Inside the Pittsburgh terminal as the C-46 taxied up to the building with its small-paned windows looking out on the tarmac, were the 29 Florida-bound passengers all believing their plane was arriving from Buffalo and would load them for the direct flight to Miami. As they waited during the 9 pm hour for what should have been their plane in the 5 pm hour, the flight crew made decisions that would lead to the disastrous crash.[47]

Thirty-one of the 35 passengers from Miami got off in Pittsburgh. The four Buffalo-bound passengers, Audrey Malcom, 24, Marine Corporal Richard J. Martin, 20, Army Sergeant David E. Arnold, 23, and Dorothy Berman Bruce, 23, were asked to remain on the plane for a quick turnaround. At this point, a decision was relayed by Captain Harris to senior stewardess Pearl Moon and SkyCoach Air Travel Agency in Pittsburgh, the ticket booking agency for Continental

---

[47] Twenty-eight had tickets. The 29th was a baby riding on his grandmother's lap.

Charters, to load the Pittsburgh to Miami passengers on the plane. They would first fly to Buffalo and then, deviating from the original schedule, fly directly to Miami, thereby saving time. Whether or not all the passengers were informed of this change in the flight schedule is still debated six decades later. Said Stewardess Dolores Beshears, "I told the passengers we would be in Buffalo in one hour, and everyone is expected to leave the plane there so it can be cleaned for the return trip (to Miami)." Beshears said she wasn't aware that she was telling the biggest lie of her life. Two other key decisions made by Captain Harris upon arrival in Pittsburgh were to deviate further from the original flight plan and cancel the instrument flight from Pittsburgh to Buffalo for a faster visual flight for the one-hour night-time trip. There was only one problem with this plan. Because of the weather, visual flight was not possible.

An instrument flight would have required the plane to fly north to the shore of Lake Erie, and then northeast into Buffalo. It also would have required the crew to take the time to load more fuel in Pittsburgh because instrument flights required a larger reserve of fuel for a final destination and alternate airport. In Pittsburgh, Captain Harris decided to get moving quickly, load his fuel later, and without consulting a weather forecast, make a straight-line night-time visual flight to Buffalo Municipal Airport with 33 passengers and six other crew members on board.[48] The plan was ill-conceived, ill-advised, and, as it would turn out, deadly.

As the passengers were loading George Albert, and his mother, Elizabeth switched seats. At the same time, passenger Eva Woodward wanted more space for her small dog. She arranged to exchange seats with reserve co-pilot Gus Athas. Woodward went to the back of the plane and Athas went forward to sit with reserve pilot, CJ Webber. The decisions made by these passengers proved fatal, for two of them.[49]

---

[48] At the time of the crash there were 32 ticketed passengers and a baby riding on his grandmother's lap for a total of 33 passengers. With seven crew members, the total number of people aboard the plane was 40.
[49] Although he was the reserve pilot, Athas is referred to as a passenger at this time because he was riding in the passenger cabin.

CHAPTER 3

GEORGE ALBERT

THIRTY-YEAR-OLD GEORGE ALBERT adored his mother and wanting her to experience the life he was living in the warmth of South Florida after he returned home from World War II, moved her to Miami from their previous homes in western Pennsylvania and northern New Jersey. Even as they boarded the Continental Charters C-46 in Pittsburgh on December 29, George was thinking of his mother. He agreed to switch seats with her so she would be warmer and so she could have a window over her shoulder for which to see the view. It was also a seat in the single row where she could sleep without the intrusion of a neighboring passenger. As it turned out, she didn't see much of anything as they took off from Pittsburgh, because of the weather.

George recently found financial success running a new restaurant in Miami that he and his mother, Elizabeth Albert, called *The Patio*. George also met a young woman there that he planned to marry. For the 1951 Christmas holidays, he wished to take Ava G. Isley home to Pennsylvania with him to meet the rest of his family. Ava demurred, however, feeling uncomfortable about the invitation, so she stayed in Florida with her two children from a marriage in Asheville, North

Carolina. She had not yet finalized her divorce. George and his mother decided to go anyway, and they purchased inexpensive plane tickets that would make the trip much faster than taking a train. It would also allow them to return before New Year's Eve so they could rejoin the staff at *The Patio*.

George Albert was born in Josephine, Pennsylvania on October 17, 1921, to Syrian immigrant parents, Abraham (Abe) and Elizabeth H. (Betty) Albert.[50] The Albert's emigrated from Syria between 1905 and 1907 during a wave of Ottoman Turk migration to North America. Josephine was a small company town built by the Corrigan and McKinney Company, which in 1905 purchased large tracts of coal and iron ore fields along the tributaries of the Conemaugh River in Indiana County, about 40 miles east of Pittsburgh. Corrigan and McKinney constructed a one million dollar iron works plant on a horseshoe curve of the Black Lick Creek with access to the Conemaugh Division of the Pennsylvania Railroad and the Buffalo, Rochester, and Pittsburgh Railroad. The business of Corrigan and McKinney was burning coal from the nearby mines and fields into coke which was then poured into the furnace with iron ore and limestone for blast burning the raw materials into liquid iron. When cooled, iron ingots were shipped by train to the big steel mills of Pittsburgh. To support its large investment in the blast furnaces, the company constructed a patch of more than 150 small wood frame workers' houses, the Josephine Supply Company store, post office, bank, and train station on a neatly arranged grid numbered from first to fifth streets. In just a few months, the company created an entirely new town, although it was hardscrabble and threadbare, with a population of newly emigrated Europeans who arrived mostly via Pittsburgh. The Albert family followed them as independent merchants.

This community may have seemed like a prison to the multitude of foreign language-speaking immigrants who moved in with their families to work the blast furnaces. They were blocked in on three sides by the creek, railroad, and hot furnaces, and on the fourth side by the forest and coal fields. Paid a pittance and running up substantial debts at the

---

[50] George Albert did not have a middle name.

company store, they were trapped in their jobs with little hope of earning enough to move upward on the social and economic ladder.

While the large, hot and smoky Josephine blast furnaces were next to the workers' houses, about 15 larger homes were built for the furnace managers, company directors, and priests along nearby Indiana Road. Among these larger homes that the Poles, Czechs, Lithuanians, Italians, Irish, German and Russian immigrants called *"Millionaires Row,"* were several shops and stores, one specializing in dry goods, and owned and operated by George's father. It was appropriately called the *Abe Albert Store*. Albert sold ready-to-wear clothing, especially women's clothes, fabrics, sewing supplies, and various household items such as dishes, and pots and pans. The Albert family was recorded as living along Indiana Road, the location of the dry goods store, in 1920 and 1930, apparently on the upper floors. Josephine flourished with activity when the blast furnaces ran around the clock, and Abe Albert prospered, the value of the family's home and store grew to about $6,000 by 1930. During these early years, they were the only Syrians among the diverse European immigrant population of Josephine.

George attended nearby Blairsville High School and played on the football team but by the end of the Depression, the blast furnaces had long been shut down. More than 500 residents of Josephine had moved away; furnace workers and their families left town almost every week until first through fifth streets were deserted. With only a few regular customers remaining in town, the Albert family store was forced to close too.

By 1940, with George only recently out of high school, Elizabeth Albert was raising the children on her own in a 3-story rental apartment building at 140 Belmont Avenue in Paterson, New Jersey. They included George and his siblings, James, Rose, Dorothy, and Joseph in April 1940. It was quite a change from their mercantile family life in Josephine where Abe remained until at least 1942 and from where he filled out his mandatory World War II draft registration card. Albert wrote on the card that he was 47, born in Tripoli, Syria (today in Lebanon), had no telephone, lived alone, was unemployed, and disabled.

In New Jersey, Elizabeth Albert supported the children by working as a machine operator in a dress factory. She was now sewing the dresses she and her husband formerly sold in their store. George, at 19, and the oldest, may have been working in the same factory; his occupation was listed as a shipping clerk in a textiles plant that made bedspreads. Like most other single young men of his generation, George joined the fighting force when America entered World War II. He joined the U.S. Army Air Forces in September 1942 reporting to Roswell, New Mexico, site of a flying school at Roswell Army Air Field. After training, he was shipped to the South Pacific where he served as an Army Air Forces Staff Sergeant. Upon being discharged from the Army in 1945, George moved to Florida to begin a new life, quite different from where it had begun in the backwoods of rural Pennsylvania. Portrayed in newspapers as a dashing and cosmopolitan South Florida restaurateur, the press wasn't aware that George knew his way around the northern forests from his childhood in Josephine.

By Christmas 1951, George Albert's family was scattered from western Pennsylvania to New Jersey and Massachusetts. For the holiday, they all gathered at sister, Dorothy's home in Josephine to celebrate with their mother. By this time, however, most of Josephine was a ghost town, torn down or abandoned and desolate. Having lived for the past six years in exotic Miami during a time of explosive growth and exciting development, except for being with their family, returning home in 1951 to drab Josephine in December may have seemed gloomy and depressing for both George and Elizabeth. Unable to make a late reservation on a major, scheduled airline, Elizabeth purchased two inexpensive tickets on nonsked, Continental Charters, and hoped it would fill up fast enough to get them to Pittsburgh and then back to Miami in time for the New Year.

Initially, everything went as planned. While reminiscing over the Christmas holiday, the Albert siblings posed for what would become their last family photograph with their mother. In the photo with all of them sitting on a sofa, the two youngest, Dorothy and Rose are in front attractively displaying bright, cheerful smiles and fashionable hair styles with white cotton blouses, collars cinched up high around their necks. George is more casually dressed in a bright white cotton T-Shirt that accentuates his dark features, his wavy, curly black hair appearing unbrushed, his trim torso slightly bent with his right hand resting on his sister's back, and his left, muscular arm around his mother's waist. He's clean shaven, but there's no smile, although it doesn't detract from his handsome appearance. James and Joseph are in the background of the photo with collared shirts, arms draped over the back of the sofa, and nearly expressionless. In the middle, with glasses, and dark hair appropriately styled up for a middle-aged woman in 1951, sits Elizabeth Albert, mouth partially open to not quite a smile but in a friendly pose, hands grasping her daughter's shoulders, and with embroidery around the neckline of her dark dress. Next to Elizabeth is her estranged husband, Abe, still wearing his wedding band, slightly balding, in a two-tone long-sleeved sweater over a button-down shirt and a collar around his neck. Like his sons, Abe Albert is nearly expressionless. George would keep this last photograph with his mother for the rest of his life. It haunted him for years.[51]

ARRIVING BY EARLY AFTERNOON on December 29 at the airport near Pittsburgh, George, and his mother joined all the other Continental Charters passengers who checked in with the ticketing agent, SkyCoach and discovered their plane was several hours late. Eager to get home to Miami, they waited.

Also waiting at the airport that day was 33-year-old Pittsburgh mother Anne Frankel, and her two young children, Mark, 7, and Judy, 2, a precious blond haired little girl a few days away from her third birthday. They were traveling to Florida to see their brother and son, Manuel "Manny" Frankel, a patient at the National Children's Cardiac Hospital in Miami nicknamed, Heart House. Manny had been living at the campus-style hospital since October 1950 because of a bout with Rheumatic Fever, but he wasn't totally alone in Miami. Nearby were his grandmother, two aunts, and several nieces. Anne Frankel's husband, Jack, a Pittsburgh restaurateur was afraid for his family to fly because of all

---

[51] The photograph and comment about it haunting George were provided by Cattaraugus County, NY blogger Jacklyn Hoard Beal via George's sister, Dorothy, and his ex-wife, Ava.

the plane crashes he'd been reading about in the newspapers throughout 1951. He initially forbids them from going but because they made it safely on a flight to visit Manny the previous winter, Anne convinced her husband to allow her and the children to take the inexpensive Continental Charters Flight on December 29. At age 11, Manny Frankel was also aware of the many crashes in 1951 and, he too, was scared to have his mother and younger siblings get on the plane. However, there was little that could tear Anne Frankel away from going to see her ailing son, with whom she had not visited in a year's time. Jack drove them to the airport late in the afternoon from Pittsburgh's Squirrel Hill neighborhood. They waited several hours for the plane.

U.S. Navy Lt. William W. Bischof also arrived at the Pittsburgh airport for the flight to return to his post in Key West, Florida. The 26-year-old commander of a submarine patrol boat and veteran of the war in the Pacific had been home in Johnstown, Pennsylvania for the holidays to visit his wife, Irene, and their infant son. Ideally suited for the Navy, Bischof was a natural leader. He was traveling in his Navy uniform which still elicited great respect six years after the war and at the height of the new conflict in Korea. His black leather shoes were expertly shined.

Pittsburgh printing company executive Robert Geyer, 34, arrived at the airport at 5:45 pm for the scheduled 6:30 pm flight to Miami.[52] He was going to spend a week relaxing and fishing from the family's vacation home in Fort Lauderdale. In his baggage, he carried a photograph of his wife Evelyn and their children, who had been forced to stay home because of illness. When Geyer was told of the flight delay, he kept pestering William S. Herr, the SkyCoach ticket agent, for a revised departure time because if it were going to be much later, he would rather have waited at his home nearby in Mt. Lebanon. He never got an answer, so he waited at the airport.

Twenty-two other passengers joined Lt. Bischof, the Frankels, Geyer, and the Alberts, and crowded the terminal departure door in Pittsburgh. Eventually, they would replace the fortunate passengers who got

---

[52] The 6:30 pm Pittsburgh departure time would have accounted for the plane having already flown to Buffalo and back to Pittsburgh on an uninterrupted schedule.

off in Pittsburgh and wouldn't hear about the crash of their plane for three days. Already more than five hours behind schedule and with the long flight back to Miami still ahead of them, Captain Harris made key decisions that sealed their fate.

First, to save time, Harris decided to skip the scheduled stop at Pittsburgh on the return flight from Buffalo to Miami. Because all the Miami-bound passengers were already waiting at the terminal, load them now, he told senior stewardess Pearl Moon, and they would fly directly to Miami from Buffalo. Second, he decided to save time by skipping the company's mandatory check of fuel in the plane by sticking the wing tanks of the C-46. This would have required Harris or Rutz to walk out on the plane's left wing and, poking a measuring stick into the fuel tanks' filler neck tube, determine the amount of fuel remaining in the six interconnected tanks spread throughout the wings. It was a backup check for the cockpit fuel gauges and along with a check of the tanks' cross-feed and selector valve controls it likely would have consumed another 10-15 minutes, at least, to accomplish this task. Further, Harris did not properly manage and record his fuel consumption on the flight manifest originating in Miami. He filled his tanks with 1,200 gallons of fuel in Miami and after twice taxiing and running the engines during the long-delayed takeoff procedures, and circling the airport a few times; he consumed 100 gallons of fuel before their final departure. His Miami calculations estimated he would have 450 gallons of fuel remaining in the tanks upon arrival in Pittsburgh for a flight to Buffalo, or three hours of flight time. However, in his new manifest filed at Pittsburgh, he changed this estimate to 400 gallons of fuel. In his apparent guesswork, Harris was going to be far short of the fuel required for a safe flight.

Continental Charters' operations manual required Harris to calculate his fuel consumption rate at 150 gallons per hour for the C-46. At that rate and with the flight time of five hours and 35 minutes from Miami to Pittsburgh, Harris should have recorded his fuel consumption as 838 gallons, leaving only 262 gallons in the tanks when they landed in Pittsburgh. Flight regulations required adequate fuel plus a reserve amount should the pilots be forced to an alternate airport in the event of bad weather or the unexpected closing of the destination airport. This amount of fuel to be kept in reserve varied depending upon a visual or instrument flight. Harris' flight plan filed in Miami early that morning indicated an instrument flight from Pittsburgh to Buffalo, which meant a slightly longer and higher elevation along the Lake Erie shoreline to Buffalo. Four hundred gallons of fuel was enough for an instrument flight and adequate reserve, 262 gallons was not. Assessing his risk, or masking it, and perhaps recalling his orders to "get that plane in the air," Harris made a decision for a low elevation visual and a direct flight to Buffalo. It was the fastest way to get there but perilous. For the one-hour flight to Buffalo, his estimated 400 gallons of fuel would have been depleted to 250. If he had only 262 gallons on board when he took off, he would have been left with only 112 gallons in the C-46 tanks when he arrived in Buffalo, or a mere 45 minutes of flight time. It was a razor-thin margin, and it was against the regulations for both his airline and the CAB. Third, and perhaps the most fatal decision, Harris skimped on his weather report. All pilots flying from Allegheny County Airport had weather forecasts available to them by the Flight Advisory Weather Service, the forecast and observation service maintained by the federal government's Weather Bureau.[53] Incredibly, neither Harris nor Rutzebeck made any attempt to get a weather briefing from the Flight Advisory Weather Service in Pittsburgh. If they had, they would have been told that visual flight to Buffalo was impossible because of the weather and that it was worse over the higher elevations of the plateau just east of their direct route. At 9:24 pm, either Harris or Rutz called Pittsburgh Air Traffic Control to file a visual flight plan to Buffalo. The controller voluntarily gave them a weather briefing for Pittsburgh and Brookville, Pennsylvania, and even Buffalo, and warned against a visual flight, telling the caller that all other pilots out of Pittsburgh that night filed on instruments. The advice was ignored. The two pilots, who had become fully certified for their jobs a few months earlier, decided to fly by old-fashioned, seat-of-their-pants navigation into bad weather-notorious Buffalo in the dead of winter.

IN PITTSBURGH ON THE night of December 29, 1951, as the pilots of Flight 44-2 decided to make a run for it to Buffalo they were low on fuel

---

[53] The Weather Bureau was renamed National Weather Service in 1970.

and there was bad weather along their route. The weather ceiling was 2,400 feet, visibility was ten miles, and the wind was from the south at 10 miles per hour. All are suitable conditions for safe visual flight. In Brookville, Pennsylvania, with a light rain, the ceiling was 1,900 feet, visibility was five miles, and the wind was from the south-southwest at nine miles per hour. Conditions here were also suitable for safe visual flight. At Buffalo, the ceiling was 2,000 feet, visibility was seven miles, and the wind was from the south-southwest at 21 miles per hour. There would be no problem for a visual landing in this kind of weather in Buffalo. Bradford, Pennsylvania and Jamestown, New York, however, the two closest weather reporting stations east and west of the midpoint of a direct route, were reporting ceilings of below 500 feet because of low clouds and fog – a heavy and unusual fog. It was not just settled in the valleys. It was everywhere. This kind of weather required instrument flight and was simply not safe for flying visually, especially through uneven terrain.

As if the bad weather weren't enough, Captain Harris also took off from Pittsburgh for Buffalo with a misguided perception there were no mountains along the way. The information was provided by Continental Charters. Although Harris would be flying over the western edge of the Allegheny National Forest in Pennsylvania, many don't consider the Allegheny Mountains to be as far west as the direct route from Pittsburgh to Buffalo. While there are tall hills along the direct route, the mountains in Pennsylvania and the Allegheny Plateau in New York State, most believe, lie about 20-30 miles east of this direct route.

Because Flight 44-2 eventually flew 11 miles east of true course, it encountered the mountains in northwestern Pennsylvania. They are neither the Rockies nor the Andes, but they are mountains, none-the-less. North of the New York State line, however, the mountains give way to the plateau where long tall ridges, or spurs from the mountains, are oriented northeast to southwest extending well into the state on the north side of the Allegheny River. Since there are no true boundaries for the mountains, most people refer to these ridges of the plateau as part of the mountains and many local names reflect this custom.[54]

---

[54] Many geographers and historians will debate the difference between the Alle-

The highest point in the New York State portion of the plateau is Clare Mark in the Town of Allegany, near the city of Olean, about 50 miles east of Jamestown and two miles from the Pennsylvania state line, at 2,430 feet. The highest point in the hilly region closest to the flight's direct route is Shutts Hill in Napoli, Cattaraugus County, where a bronze triangulation tablet embedded in the ground shows an elevation of 2,410 feet – it's only 20 feet shorter. Certainly this is a mountainous peak, and it's slightly northwest of Bucktooth Ridge, which is only 30 feet lower than Shutts Hill, at 2,380 feet. In contrast to these high points, the elevation at the Jamestown Airport is 1,719 feet, although a peak known as the Gurnsey Benchmark southeast of Jamestown and on the visual direct route of Flight 44-2 has an elevation of 2,195 feet. Most people will consider a peak of this elevation to be a small mountain or, at least, mountainous. But not everyone did.

Continental Charters obtained its flight charts from the CAA Aviation Safety District Office in Miami. For this flight route, the CAA Miami office did not classify the area as mountainous. However, the CAA main office in Washington did. If the faulty CAA records in Miami had matched the accurate CAA records in Washington, would there have been a crash? The answer will never be known.

In 1951, the CAA manual required a night visual flight to remain 2,000 feet above the highest point five miles either side of the flight's direct route. With the Gurnsey Benchmark within the five-mile easterly range of the direct route, Flight 44-2 should have remained higher than 4,195 feet. Because the nearby Jamestown Airport was reporting ceilings below 500 feet, this would have been impossible on a visual flight. True to the eyewitness reports, Captain Harris would have been forced to drop well below 2,219 feet (even below 500 feet) just to be able to see the ground, literally skimming the treetops. If this complication weren't enough, Harris took off from Pittsburgh with malfunctioning altimeters in Continental Charters' new C-46.

---

gheny Mountains and Allegheny Plateau. Some refer to this area as part of the Appalachian Mountains. Local names and references reflect everything from mountains to hills, to peaks and ridges. Whatever called, it is a hilly, mountainous region.

CHAPTER 4

CURSING AT THE COCKPIT DOOR

WHEN BOARDING THE CONTINENTAL Charters plane in Pittsburgh, some of the passengers said they were not told that they were first flying to Buffalo before heading south to Miami. This became an issue only later when several lawsuits against Continental Charters were settled for hundreds of thousands of dollars. It was only part of the confusion surrounding Flight 44-2.

After boarding and giving his mother his seat in the front, George Albert settled into the tail of the plane next to Lt. Bischof, near the rear door.[55] The two military veterans with western Pennsylvania boyhoods immediately became friendly, and they began conversing using their first names. Directly behind them were two seats in the farthest rear of the plane reserved for the on-duty stewardesses, Pearl Moon, and Delores

---

[55] The rear door was the main entrance and exit door on the C-46. Because of the plane's lower tail landing gear, this put the rear door closest to the ground when the plane was parked. Access was made by climbing a hanging ladder if an airport did not provide portable stairs.

Harvey. However, because Harvey was servicing the forward section of the plane and because the flight was not completely full, she had taken an empty seat near the front. Therefore, reserve stewardess Dolores Beshears was sitting next to Moon in the rear. Rounding out the passenger list in the rear of the plane were Mary Battista, 28, Weirton, West Virginia; Albert Dichak, 29, Canonsburg; Robert Geyer, 35, Pittsburgh; Mary Messerlos, 45, Pittsburgh; Marie Norcia, 47, East Liberty; Thomas Patterson, 21, New Castle; Anna Piso, 52, Crafton; Edward Wessel, 19, Pittsburgh; Eva Woodward, 62, Miami, (with her dog); and Joseph Wozniak, 33, Canonsburg.

The reserve pilots, CJ Webber, and Gus Athas were seated in the front of the plane, by their prestige and need for preparation for the trip back to Miami. As the most experienced and longest-employed pilot of Continental Charters among them with three years, Webber had flown the Pittsburgh to Buffalo run in the company's other C-46s. He knew the routes for both visual and instrument flight, and he knew the terrain. However, at this stage of the flight the pilot with the most experience with a C-46 was merely a passenger like all the others.

Flying the Curtiss C-46 Commando was not easy. The plane was packed with power with 18-cylinder Pratt and Whitney Model R-2800-51 double-row, radial, air-cooled engines. They contributed to its massive fuel consumption rate, often 50 percent greater than that of its main competitor, the C-47 (DC-3). It was impossible to fly when an engine was lost during takeoff, which often happened. It was extremely difficult to fly when an engine was lost in flight, especially the left engine, which provided the hydraulic assist for the controls. Better suited as a cargo plane than for passengers, the C-46 initially had 2,640 cubic feet of capacity – greater than what could be stowed in a 36-foot railroad freight car.[56] When the huge plane sat on the ground, its nose was high in the air because it used a tail landing gear wheel. The plane was equipped with a 24-volt electrical system with two main storage batteries and two 200-amp generators. The heating system utilized fuel from

---

[56] From the book, *C-46 Commando in Action*, Terry Love, author; Squadron Signal Publications.

the main tanks to provide warmth in the cockpit and main cabin. An ice elimination system included rubber de-icing boots on the leading edges of the wings and tail surfaces, anti-icing fluid slinger rings for each propeller, defroster vents, fluid spray and windshield wipers, and a carburetor heating system. For emergencies, if a fire should break out, the C-46 had a carbon dioxide fire extinguishing system in each of the engine's nacelles and hand fire extinguishers in the cockpit and cabin.[57]

The C-46 was loaded with all the latest instrumentation and even came equipped with a skylight for celestial navigation in the event the sophisticated (for the 1940s) instruments failed. Heated pitot-static tubes protruded from the bottom of the fuselage beneath the cockpit for the instrument sensors that calibrated airspeed and rate-of-climb. Altimeter, magnetic compass, aperiodic magnetic compass, artificial horizon, and directional gyro indicator were vital instruments for the pilots as were the tachometer, oil and fuel pressure gauges, the radiant cooler thermometer, engine cylinder head temperature gauge and the manifold pressure gauge.

Despite these high-tech sounding devices, the cockpit in a C-46 looked more like an early industrial factory control panel with wheels, tubes, levers, and switches, in contrast to modern airplane's computer screens and joysticks. And, there was still room for a relaxing pilot to hoist up his leg to rest his foot on the instrument panel during a long auto-pilot flight. The only problem was the deafening noise from the piston-driven engines. Pilots often couldn't hear each other unless they talked through the plane's intercom.

Pilots initially recoiled at the sheer size of the large, bulky plane with only two engines and heavy controls. Curtiss and the Army stressed the importance of a properly distributed load or the plane had a tendency for vertical hunting because of the sensitive action of the control boosters.[58] These were similar to power steering that would soon be utilized in automobiles. The control boosters gave a 3:1 advantage over purely manual control, declared the Army in its pilot training manual but even with the

---

[57] An engine's nacelle is the aerodynamically shaped cowling that surrounds it.
[58] Vertical hunting is a plane's tendency to nose up or down.

boosters, the foot pedals, and yoke were moderately heavy. With the control boosters off or with the loss of the left engine, the airplane was extremely heavy on the controls. It took pilots who were used to the ease of flying the C-47 some time to get used to this.

More unique characteristics of the C-46 involved the loss of an engine on such a large and heavy plane, and night flying, which caught many pilots off guard. While stall speeds in the C-46 with both engines functioning were anywhere from 88 – 67 mph, depending upon load, landing gear and flaps configuration, the stall speed on one engine jumped dramatically to a minimum of 105 mph and as high as 125 mph.[59] *"Because of the weight of this airplane it is imperative that you keep adequate airspeed with sufficient power until you are absolutely sure of reaching the field,"* warned both Curtiss and the Army.

Night flying presented its own unique set of circumstances in the C-46. For some unexplained reason, many of the gauges and controls in the cockpit were not illuminated. Flashlights were required, and the co-pilot was warned not to change any controls without first being ordered to do so because the captain wouldn't be able to see the changed settings at night without a flashlight. The pilots were warned that all night flying in the C-46 was instrument flying unless they could see a clearly defined horizon or ground lights were properly grouped to provide an unmistakable reference point. Additionally, most C-46 designs set the beam of the right landing light along the line of flight so the approach would follow the light beam, contrary to the procedure in most all other airplanes where the wing-mounted light beam was positioned straight ahead. This would prove to be problematic for the pilots of Flight 44-2 flying in the fog as the light beam produced a visual vortex.

Flying in bad weather presented unique challenges in the C-46 as well. The cockpit displayed two complete sets of flight instruments (gauges) on the panel. One was in front of the pilot while the co-pilot used the autopilot instruments. Because the plane had great stability,

---

[59] A stall occurs when an airplane's angle of attack is so dramatically altered, and its airspeed is so greatly reduced that the wings no longer provide lift from the flow of air across their leading edges. It does not mean an engine has stalled.

the pilots could fly on instruments as smoothly and with as much precision as flying contact, or visually monitoring the ground. Ice buildup on the wings affected the C-46 as it does any other plane by increasing weight and stalling speed. Some reports from WW II about four feet of ice built up on the wings were exaggerated, but there's no question the C-46 could carry large amounts of ice safely.[60] However, once ice accumulation began, pilots had a tendency to pull up the nose to maintain altitude. When this happened, nodules of ice formed on the rivet heads on the bottom surface of the plane. These airborne barnacles increased drag and caused a dramatic increase in fuel consumption. Pilots were warned to increase power and airspeed to 180 mph during ice buildup to maintain a proper flight attitude. The rubber de-icing boots on the leading edges of the wings and tail surfaces were very effective at removing chunks of ice which often flew into the fuselage with a loud thunk. It took pilots time to get used to this.

Another common problem during poor weather was carburetor icing although the fuel injector carburetors on the C-46 tended to be more ice-free than most others. When flying through rain or snow or in the moisture-laden air, the Venturi effect (fluid flowing through a pipe constriction) would cause ice to form in the C-46 carburetors in temperatures as high as 59 degrees Fahrenheit. Manifold pressure would drop, fuel flow gauges would fluctuate, and engines would surge or even backfire. In serious conditions, it could cause loss of the engine. The icing was most likely to occur at small throttle openings when descending through overcast skies or during approach for landing. Carburetor heat, to alleviate icing, was supplied through the hot exhaust from the engine and its use resulted in a slight loss of power. These conditions could have caused a problem, if only momentary, for the pilots of Flight 44-2.[61]

Two types of autopilot were also provided on the C-46s produced by Curtiss during the war. They were either Sperry A-3s or Jack and

---

[60] Four feet of ice build-up on a wing was most likely pilot hyperbole.
[61] Such a problem at high speed and low elevation would leave no chance for correction.

Heintz A-3A autopilot mechanisms. Nicknamed "Elmer," the Army reminded pilots that autopilot could keep the plane on course with greater accuracy than any human and to use it whenever needed. However, the training manual explicitly warned pilots not to use autopilot below 2,000 feet or 140 mph, in the extremely turbulent air, while de-icing boots were engaged, and unless both engines were producing normal power. All of these conditions were present during Flight 44-2's trip toward Buffalo.

Other features of the C-46 were also commonly installed on other cargo and transport planes of the time period specifically five different types of radios, including portable emergency radio, marker beacon receiver, intercom, and ID signal transmitter. Miscellaneous items included an oxygen system for high elevations, fuel crossover valve systems for moving fuel from spare to main tanks, and a glider towing mechanism. Also, life rafts and oars, first aid kits, emergency rations kits that included food and water, lamps, machete and even a gun, flares and flare gun, and a fire ax. Some also included parachutes that remained stowed away in the planes long after they were discarded by the military. Because crew members during the war were all men, a small portable toilet was carried along, sometimes exposed to full view in the cabin. Some cockpits even had a small relief tube porthole so pilots could urinate without ever leaving the flight deck.

Typically flown with a crew of three or four; pilot, co-pilot, navigator, and sometimes with a flight engineer-radio operator, the C-46 was the largest airplane in the world at the time of its development during the war, bigger than the notorious B-17 bomber. It was a whopping 21 feet nine inches off the ground at the tip of its nose and the wings stretched for 108 feet one inch. From nose to tail it was 76 feet, four inches and could hold 10 to15 thousand pounds of cargo (many more were often loaded).

While the C-46 had a maximum speed of 270 miles per hour, its cruising speed was 183 mph. The airplane's rate of climb was impressive. With 2,000 horsepower at takeoff from each engine, it took just 17.4 minutes to reach 10-thousand feet. It was rated for a ceiling of 27,600 feet although many pilots flew the plane much higher. The normal range for this new plane with full wing fuel tanks was 1,200 miles. However, with portable barrel tanks fastened in the cargo hold, the C-46 could manage an incredible 3,150 miles before refueling. It's no wonder Hap Arnold wanted this airplane for the U.S. Army leading up to World War II. It was ideal for war but not for hauling civilian passengers over North America.

THIRTY-THREE MINUTES INTO Flight 44-2's low elevation trip out of Pittsburgh, Pearl Moon recalled that after her final check of seat belts from the warning for turbulence, the plane began shaking. Suddenly, reserve pilots Webber and Athas leaped from their front seats and rushed the cockpit door. Pearl was returning to her seat from the midsection of the plane where little Judy Frankel and Judy's older brother, Mark were sitting. They had fallen asleep upon departure from Pittsburgh. Now, they were wide awake, terrified, and standing up in their seats. The plane pitched and rolled through the darkness. Pearl had to force the children to sit down. In a split second, Pearl cinched up their seat belts and then turned to get herself back to safety. Pearl struggled as fast as she could to get into her own seat in the rear of the plane. Passengers grabbed her arms as she pulled herself down the aisle, demanding to know what was wrong. "I don't know!" she blurted within her orders to tighten seat belts and lean forward. This was no time for company-mandated composure. They were in a critical emergency.

Glancing toward the front again, Pearl saw Webber and Athas yank open the cockpit door and, despite the roar of the engines, she heard them shouting and cursing. She believed Webber entered the cockpit and declared, "Goddammit, I know how to do this! We'll get out of it." Whatever, it was. Athas, Pearl recalled, remained just outside and gripped the cockpit door, perhaps because space was limited or because he deferred to the senior pilot, Webber. Between the two reserve pilots and the pilots flying the plane, there were a lot of hollering and hands flying around. Pearl noticed that Athas and Webber were crouching and leaning into the surging rolls of the airplane to maintain their balance as the plane swayed and bounced wildly, up and then down. Pearl was confused. "The pilots were all grabbing this and that," she said. With their hands waving around and with loud profanity from the cockpit, it appeared to Pearl as if all four pilots were trying to fly the plane. In a flash in her mind, her stewardess instincts questioned, why weren't Webber and Athas buckled in? It all happened within seconds. "I knew (we were) going down," Pearl said. "I realized it at that very minute, and I felt I was saying goodbye."

Pearl and some of the survivor passengers reported hearing an engine "sputter" or begin to "conk out."[62] Lt. Bischof had experience flying in war planes but he recognized that the bouncing around was abnormal. He also noticed the pilots "gunning the engines," as he described it. Lt. Bischof and George exchanged nervous glances. Then they strained for a better view toward the cockpit and the unusual circumstances of Webber and Athas grappling and cursing at the cockpit door. The reserve pilots' sudden appearance in the cockpit in this moment of severe stress would probably have initially startled but then reassured the pilots that they could regain control. Or, it could have confused and further distracted them at the controls.[63]

Whatever the problem, the pilots simply didn't have the altitude to make a correction fast enough, even with help from a seasoned veteran like Webber. His sudden leap into the cockpit just before the crash, when he was traveling as a reserve pilot in the passenger cabin, may have been a factor in many early false reports that he was the pilot-in-command. Even Pearl was quoted by reporters as saying that Webber was flying the plane at the time of the crash, when he clearly wasn't. Many years later Pearl would renounce her initial claim and declare that if the highly-skilled and cautious CJ Webber had been flying the plane the tragedy would never have happened. "He was a man who said do it right or don't do it at all," Pearl lamented.

---

[62] Pearl and the other passengers gave conflicting reports about which engine it was. It's possible that the passengers confused the engine surging with a momentary loss of power. Both engines were developing full power at the time of the crash, according to the CAB investigation.

[63] Whatever the reserve pilots were trying to do to regain control of the airplane will never be known. This was before flight data and voice recorders or "black boxes" were installed in airplanes.

CHAPTER 5

SILENT NIGHT, SILENT CRASH

INCREDIBLY, THE VIOLENT CRASH of Continental Charters Flight 44-2 took just four seconds. The huge plane, once billed as the largest passenger plane in the world, tore through treetops on a small mountain ridge along a path of 933 feet, smashing, grinding, scraping and gouging the earth as it tossed over and over before coming to rest in several pieces. It mowed through the bare hardwood trees just below the top of Bucktooth Ridge in the tiny farm community of Napoli, New York during a slight winter warming spell that produced a noise-canceling fog in the deep, heavy snow. With both engines thrusting at nearly a full power roar, the crash made a tremendous noise but no one on the ground heard it.

The C-46's first impact with the treetops was like a buzz saw. The cockpit of the plane split the distance between two 60-foot tall maple trees with the engines doing a prop-chop through the top branches of the deciduous trees about 100 feet below the peak of the 2,380-foot high ridge. Shards of branches flew from the props into the side of the fuselage causing snapping and popping sounds inside the cabin. It sounded like hailstones peppering the wall and ceiling. This dual prop-chop was the first of a few tell-tale signs that both engines were producing power at the time of the crash. Within another second the plane dipped and dove through the tops of the next two trees, spewing wingtips, shattered windshield glass, antennae, and ripped aluminum from the underbelly, across the snow. The splintered branches scattered on the snow-covered ground like an attack from hundreds of sharp spears. From this point onward, fuel and oil sprayed along the ground and painted the snow an unusual color of dark greenish-purple.

Four-hundred feet beyond its first impact with the trees, passengers who weren't already knocked out felt a sickening lurch as a large maple tree measuring 30 inches in diameter was sheared near the stump. The tree apparently caught the plane along the right side of the fuselage because pieces of prop blades from the right engine splintered to the ground. The cockpit jump seat, instrument panel from the flight engineer/radio operator's position, and front gas tank were ripped from the plane. The next maple tree the plane hit was 80 feet high and also had a 30-inch trunk. It stood. The impact, however, ripped off both engines and hurled them rolling and gouging more than 100 feet away with one prop blade on the left engine folding over from the impact. The forward section of the plane, holding the cockpit, was driven downward and crunched like the bellows of an accordion into the base of several clustered oak trees. There, all four pilots (the reserve pilots weren't strapped in) were either crushed among the heavy instruments, ductwork, tubing and wiring of the cockpit and the main landing gear wheel wells or thrown, to their deaths. The compaction of the cockpit was so complete that only the on-duty pilots' arms, displaying gold stripes on their dark-colored jacket sleeves, were visible as they were extended into the snow. The plane's tail wheel, large rudder with black lettering, *N3944C*, another gas tank, right engine nacelle, pieces of flaps, engine firewall, cockpit controls, pilot seats, pedestal, and oil tanks were ripped out and thrown to the ground. The long flat wings splintered into several large pieces.

When the nose fuselage hit the last large tree dead-center, the rear section of the cabin, holding Pearl and 12 others, did a giant life-sparing cartwheel and landed at the farthest point, 933 feet, from where the first tree tops were prop-chopped. Among it were flaps, the left engine nacelle, more fuel tanks, the elevator, and stabilizers. Everyone on board the plane was either killed or knocked unconscious, except for one.

AT FIVE SECONDS FROM impact, the mangled airplane sat in total darkness and near silence with only hissing from the hot engines melting the snow into steam. The wind blew, and the bare trees swayed together with the strongest gusts creating a hollow knocking sound -even creaking. The worst was over. Or was it just beginning? There was only one passenger survivor who could attest to the sudden quietness of the woods in the seconds after the crash. Stewardess Dolores Beshears later discovered that she was the only survivor who remained conscious throughout the impact. "I was thrust forward against my belt. Then I was slammed back against the seat. My seat came loose and bounced through the plane – with me in it." Several passengers, in fact, were thrown from the wreckage still strapped into their seats. Beshears said she called out to the others, but there was no answer. She unfastened her seat belt and stood up, realizing then that she didn't have any shoes. She could feel softness beneath her feet. "I was standing on a body," she said.

Within moments, the only sound on the top of the mountain ridge, the wind, was pierced by the moans, and then cries, then shrieking of critically injured passengers who realized they were still alive but trapped and might soon be dead. Seventeen passengers and Pearl's on-duty stewardess partner, in the middle and front sections of the plane, were instantly crushed, impaled or thrown to their deaths, some whose lifeless bodies were straddling branches in the trees. Other bodies were in pieces. The infant being held in his grandmother's arms was catapulted from the cabin and killed. At least one of the buckled-up children was thrown too. Adult passengers, depending upon where they were sitting, were either thrown clear or rammed into the heavy metal seat frames in front of them with such force it broke their legs, crushed their chests, fractured their skulls, and snapped their necks. Others were impaled with metal objects or slit with sharp edges of aluminum shards of the plane's framing and would soon die from the blunt force trauma and bleeding. Two were decapitated. The bodies of those who were killed instantly by the impact and thrown clear were dispersed over nearly an acre of ground. Some bodies were half-buried beneath broken limbs and branches, snow, gouges of dirt and ripped shreds of aluminum. Body parts – appendages – were scattered. Oil, gasoline, and heavy hydraulic fluid dripped or oozed everywhere. The distinctive odor of leaking gasoline, the putrid odor of burned gear oil, quickly permeated the cold mountain air.

Pearl was one of the few lucky ones. Still strapped into her bulky aluminum, dark blue vinyl, and wool-cushioned plane seat, she was cartwheeled with the rear fuselage and then thrown out of the wreckage. When she awoke in the snow, she didn't know where she was for a moment. She felt severe pain on the right side of her face, but she realized she could move and didn't hurt anywhere else. From her seat which was embedded in the snow, she could see a light in the distance through her severely bruised eyes and it brightened her hopes to find help. Unsnapping the buckle from her waist, she pulled herself up from the wet snow and immediately discovered passengers George Albert and Lt. Bischof, who had been sitting in front of her. They were thrown from the wreckage in the same manner as she and all they had to do was unstrap and crawl to their feet for safety. Fortunately, the plane did not catch on fire because the hot engines had been sheared off and thrown away from the volatile gasoline in the wing tanks.

Confused and disoriented but not seriously hurt, Pearl, George, and Lt. Bischof discovered that the light Pearl saw in the distance was not from a home where they thought residents might offer help and safety but from a small green, steel encased L-shaped Army flashlight. It was from the cockpit and was used to illuminate dark gauges. It snapped on when it was thrown from the crash into the snow.

Suddenly alone in the silent night of the fog-covered mountains, together they slogged through the heavy snow to retrieve the flashlight. Playing the light beam on the wreck for the first time, the sickening cries for help from several injured passengers trapped inside the once mighty twin-engine C-46 came to life and resonated in their ears from many directions. Saved only by the circumstance of riding in the back of the plane, Pearl, George, and Lt. Bischof realized at that moment that they were the only ones able to help.

CHAPTER 6

SEARCHING AND WAITING

WHEN CONTINENTAL CHARTERS FLIGHT 44-2 didn't show up for its scheduled landing in Buffalo at 10:47 pm and there were no radio communications from the plane, Buffalo air traffic controllers knew they had a problem. After exhausting several more attempts to raise the pilots on the radio, they eventually called for help from the local CAA office which then relayed notice to its counterparts in Pittsburgh, New York, and Washington. However, the timing of the initial warning about a missing passenger plane was considered a bit late. It took more than an hour after the scheduled arrival time in Buffalo for controllers to declare Flight 44-2 as missing.

By the end of 1951, there had been so many crashes that the Washington and New York CAA offices were getting used to calls about downed airplanes. But, this one was different. Instead of a report that another plane had crashed, it was just missing. Investigators were dumbfounded.

The first of many witnesses who reported the Continental Charters plane's trouble was 74-year-old retired Pennsylvania machinist and farmer, Edward Frampton. He told police he heard a low-flying plane over Clarington, Pennsylvania just before he heard a loud crash. "The engines roared loud and then quit, dead," he said. That caused Pennsylvania State Police to send a half a dozen squad cars to Frampton's remote countryside in Forest County for a search. They found nothing. It was only the first of many false alarms. In nearly a straight line from Pittsburgh to Steamburg and Randolph, New York, witnesses called in by telephone (some even waited until morning) to local and state police in both states to report seeing or hearing a low-flying plane.[64] One witness reported hearing a plane flying "very low" over Sarver, Pennsylvania, just 28 miles northeast of the Allegheny County Airport. By this distance, the plane was already three miles east of its intended true course for Buffalo. The next report had the plane eight miles off course over Cowansville, Pennsylvania, some 40 miles northeast of the airport. Observers here reported hearing, but not seeing, the plane flying low above them. At Rimersburg, Pennsylvania, people reported hearing the plane flying low, still about eight miles off its course. When witnesses saw the plane "entering a fog bank" near Sheffield, Pennsylvania, it was about 15 miles off its intended course.

Through all of this rural and forested countryside in northwestern Pennsylvania, Flight 44-2 flew high enough to clear the tallest mountains of the Allegheny National Forest in Warren County at 2,231 feet and in McKean County at 2,460 feet. After crossing into New York State south of Steamburg in Cattaraugus County, the plane flew high enough to clear Jones Hill and Round Knob, both with an elevation of about 2,100 feet, before flying over the village of Steamburg in the Allegheny River Valley at 1,410 feet.[65] This is about the location where witnesses, Luther Dickson and Lillian Pierce of Onoville, Eli Jimerson of Quaker Bridge, and John and Florence Jackson of Steamburg, reported hearing the plane flying very low in foggy weather. The Jacksons said the plane was so low they could see the lighted passenger windows.

---

[64] None of these reports of a low-flying plane came from locations farther north than the Town of Randolph, which should have tipped off investigators to a general search location.

[65] These numbers indicate terrain elevation above mean sea level and not the elevation of the plane.

Next in line from Steamburg the terrain rises sharply to the northeast where there was one last observation from 65-year-old William A. Fargo in the southeastern section of the Town of Randolph, adjacent to Napoli. From his farm on Ireland Road, Fargo said he heard the plane flying low in very foggy weather just before 10:30 pm. No one closer to the scene of the crash reported hearing or seeing anything, except for Ruby Bryant. She heard the plane but didn't report it until much later.

WITH THE PLANE OVERDUE in Buffalo, controllers there first called Pittsburgh controllers to determine if the plane had taken off on schedule and to confirm its flight plan. Investigators later reported that Buffalo controllers, *"within a reasonable time after (the flight's) estimated time of arrival,"* simultaneously contacted the adjacent Williamsville, New York office of the CAA, the Pittsburgh CAA and the New York State Police in Batavia.[66] It was later revealed that the initial call to the Buffalo CAA office was placed just after midnight, a full one hour and 13 minutes after the flight's scheduled arrival time! Without radio contact with the plane, this rather lengthy lapse in time was never held accountable. It's reasonable to conclude, however, that controllers may have busied themselves during this time calling airports in Niagara Falls, Rochester, Dunkirk, Jamestown, and Syracuse in New York, and even Bradford and Erie in Pennsylvania, and Cleveland, Ohio, to determine if the plane had landed at those locations. Discovering that the C-46 with 40 people on board had not landed at any other regional airports, CAA officials in Buffalo placed calls to Continental Charters in Miami and the U.S. Air Force at its nearest emergency rescue team, the 5th Air Rescue Squadron at Westover Air Force Base in Amherst, Massachusetts. Westover sent refitted B-17 bombers to arrive in Pennsylvania at daylight with parachute-equipped medics on board. However, the weather was so bad that they circled a few times over northwestern Pennsylvania and the location of the first false sighting and then landed

---

[66] New York State Police Troop-A headquarters in Batavia sent teletypes to its outpost barracks each time a plane sighting was reported. The teletypes piled up, and each one had to be checked out. The nearest outpost to the scene of the crash was in the Town of Allegany.

in Pittsburgh. It was late Sunday, December 30 before the Westover planes could do an extensive visual search and then it wasn't very productive because of poor visibility.

By five am Sunday, December 30, the CAA also notified the Civil Air Patrol (CAP), a large national group of private plane owners who served as spotters and conducted search and rescue missions during World War II. Several small CAP planes from airports around Pittsburgh were prepared to search but couldn't take off because of the weather. By this time, Pearl, George, and Lt. Bischof, had gathered all the survivors who could move and settled in the snow some distance from the plane's wreckage. They were waiting for rescuers whom they believed would arrive by daybreak.

Waiting at the Buffalo Airport, were family or friends of the four passengers who had spent more than 12 hours trying to get there from Miami.[67] The four overdue passengers were Audrey Malcom, a restaurant waitress who had separated from her husband and left her home in Lockport, New York to find work in Miami; Sgt. David E. Arnold, an Air Force enlistee from Miami flying to Buffalo to see his girlfriend before transfer to Japan; Marine Corporal Richard J. Martin, of Buffalo, who had taken leave from the Navy base in Key West to fly home to visit his parents; and Dorothy Berman Bruce. That December Dorothy and her husband were returning home to Kingston, Ontario, Canada from an extended work-related visit to Nicaragua when Dorothy took the side trip on Flight 44-2 to see her mother in Buffalo. Audrey Malcom was the young woman who expressed concern to a Pittsburgh-bound passenger on the plane that she couldn't contact her parents about the extreme lateness of the flight. Tearfully, before dawn Malcom's mother told reporters at the Buffalo airport that she and her husband were giving up on the long night's wait and going home to Lockport without their daughter. It was Audrey Malcom's first time on an airplane.

---

[67] Passengers were also waiting in Buffalo to board the plane for its return flight to Pittsburgh and Miami. There were to be approximately 18 empty seats available when the flight reached Buffalo. How many were planning to board there has never been determined.

Meanwhile, the B-17s from Westover were joined by pilots from the Niagara Falls Naval Reserve Station and the Air Force's 136th Fighter Interceptor Squadron, also based at Niagara Falls, under a large group from the Air Search and Rescue Command, Selfridge Air Force Base, in Harrison, Michigan. As the planes flew over western New York State, the crash survivors kept hearing them on Sunday and even early Monday, December 30 and 31, but it was too foggy to see anything. Their hopes were dashed each time they heard the low droning sound of a plane flying off – away from their location.

One plane, a twin-engine Beechcraft, flown by naval reservists from Niagara Falls dropped to low elevation along the Lake Ontario shoreline all the way to Rochester but didn't see anything. Large military planes from Griffiss Air Force Base in Rome, New York searched through the Finger Lakes and along New York and Canada's Niagara Escarpment. Amphibious planes from the U.S. Coast Guard in Cleveland continued flying low over Lake Erie, and planes from the Royal Canadian Air Force in Trenton, Ontario searched over Lake Ontario and the northern shore of the lake. More than 100 military planes were available to search, but the fog was so thick over the large area that they were essentially useless. So, for much of the time, the search planes waited on the ground. The crash survivors waited too.

The Coast Guard sent search and rescue crews in boats and small ships into Lake Erie from its Buffalo and Erie stations while Coast Guard Auxiliary units dispatched search boats from Dunkirk. The Canadian Coast Guard also launched a water search, in Lake Ontario. Visibility on the lakes was still poor, but the vessels were not nearly as restricted by the weather as were the Air Force and Coast Guard planes.

Because so many reports poured into police agencies about a plane crashing in northwestern Pennsylvania, state police there spearheaded the initial ground search with headquarters set up first in Clarion, and then in Marienville, Forest County. There, a man told police he saw a plane flying so low overhead at about 10:15 pm on Saturday, December 29 that its lights reflected off the snow on the ground. Military planes from Pittsburgh and Middletown, Pennsylvania's Olmstead Field, an Air Force Base that became Harrisburg International Airport, flew out to Forest County but encountered fog so thick they had to turn back. When the Pennsylvania CAP joined the fray with volunteer pilots readying their small single-engine planes at local airports and grass landing strips throughout western Pennsylvania, one CAP group from New Castle had no idea that one of the missing plane's passengers, 21-year-old Thomas Patterson, was from their small town. Even the Pennsylvania Flying Farmers, a well-organized group of farm owners who flew small planes from their pastures and hay fields, volunteered to help, along with ham radio operators offering ground and aerial communications. All were of little use, however, because of the poor weather. Some of these small planes managed to get into the air during a slight clearing of skies late on Sunday, December 30, but they soon were grounded when a thick fog rolled in again between Pittsburgh and Buffalo.

With all planes grounded, the search task fell to Pennsylvania State Troopers and a small but rapidly growing force of volunteers who could more accurately be described as sightseers eager to be the first to find the missing plane. They simply drove their cars dangerously fast to the next location where someone claimed to have heard a low-flying plane and a crash. In Clarington, Pennsylvania, a press photograph shows several spectators crammed in behind State Police Sgt. Steve Banks and Pennsylvania Forest Ranger Art Van Nort as they spread a map across the hood of their 1950 State Police cruiser. Van Nort warned the volunteers that some parts of the forest in northwestern Pennsylvania were so dense that deer and bear hunters were known to get lost within a few hundred feet of their parked cars. Regardless, adrenaline filled the gawkers who, in the picture, appeared ready to race to the map point at the tip of Sgt. Banks' finger, on a moment's notice.

AS SEARCHERS WAITED ON Sunday for the weather to improve, Continental Charters president John Belding arrived in Pittsburgh on another of the airline's C-46's and motored immediately to Brookville, Pennsylvania where it had been incorrectly reported that the plane had crashed. Belding chose Pittsburgh to land with his company's plane because Buffalo Parks Commissioner James Hanlon, as part of his authority over Buffalo Municipal Airport, banned all Continental Charters planes from landing at or taking off from the Cheektowaga airfield. It was depicted by the Buffalo press as an overreaction because of fear and panic for the notorious C-46. Hanlon claimed it was simply a precaution until the missing plane was found. Belding met with reporters and emphasized that five-year-old Continental Charters had never had a fatality and that "we know the plane had a first class pilot-in-command, Capt. CJ Webber, plus a well-qualified crew. I came to find that plane," he declared. Belding got it wrong about which pilot was at the controls and in command, but he was correct about Webber being a first class pilot. He also further fueled the confusion by incorrectly telling reporters that the extra flight crew was to be dropped off in Syracuse to pick up another plane.[68] At the time, Belding was not fully truthful about his company's accident history, either. He failed to inform reporters that his company had suffered one non-fatal C-46 crash on May 9, 1949, with a three-man crew on board while taking off from St. Thomas, U.S. Virgin Islands. Belding correctly confirmed, however, that the Miami to Buffalo trip was only the second flight for their newest C-46 since they had leased and fitted the plane for passenger use a few days earlier. In fact, its maiden flight on the nonsked airline had taken the same route with 21-year-old William Kronick, Jr. as one of the pilots. Before he could be considered for the second flight in the new plane, Kronick decided to spend the holidays in Albany with his parents.

Also arriving in Pittsburgh late Sunday, December 30 was the New York regional crash investigator for the Civil Aeronautics Board, Joseph O. Fluet. Already a veteran of plane crash investigations since 43 people were killed in the 1948 fatal crash of a United Airlines DC-6 over Mount Carmel, Pennsylvania, Fluet flew to Pittsburgh on a CAB plane straight from the Newark Airport. He had spent the previous two weeks investigating the December 16 fatal crash in Elizabeth, New Jersey involving the Miami Airlines C-46 that killed everyone on board. To make matters worse, by the time Fluet arrived in Pittsburgh he got

---

[68] The extra crew was required to fly the plane back to Miami because the flight crew would have gone beyond the time allowed to fly in one trip. Why Belding said the extra crew was to be dropped off in Syracuse, which was not on the flight's itinerary, remains a mystery.

word that still another plane, a C-47 Air Force troop carrier (DC-3 civilian plane) crashed into a mountain in Arizona, killing all 28 on board. Most of them were cadets from the U.S. Army Military Academy at West Point. Then, another C-46, from nonsked Transocean Airlines, with four people on board went missing while flying to Fairbanks, Alaska over 4,421 foot high Chena Dome.[69] Fluet's professional life over the next few weeks would be pure hell as he spearheaded crash investigations and as fear of flying spread throughout the nation. Over his shoulder at the CAB were the mounting political demands for safety and accountability originating at the White House.

SO MANY REPORTS CAME from Pennsylvania about a plane crash that passengers' family members began driving there hoping their loved ones would be found. Audrey Malcom's mother drove to Hallton, Pennsylvania with friends after hearing a report that the Continental Charters plane had crashed there. Dorothy Berman Bruce's mining engineer husband, Angus, left his home in Kingston, Ontario to drive to the mountains of western Pennsylvania where the plane had incorrectly been reported to have gone down. Each of these family members found nothing but a sleepless night in small hotels, waiting for news about the plane.

Poor weather continued into Monday morning, December 31, and small special teams of local men, familiar with the Pennsylvania terrain, were sent out from Marienville to scout the forest for any sign of a crash. Their efforts were futile, however, because they had no leads to point them to where a plane may have gone down. At the height of the Pennsylvania search effort on Monday morning, more than 300 police officers, forest rangers and mostly volunteers had gathered in an area bounded by Clarington, Hallton, and Rimersburg on the southern fringe of the Allegheny National Forest some 80 miles northeast of Pittsburgh. They found nothing. No one in Pennsylvania, it appeared, seemed to grasp the significance of the fact that of all the many reports

---

[69] The wreckage from this crash was still on the mountain in 2015 and has been photographed by hikers trekking to the treeless peak of Chena Dome.

of a low-flying plane on the Pittsburgh to Buffalo route, the northernmost report came from the farm country around Napoli, New York. No one farther north than Napoli made a call.

THE FIRST INCORRECT REPORTS of a plane crash in New York State came early on Sunday, December 30 from along the Cattaraugus and Chautauqua County line, southwest of Napoli. Police and volunteers went to Leach Hill near the small community of Kennedy where residents thought they heard explosions. Again, nothing was found. Meanwhile, from Pennsylvania, the search area was quickly shifting to New York State and was expanded Monday morning, December 31, two nights after the plane disappeared. With the first break in the weather, military and civilian planes began flights over Lake Erie and Western New York State, the western and southern half of Lake Ontario, as far eastward as Syracuse, the New York State Route 11 corridor and Susquehanna River Valley, south to Binghamton, and back westward along the Pennsylvania state line. Still, no one spotted the missing plane. It was as if the airliner and passengers had been swallowed somewhere within 60-thousand square miles. The massive search, however, brought no one except for those aboard a few airplanes, anywhere near the Town of Napoli where the plane had actually crashed.

Despite the fact that three searches were going on simultaneously for lost aircraft in different parts of the nation, missing Flight 44-2 became the biggest mystery of modern aviation.[70] Never before had such a large plane with so many passengers disappeared in the continental United States where no one could find a trace of them.[71] Speculation about the fate of the missing plane and the 40 people on board was rampant. One CAA official in Pittsburgh said that if the plane ran out of fuel with a strong westerly

---

[70] Along with the crash of Army Cadets into an Arizona mountain, another C-46 with four people on board crashed in Alaska during this time period. Investigators, however, knew the approximate location of the Arizona and Alaska crashes and were attempting to get to the scenes.

[71] Earlier in 1951 a Canadian Pacific Airlines DC-4 flying from Vancouver to Tokyo via Anchorage with 37 people on board, disappeared along the Alaskan panhandle and had never been found. This plane disappearance, however, was outside the continental United States and before Alaska achieved statehood.

wind, it would have dropped the plane in the 800-foot depths of Lake Ontario. Another CAA official, talking to reporters in Pittsburgh, speculated that if the pilot had been on a visual flight, "he may have gone down too far and smashed into a hill." Reporters dutifully relayed this sound reasoning in their newspapers but expressed hope that it was wrong.

By Monday morning, December 31, frustration crept into the hearts and minds of searchers, CAB investigators, Continental Charters, and Americans closely monitoring news reports. Pennsylvania Congressman James G. Fulton, representing suburban Pittsburgh's 31st Congressional District, publicly expressed the growing vexation when he declared the search was "tragically haphazard." Fulton's district in 1951 included Crafton, Coraopolis, and Mt. Lebanon, hometowns of passengers Anna Piso, Roy Hemphill, and Robert Geyer. In fact, the Congressman was a personal friend of the Geyer family, which ran a large printing company in Pittsburgh, and his close relationship may have contributed to his awkward outburst. Trapped in the wreckage on Bucktooth Ridge, Geyer could hear the search planes overhead but the planes' pilots couldn't see the crash site. Fulton charged that no helicopters were being used by the Bell (Helicopter) Aircraft Corporation near Buffalo. Bell officials responded that it was impossible to launch a helicopter because all of their aircraft had been moved to their new Fort Worth, Texas facility earlier in the year. Without consideration for the danger from unorganized multiple airplane searches in extremely foggy weather, Fulton foolishly declared that he would pay for the fuel of any pilots who would take off in their small planes to search. His challenge was useless, however, because no one could gain clearance to take off in the fog even if they were daring enough to make an attempt.[72]

IN NEARLY EVERY NEWSPAPER across the country, the search for the missing airliner was the large banner headline across the front page. It pushed

---

[72] Congressman Fulton later called for the U.S. House Interstate and Foreign Commerce Committee to investigate the nonskeds for safety equipment on planes, their scheduling techniques, and safety registrations. Before the committee could act, however, the CAB instituted a variety of safety regulations on the nonskeds.

other big stories, such as Prime Minister Winston Churchill being stranded aboard the Queen Mary by a ravaging Atlantic storm and a stuck anchor, below the fold of the wide front pages. Appearing in newspapers on the last two days of the year, it seemed like the final nail in the coffin for the notoriously deadly C-46 passenger planes of the nonskeds. *Fog Blocks Search For Airliner* hawked Albany's *Knickerbocker News*. *C-46 Airliner, With 40 Aboard Disappears*, declared the *Long Island Star-Journal*. *Airliner is Lost with 40 Aboard in Pennsylvania*, trumpeted *The New York Times* above a story from the *Associated Press*. The *Times* and the *AP* were wrong about the state. Pittsburgh and Buffalo newspapers jumped all over the story from the very beginning, but reporters and photographers locked into the hand straps of their bulky Speed Graphic press cameras with high-intensity flash bulbs didn't know where to go. One reporter for the *Pittsburgh Sun-Telegraph* drove over back roads through the fog and snow on December 30 to get to northwestern Pennsylvania only to be pressed onward into western New York State before being ordered back to Pennsylvania by his editors. Edward D. Bell would follow radio reports or make quick stops to telephone his newspaper office for additional instructions. He was on a wild chase. While backtracking north on Pennsylvania's Route 62 near Warren, Bell finally decided to stay in his car in one place next to a public telephone and monitor the radio news. Bell had just become a crack spot-news reporter earlier in 1951 for the *Sun-Telegraph*. His experience during World War II as a radio operator and airplane Bombardier may have helped him decide to stay put with his car gassed up and ready to go. He chose the Pennsylvania-New York border between Cattaraugus and Warren counties. As a result, Bell and his photographer, Dave Evans, were two of the earliest large newspaper men (only one was a woman) to reach the crash scene. Bell's first-person description and Evans' graphic photographs for the *Sun-Telegraph* were gut-wrenching for readers who followed them for days to find out what happened to the plane.

NEWS OF THE MISSING passenger plane also immediately caught the attention of federal aviation officials in Washington. With two other major C-46 crashes in just the past 15 days, politics would soon enter the picture as the Truman Administration sought to calm the fears of Americans it was so diligently persuading to fly. More airplane passengers justified increased federal funding to expand airports, and it was believed that more people flying would reduce the airlines' reliance on federal mail subsidies. It was believed the crashes would scare people away from the airports. And, to make matters worse, even though many of the spectacular crashes involved the nonskeds, most people didn't know the difference between a nonsked and the major carriers. To them, an airplane was an airplane. They began canceling reservations on all airlines or insisting they would fly only on safe airplanes. In 1951, just as more people wanted to try them, it seemed like planes were crashing every few days.

DESPITE THE RISK OF flying, however, Americans were flocking to the airports, still small, dirty and dingy from years of neglect during World War II. In the first six months of 1951, airplane travel was up by 56 percent over 1950 to nearly 12 million passengers. By December, that number had nearly doubled.[73] Air travel presented a technological advance into the future in 1951; President Truman was an aficionado of aviation, and most Congressmen and Senators eagerly grabbed federal funding for new or expanded airports in their home districts while pointing to all the new passengers to justify the expenditures.

On the morning of December 30th, however, jittery travelers all over the country were focused on one thing: finding the missing Continental Charters plane and determining if any passengers were still alive. All through that Sunday and into Sunday night the search continued. At dawn, Monday morning, December 31, the planes were back in the sky but visibility didn't begin to clear until mid-afternoon. By then the survivors had given up on rescue and taken their spared lives into their own hands. For the search planes, it was too late.

---

[73] Air travel statistics were compiled in August 1951 by Eastern Airlines from reports by all airlines in America. The rate of two million per month indicated about 24 million annually. In 2015, there were nearly 800 million annually. The Federal Aviation Administration predicts nearly one billion passengers annually in the U.S. by 2025 and 1.15 billion by 2034.

CHAPTER 7

"They're Never Going to Find Us"

ON THE EDGE OF the Allegheny Plateau in western New York State, hunters and farmers have long known that if you get lost in the woods of the tall ridges you simply walk down into a valley and follow a stream where you'll eventually find a road. Or, the stream will take you all the way to the Allegheny River and civilization. The stranded passengers, however, were from Miami and Pittsburgh and guided by stewardess Pearl Moon. Her training taught her to stay with the plane and wait for rescue. Stranded on the tallest ridge in Napoli and uncertain about which way to go, Pearl maintained that it would have been an exhaustive, dangerous and risky venture to walk out to find help. She forbade it. They stayed put.

Far below Bucktooth Ridge is the small community of Salamanca. Sprawled out in a wide valley southeast of the ridge lines of Napoli, Salamanca's origins are traced to the confluence of the Allegheny River and Little Valley Creek in West Salamanca at what was originally named

Hemlock, and then *Bucktooth* after an Indian who lived in the area.[74] The name *Bucktooth* was changed in 1862 to *Salamanca,* after the Spanish Marquis Jose De Salamanca, an investor in railroads, and eventually the city growth occurred in East Salamanca, site of the present community. Home to the Seneca Indian Nation, *Salamanca* was a lumber town until it became an important junction for the railroads. The main line of the Erie Railroad ran through the city, and it served as a major crossroads for trains traveling from the oil and coal fields of Pennsylvania to New York, Buffalo, Rochester, Cleveland, and Chicago. In its heyday as a junction town, whistles from steam locomotives of the Erie, Pennsylvania, Baltimore, and Ohio, and Buffalo, Rochester, and Pittsburgh railroads echoed through the valleys. From high in the wooded hills, a local farmer could orient himself just by hearing a whistle at a crossing, and he often knew exactly which train was blowing.[75] As the trains approached a grade crossing, sign posts with a large W warned the locomotive engineers to blow their whistle or horn.[76] The sound would bounce across the valleys and the hills of the plateau. Some called Salamanca *"the greatest railroad town you never heard of."* It was the railroad that saved the passengers of Flight 44-2.[77]

West of Salamanca along the Allegheny, the first hollow is Bucktooth Run and then, farther west, is Sawmill Run.[78] Slightly more than a mile up Bucktooth Run, the creek splits into East and West Bucktooth Run with Bucktooth Ridge draining into both creeks. The high elevations reach well into the Town of Napoli along Route 242 to an area known as The Narrows, a gap through which early travelers discovered easier access

---

[74] Native Americans named Bucktooth were still living in the Seneca Indian Nation in the 21st century.

[75] Trains had unique-sounding whistles from different manufacturers and the farmers got used to hearing them on regular schedules.

[76] A whistle came from a steam locomotive with a high pitch tweet. A horn was a low pitch blast from a diesel engine, which had replaced most, but not all, steam locomotives by 1951.

[77] The phrase has been repeated in so many publications it's difficult to determine its origin.

[78] A run is a creek that drains from the mountains, as in water running down the mountain.

for their livestock and wagons through the hilly region. Largely second and third growth forest on the ridge in 1951, much of this rolling landscape of former hardscrabble farms is now the Bucktooth State Forest. This remote, wooded and inhospitable country is where the survivors of the crash of Flight 44-2 were trapped. They had no idea where they were and, on the long flat ridge in the fog, they couldn't see anything that might point them where to go to find help.

It was here on a peak elevation in the 1870s that Randolph, New York honorary medical doctor Frederick Larkin reported finding an Indian burial mound about 120 feet in circumference and with a stone hut about six to eight feet high. Within what Dr. Larkin described in his 1888 report, *Ancient Man in America*, as a 'stoned-up vault" were several Indian skeletons sitting in an upright position with "gorgets, spearheads, and Celts." While the steep and rocky ridges and deep hollows of this section of Napoli were inhospitable for permanent living, it's believed the Seneca, and Erie Indians before them, used these forested ridges for burial ceremonies to ward off evil spirits. The 26 plane crash victims who were crushed, thrown, decapitated, or bled to death were not the first bodies on Bucktooth Ridge.

ONLY BY A MIRACLE and because the rear of the plane's fuselage was cartwheeled over the crushed forward section and the cockpit, were Pearl, George, and Lt. Bischof still alive. Although badly bruised, they were not seriously hurt. Grabbing the flashlight that had snapped on during the crash and bounced into the snow, the three survivors began shining its beam on the wreckage from where the shrieks and cries for help were loudest. Enveloped in complete darkness because of the fog that blocked out any ambient light from the nighttime sky, they relied on that one flashlight to see. George took it first. He was the only one of the uninjured survivors who had been traveling with a companion, his mother. He immediately set out to find her but was detained along the way by the desperate cries of others. Crawling around in the forward section of the plane, George used a small knife-tool device from his pocket that he called a "seven-in-one," to cut two survivors from their seat belts and drag them from the wreck. He never revealed who they were and wouldn't further discuss them with reporters, leading to the presumption that they were later counted among the dead. George then crawled into the plane where he found passenger Robert Geyer, who had taken a seat next to the emergency hatch. Geyer was just regaining consciousness and while sitting immobile at the edge of the wreckage he witnessed one of the most intimate and dramatic scenes imaginable.[79]

George found his mother's lifeless body in the seat that he had given up to her. "He lifted her up and began to cry," Geyer narrated to reporters. Guilt, from which he would never escape, flooded George's body. Geyer, in his own anguish, could barely hear George's low tones, but he determined that George kept repeating his regret that he had changed seats with his mother just before the plane left Pittsburgh.[80] "Sit here, mom," he had said. Those words deeply pained him. Elizabeth Albert was impaled with a brick-sized metal object driven into her head.[81] Her blood, still warm from death just moments earlier, smeared George's shirt as he cradled her in his arms and wept. George Albert's wife revealed years later that George kept the blood-stained and unwashed shirt in his closet for many years after the crash. It served as a constant reminder of that last moment of anguish with his dead mother in his arms. Within a few moments, Geyer explained, George set aside his mother's body and covered her as best he could. He quickly hunted around her seat and found her valuables, in her hand-stitched alligator-skin bag. He draped the bag over his shoulder and kept it safe with him throughout their struggle.

Rejoining the others, George, Pearl, and Lt. Bischof continued crawling around inside the wreckage somewhat aimlessly through the

---

[79] Robert A. Geyer was the only survivor who was not riding in the back of the plane. His seat near the emergency hatch was at a point where the center fuselage broke apart from the rear section. He was found at the very edge of the ripped fuselage.

[80] Geyer dictated in great detail about this scene in a first person account for a newspaper.

[81] Some of these details were written in a blog, since removed from the Internet, by Salamanca resident Jacklyn Hoard-Beal from information provided by George's sister.

darkness and pushing their single flashlight beam up close to where they heard human sounds; groaning and weak cries for help. One by one they found more survivors. The most seriously hurt, Thomas Patterson, Mary Messerlos, and Geyer, were so embedded into the twisted shards of aluminum, they couldn't move on their own. Geyer and Patterson were going in and out of consciousness. George and Lt. Bischof tried to pull them out of the wreckage, but they were in too much pain. The best they could do was carefully lift Geyer a few feet to the edge of the fuselage so they could get in and out without stepping on him. He had multiple fractures in both legs and a broken bone in his hand snapped by the metal seat framing. Patterson had a critical head wound with a fractured skull on his forehead from being slammed into the seat in front of him. Messerlos had a fractured pelvis and was in intense pain. She was never moved. George and Lt. Bischof paused to help make them more comfortable and assure them that rescuers would be showing up at any moment. Then, it was Pearl's turn. Taking their only flashlight, Pearl went in search of the rest of her crew for much-needed help to deal with the tragic disaster. She kept calling out the names of the pilots, but there was no response. "They just didn't answer me," she said, fearing the worst. "The passengers were all calling for help, but I knew I couldn't help them," she sobbed.

When Pearl found the on-duty pilots, Victor Harris, and Hans Rutzebeck, in the cockpit, which had nosed into the ground and was wedged between mid-sized oak trees at a 60-degree angle, the metal wreckage was so compressed she could barely see them with the amber glow of the flashlight. She initially recognized the gold stripes on their jacket sleeves as their arms were splayed out into the snow. There were no signs of life among the two pilots crushed in the cockpit, what parts of them she could see. Shining her light beyond the wreckage, Pearl found the two reserve pilots, CJ Webber and Gus Athas, dead, their unsecured bodies thrown out of the flight deck. Then, peering around the cockpit and into the trees, Pearl spotted her co-stewardess, Delores Harvey, who had been on duty and was sitting in the front of the plane during the crash. Her body was hanging from her seat belt which appeared to be nearly cutting her through at the waist. She was doubled over in her dress uniform with her lifeless and long slender legs and arms dangling nearly to the ground among the branches and snow as if she were a circus acrobat in a suspended twirl. The impact was so great her long brown hair was thrown forward covering her ears and face and revealing the backside of her bare neck. It had been snapped instantly, the coroner determined. Her body never left her seat.

It was about this time that Pearl, discovering she was the highest-ranking crew member alive, fully realized the extent of their predicament. She was now in charge of all the passengers. Searching a bit further, since she was the only one at this moment with a flashlight, Pearl heard crying sounds and discovered two men, trapped in their seats in the main fuselage, and still alive. "Help us, help us," they cried while looking at Pearl with the flashlight. However, it was useless. They were too severely injured and trapped. "Those two men sitting together had their throats cut, and I knew they weren't going to live. I got blood on my hands," Pearl revealed for the first time while shaking and crying nearly hysterically during an interview 60 years later. "They were two nice men, and I couldn't lift one of them and I just put my hand there to stop the bleeding. They just didn't have a chance. They were just crying for help." Pearl was a thin, frail 83-year-old woman at the time of this interview and her head fell into her breast as she sobbed uncontrollably from the painful memories of so long ago. It was obvious that she had never gotten over the horrible moments after the crash.

After a few minutes trying to staunch the flow of blood and realizing the men could not be saved, Pearl somehow managed to turn away and leave them. When I asked her how she drew the strength to do it, she just waved her hand, shook her head and cried. The two men were later counted among the victims but who they were was never revealed, and Pearl simply didn't know.

Covered with blood from her effort to save them, Pearl returned to George and Lt. Bischof near the rear section of the plane where they could all share the flashlight. The 24-year-old-year-old stewardess from rural North Carolina summoned all of her courage to continue pushing and poking into the deep recesses of the wreckage for more survivors. Pearl's attention was now focused on finding the children she had been tending only minutes earlier. Fourteen-month-old Jeffrey Evans was the youngest on the flight. When the plane took off he was being cared for by his grandmother, Gertrude McLain, 54, traveling with her husband, Roy H. McLain, 59, from their Morgantown, West Virginia home to Florida. The baby's father, Sidwell L. Evans, and mother, the McLain's daughter, Constance McLain Evans, were University of West Virginia sweethearts who married in 1949. They had driven to Florida a few days earlier leaving their little boy to ride in the airplane with his grandparents.

Unsecured, little Jeffrey Evans' tiny body was thrown from the crash and was later found wedged in a tree. Roy McLain was killed in the crash. Gertrude McLain survived the crash but died from what Pearl described as "horrible injuries" just before the first daybreak, still fastened in her seat. She was so critically hurt the others didn't dare remove her. They simply dragged the seat, with Gertrude in it, from the wreckage across the snow and covered her legs and torso with clothing. They all watched her die.

Pearl grew determined to find the Frankel children, so fresh in her memory of cinching up their seat belts just before the plane hit the ridge. With help from George and Lt. Bischof, she played the beam of their flashlight through the woods until they found both Mark and little Judy. There was no sign of life for 7-year-old Mark whose body lay crumpled in a heap on top of the snow. But, they found a pulse for Judy and scooped her small frame into Pearl's arms where she cuddled her close to her chest for warmth near her heart. Pearl waited like this until George and Lt. Bischof found a large wool coat from near a victim's body. They wrapped and buttoned it around Judy's tiny unconscious and curled figure, now cradled in Pearl's arms. From whom they got the coat is speculation but both men later told reporters they were forced to remove outerwear from near some of the bodies just to keep everyone warm. Many of the passengers had been wearing their coats or had the garments draped around them because the cold plane had taken so long to warm after takeoff.

Reports from newspapers, and from Pearl, herself, are conflicting about how the Frankel children died. Initial reports quoted Pearl as saying that she, George and Lt. Bischof found Judy Frankel in the snow, unconscious and with apparent internal injuries. Other reports and Pearl, during her interview 60 years later, said it was 7-year-old Mark Frankel who they found unconscious in the snow, but still alive. The children's mother, Ann Frankel, so confident about flying and eager to get to Florida to see her other son, Manny, was killed in the crash.

Shock, grief and the passage of time often impact one's memory. Because there were so many independent reports in agreement, I've concluded that it was Judy Frankel, who would have turned three on January 3, who was found alive and then cradled by Pearl and wrapped in the wool coat. It's not likely that a woman of Pearl's thin stature could have held a 7-year-old boy easily in her arms and walk around in the deep snow. It had to have been little Judy, small, lightweight, and easily swaddled in the overcoat to keep her near lifeless frame warm. Pearl held the unconscious blond-haired girl tightly in her arms. She apparently had severe internal injuries. Some of the survivors recalled hearing a woman shouting in the seconds before the crash. The voice was reported to have come from a woman shrieking in panic. It must have been Anne Frankel in a final moment of life as the plane struck the tops of the trees on Bucktooth Ridge. "Take care of my baby," she yelled.

Stewardess Dolores Beshears had joined the small group of survivors by now, and she helped Pearl comfort the unresponsive little girl. Beshears had been strapped into a seat next to Pearl, but she doesn't remember hearing anything during the crash. "Beshears said she called out to the passengers but got no answer. "I didn't think anyone was badly hurt because I wasn't," she said. Beshears later determined that she was the only one among the survivors who remained conscious during impact. A tiny woman, Beshears still helped George and Lt. Bischof move and comfort Robert Geyer inside the forward section of the fuselage. When she joined Pearl to help care for Judy Frankel, she had just come from inside the wreckage where she had been providing comfort to Thomas Patterson. Like Lt. Bischof, the Navy Quartermaster was also returning to Key West, his duty station aboard a Destroyer Escort. With a fractured skull and lacerated scalp, he was in such intense pain that he couldn't get out of the wreck. Beshears stayed with him. She said that Patterson gripped her hand so tightly she had to pry it loose. He went in and out of consciousness several times until much later when the other survivors were finally able to get him out of the plane.

When everyone who could be moved was out of the wreckage, George, and Lt. Bischof made another quick survey and then decided they must move everyone, especially immobile Judy, away from the plane in the event of an explosion and fire. Beshears warned everyone not to light cigarettes with their matches because they could smell gasoline dripping from the fuselage. Lt. Bischof took the lead here, pulling George, Pearl carrying Judy, and a few others away from the plane and into the woods. After a short distance, they turned and looked back at the wreck. George felt they had gone far enough but Lt. Bischof, displaying his naval leadership, pushed them farther. Several times they repeated this procedure as Bischof continued pushing them farther into the woods until they were about 150 yards from the wreckage. Finally, he pronounced them safe from any fire and gathered them around. Lt. Bischof settled Pearl into the snow with Judy in her arms and together, he and George took the flashlight and made return trips to the plane to carry or help the other survivors who could move, cross through the woods to their safe location. Whatever stewardess Pearl Ruth Moon was thinking while sitting in the dark woods with a near lifeless little girl in her arms is beyond imagination. When I asked her about this, she simply waved again and sank crying into her chair, speechless, and in the absolute defeat of finding any way to describe it.

Twenty-eight-year-old Mary Battista of Weirton, West Virginia was able to join the group on her own, despite a broken knee, cuts and bruises, and bare feet. Seated next to a window on the right side of the tail for her first flight on an airplane and a Florida vacation, the National Steel Corporation inspector lost her shoes in the crash. Battista said in a first-person newspaper account of the incident that she remembered little of the impact except for the seat belt warning, a scratching sound, and sparks shooting from the wings of the plane before it hit the ground. She also blacked out, and when she recovered, she hollered toward the silhouette of what turned out to be Lt. Bischof holding the flashlight. He helped her get out of the wrecked tail section and through the woods to safety. One by one they arrived at the safe location until the group of survivors outside the plane was a band of 11. At this stage, five others remained alive, in or around the plane's wreckage, either too injured to move or trapped. Gathered in a semi-circle, they assessed their injuries, certain that rescuers would come running for them at any moment.

Among the group in the woods, aside from the unconscious Judy Frankel, Marie Norcia, 47, of East Liberty, Pennsylvania, and Battista appeared to hurt the worst. Norcia had fractures in her left leg while Battista's fracture was in her right knee. Stewardess Beshears had only contusions to her chest, shoulder, and neck. Pearl had severe contusions to her face from being ejected from the plane. Anna Piso had a shoulder injury. Joseph Wozniak was in pain from chest injuries, Edward Wessel had a fractured right thumb, and Albert Dichak had only contusions and bruises. George Albert had a bruised shoulder and chest while Lt. Bischof had just a few bruises throughout his body, mostly to his legs and back.

Still in the wreckage were Mary Messerlos, with a fractured pelvis; Eva Woodward, with chest injuries and possible broken ribs; Thomas Patterson, with a fractured skull and a badly lacerated scalp. Robert Geyer had been in and out of the plane despite multiple fractures of both legs, his broken hand, and lacerations on his face, and Gertrude McLain was still strapped in her seat but outside the plane with injuries so severe she wouldn't live through the night. Her husband Roy, and everyone else who had been sitting in the forward section of the plane in front of Geyer at the emergency exit was already dead.

Despite the pain in her right eye and bruises on her face, Pearl was not hurt for the rest of her body. Sitting in the woods, surrounded by the other survivors and illuminated only by the weak beam of their flashlight, Pearl held tightly to Judy Frankel as Lt. Bischof assumed leadership and started planning for their survival. They first focused on the precious little girl. "I held her for at least an hour," Pearl recalled. Each of them looked in closely as Judy lay nearly lifeless in Pearl's arms. Then, they took turns cradling her in their own arms, trying to hold her without the slightest movement to control what they guessed was internal bleeding. It appeared hopeless. The time moved ever so slowly.

When little Judy died in Pearl's arms during the night, she didn't want to believe it. Tears flowed down her cheeks, already swollen and turning black and blue from the crushing blows of the crash. "I wasn't positive she had died at first, and I didn't want to put her on the wet ground," Pearl told reporters. Eventually, she swaddled the little girl's lifeless body in a blanket and tightly wrapped it in the wool coat. One of the men then laid Judy Frankel upon the driest spot of ground they could make with leaves and twigs. Many years later Pearl could still see images of little Judy as she died in her arms. Images of the bloody men trapped in the plane still flashed in her mind, too. "I have to cut it off in a hurry," she sobbed. "I just can't take it." The rest of her life was haunted by those images.

With the death of Judy Frankel, the group, was now down to ten in the woods some distance away from the plane. When Gertrude McLain died still strapped in her seat, it left just four still trapped in or near the wreckage. Down to 14 survivors from a horrendous and sudden crash of their low-flying passenger plane just 48 hours from the New Year, it was now approaching dawn on December 30 in the wild mountains of the Allegheny Plateau of western New York. It was silent again in the woods atop Bucktooth Ridge. All around them the cold night air was whisper quiet except for the occasional knocking sound of the tall bare hardwood tree branches in the breeze. The wrecked plane could no longer hurt them. Their main enemy now was the weather. And the rain was steadily falling faster. On the cold ground, it was turning to a crusty ice.

IN THE VALLEY BELOW the wreck, Ruby Bryant awoke on the morning of the 30th and stoked the wood fire in her farmhouse stove for more warmth. Four of her five boys lay snug in their beds upstairs. It may have warmed to just above freezing outside their farm overnight, but that was still plenty cold, and it required the old kitchen cook stove to get roaring with heat again. Ruby was extra careful loading the chunks of firewood. The pain in her breast had interrupted her sleep many times during the night.

ACROSS THE VALLEY and nearly atop Hoxie Hill, David Shenefiel was still in the barn before dawn, finishing his milking chores and laying down new bedding for the cows. His next assignment would be to take a quick drive around the Town of Napoli for a road inspection as part of his job as highway superintendent. He didn't suspect any serious problems, though, because the slight thaw, rain, and fog were melting some of the snow from the many gravel roads. He did, however, anticipate a lot of mud. On his drive, there would be no view of Bucktooth Ridge.

SALAMANCA DISTRICT HOSPITAL WAS slowly coming back to life after a quiet night, despite the fact that only 12 of its 52 beds were empty. And, at the Cattaraugus County Courthouse in Little Valley, offices were closed on this Sunday except for the Sheriff's Office and jail, attached to the sheriff's house, and beginning to stir, starting in the kitchen.

AT 9:30 THAT MORNING, the Erie Limited, a diesel-electric passenger train, departed its terminal in Jersey City filled with passengers who had crossed the Hudson River from Rockefeller Center Terminal in Midtown Manhattan.[82] It pulled north through New Jersey and into lower New York State for its 24-hour journey to Chicago.[83] Traveling across the Southern Tier, the Limited made passenger stops in several communities and was scheduled to arrive in Salamanca by 7:32 in the evening.[84] After a ten minute stop for loading passengers, it would continue westward where it would sound its horn for grade crossings at Sawmill Run Road and again at Steamburg just before 8 pm. Train horns are like fog horns. Their tone and decibels are designed to be heard under any conditions. The Erie's horn was loud enough to be heard on the top of Bucktooth Ridge.

---

[82] The Erie Limited passenger trains were all converted from steam engines to GM's Electro-Motive Diesel (EMD) E8 locomotives by December 1951.
[83] Utilizing its own mainline tracks, the Erie Limited took considerably longer to reach Chicago than did the high-speed trains of the New York Central and the Pennsylvania Railroad, which took only 16 hours for the trip. However, passage on the Erie was much cheaper.
[84] The Southern Tier is a common term for the southern counties of New York State along the Pennsylvania border.

NO ONE AMONG THE 14 survivors slept at all through the cold first night in the rain at the crash site. With temperatures just below freezing at the top of the ridge, the shivering of their poorly dressed and wet bodies set in soon after their adrenalin subsided. They needed warmth. Several times the uninjured survivors returned to the wreckage from their safety circle to search for warm clothing and the emergency supplies that Pearl said were packed away on the plane. Also, at the Pittsburgh airport, she had loaded small box lunches into the galley, intending to hand them out during the overnight run to Miami. In the compaction of the several large pieces of wreckage, however, they couldn't find them.[85] At first, Lt. Bischof, Pearl and George searched for two complete first aid kits that were on the plane. In the C-46, one was stowed in a canvas bag behind the pilot's seat, and another was stowed by the stewardess in or near the galley. Eventually they gave up, deciding that the first aid kits must have been crushed in the wreckage and destroyed. They drew the same conclusion for the box lunches. Lt. Bischof also searched for the emergency flares that he knew had to be stored in every airplane, but, again, he could not find them. There was a signal pistol and flare cartridges stowed above the map and data case hanging on the cockpit fuselage to the left of the pilot but, like the first aid kits, it couldn't be found because the cockpit was so compacted and inaccessible. Despite the fog, Lt. Bischof had hoped to fire the flare gun in the darkness as a signal for help. Returning to the survivors, his failure to find the flares left him shaken because he had been searching among the pilots' crushed bodies.

In the scattered heap of suitcases, they poked around with their flashlight and found dry clothing. They passed out coats and shirts among the wettest of the survivors. They also draped dry clothing over the four severely injured passengers still in the plane's wreckage. Pearl found pink napkins and some matches from the flight's food service trays. During a short walk around the woods, George, and Lt. Bischof stumbled into an old galvanized metal trash can. Gathering up some of the branches that had been buzzed to kindling-sized wood by the whirling

---

[85] The plane's galley was located directly behind the cockpit and was crushed.

propellers, and with the matches and napkins, they managed to get a small fire going in the trash can. Their circle of survivors now resembled a crude campsite. The fire provided some more light beyond their weak flashlight but little warmth. The plane was still in the dark.

The wrecked C-46, which delivered 26 passengers and crew to their deaths, proved to be a lifeline for the survivors. Inside the wreckage, they also found a cup in which to melt snow and some blankets that Pearl had handed out to the passengers while they were still flying. One of the able-bodied men released the snaps of a leather suitcase and found a pair of slipper socks for Mary Battista's bare feet. They couldn't find her shoes. Retrieving her purse from the wreckage, Battista opened it and produced two candy bars. She cut them into small pieces and shared them with everyone. They each got two bites.

Part of the wreckage also proved to be beneficial to Robert Geyer, who spent most of the first night in the cold and rain sitting up against the stump of a tree sheared off by the plane's wings. Because Geyer's badly fractured and bloodied unconscious body partially blocked an entrance to the largest part of the forward fuselage immediately following the crash, George, Lt. Bischof, and Dolores Beshears had moved him only to the edge of the opening where he lay in the snow. Regaining consciousness, Geyer had blood clotted over his right eye, partially blocking his vision. Discovering his broken hand and two badly smashed legs, he managed to use his one good hand to scoop snow and wash the blood from his eye. Reaching for his coat and hat that he had placed on the seat beside him, it was about then that Geyer realized he was no longer inside the plane. Thinking he had been thrown from the wreckage, only later did he discover that his unconscious body had been carefully dragged to the edge of the fuselage. At some point soon after the crash, Geyer became aware of the other survivors searching for matches to start a small campfire. Using his good hand, he managed to drag himself further away from the wreckage because he was afraid the others would carelessly catch the plane's dripping fuel on fire. Through the rainy night, he just sat there on the tree stump. "By morning I was soaked, and I knew I was freezing," he said. "I dragged myself back into the shelter of the plane using my one good hand, a few inches at a time. It must have taken an hour."

Geyer made a makeshift bed out of suitcases, and the clothing stashed in them. The others helped him pile more suitcases around him to block the wind and there, under the somewhat dry overhang of the unsteady hulk of the fuselage, he remained. Although his body was badly broken, he offered advice and encouragement, and then, the final inspiration that spurred the others to take action.

With enough dry clothing to ward off the rain for a few hours, the survivors then began searching for more food. In the baggage, they found some oranges, nut rolls, sausages, and some bread but they could not find the main supply of food and drinks packed away on the airplane for cabin service. They never found it. They did, however, find the plane's jar of instant coffee and with the cup held over the fire by a coat hanger from the plane, they warmed water from a spring found nearby and managed to serve lukewarm coffee, which they rationed and drank while sitting on suitcases around their small campfire. Their food was rationed too. At least, they tried to ration it. Pearl said that a few times there were arguments over the bite size of bread and nut rolls and who took a bigger sip of coffee from their shared cup. However, she attributed these small outbursts to the stress, fear and shock of the crash and their dire predicament rather than hunger or thirst. How, she recalled wondering silently to herself, would they get along when the food and coffee ran out?

Because it continued raining on Bucktooth Ridge on Sunday, December 30, they returned to the wreckage again where Lt. Bischof made a long, exhaustive search and found a large parachute that was left over from the days of the cargo plane's use in World War II. Snapping off long saplings, he set up the White Nylon parachute as a makeshift umbrella at their campsite to ward off the raindrops. He used a couple of metal rods from the plane too. It wasn't very effective but the appearance of a roof above their heads provided the illusion of shelter and comfort, and it did block some of the rain. Lt. Bischof also established one location for the group's latrine and requested they not wander off the ridge to relieve themselves (for those who could move). If they were to become incapacitated, even while urinating in the woods, he wanted to know where to go to find them. For the mobile passengers, having to walk off into the woods to find a measure of privacy to urinate and defecate was disconcerting enough. The four still trapped in the plane had no choice but to go in place. For them, it was embarrassing and demoralizing.

LT. BISCHOF WAS USING his extensive naval training, and the others began to respond to his leadership skills. Only 26, Lt. William W. Bischof was a graduate of Pennsylvania State College and served in the Pacific during World War II. From the upscale residential Moxham neighborhood along the Conemaugh River in Johnstown, an area spared by and built mostly since the great flood of 1889, Bischof only recently attained the rank of Lieutenant upon transfer from the U.S. Naval Base in Charleston, South Carolina to Key West. He had assumed command of the 136-foot-long submarine chaser, *USS PCS-1384*[86] Lt. Bischof was accustomed to leading and giving orders. He also had his wife, Irene, and recently born infant son, Frederick William Bischof, at home inspiring his fight for survival. While maintaining their fire, steadying the parachute, and tending to the injured in their small circle, Lt. Bischof, George, Pearl, and Dolores Beshears also kept returning to the plane to offer comfort to the four survivors still stuck inside. They replaced wet clothing and blankets with dry and tried to keep their spirits up. At one point on Sunday, Lt. Bischof and George tried to move Geyer to their campfire. Grabbing around him in a bear hug, they tried lifting him but the Pittsburgh printer was in too much pain. "My God, man, let go. I can't do it," he cried out. Settling back into his makeshift bed, Geyer began pawing through the suitcases piled around him with his one good hand. His other was not only broken but severely frostbitten. He found a breakfast cake in one of the suitcases, "a frosted one in the Viennese style," he said. Shouting off toward the campfire, he invited anyone who could to come and share the cake with him. Sitting there in the plane, bloodied and immobile, Geyer remembered what he had stashed away in his own luggage as he packed for his Florida vacation. With George's help, they found his suitcase and dug out a photograph of his wife, Evelyn, and their children, all under the

---

[86] The Patrol Craft Sweeper was later named USS Eufaula.

age of six. Pamela, Robert Geyer, Jr., and their infant daughter, Joyce, had all come down with the mumps. If the kids had not been sick, Evelyn would not have stayed home. She would have been on the plane with him. Carefully, he placed the photograph in a chest pocket of his coat. Geyer's mother had suggested he take the picture with him on vacation and now, with his family nestled close to his heart and no rescue in sight, Geyer settled in for what he considered might be the final hours of his life. And then, with George Albert, whom he had quietly watched as a stranger just the night before in a personal moment of absolute anguish and guilt over his dead mother, Geyer shared his private feelings of despair. "They're never going to find us," he told George in an emotional display of discomfiture. "You've got to go out and get help," Geyer implored. He offered George his dry clothes including his pants and socks. "I won't need them," he said.

CHAPTER 8

THIEF

THE SEARCH FOR DRY clothing was non-stop for the survivors. Their parachute umbrella was nearly worthless and as it collected rainwater, George, and Lt. Bischof would slosh the pools of water off the sides where they just got wetter. They desperately wanted to get dry.

It was during this time on Sunday, the day after the crash, among the survivors who managed to walk or crawl to the crude campfire site, that someone returned to the wreckage and began closely examining the dead in the fuselage and removing dry clothing from on or near the bodies. Such an act of desperation with an article of clothing needed to sustain life is perceived as acceptable in a civilized society. It was cold, they were wet and injured, they feared death from hypothermia, and the dead, their bodies dry inside what little remained of the airplane, could no longer benefit from the clothing. A wool coat had already been removed from the side of a dead passenger for wrapping around little Judy Frankel. Her lifeless body was still cocooned in the coat, and it was lying on some branches and leaves uncovered from the snow. All of this was necessary in a case of life or death. What happened next, however, was not. Perhaps it was hidden by the gray dusk or darkness late in the day but it happened on Sunday, December 30th as the survivors realized they would spend another night alone in the cold rain and snow on the mountain. Someone, either searching for clothing or food among the suitcases and the corpses, reached into the breast pocket of one of the dead women passengers to find a cache of more than $700 pinned inside the woman's jacket. In the quiet of the wreckage, hidden in the woods near the top of Bucktooth Ridge and apparently with no one watching, the thief unpinned the many paper notes from the fellow passenger's cold, lifeless body and slipped them into a pocket on his or her own living, warm body. He, or she, never uttered a word about it.

There were nine women who perished in the plane crash but only five who were likely to have had such a large amount of cash during the flight. Only two were very likely to be carrying this large amount of cash, based on their stature and travel plans, which were revealed after the tragedy. Dorothy Berman Bruce was in the process of traveling home to Kingston, Ontario, Canada from an extended foreign trip and, on a side trip to see her mother in Buffalo during the crash, was one of the two women most likely to have been carrying a large wad. Gertrude McLain was traveling to Florida for the winter months and was also likely to have been carrying this amount of cash. Because she survived the initial impact of the plane crash and died soon afterward, the other survivors who were at McLain's side giving her assistance, could have noticed or felt a clutch of bills. Perhaps because the only authority figures from the flight, the pilots, were all dead, did the thief feel that he or she could get away with it. Only days later would this criminal act be discovered when the victims' family began whispering among themselves that a large fold of cash was missing. Their whispers spread throughout the rural Cattaraugus County communities and would eventually reach the ears of the sheriff.

CHAPTER 9

TRUST THE PILOTS

USUALLY THERE IS NOT one single crash-causing mistake in an airplane. It typically is a series of mistakes over an extended time which, when all combined, leads to a situation from which the pilot cannot recover. That was the case with Flight 44-2 as the pilots in the cockpit seats, and two more at the cockpit door, struggled to save a large airliner with 40 people on board that was doomed from the moment it took off. Even 60 years after the fatal crash, Stewardess Pearl Moon repeatedly insisted that if Continental Charters' most experienced pilot had been flying the plane, the crash would not have happened. This remained her wishful thinking. She was referring to the pilot they affectionately called the old man, CJ Webber.

CJ Webber, Reserve Pilot

Originally, the Webbers of Luverne, Minnesota had only one B in their name, indicating their German heritage. The rise of the Nazis caused them to quietly change it.

Clarence Joseph Weber was born on September 26, 1913, in Luverne long before many German-Americans began distancing themselves from their homeland. His parents, Aloysius Joseph and Olena Knudtson Weber, were first generation Americans whose parents arrived from the Kingdom of Prussia, and Norway. They already had a 12-year-old daughter, Florence Katrina, when Clarence was born, and father, Joseph or "Big Al" as he was sometimes known, worked as a saloon keeper and grocer in Luverne and Hardwick, tiny farm towns closer to Sioux Falls, South Dakota than Minneapolis. Lena Weber stayed at home and raised the children. The nickname CJ was adopted at an early age and in the 1930's the family's last name was Anglicized with a second B to rid the family of anti-German sentiment that was growing in the years leading up to World War II.

When he was about nine, CJ moved with his family to Bedford and then Madison, Wisconsin. These were times when newspapers were filled with heroic events surrounding the race to fly solo or non-stop across great distances. Like many Midwestern boys, CJ became especially enthralled with airplanes when Charles Lindbergh flew solo across the Atlantic Ocean. For a boy from Wisconsin, who, no doubt, had seen barnstorming pilots bombard local farm towns with daredevil loops and wing walkers, it was enough for him to be hooked. CJ applied for his student pilot's license in June 1931 at about the same time he was graduated from West High School in Madison. By this time, however, the Depression interrupted his budding career in aviation and left him grounded, as a bus driver.

In his spare time, CJ was an airport kid who hung out at the Madison Airport with manager Walter Blake. Another airport kid, Fred Liedel, recounted how Blake would take them up flying "just for the fun of it or as passengers when he was teaching." Liedel counted CJ as a friend who was also a part-time pilot and who jiggered the fare lever on his bus so Liedel could ride around Madison for free. For CJ, however, flying was no part time vocation. Even while driving the bus, he accrued 700 hours in the cockpit by April 1939 when he ended his bus driving career and attempted to make a living by flying full-time.

It was about this time that CJ met Pearl Jensine Quam. Pearl was a farmer's daughter from Stoughton, Wisconsin, who captivated CJ on a double date (he was with the other girl) while she was attending the University of Wisconsin at Madison. Their courtship was long, 11 years! CJ was flying in air shows throughout Minnesota and Wisconsin but not making very much money. And, because she was a teacher, Pearl could not be married and keep her job. During one show, CJ wrote home to Pearl in Madison that he gave passengers rides in his "crate" until 12:45 am and that they lined up cars on each end of the grass runway with their headlights on to illuminate the field for landing. He also relied on the light of a full moon to get back on the ground safely. CJ earned his private pilot's license in October 1938 when he was 25 and his commercial license a few months later, in 1939.

CJ Webber, as he now spelled his name, also demonstrated his skill as a pilot. In May 1939, The Wisconsin State Journal reported that CJ saved three passengers and himself when the motor of his *"six-passenger cabin job"* conked out over a marsh near Madison. His first crash was a *"perfect three-point dead stick landing in the soft bog."* They all walked away.

By 1940, CJ was in Miami flying a Piper Cub J-3. The J-2 and J-3 were the primary trainers for the Civilian Pilot Training Program (CPTP), sponsored by the federal government to get more civilians in the cockpit as part of military preparedness for World War II. Later in 1940, at the age of 27, CJ found himself in East Lansing, Michigan as part of the Art Davis Air Show in Michigan and Minnesota. He flew a Taperwing Waco, a three-seat biplane with a Wright 250 HP Whirlwind engine that produced a gentle 3-G's in a loop; a Hansen Baby Bullet racer; and another Piper Cub J-3. CJ was earning his wings and learning how to handle an airplane upside down too.

The stunt pilot and air show life was exciting for CJ, but he also needed to earn a better living. He was planning to be married to Pearl soon, and he needed more money. In early September 1940, CJ received an invitation from Canadian Army officials to join the British Air Transport Auxiliary (ATA). The ATA was a squad of civilian pilots used to ferry newly built British warplanes from the factories to the front for British pilots in the early days of World War II. CJ left his air show flying and submitted to ATA testing in Toronto. He had never flown heavy aircraft, and if he was to advance to become a pilot ferrying Hawker Hurricanes and Lockheed bombers to the front, he had to take refresher courses in twin-engine aircraft and obtain his instrument rating. Soon, CJ began delivering war planes from Canada to England and throughout England and Scotland. Some of them were American planes. To maintain its official neutrality before the United States' entry into the war, American-built planes were flown to northern New York State and then towed across the border to Canada from where they were either shipped or flown to Great Britain. Twice CJ encountered close calls with war activities while delivering planes to the RAF such as the Bristol Blenheim, a twin-engine light bomber that suffered such heavy losses in the war. CJ once flew a "Blenburgher" (nickname for the Bristol Blenheim) into a British airfield and, as he stepped from the cockpit, was surprised to see no signs of life. He immediately heard and then felt the whoosh of a bomb. It exploded less than 100 yards away and knocked him to the ground. His chin was struck by shrapnel, and a scar from the wound was so pronounced that it was later noted in his travel documents as an identifying feature.

CJ capitalized on his training and flew 32 different aircraft to the RAF; Beaufighters, Spitfires, Whitley, Wellington, and Beaufort bombers, and many more. He listed the manufacturer, size, weight and number of engines of each plane in the back of his thumb-worn aviation logbook. He also wrote notes about rain, fog, aerobatics he performed when out of sight of superiors, the aerodynamics of each plane, and encounters with fields of barrage balloons used to prevent low-level bombing runs by the Germans.

These were situations that were turning CJ into an undisputed expert pilot in all conditions and airplanes. Although not fighting in the war, he was playing a key role. When the infamous German battleship *Bismarck* sank the British *HMS Hood* on May 24, 1941, CJ was the chief pilot of a Lockheed Hudson bomber flying from Canada to England as British warships were chasing after the damaged *Bismarck*. He encountered jamming of signals on his radio when he called for his bearings from an airfield in England. Unable to obtain an accurate fix on their position, CJ's navigator finally determined that German radio operators in the Atlantic had given them false bearings that sent them toward German anti-aircraft guns on the occupied French coastline. If they hadn't discovered their mistake and changed course, they would have been blown to bits. It was another lesson learned that would be useful to CJ later as a commercial airlines pilot.

CJ also learned what every pilot experiences first hand if he stays in the cockpit long enough – the loss of close friends. A lack of instrument training caused many of his pilot friends to crash. As a result, CJ wrote to Pearl that he often flew on instruments for practice and because he had to long before he became certified. *"I'm getting, so I can fly instrument as well as I can contact (visual flight),"* he explained to Pearl. *"(It) should be very useful sometime."*

A full year after CJ signed up, he made his final flight for the ATA. The entry in his log expressed his feelings, *"Spitfire AB986 – Captain – Birmingham to Kenley – (aerobatics) – My last delivery – a year well spent."* Apparently the British felt less urgency sending ATA pilots back home after their tours than they did transporting them to England. CJ returned to North America on a whaling ship in October 1941. Packed in his luggage were his logbooks filled with hour after hour flying some of the most sophisticated single and twin-engine airplanes in the world. And tucked into a small box was a diamond ring that Pearl Quam Webber would wear on her finger until she died 43 years after their marriage. After their wedding, CJ and Pearl left home immediately for Miami where he landed a job with Pan American Air Ferries (PAAF), a company that flew American warplanes from the United States to Africa, the Middle East, and Europe. CJ piloted Lockheed Hudson and Ventura bombers, Douglas A-20 Havocs and C-47 Skytrains, Martin A30 light bombers, and many other twin-engine planes from Florida via Central and South America to Africa and the Middle East. By the end of the war, CJ Webber, a saloon keeper's son from rural Minnesota and Wisconsin, had mastered more airplanes than most any famous fighter pilot or bomber crew. He claimed to have set both the South Atlantic speed record crossing from Natal, Brazil to Ascension Island for the Martin A30 (5 hours and 51 minutes) and made 28 trips across the South Atlantic air ferry route, the greatest number of any pilot during the war on all types of aircraft.[87]

---

[87] This record is according to CJ's logbook only and cannot be independently verified. Such records were not kept for these flights – it was up to each pilot to keep track in his logbook.

CJ returned to the United States on May 4, 1945. He officially obtained his instrument rating (although he had already flown by instruments on many flights) and began ferrying airplanes between Miami and Central and South America. On at least one trip, he was carrying cows on his transport plane. By 1947, and already an expert at ferrying planes south of the equator, CJ became associated with a Miami produce exporter-importer named Charlie Winters. From February 1947 through June 1948, CJ's logbook indicates that he continuously flew war surplus B-17s between Miami and South America, Puerto Rico, and the Bahamas. Pearl described his business with Winters as going to South America to find airplanes to refurbish and sell. On one trip in a B-17, he apparently had to outrun a large hurricane while Pearl, pregnant with their second child, was with him on the plane.

Charlie Winters had been using three American war surplus B-17 bombers to haul fruit and vegetables between Puerto Rico, the Bahamas, and Miami. As a business partner, CJ frequently flew the planes.[88] Another pilot who flew the B-17s on the fruit and produce runs was Harold "Hal" Rothstein, a veteran bomber and fighter pilot who also became a pilot for the nonscheduled airlines of the early 1950s. Rothstein recalled, at the age of 91, how he crash-landed a nonsked C-46 when he was 29 and flying a load of 36 Air Force airmen from the west coast to Mississippi and Alabama. Rothstein made a belly landing after losing an engine on the C-46 while taking off from a refueling stop in Prescott, Arizona. His skill saved his life and 40 others on board the plane.

Perhaps the produce flying business was not successful enough because Winters agreed in 1948 to either sell or donate their B-17s to the cause of independence for Jews in Palestine, leading to the creation of the state of Israel during the Arab-Israeli war of 1948. Winters had become friends with a flight engineer named Al Schwimmer, known as the father of the Israeli Air Force, and it was Schwimmer who convinced Winters, an Irish Protestant from Boston, to provide his produce

---

[88] The unpainted surplus B-17s initially displayed a logo of interlocking W's for Winters-Webber.

hauling B-17s to Israel through an intermediary, Irving L. Johnson of Miami.[89] Taking off from Miami on June 11, 1948, the three planes were flown to Puerto Rico and refueled as they often did on their routine fruit and produce hauling runs. But, instead of returning to Miami the planes were flown on a grueling 33 hour-long trip to the Azores and Zatac, Czechoslovakia where they were refitted back to bombers and flown on bombing runs over Cairo and Rafiah, Egypt.[90] They became the first three heavy bombers of the new Israeli Air Force and played a role in turning the war for independence in Israel's favor.

Sending war planes to Israel was a violation of the Neutrality Act of 1939. By the time the planes arrived in Puerto Rico, the FBI was already on to their mission and trying to stop them. As one of the pilots, Rothstein had a friend in the San Juan airport tower who called him late that night and warned him, "you'd better get your ass out of here because the FBI is going to shut you down." They took off right away. Rothstein identified the other daring pilots as Naron H. "Smoky" Lee and R. Weid Mayer of Miami. After more than 60 years, he couldn't remember the names of the co-pilots who didn't do much actual flying anyway. Rothstein's friend and the other airport tower controllers at San Juan followed FBI orders and called on their radio for the B-17 pilots to return.[91] Rothstein said they kept going and even threw old life rafts and other non-essential items out of the planes into the Atlantic Ocean to suggest they had crashed. They radioed maydays, reported engine fires and that they were ditching in the ocean. It was all a ruse to throw off any efforts to find them before they got to Europe. When they arrived over the continent and flew over German air space, Rothstein grew nervous at the sight of American fighter planes that flew up to check them out. "They saw the N numbers in our B-17s and left us alone," he said.

---

[89] The name has been spelled different ways in reports from the 1950s. Irving or Erving L. Johnson may also have been a fictitious name.
[90] Such long flights were possible only with extra fuel tanks fastened in the cargo hold of the planes.
[91] Naron "Smoky" Lee was also aboard the nonsked C-46 piloted by Rothstein when it crashed in Arizona on August 31, 1952.

The telephone number for Winters' Miami air transport business, Charwin Sales, was connected to the telephone at CJ and Pearl's Miami El Portal neighborhood home in the 200 block of Northeast 86th Street. Federal agents came knocking on their door looking for CJ because his name was on the flight customs documents and agents initially believed that he had been one of the pilots of the Palestine-bound B-17s. With two little children at her side, Pearl Webber nervously told the agents CJ wasn't home and that she didn't know where he was at the time. Later, she thought, "maybe Czechoslovakia!"

CJ was never arrested or charged in connection with the B-17 caper, but he was identified as the man who hired "Smoky" Lee to fly one of the planes. Clearly, he played a role, albeit minor. Winters was charged, convicted, fined $5,000 and sent to prison for 18 months. In Israel, and among prominent American Jews, Charlie Winters is considered a hero of the 1948 war. After his death in 1984, Winters' ashes were scattered from Mount Tabor and buried in a Christian cemetery near the Knights Templar cemetery in Jerusalem. On December 23, 2008, he was posthumously pardoned by President George W. Bush. Schwimmer and another man convicted of the conspiracy with Winters, Herman Greenspun, were pardoned by Presidents Kennedy and Clinton respectively. Of the three, Winters was the only one who served time in prison. Despite his close business association with Winters, CJ was never directly involved in smuggling the B-17s to Israel. He knew he was in a dangerous profession and, with a growing family, perhaps the risk wasn't worth it. His family believes that Winters purposely left CJ out of it when the FBI came sniffing around. From his notes in his logbook, CJ also believed that he would die before he turned 39, as had three of his close friends. He wisely kept a low profile in the B-17 smuggling caper.[92]

The events of 1948 ended CJ's job as a cargo pilot, and he soon undertook a major change in his flying career, piloting commercial passenger

---

[92] Much of the information about Charlie Winters is confirmed in a formal letter from Florida Congressmen Connie Mack and Ron Klein to a U.S. Department of Justice pardon attorney in 2008. They called Winters' conviction and prison sentence for his role in the 1948 Israeli Independence War an *"injustice."*

airplanes. On April 24, 1950, CJ's logbook indicates his first flight in a C-46 for Continental Charters of Miami. CJ had accrued more than 6,000 hours of flight, and he achieved an aircraft rating which allowed him to serve as pilot-in-command for commercial operations. He was a tremendous asset for Continental Charters because of his vast experience flying multi-engine aircraft. It's likely that CJ would have been a key pilot for Continental Charters' flagship four-engine Boeing Stratoliner before the high expense of the now infamous plane forced the company to unload it to obtain another cheaper C-46, the plane that killed him. Ironically, by 1951 CJ and Pearl Webber had three little children at home in Miami and they considered this time the safest flying in his career.

Gus Athas, 25, Reserve Co-Pilot

The youngest pilot for Continental Charters among the four on Flight 44-2 was 25-year-old Gus Athas. He was Frank Sinatra handsome with an engaging smile. He loved fast motorcycles and his wife. Gus may have known more about the plane they were in than the other three pilots because he was the company pilot-mechanic who went to Texas several days before the crash to supervise the refitting and retrieve the C-46 for Continental Charters. He was the first to fly it when he ferried it from Dallas over the Gulf of Mexico to Continental Charters' home airport in Miami.

Pearl Moon described Gus as "the young kid" (even though he was a year older than her) because his good looks made him appear younger than his 25 years. He was also described as a very good pilot. Born in 1926 in Wheeling, West Virginia to Peter and Anna Raschek Athas, Gus moved with his parents and his brother, Theodore, sister, Georgianna, and his 70-year-old grandmother, also named Anna Raschek, to Raymond Avenue in Rutherford, New Jersey, before 1940, where Peter worked as an advertising salesman. Peter Athas' father was raised in Wheeling where he worked as a waiter and *"proprietor"*, but he was born in Platana, Sparta, Greece. Gus' mother, Anna, was raised in St. Louis. His name was just Gus, but it may have been a short version of his maternal grandfather's name, August Raschek, a Bohemian national who worked as a machinist after migrating to America. At East Rutherford High School, Gus was voted best-looking boy in his graduating class of 1945. He easily won the prize with his Sinatra features. With thick dark hair from his father's Greek heritage and a wide smile from his mother's Bohemian ancestry, Gus was popular among the girls of Rutherford and East Rutherford, especially when he put on his leather helmet, stripped down to his white T-Shirt, and climbed aboard his fast and beloved Indian motorcycle. Gus learned to fly with the Civil Air Patrol at the age of 16. Although he was active in the Army after joining the Army Air Forces in Newark, on January 2, 1945, before he finished high school, Gus was not directly involved in the war. He was stationed in Biloxi, Mississippi and Fort Myers, Florida. Gus married his high school girlfriend, Joan Harrison, and after he was discharged from the Army, they found themselves living in an apartment house on NE 55th Street in Miami. Gus worked as an airplane mechanic for Continental Charters. He further trained on the GI Bill to fly, and eventually became a licensed twin-engine co-pilot.

During their time together in Miami, as Gus worked for Continental Charters, he and Joan produced two sons, Gus Michael Athas, who was five in 1951, and James Jay Athas, who was three at the time of his father's fatal crash. Although with a deep retrospective interest in the aviation events of 1951, neither remembers much of anything about their father. Because he was not on duty and was not flying the plane when it crashed, Gus's flying history and hours were not included in the accident investigation report, and his pilot's log book was long ago lost. Pilots often took them on flights, and it may have been destroyed in the crash.

In 1951, a long-distance flight scheduled to return home on the same day required a second crew. Because Continental Charters was such a small airline, the reserve crew had to ride along on the first leg of the trip; there were no pilots waiting in Buffalo to take over the flight duties of the plane. There was little that a reserve crew could do on a flight but ride and rest and wait for its turn in the cockpit. Joan Athas was told by investigators that Gus started out sitting in the back of the plane but switched seats with a woman from the front who complained about being cold.[93] The switch placed him next to his pilot mentor, CJ Webber, and near the cockpit. It cost him his life.

Hans E. Rutzebeck, 33, Co-Pilot

"Rutz" was a nickname and everyone who knew Hans Rutzebeck used it, even his wife. No one ever called him Hans. That was his father's name although Rutz was not a Hans, Jr. and his somewhat famous father didn't go by the name Hans either, he used his middle name.

Hans Edmund Rutzebeck was born on July 13, 1918, when his adventure-seeking Danish father, Hans Hjalmar Rutzebeck, and Kansas-born mother, Margaret Johnson Rutzebeck lived in Alaska. The Rutzebecks soon after moved to Los Angeles, where they lived in 1920, and then to Paradise, California, in the foothills of the Central Valley near Chico, to raise and sell fruit and produce. Here, Rutz was joined by four siblings.

Why the Rutzebeck men didn't use their first names may have been to avoid confusion. The name Hans was handed down from Hjalmar's grandfather in Copenhagen, Denmark. This Hans was the captain of a mail sloop and later for a steamship line. Hjalmar's father, Hans Julius Rutzebeck, apparently went by his middle name, Julius, passed down to Rutz's uncle.[94] Hjalmar Rutzebeck ran away to the sea from his Copenhagen parents and eight siblings at the age of 12 and eventually jumped ship in the Alaska territory in 1910 where, without any citizenship papers in Haines, Alaska, he joined the U.S. Army before America's entry into World War I. He displayed a tattoo of the Norwegian flag on his right arm, but he was declared a U.S. citizen in 1922 through a special act of the Territory of Alaska delegation to Washington.

After the war, Hjalmar wrote Jack London-style Alaska adventure stories for newspapers and magazines, and books based on his own early

---

[93] This was all Joan Athas was told about how Gus died. Few other details were provided to her by the CAB.
[94] Rutz's only son was named Lief Alexander Rutzebeck, possibly after another of Hjalmar's brothers, Lief Hans Rutzebeck.

life on the gold rush frontier. *Alaska Man's Luck* and *My Alaskan Idyll* are two titles among them. And, from his experience as a fruit grower in California, he worked as a union and commune organizer with socialistic views, as a tax consultant, and occasionally as a real estate broker. He was an organizer of the self-help movement during the early 1930s in the San Francisco area working with the Unemployed Exchange Association (UXA) of Oakland, a bartering cooperative designed to offset the economic challenges of the Great Depression. His stories and Shanties of his early seafaring and Alaskan frontier life were recorded for Folkways Records as late as 1980 when he was 91. A photograph of Hjalmar with Hans Edmund Rutzebeck, in early 1920s Southern California, shows a beaming father holding his long blond-haired toddler boy on his knee beneath a palm tree. Those happy times wouldn't last.

Rutz had a brief marriage in 1937 in Ormsby, Nevada, which produced a daughter. After a divorce, Rutz joined the U.S. Navy in July 1943 where he became a machinist mate through World War II, a time when his ancestral Rutzebecks, who remained in Denmark, lost everything to the invading Germans. In the fall of 1945, Rutz was on his final military stint in St. Johns, Newfoundland where, at a USO dance, he met and began dating a young Royal Canadian Air Force Women's Division corporal who worked as an airplane spotter. Ruth Isobel Stewart's job was to help Canadian military air traffic controllers track planes being ferried to Europe for the war and to look out for enemy planes that might arrive from over the North Atlantic.[95] Upon their discharges from the military after the war, Rutz returned to his family adventures in Fairbanks and Barrow, Alaska, and Isobel returned home to her family in Edmonton, Alberta.

Soon enough, however, a letter arrived for Isobel proposing marriage and to join Rutz for an Alaska adventure. Isobel, who had once tricked Rutz into thinking she was her identical twin sister, accepted the proposal and on August 12, 1946, she and Rutz were married in Edmonton.

---

[95] Ruth Isobel "Izzy" Stewart went by her middle name and hereafter is referred to as Isobel.

Soon afterward, the newlyweds set off for Alaska traveling in an old car up the recently constructed gravel Alcan Highway through British Columbia, Yukon Territory, and into Alaska.

They spent nights in camps built for the Alcan workers because there were no hotels. They passed by broken down cars and trucks and suffered only one flat tire, themselves. An experienced Alaskan traveler, Rutz had prepared the car well, even removing the engine and cleaning it before the trip. On one stop at a construction camp, they found just two fold-out cots in a small room of a wood and tarpaper shack. "It was so cold, and we had one blanket each, so we got into one cot to snuggle up and get warmer," Isobel fondly recalled more than 60 years later.

Upon arriving in Fairbanks, Rutz took a job operating excavation equipment for construction of Fairbanks International Airport, which opened in 1951. He also took his first flying lessons at Seltenreich's Alaska Flying School in the fall of 1946. His first lessons were in an old Taylorcraft plane, with rear-wheel landing gear, at the former Fairbanks' Weeks Field. He earned his student permit on September 7 and his private flight certificate on October 10, 1946, from Bud and Fred Seltenreich, organizers of the flight school. Rutz immediately recognized that he could make money flying a plane in Alaska. He scraped together $500 to buy a small single-engine Aeronca with high wings and tail landing gear, and he began flying between Fairbanks and the Yukon-Koyukuk region of west-central Alaska. Isobel sometimes flew with Rutz in this old plane. "I liked it until he wanted to do loops," she said. "He liked to do loops."

In the winter, Rutz would fly Indian trappers to their interior Bush trap lines, landing with skis on frozen lakes, where they would spend weeks at a time harvesting bales of valuable beaver, mink and marten pelts. It was tricky flying that taxed his every skill in all kinds of weather. He flew for Koyukuk trading post owner Dominic Vernetti, who managed the Indian trappers and purchased the furs that returned in Rutz's plane. One of Rutz's trappers was Sidney Huntington, who told his Alaska adventure stories in a 1993 book, *Shadows on the Koyukuk*. Huntington reported that from the $11,000 in fur pelts harvested one winter in the late 1940s, his flying bill from Rutz amounted to $2,800.

In the summer, Rutz would fly between Fairbanks and the gold mining camps of the Livengood region. His primary client was Carl G. Parker, owner of the Olive Creek Mines. Rutz flew passengers and mining machine parts and sometimes flew Parker to Fairbanks with old rags wrapped around bags of gold for deposit in the bank. Rutz proved to be useful to Parker because when he wasn't flying he could operate excavators, scooping up the pay dirt and dropping it into the sluice boxes for sifting out the gold. It was a job similar to that portrayed on the Discovery television network's *Gold Rush,* in 2015.

At Olive Creek, Rutz and Isobel bunked in the gold camp's original miners' cabin where Isobel worked as a school teacher for the few children at the camp. Isobel recalls teaching the kids to climb into the rafters when Grizzly Bears came sniffing around and where they would hide with the safety of a gun hanging on nails near the ceiling. When the camp closed for the winter of 1947-48, Rutz bought a Taylorcraft airplane, and together they moved westward to Koyukuk for more bush flying along the Indian trap lines.

With business partner and fellow pilot, Al Wright, who later founded Wright Air Service in Fairbanks, Rutz formed a small flying company with which they amassed five planes including the Taylorcraft, a CallAir and a larger plane to haul cargo between Koyukuk and Fairbanks. He also earned his commercial license on July 30, 1948, and his instrument rating on September 28, 1949. Between the winter of 1947 and spring of 1951, Rutz would fly tourists from Fairbanks to see Mt. McKinley, and Indians from Koyukuk to their trap lines, always with single-engine planes that he maintained himself. He was running what the CAA considered a nonsked airline under the original Aeronautics Act of 1938. Rutz and Isobel also started their family during these years between the winter camps of Koyukuk and their small house in Fairbanks. Their son, Lief, arrived in 1949 and their daughter, Peggy, in 1951.

Rutz had a few close calls with his airplanes in the Alaskan bush. A return flight from the Bering Sea to pick up whale blubber for the sled dogs of Koyukuk was abruptly aborted when Rutz hit a chunk of ice with his landing skis, toppled over in the plane and damaged the prop and leading edges of the wings. While Rutz waited days for a spare prop to be flown to him from Fairbanks, Isobel was flown into the bush by another pilot where she trapped several beavers to help pay for repairs to the plane. Another time Rutz flew into the bush and picked up an Indian trapper with a large load of beaver pelts. Taking off on a short frozen lake, his plane was apparently too heavy for flight in the subzero temperatures, even with the treetops at the end of the lake cut off. Once again his plane toppled over and, without injuries, he holed up in the trapper's cabin. Isobel used the Koyukuk two-way radio to alert the Fairbanks airport that Rutz was several days overdue. The wrecked Taylorcraft was spotted by the pilots of a passenger plane diverted from its regular route to Fairbanks. Another small plane was sent into the bush to rescue Rutz and the trapper.

Isobel described Rutz as an "adventurist and daring" pilot. After a crash landing in the old Aeronca that damaged the wings, Rutz repaired the wood framing, and Isobel sewed on the fabric to get the plane back in the air. Flying to Fairbanks one day from the bush, the plane couldn't achieve enough altitude to clear a mountain peak. Rutz had Isobel hold the yoke steady while he climbed into the tail of the plane, made some adjustments, returned to the pilot's seat and navigated the small plane over the peak. "Whatever he did, worked," Isobel said, "and we landed safely at the Fairbanks airport." Rutz was lucky as a pilot, and he was becoming a veteran of minor plane crashes. But then, the couple's marriage hit turbulence.

Early in 1951 Rutz announced to his pregnant wife, Isobel that he wanted to go to Florida where he could be certified as a pilot for multi-engine planes. Excitement over the October 1951 opening date of Fairbanks International Airport gripped the territory, and Rutz yearned for a bigger piece of the action. His initial plan (he professed to Isobel) was to become certified for multi-engine planes and return to Alaska where he and partner Al Wright would expand their flight business with larger twin-engine cargo and passenger planes to fly between Fairbanks and Point Barrow. There may have been a different motive for the Florida trip, however, because another woman entered the picture.

On June 3, 1951, without telling Isobel, who was at their home in Fairbanks taking care of toddler Lief and one-month-old Peggy, Rutz gassed up his flight company's Studebaker car and left for Miami with the other woman. He earned his multi-engine, seaplane rating on July 6, listing his total flight hours as 6,385. Why he chose Florida for his certification isn't known. He could have done it in Fairbanks. Perhaps it was the prospect of a paying pilot's job with one of the popular nonskeds based in Miami, such as Continental Charters which he joined as a co-pilot on July 25, or simply the lustful adventure of a trip to exotic Florida with a new girlfriend. Whatever the reason for the sudden departure, Al Wright was the one who gave Isobel the bad news that Rutz, the Studebaker, and the other woman were gone from Alaska. Isobel never saw or heard from Rutz again.

Victor A. Harris, 28, Pilot

Victor Harris was the pilot in command and at the controls of Continental Charters Flight 44-2 when it crashed. There is no question about where the CAB investigators placed blame for the crash; it's in their lengthy but rather rushed crash investigation report. However, after examining all the information about Flight 44-2, Continental Charters, the nature of the nonsked business model, the CAB's lax oversight, and the still evolving rules and regulations of commercial aviation, the question remains, was it fair to blame only Harris for the crash?

Victor Arthur Harris was born on October 15, 1923, to Arthur Farr Harris and Nellie Ellen Wohlert Harris in Tom, Oklahoma, a barely noticeable crossroads hamlet of just a few homes near the most winding portion of the Red River, and the border with Texas. For an idea of how desolate the country is around Tom, watch the 1948 western cattle drive film *Red River*, starring John Wayne and Montgomery Clift. Although the film takes place in the mid to late 1800s, Tom, Oklahoma hadn't changed much by 1923 or 1951.

Father Art Harris was part Choctaw Indian and his family proudly claimed an Indian scout who served during the Revolutionary War. By 1940, however, Nellie was divorced from cattle truck driver Art, and she maintained a rented home for Victor and his younger siblings in Dorchester and Bunker Hill, Illinois (near St. Louis) where Nellie's father helped them make ends meet financially.

Victor Harris enlisted in the U.S. Army Air Corps during World War II on November 3, 1942, at Jefferson Barracks, Missouri. He had completed four years of high school at Bunker Hill and was a skilled mechanic and repairman, unmarried, and with no children. A thin, lanky man with large ears and a long chin who combed his blond and brown hair back and to the right, Harris portrayed a broad smile below his blue-green eyes that revealed dimple-like features on both cheeks. By April 1945, when he was 22, Harris was based in Florida where he was married in Manatee County (Bradenton) to Evelyn Lucille Mann, the 17-year-old daughter of a cattle ranch foreman in Polk County. They met through friends only six months earlier in 1944. Victor and Evelyn first lived in Sarasota and through the late 1940s and into 1950, they produced two children, Judith Evelyn Harris, and Raymond Victor Harris. After Harris had been discharged from the Army, the family lived for a time in Illinois where Victor worked as an automobile mechanic at a gas station. Eventually moving back to Florida, Harris obtained a job as an aircraft engine mechanic for Continental Charters (similar to the job obtained by Gus Athas), and he studied to be certified with his full commercial pilot's license. Harris began working for Continental Charters in Miami on November 29, 1948, but he didn't obtain his Airline Transport Pilot rating on a C-46 plane until March 9, 1951.[96] His first flight for Continental Charters was over the Caribbean, and it caused Evelyn to stay up all night afraid that he wouldn't return. She was extremely proud of how her husband worked as a mechanic during the day and studied at night to become a pilot. "He worked and studied, and just never stopped," she said about Harris, whom she called Vic. Even by 1950 standards among the nonskeds, Harris' ascent to captain was extremely fast.

Before this achievement, Harris flew as a co-pilot, and Continental Charters was the only airline for which he worked. Trim and fit in his company uniform of dark pants and jacket with four large shiny gold-colored buttons down the front and with two gold stripes on the sleeves

---

[96] Airline Transport Pilot rating is the highest level required for serving as Pilot-in-Command of a passenger airplane.

signifying co-pilot-in-training, Harris portrayed the dashing confidence of a prestigious commercial airlines pilot. Black tie tightly cinched up to his white cotton shirt collar; he donned his pilot's cap with gold leaf sprig and a band prominently displayed above the wide sun visor. Gold wings were pinned to his breast pocket, and his black shoes were shined to a gleam. Harris drove a late 1940s two-door sedan to the airport from their small ranch-style tract home on Northwest 17th Street near Miami International Airport. He enjoyed flying and was reportedly not one to take risks in the cockpit. He appeared to be living a swank life in the Florida sunshine, ferrying passengers through the eastern United States and to Central and South America in the Continental Charters' C-46s. The stewardesses got to know Harris well and Beshears, who flew with him many times, described Harris as one of the best pilots in the company. At the time of the crash of Flight 44-2 his logbook listed flight time as 3,107 hours.

Harris had been with the company the longest, but he was not the most experienced pilot among the four; it was definitely CJ Webber, and even co-pilot Hans Rutzebeck had more flight time, though not with twin-engine planes. Additionally, Harris and Gus Athas apparently had become close friends during the time they worked together as mechanics and pilots for Continental Charters. The good life, however, soon dropped into an uncontrollable spin.

Despite being married and with two young children, Harris began dating Athas' neighbor on Northeast 55th Street in Miami, a young woman originally from western Pennsylvania.[97] Gus liked Victor Harris and the two pilots often chummed around together and double-dated with Gus' wife Joan and Harris' girlfriend. Harris was described as kind and friendly, but, like his co-pilot, Rutz, there was obviously trouble with his marriage. Because marital problems can cause stress, leading to poor judgment, they and other domestic strife issues are part of modern plane crash investigations when pilots are believed to be at fault. However, it's an issue that CAB investigators ignored in 1952 in their rapid search for a cause of the crash of Flight 44-2.

---

[97] Harris' girlfriend's name was learned during research for *Hang on and Fly* but her identity has not been revealed to respect her family's privacy.

In contrast to the kind and friendly description of Harris, while answering the simple question, "what were the pilots like," Pearl Moon quickly and tersely described Harris as "smart and jerky," as in a smarty-pants and a jerk. Even after all these years it's a strong and bitter assessment of a man portrayed favorably by others. This is Pearl Moon's description only, based on her experience with Harris on the fatal flight and previous flights with Continental Charters. Moon obviously did not like Harris, and she resented the fact that her pilot-in-command did not provide her with much information about the flight plans from Miami to Pittsburgh and Pittsburgh to Buffalo. During an extensive interview with Moon 60 years after the crash, she still expressed anger for Harris and regret about how the events of that long and disastrous day turned out. However, aside from the fact that Harris was blamed for the crash, the reasons for her long-held bitterness toward him are unknown.

Harris was described as flirtatious, and Moon was portrayed as being romantically involved with various men (including pilots) during her time as a stewardess. If there was ever more than a professional relationship between Moon and Harris, she never revealed it. Additionally, Moon was apparently confused about who was flying the plane when it crashed. In separate, independent newspaper reports from the days immediately following the crash, Pearl was quoted as saying CJ Webber was the pilot in command, not Harris. Another person who knew Harris in Miami in 1951, and from whom I inquired about his personality and character, suggested he was very friendly but that he was also a "ladies man." A further description was cut short as if not wanting to say anything bad about the man killed at the controls of the plane.[98]

It should also be noted that stewardess Pearl Moon of 1951 was described not so favorably by this person as well. Whatever happened it appears there was some animosity or strained professional relationships between some of the Continental Charters crew which so often worked

---

[98] Harris' family also confirmed the fact that he dated stewardesses from the airline and had a girlfriend before the fatal crash in December 1951. It's relevant only because modern plane crash investigations consider marital strife when in 1951 they did not.

closely together on many long and difficult flights throughout 1951. Today, these relationships, conflicts, and personality issues would be investigated fully as a matter of routine in a plane crash probe. In 1951 and '52, they weren't even considered.

In late December 1951, Harris had a lot to contemplate as he prepared for his first flight in Continental Charters' newest C-46 airplane. He and Evelyn had been having marital difficulties since September; he was involved with another woman, and his only son's first birthday was December 27 with no party or celebration planned. Evelyn went into a Miami hospital for elective surgery on the 27th and Harris stopped in to visit her the next day. He told Evelyn he would be flying the company's new plane to Pennsylvania and New York State the following morning as captain of Flight 44-2. Despite all the turmoil, she was proud of him. Their marriage ended the same as it did for Isobel and Rutz. After that day in the Miami hospital, Evelyn never saw or heard from Vic again.

Top, clockwise, Allegheny County Airport, West Mifflin, Pa, as it appeared in 1951 when Continental Charters Flight 44-2 departed Pittsburgh for Buffalo; Ruby Bryant and four-year-old Otis Bryant on their Cattaraugus County farm, 1950; Continental Charters Stewardess Pearl Ruth Moon among the stewardess crew in 1951. The Flag behind her is from the tail of a Continental Charters C-46.

Top, an Air Force Curtiss C-46 Commando, nearly identical to the unpainted Continental Charters plane used for Flight 44-2 on December 29, 1951; below, one of four C-46 Commandos in Continental Charters' fleet in 1951. This was not the plane that flew and crashed as Flight 44-2. Note the simple ladder hanging from its port-side cargo door.

Top left, clockwise, interior of a crudely converted C-46 in 1952; thick fog on Bucktooth Ridge State Forest lands; view of Bucktooth Ridge from Hoxie Hill, looking across the Pigeon Valley in Napoli, New York. Route 242 and Windmill Road are in the foreground. Crash scene is to the left of and beyond the communications tower.

From atop Hoxie Hill in the 1950s, David Shenefiel looks out to Bucktooth Ridge and the scene of the crash of Continental Charters Flight 44-2. Heavy snow was often a problem in the mountains of Cattaraugus County for small towns such as Napoli. The winter of 1951-52 produced especially deep snow which hampered the rescue efforts for the survivors of the plane crash.

The last Albert family photograph with their mother, Christmas 1951 in Josephine, Pennsylvania. Bottom row, l-r: Rose and Dorothy. Middle row, l-r: George, Elizabeth and Abe. Top row, l-r: James and Joseph.

Ruby and Otis Bryant on the back steps of the Bryant farmhouse on Sawmill Run, 1951; the back of the Bryant's farmhouse, with Tippy, the family's dog, about 1951. The slope leading up to Bucktooth Ridge is in the background.

Top, clockwise, the first production C-46 Commando is rolled out of the Buffalo Curtiss-Wright factory on April 11, 1942, painted camouflage green and beige. More than 3,000 C-46s would be produced for the war; at the height of production in Buffalo, many Curtiss-Wright employees were women, pictured with hair wrap in the nose of the plane.

Top left, clockwise, a C-46 flying over The Hump, Himalaya Mountains in 1945; Carl Constein, Pennsylvania C-46 pilot flew 96 missions over The Hump during WW II, posing in one of the few C-46s still flying, *Tinker Belle*, in 2012; cargo of aircraft tires flying The Hump in a C-46; inside a C-46 air ambulance during the war; the cockpit of a C-46 Commando in 1945.

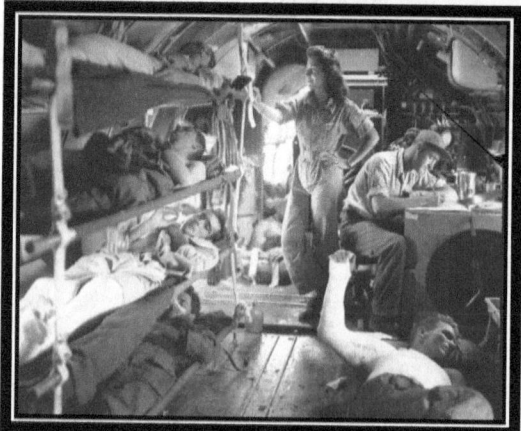

Top left, clockwise, Randall and Margaret Shenefiel at the David and Rosa Shenefiel farm in Napoli about 1951; Hoxie farmhouse in winter, late 1940s; the Cattaraugus County village of Randolph with Hoxie Hill and Bucktooth Ridge in the background; village of Randolph in the 1940s; site of Flight 44-2 crash investigation hearing in the old Cattaraugus County Courthouse with the sheriff's home next to courthouse in Little Valley, NY.

Top left, clockwise, The Oscar and Helen Shenefiel farm in the valley below Bucktooth Ridge; David Shenefiel driving the Napoli snow plow on Hoxie Hill Road, early 1950s; snow-filled and slightly plowed Hoxie Hill Road; David and Rosa Shenefiel farm and Hoxie Hill in the 1950s, top, from where there was a clear view of Bucktooth Ridge; 1951 S & S hearse identical to Myers Funeral Home hearse-ambulance driven to the crash of Flight 44-2.

Top left, clockwise, the Continental Charters C-46 flown to Pittsburgh and Buffalo by company president John Belding, right, after the crash; Continental Charters' infamous Clipper Flying Cloud as delivered to Pan Am in March 1940; Miami International Airport in the early 1950s; Flight 44-2 pilots Victor Harris, Hans Rutzebeck, Gus Athas, and CJ Webber in the 1940s; three of four passengers riding on Flight 44-2 from Miami to Buffalo, Dorothy Bruce (flowered dress), Richard Martin, Dave Arnold (with hat), Stewardess Dolores Beshears.

Top left, clockwise, George Albert from Blairsville, Pa High School; Lt. William Bischof, US Navy; Manny and Judy Frankel at National Children's Cardiac Hospital in Miami; Anne, Manny, and Mark Frankel in Miami; Anne, husband Jack, and Judy Frankel in Pittsburgh; Mark Frankel; Judy Frankel, all in 1951.

Top left, clockwise, Pennsylvania State Police and Forest Ranger consult a map during search for missing Flight 44-2, December 30, 1951 in Clarington, Pa; Buffalo Municipal Airport, destination of Flight 44-2 with the Curtiss-Wright airplane factory at bottom right; headline and map from *The New York Times* reporting Flight 44-2 lost in Pennsylvania; *The Bradford Era* headline, December 31, 1951; search and rescue B-17s from Westover Air Force Base were useless and mostly grounded because of fog.

Top right, clockwise, Pittsburgh printer Robert Geyer was the most forward-seated passenger on Flight 44-2 who survived; Albert Dichak was one of two passengers from Canonsburg, Pa who survived; Eva Woodward was the oldest person on Flight 44-2 and carried her dog on the plane for a vacation in Florida; Mary Messerlos was so injured she remained trapped in the wreckage for three days and two nights; interior of a military C-46 showing the cockpit door slightly left of center in the forward cabin; inside a C-46 cockpit in 1952.

Top Left, clockwise, CJ Webber with a Travel Air 4000E, 1939, Madison, Wisconsin; CJ at an air show, 1940; CJ with Pearl Quam Webber, in his ATA pilot's uniform, 1941; CJ, right, in Egypt with fellow Pan Am Air Ferries pilots; in a Douglas A20B for Pan Am Air Ferries; in a converted B-17 with interlocking W's for *Winters-Webber* air cargo in Miami, 1947 (this may have been one of the B-17s flown to Palestine in 1948); holding daughter Nancy in Miami in 1951.

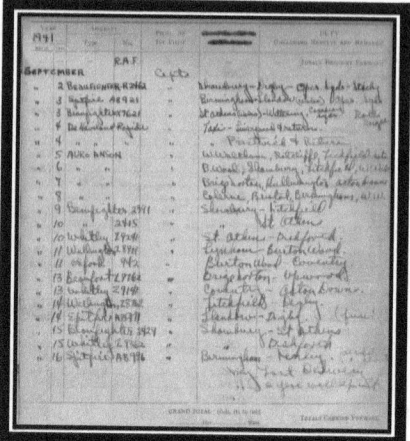

Top left, clockwise, flight logbook kept by pilot CJ Webber while flying British war planes in 1941; co-pilot Gus Athas on his beloved Indian motorcycle, about 1950; funeral register for pilot Victor Harris signed by John and Margaret Belding, January 1952; Harris in a co-pilot-in-training uniform at his Miami home 1950-51; Harris in his Army uniform during WW II

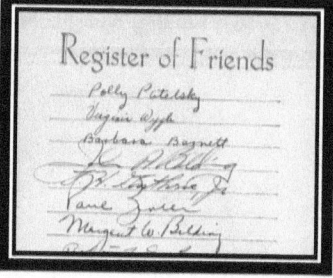

Top left, clockwise, Victor and Evelyn Harris while Vic was in the Army during WW II; poem written by Evelyn Harris on January 17, 1952 as she was mourning her husband's death in the crash of Flight 44-2; Gus Athas and Victor Harris with a companion, in New York City, 1951 (the woman's identity is concealed for privacy); Hans E. "Rutz" Rutzebeck and Isobel, in Alaska, 1947 when Rutz was flying as a bush pilot into the Koyukuk region.

> Your First & Last Flight
> You went away not long ago
> And how I've missed you, no one knows.
> The memories of years keep flooding back
> So fast and furious I soon lose track.
> Like the day you made your very first flight
> And I waited thru' a cold & anxious night.
> It was over water and I was so afraid
> until you were home & the trip was made.
> You were so proud & happy on your return

CHAPTER 10

"Go Down, Never Up"

MIDWAY THROUGH THE DAY on Sunday, December 30, George and Lt. Bischof grew uneasy about their initial plan to wait for rescue while trapped on Bucktooth Ridge. Actually, it was Pearl's plan to wait for help but the others went along because she was the authority figure from the airline. With the pilots crushed in the cockpit, Pearl was in charge of the passengers. She was adamant. She demanded they stay put because that's what she learned from her training, albeit just reading a company-supplied booklet about the duties and responsibilities of a stewardess. Pulling away from the stubborn stance of Pearl for a few moments, George and Lt. Bischof walked a few yards away from their campsite and met privately in the rain-drenched woods and re-assessed their critical situation.

The survivors heard airplanes above them, and they presumed the plane's pilots were searching for them, but it was still so foggy they couldn't see the planes. And, they knew the pilots couldn't see them either. Still hoping they would hear and see a rescue crew in the woods at any moment, George reviewed the list of names he had scribbled with the stub of a pencil on a pink Continental Charters napkin from the plane.

Most of the survivors on his list were so badly hurt they couldn't move away from their pitiful campfire. Four were still trapped in the wreckage. George feared that some of them wouldn't make it out alive if they didn't get help soon. Pearl kept repeating the dictates of her scant stewardess training to stay near the plane and wait for help. "Don't do it," she admonished George and Lt. Bischof. "You're only going to get lost."

The two men also realized the value of staying put, but they couldn't resist the urge to make a run for help. Geyer also wanted them to go. When they announced their decision to walk off through the woods, George and Pearl argued. "I'm going, and you can't do a thing about it," he snapped at Pearl. Among the stranded survivors, the authority had shifted. But the question remained, where would he go?

Based upon the time elapsed during their flight from Pittsburgh, George and Lt. Bischof determined that they were probably in New York State. Each was raised in rural communities of western Pennsylvania, and they were comfortable and familiar with a northern forest. While Pearl was steadfast in her position to stay put, the two men felt comfortable setting out through the woods to search for help, but they simply didn't know which direction to go. Finally, without full agreement from Pearl, who actually became angry that they might defy her stance, George, and Lt. Bischof decided to walk off the ridge together. "We'll find somebody to come get us," they said. Pearl and the others would have to stay behind and wait.

There was no sun visible for orientation and no sounds in the snow and fog-deadened mountains and valleys of the plateau that might lead them in the proper direction. Without much preparation except for taking the napkin with survivors' names on it and a few matches for starting a fire, they simply began walking down the ridge. Both men were wearing black leather shoes. Lt. Bischof's shoes were part of his Navy-issued uniform. They had long lost their shine and would prove to be a problem. Their street shoes didn't provide much protection from the snow, ice, water, and mud on Bucktooth Ridge. They couldn't keep their feet dry and warm. They were a tremendous handicap.

Walking off a 2,380-foot tall mountain ridge is not a simple journey. No sooner had the two men walked down into a ravine then they would have to cross over a spring seep or small stream from melting snow and then grasp saplings, roots and rocks to climb up the other side. The entire western slope of Bucktooth Ridge was pockmarked with these drainage ravines in the winter. Making matters worse, Lt. Bischof, bruised and battered from being thrown from the wreckage, had done the bulk of the heavy lifting of injured passengers, preparation work for their campsite, and searching among the wreckage. His body was stiff and sore. Furthermore, without much food and water, Lt. Bischof was already exhausted and had slight pain in his legs and his back. The snow was up to the men's' knees for most of their hike, it was raining steadily, and they kept stepping into piles of snow which would suddenly give way under their weight and drop their feet into cold cavities of water. All the while, "we were yelling and shouting but got no response," Lt. Bischof recalled. The forest of Bucktooth Ridge looked different from when much of the Allegheny Plateau was denuded of the hardwood trees, for sawmills, and the hemlocks, for tanneries, but the slope was still thick forest, grown back a second and third time, and it made their journey difficult, too difficult.

After more than two hours of high-stepping through deep snow, jumping, pulling and sliding along the steep ridge, both men could no longer feel their freezing feet. They estimated they had walked for two-and-a-half miles in the snow. Having no idea where they were and even in what direction they were headed, they decided together to give up their quest to find help and to backtrack to the campfire near the wreckage. However, this time, going uphill, the trek took them even longer and by the time the other survivors, still huddled together around the fire, spied two men walking toward them it was nearly dark in the cloud and fog-shrouded mountains late in the afternoon on December 30. Their effort to find help had failed. The crash had spared them, but their feet were killing them.

Realizing it was George and Lt. Bischof trudging back into their camp and not rescuers, Pearl felt the return of her fear and then more anger that the two men had come back without finding help. She had told them they would get lost, and she felt that her admonishment was vindicated. Quickly setting aside her disappointment, she began tending to the men as they rejoined the doomed group, handing them small cups of the lukewarm, instant coffee. The men described their efforts in the woods, the echoes from their voices shouting for help, the eerie silence, and the hopelessness they felt from not knowing where to go. Cold, wet, dispirited, bone-tired, and even angry themselves, George and Lt. Bischof dropped into their sitting positions around the fire and tried to hide their shame and disappointment as they explained to the other survivors how there appeared to be no way off the mountain.[99] What they didn't realize until much later was that they had come within a half mile of finding the only road, Sawmill Run, on the downward slope of the west side of Bucktooth Ridge. Resigned to their fate, they removed their shoes, and Pearl wrapped their numb feet in blankets from the plane. They settled in for yet another night on the ridge. George even caught a few minutes of sleep. Sitting there watching the two war veterans rest and regain composure by the campfire, Pearl developed an idea from wrapping their freezing feet in the blankets.

George was clearly the strongest and healthiest among them and ideally the one to make another attempt to walk off the mountain for help. Exhaustion and minor injuries had taken their toll on Lt. Bischof, and George realized that what forced them to return to the campsite were their freezing feet. He discussed with Pearl his determination to try again. She was against it, at first, still demanding the group stay together until help arrived. George was adamant, however, and giving in, Pearl finally resigned to give it another try. She then presented her idea. She would wrap his feet before the second attempt. They would do it tomorrow.

A SHORT TIME LATER, sitting around the puny campfire in the early darkness of the final hours of December, they were contemplating their dwindling supply of food and instant coffee. The corpses of their fellow passengers and crew were inside the wreckage of the plane or still hanging in the trees. The gravely injured passengers were tormented by thoughts of dying in the woods. Then, they heard an encouraging sound from outside their mountaintop tomb. It was muffled and weak,

---

[99] They continually referred to their location as a mountain.

but off down the ridge in the valley below it was the unmistakable sound of a train whistle.[100] That meant civilization, and on what would be their third day, and the longest stretch ever for a large group of North American plane crash survivors lost in the woods, George became even more determined to make a run for it and find help. Lt. Bischof did the best he could to keep the fire going with wet branches. Pearl, George, and Lt. Bischof rudely forbade anyone from going to sleep for more than 10 minutes fearing the reduced heart rate of a sleeping body would cause slower blood circulation and lead to frostbite, especially in their feet, or uncontrollable shivering and death from hypothermia. Able to wrap each other with blankets, extra clothing and coats they scavenged from the victims' bodies and their luggage there was little they could do for their feet because once their shoes got wet they never dried out sufficiently to keep their feet warm. Additionally, no one was equipped with boots because everyone had been headed to warm, sunny south Florida. Because darkness had set in soon after four pm, it was to be their longest night on the ridge.

After dark around their camp fire, the survivors moved closer together to share body warmth with arms around one another, legs over legs while sitting on the hard-surfaced luggage to insulate their buttocks from the cold, wet snow. The scavenged suitcases were packed in tightly, some covered with the plane's blankets for added insulation. Others were cracked open and pawed through. Black loafers, two-tone brown and white saddle shoes and oxfords were scattered about, used when

---

[100] While each of the survivors described the sound like a train "whistle", they probably were using generational vernacular for the whistles of steam-powered trains of their recent past. Because they heard the "whistle" in the evening, well after dark on December 30, it was the air horn of the Erie Limited passenger train that pulled westbound out of Salamanca at 7:42 pm. Operating on a General Motors Electro-Motive E8 diesel which typically ran Erie passenger trains in 1951, the engineer would have been required to sound his horn at the grade crossings for Sawmill Run Road, and Lebanon Road in Steamburg. For the survivors on Bucktooth Ridge, this would have placed the horn sound coming from the southwest. Erie E8's were equipped with *Leslie* A-200 or *Nathan* M-3 horns which produced a low-pitch "blat" sound. It's also possible that the train was equipped with an electric *Airchime*, a horn designed by Robert Swanson and sold to *Nathan* to sound like a whistle.

someone needed to walk through the snow to their latrine site. Women's flats and heels were also among the luggage, but they were useless in the snow. To keep their spirits up and to ward off sleep, they talked about how rescuers must be looking for them and would arrive soon. They talked incessantly through the night about being rescued failing to comprehend that no one in the search planes above them could see them and that they were lost. Surprisingly, no one really got to know each other. They never discussed their families or what they did for a living. They all later reported how they just talked continuously about how they would soon be rescued. The thought of rescuers consumed them. One of them, however, remained silent about the $700 in cash stolen from a corpse in the plane, in his, or her, pocket.

THE TEMPERATURE ON BUCKTOOTH Ridge dropped to about 26 degrees before dawn on the morning of New Year's Eve 1951.[101] Rain continued falling through warmer temperatures aloft, and when the droplets hit the ground, they turned the snow on the ridge into a crusty glaze. As the first gray light of dawn revealed the semi-circle of survivors huddled around the trash can campfire, they were near desperation to find a way off the ridge. Even their wool coats and blankets were glazed over with a thin, stiff and crunchy crust of ice. Where there had been ice and snow beneath their parachute was softened to slush and mud from their dwindling body heat conducting into the ground. After two nights on the mountain, they feared the danger of hypothermia. Unlike the rapid death of the other passengers from the crash trauma, the survivors believed that someone among them could literally freeze to death. Without the rescue, they had once believed would happen right away, they now feared they wouldn't be found at all. They had water because George discovered a spring bubbling from the ground in the forest, but they were running out of food. Something had to be done.

---

[101] Weather reports and temperatures were printed in all local newspapers for these dates. The ridgetop temperature was estimated based upon overnight temperatures in surrounding valley communities.

Daybreak found nearly all of them, (by now using each other's first names) Al Dichak, Anna Piso, Dolores Beshears, Ed Wessel, George Albert, Joe Wozniak, Marie Norcia, Mary Battista, Pearl Moon, and Bill Bischof, gathered around the campfire facing yet another day stuck on the mountain. Mary Messerlos, Ava Woodward, Tom Patterson, and Bob Geyer were still in the wreckage. The survivors at the campfire, who were capable, visited the plane frequently, offering food and water, and inspiration to the four who couldn't move. By this time, however, there was no more dry clothing to be found without prying open the crushed fuselage for more suitcases. Everything was saturated from two nights of cold rain. Geyer said that George and Lt. Bischof kept trying to help him get to the campfire, but Geyer wanted George to go find help. "Save your strength," he warned. By then, George was the only one with any strength left.

Deciding when to leave such a predicament where help might arrive at any moment presented a quandary. Pearl had reverted to her original stance during the night, and she continued arguing, sometimes loudly and vociferously, to remain in place and wait. She was afraid George would get lost before getting help, and the rest of them wouldn't know it. Geyer, George, and Lt. Bischof favored going out to find help. The others acquiesced to whatever decision was made.

Discussing the train whistle they had heard the night before, it was decided that George would go alone and in the direction of the whistle where, perhaps, he could flag down a train.[102] Lt. Bischof was suffering from a stiff and sore back and found it difficult to walk. Not wanting to hold up the emboldened effort, he decided to stay behind. Rummaging through the victims' luggage again for scraps of clothing, Pearl and George found cotton dresses and shirts that they ripped into long strips. Leaning back and holding his feet off the ground, George sat while

---

[102] If George had found train tracks and flagged an Erie Railroad train, the engineer most likely would not have stopped. But, he would have been able to use his rather a new radiotelephone to call the Erie office in Jersey City, even from Salamanca, via several relay stations along the tracks. Whether George knew about the Erie's ability to place a telephone call from a train is unknown. It was high-tech communications for 1951.

Pearl wrapped the strips of cloth around his cold, wet leather shoes and tied them around his ankles. She made several wrappings, each one carefully flattened so the bulk would not impede his gait.

When she finished, they agreed on the direction from which they all heard the train whistle in the dark and wrapped George with a warm but wet wool coat (pilfered from victims' luggage) over his brown gabardine suit. George declined a pair of gloves, choosing to leave them for the others. They ended up on Tom Patterson's hands. When a pocketful of the last of their food was offered, however, George took it. He recognized that he needed extra nourishment for strength. He also took their matches to build a fire in the event he got lost. Pearl pointed him toward the valley and the train whistle. "Go down, never up," she warned, from her stewardess training.

IT WAS JUST AFTER 11 am on New Year's Eve as they quietly watched George disappear into the woods, his wool overcoat, and thick wavy black hair slowly blending into the brown and black bark on the trees. Each of the 13 survivors left behind silently prayed that he would find help. Pearl believed she would never see him again.

George said his decision to leave the group to find help was made easier after the second night in the woods because he was not certain some of them could survive a third. "I had no idea where we were," he said. "I thought we were in New York State, but we couldn't be sure. The pilots were dead. They were the only ones who knew. So, I took off."

Lt. Bischof, too weary and even suffering from vision problems due to exhaustion and campfire smoke, lack of sleep and food, frostbitten toes, sore back, and tending to the injured survivors and their campfire, was glad he stayed behind. He knew that by going along he would have slowed the pace of the more physically able George. He and Pearl had kept them all alive to this point, now it was someone else's turn to lead, he rationalized.

Despite the fact that he ran a restaurant in cosmopolitan Miami, George Albert had plenty of experience walking in northern woods. Alone in the quiet of the mountainside on Bucktooth Ridge, he said he thought of his boyhood in Josephine playing in the forest with his siblings along Black Lick Creek. Only days earlier he had been with them all, enjoying

Christmas with his family together again in what was left of old and decrepit Josephine. As he trudged through the snow, following the same tracks he and Lt. Bischof made the day before, George focused on walking in the direction of the train whistle. For the first time, however, his muscles stiffened, and soreness, even pain crept into his legs and his tightly wrapped feet. Recalling Pearl's advice, he discovered that when he walked downhill, the pain subsided. When he had to lean forward to push up the side of a gully with his nearly frozen toes, the pain intensified.

Finally, after finding a deep ravine with water flowing downward through the middle, he departed from the path him and Lt. Bischof created the previous day and followed the rivulet of water, discovering that walking downhill became easier with each step. He stumbled on in a zigzagging path, falling into the deep snow several times from sheer exhaustion and snapping off saplings and branches as he grabbed them to hold his balance. Unlike Sunday's attempt, this time he was more determined to make it.[103] The wrappings around his shoes were a good idea, he realized.

Back at the makeshift campsite the remaining survivors lay and sat around the smelly fire with its smoke from the wet branches slowly curling up through the trees until it was wafted away by the breeze and was lost in the low hanging clouds. On the ridge, the wind never really subsided and in their wet clothing from two days of rain, none of them ever really got warm.

They wondered if George would make it. Where was he now? Would he be forced to return like he did yesterday? Would they ever get off this mountain? Could they still be in Pennsylvania or had they made it to New York? They simply didn't know. And no one else did either.

Before leaving, George had finally convinced Tom Patterson to get out of the plane. He and Lt. Bischof half-carried, half-dragged the lanky sailor to the campfire where he laid down across the suitcases, barely conscious. Dolores Beshears continued holding Patterson's hand as she

---

[103] George's trek down the hill was described by Bob Lilienthal as he hiked up the ridge using the same path. Lilienthal saw the zigzagging and broken branches left behind by George's effort to find help.

had when he was stuck on the plane. They used one of the cloth strips that Pearl ripped from a dress to wrap carefully around Patterson's fractured head. He winced, but it stopped the bleeding. They gave him the wet gloves that George refused to take, but they made no difference, his hands were still freezing cold. They turned up the collar of his wool overcoat and cinched it tight with the top button. He looked miserable in his bloody head wrap, wet, too small gloves, and tight-fitting overcoat pulled up around his neck, but they all felt better just trying to make him feel more comfortable. One of the men had a small pocket-sized Bible, and he read verses to the others as they lay around the campfire. When they tired of the Bible verses, someone started singing Christmas carols, and they all joined in. Even though Christmas was over, singing carols unified their spirit and hope. Mary Battista clutched her rosary beads and prayed that George would find help.

After about two hours, they decided that George wasn't coming back. It led to a bit of excitement when they realized that he probably would find help, but their hopes waned when they also thought about how he might have fallen or gotten lost in the woods. Getting lost is what worried Pearl the most, and she began second-guessing her decision to let him go. Together, they continued talking about a rescue to keep their spirits up. Still cloudy and foggy, the woods around them brightened a bit as the hidden sun reached its apex for the day, their third calendar day on the ridge. They heard another airplane but still couldn't see it. They settled in to wait. George had promised he wouldn't come back without finding help. Deep inside, they wanted to believe him.

After a few hours of walking and frequently falling in the snow from near exhaustion, George noticed that the terrain on the ridge changed. It flattened out somewhat but still flowed downhill. It became easier to walk. He slogged on in the direction he thought was the location of the train whistle. Then, he noticed what appeared to be an open field and a farm in the far distance – uphill. George couldn't do it, so he continued down the slope for a time and through the woods where he came across a pile of rocks. Climbing over the rocks on all fours, he fell down into a shallow ditch. Getting back onto his aching and wrapped feet again, he stepped onto an open path covered with snow and ice. It was a road! What he saw next warmed his heart and made him burst into a wide smile.

Kneeling down in the road, George closely examined tire tracks in the packed snow, ice and mud. In fact, he could make out the tread grooves from the narrow tires that sunk deeply into the unplowed road and spit out the long thin ribbons of snow in their path. It had taken him three hours; he would later learn, but he found a road, Sawmill Run Road, a narrow, seldom-used single lane through the hollow that split Bucktooth Ridge and the Towns of Napoli and Cold Spring. "The big thrill for me was coming out on that road with fresh tire tracks on them. That meant it was only a question of time before I found a house," George said.

George first walked a short distance up the long gradual slope of Sawmill Run Road, flanked on both sides by the thick woods of deciduous and fir trees, and by the fast flowing creek. It was in the direction of the farm he had seen while dropping down through the woods. However, it pained his feet so much to walk uphill that he turned around and walked back down the hill. Then, to make it easier, he removed Pearl's fabric wrappings and stood on the soles of his wet and frozen shoes. He threw the fabric off to the side of the road and trundled on down the hill to find the help he had promised the other survivors.

Having already staggered about two and a half miles through the woods, within another half a mile or so, George's heart rate quickened again as he found a small cabin on the side of Sawmill Run Road with the creek running in front of it. He noticed a wire strung to the cabin from telephone poles along the road. Dropping off the lane and onto a makeshift driveway over a small bridge, George cut a new path to the cabin in the snow because no one had been there since the last few snow storms. He walked around the cabin, stopping at each window and peering inside. He stepped up to the door and found it locked. He moved on, making his tracks out the driveway and back onto Sawmill Run Road.

Had he gotten inside, whether by breaking through a window or the door, George would have found a telephone. It was an old wall-mounted telephone with which you first had to crank a lever to create an electrical current to ring a bell at the local telephone Operator's office. She would then have placed the call. And it was on a party line with the few homes on Sawmill Run. Randolph, New York mortician Fred Myers had installed the old phone in the camp because a funeral director must be reachable at all times in the event of death and the Operators knew how to reach him. It was the one luxury in the scantily outfitted cabin that the Myers family used for weekend escapes. George never got in to use the hand-crank telephone and even if he did he would only have been able to tell the Operator he was in a small cabin in the woods along a dirt and gravel road and at the end of a line of telephone poles. In vast Cattaraugus County alone, that could have been a hundred different locations. Back on Sawmill Run Road George continued walking downhill, following the telephone line, in search of help. He had less than a mile to go.

CHAPTER 11

Diagnosis Interrupted

FOR RUBY BRYANT, CHRISTMAS was over but the small lump in her breast was still there. Heavy snow filled Sawmill Run and covered Bucktooth Ridge on the last day of December, but there was some warmth in the air and it brought rain and fog. Finally, though, she could focus on her health crisis. With the pain persisting in her breast and armpit, Ruby was scheduled to see Dr. James Fleming at Salamanca District Hospital at the end of the week, on Friday, January 4th. There was nothing she could do to get in earlier she rationalized, because of all the family events and Christmas, in December. And now, with the New Year upon them, things wouldn't get back to normal until at least January 2. Friday the 4th would have to be soon enough, she reasoned.

Ruby resumed her daily routine in the Bryant farmhouse. She was intent upon finishing up her regular chores in the kitchen before going off to the doctor. Ruby was fastidious about completing the household chores. During her work, she thought deeply about the pain and swelling she had only recently discovered in her armpit and chest. Her sleep had been restless the past few nights because the pain made it difficult to lie on her side. She had managed to get a few chores done, however, on this final day of the year, including taking down their Christmas decorations.

After dismantling the family's Christmas tree, Ruby hauled it outside to the back of their yard. Wrestling the tree to the burn pit, Ruby was careful not to bump herself anywhere because of the pain. She was only 45 and terribly scared. She had no training in how to examine herself but by following tips in a *Reader's Digest* article, she felt her breasts and nipples, found the small hard lumps and was sure it was breast cancer. Earlier in December she also read another *Reader's Digest* article about a man who beat cancer and then convinced the U.S. Congress and President Truman to pass a law so he wouldn't be medically discharged from the Navy. Her confidence ebbed and flowed and once or twice that month a few tears did too.

Ruby wasn't so much worried about what would happen to her older boys if she had cancer; she was mostly worried about five-year-old Otis. In her diary she wrote, *"those old enough to enjoy life and able to take care of themselves won't need me so much but little Otis, what of him? I hope I can stick around a while to love and care for him."* Otis had been born a full ten years after what she thought was the last of her brood. Accidental or not, how she adored his bright blue eyes and singing from the moment he woke up. *Don't Just Stand There* by country music singer Carl Smith was his favorite song with lyrics, *"You gotta laugh and dance and sing, you gotta get that gal a ring,"* that he would chirp as he toddled about the house full of adults.[104]

Ruby also felt guilty. She hadn't been so good to Otis lately. She was impatient with him as he grappled for her attention because she had focused on her oldest boy, who had left home and might end up in the war and because she was preoccupied with her breast pain. Even at his age, she recognized that little Otis noticed something different about her.

All through December Ruby worried about the fate of her oldest son, Benton. Only weeks earlier he had returned to military training in Washington after visiting home while on furlough. He had been drafted

---

[104] These musings were all contained in Ruby's personal diary in which she wrote daily during her crisis with breast cancer.

into the Army the previous year for the war in Korea. In early December, on the night before they took Benton to the train station in Olean for the long ride to return to his post, they took pictures with the boys playing their musical instruments. Rodney, with a mound of brown hair, brushed back on his head, wrapped his arms around a guitar. And Benton, wearing a broad rimmed cowboy hat, held a bow to the fiddle tucked under his chin. They played mountain music together in some of the best times of their lives. Soon enough, however, this close-knit family living a nearly solitary life in the hollows below Bucktooth Ridge would be thrust into the international headlines and then torn apart in the worst ways imaginable.

Returning to the warmth of the house, Pearl then focused on getting the boys to participate in their chores. Her emotional misgivings continued.[105] Ruby counted again the days until she could see the doctor. It was a Monday, but it was also New Year's Eve. She had to get some more of her cleaning and laundry done because, by Friday, she dreaded, she would probably know for sure if it was really cancer. In minutes, she would enter the most dramatic and unmanageable week of her life.

THE BRYANT FAMILY FARM was a lot like Ruby's childhood home in West Virginia. Born on March 18, 1906, in Garretts Bend, in the rich valley farmlands of the Hayzlett Fork and Trace Fork creeks west of Charleston, Ruby Jewel Bowles was one of ten children of John and Isabella 'Belle' Meadows Bowles. When Belle died in 1915 just hours after giving birth to Ruby's youngest sister, Joyce, nine-year-old Ruby joined her older sisters as mother and housekeeper for the Bowles family.

Ruby married Charles Eugene Bryant on April 5, 1928, and she moved onto his 134-acre farm, which was mostly forest. Charlie, as he was known, bought the farm from his younger brother, Rollin. It wasn't much of a farm, really. It was well off the main road between the county seat in Little Valley and Salamanca where the mainline Erie Railroad tracks ran alongside the Allegheny River. Their one and a half story

---

[105] Newspaper accounts have depicted Ruby as disposing or preparing to burn the Christmas tree in the yard when George found her.

1800s-era wood-frame house was covered with tar paper and brown interlocking shingles that resembled bricks and had a small lean-to wood shed on the back. Four crude steps leading up to a small narrow side porch provided Ruby with a seat from where she often watched her boys play in the yard, which more often than not, was overgrown with tall grass and weeds. The creek ran behind their house, and they had to cross it to reach their large patch of vegetable gardens. Selling vegetables in the summer and autumn was a big source of their income. Ruby decorated the walls inside their house with flowered paper and family photographs. It was a simple farmhouse but suitable for the needs of their boys and her extended family which often visited from West Virginia. There was no TV or central heating, but by 1951 they did have running water and a bathroom in the house, still considered a novelty because they had only recently been installed. A barn of rough-cut, sun-bleached lumber along with a few outbuildings were behind the house where the Bryant's kept their farm animals; a cow, pigs, chickens, and until they were destroyed by a pack of wild dogs, sheep. Rollin also lived on the farm and together he and Charlie sold their market vegetables in Salamanca and other nearby communities. Their parents, Frank and Mary Bryant, had started the family in the vegetable garden business a generation earlier. It didn't provide a lot of money, but it was enough to get by until the Depression. Then, people stopped buying, and the Bryant's quickly ran out of money.

In the autumn of 1929, the newly married Charlie and Ruby, along with their first little baby boy, Benton, and Rollin, drove their Model T Ford all the way to Washington State where they picked apples and trapped for animal furs through the winter in an attempt to make a better living.[106] They nearly starved a few times as did many transient workers during the Depression. Soon enough they returned to Sawmill Run to give their vegetable farming another attempt.[107] Not long afterward, the

---

[106] Ed Wilkes, a friend of the Bryant's wrote in 1958 about a 900-mile-long trip he once took with Charlie and Rollin Bryant in which they slept under the stars and "roughed it." It was a trip down the Allegheny River system from western New York State to Kentucky in the early 1920s.
[107] Starved is hyperbole passed down through the family as the story of their Washington State struggles has been retold many times.

other boys came along. The second born was Rodney, in 1931, then came Stuart in 1934, John in 1936, and lastly, ten years later in 1946 came the youngest, Otis. In those early years, before running water and electricity, using an outhouse for sanitation, wood parlor stove for heating, and cooking over a wood-fired kitchen stove, the Bryant's ran their small farm with large draft horses, Maud, and Tom. They pulled the plows and tillers in the vegetable plots across Sawmill Run. In 1948, Charlie went to work for the New York State Conservation Department. He cut and pruned trees, and maintained firefighting trails in state forests along with other early land conservation work, leaving many of the chores at home to Ruby and their growing boys

The Bryant farm was in such a remote section of the county that they didn't get electricity until 1948, and they only got it then because their neighbor, Lee Earle, helped the boys install wire in the old house when power was finally extended along the road by the Niagara Hudson Power Corporation. It didn't provide much amperage, but it was enough for a few electric lights, and when combined with their long-used kerosene lamps, it really brightened up the old house. They had enjoyed a telephone for several years because it was necessary to take market orders for their farm-raised vegetables.

After World War II and during Ruby's daily routine of cooking and canning fruits and vegetables, collecting chicken eggs, milking the cow, and tending the vegetable gardens, she would have seen airplanes fly over the farm to cities farther upstate in New York, into Canada, and east to Boston, New York, Newark, and Philadelphia. At first, it was a new experience. To people like Ruby they were simply flying overhead, somewhere. Gradually, farm families of the plateau became accustomed to the sound of a plane but Ruby had never flown in one, herself. In fact, for a typical cash-poor family like the Bryant's, spending extra money on an airplane trip to somewhere they didn't need to go wasn't even considered. Still, when the DC-3 mail plane from Pennsylvania Central Airlines flew overhead, most farmers in Napoli looked up and watched until it cleared the mountain ridges. The magic of flight was still the world apart from their simple lives on the ground.

Never quite losing her West Virginia drawl, Ruby could be heard singing around the farm while doing her chores. Rollin had a large battery-powered farm radio in the house from their pre-electricity days, and Ruby would sometimes sing along to the songs they heard on the radio when the batteries were charged. They didn't have a battery eliminator, a device used to convert the household electric alternating current to direct current to operate the radio. Otherwise, it was used to get the news. In what little spare time she had, Ruby also enjoyed reading and exploring nature around their farm. She could identify all the birds, and she kept track of their seasonal appearances in her diary: chickadees, juncos, killdeers, robins, downy woodpeckers, and even the scavenger crows. She also kept track of the weather. That winter, through December, was already turning out record snowfall in western New York State.

A quiet woman with sparkling blue eyes, Ruby normally kept her dark brunette hair long and straight, but sometimes she pulled it back in pigtails. She ran the household full of men and boys, and she often used her soft-spoken voice to put them in their place when they needed it. She barely tolerated the occasional drinking of beer or the *Lucky Strikes* and hand-rolled *Bull Durham "twisties"* smoked in the house by Charlie and Rollin.[108] Her favorite part of the long snow-filled winters at Sawmill Run was when their mailmen delivered letters from her sisters in West Virginia and Ohio to their mailbox along the road. If there was a letter that they knew Ruby was waiting for they would toot the horn and she would go tramping out through the snow to get it. In the gloom of their remote hollow when early winter darkness fell by four pm, the letters brightened her days.

Just below the Bryant farm, toward Salamanca, the road turned from gravel to macadam. In the other direction, however, uphill past the hunting camps and into Napoli, the gravel turned into the dirt (mud in the spring) with a long strip of grass growing down the middle during summer months. No one ever really walked on Sawmill Run

---

[108] *Twisties,* also known as *quirlies,* were cigarettes rolled from a can or bag of chopped tobacco with rolling papers. The ends were twisted to close them off, hence the nick-name.

Road, especially in the winter when it was seldom plowed all the way through. And, when a car drove by, Charlie, and Ruby and the boys could often tell whose car it was by the rattling and pinging sound it made from the gravel being thrown up into the undercarriage. As the road climbed in elevation along the creek and in the morning shadow of Bucktooth Ridge, the hunting camps sprang up after the war. There remained only two other permanent homes up the hollow; the Johnson house, just past the Bryant's, and the Kenneth and Margaret Herrick farm, near a sharp curve at the Napoli end of Sawmill Run Road.

In 1951, the camps were used mostly during the short deer season from November 22 through December 6 and then locked up for the remainder of the winter. They straddled Sawmill Run as it meandered along the road down to an old bridge just upstream from the Bryant farm. Only during special events, such as opening day of trout season in April and deer season in the autumn, did more than a dozen cars a day ever drive along the entire road. Deer season was, by far, the most popular. In 1951, some 1,673 bucks were shot by hunters in Cattaraugus County, typically one of the top whitetail deer harvesting counties in New York State. This week, between Christmas and the New Year, the Bryant's were among few along their end of Sawmill Run. Even as progress and new technologies swept across America following the war, in the final days of December 1951, Ruby's rural farm life was still a dramatic contrast to an emerging urban population just beginning to fly hopscotch around the country on large passenger airplanes. It made the national news headlines from the crash even more dramatic. City travelers raining death upon farmers stuck in a rapidly disappearing era.

Ruby continued supervising the boys in the house with their work. It was midafternoon of New Year's Eve. It appeared outside as if the several days of fog were beginning to change. Colder air was moving in. The fog was dissipating. While removing Christmas decorations from the window of their farmhouse Ruby and her son John saw a most unusual sight in the road near their front yard. A strange man in a long wool coat loitered as if contemplating an approach to the house. Just by his appearance they knew he was from somewhere else. Who could that be, they wondered? Ruby boldly stepped through the front door to find out.

CHAPTER 12

"CHRISTMAS IS OVER, HUH, LADY"

"**H**ELLO, LADY" WERE THE first words that came out of the stranger's mouth. Startled, Ruby stared into to the expression-less face of a handsome young man with a dark complexion and a full head of wavy black hair spilling a curl onto his forehead. She knew immediately that he was not a local resident or from the hunting camps. He appeared to have a deep tan, and he wore city clothes; a brown gabardine suit under a heavy wool overcoat that was too big for him. His linen shirt collar flopped out from the top of his coat, buttoned all the way up as would be done only in severe, cold weather. Although she couldn't see it, he also wore a cream-colored, hand-knitted sweater vest. It may not have been his. Ruby also noticed he had no hat, gloves, scarf or mittens for the cold winter weather, and his black street shoes were caked with mud and ice. His appearance was also unusual because he had something wrapped around the lower part of his legs that made his gabardine pants billow like an 18th-century sailor's leggings. Looped around his wrist were the handles of a small blue bag with brown leather strips. The man kept putting his hands in his coat pockets and from there down the wool garment was speckled with mud. He was sweaty, dirty, exhausted, and he showed a few day's growth of a dark, stubbly beard. It didn't diminish his pleasant-looking face, but there was no smile with his greeting. Ruby was a friendly country woman, but the appearance of this strange urbane man in her remote farmyard made her muscles tense with suspicion and distrust. She wasn't the type of woman to be afraid that this was cause for concern. Thoughts of the pain in her chest disappeared. Apparently noticing that Ruby and the boys were removing their Christmas decorations, the stranger spoke again with the awareness that he had missed something. "I guess Christmas is over, huh, lady?"

So engrossed in her chores and her medical predicament, Ruby had not noticed the man walking through the snow in the crudely plowed road in front of their farm, until he arrived at their yard. She immediately recognized him as emotionally stressed and physically exhausted. How odd for someone to suddenly appear at their farm. It was miles away from the nearest community and surrounded by thick forest in the mountains. He certainly wasn't a hunter, not with those clothes, and hunting season was over. Because 118 inches of snow had already fallen in Cattaraugus County that winter, she doubted that he had driven down the road because most of it hadn't been plowed. Then, the stranger spoke again with an explanation that hit Ruby like a bomb. "We've been in a plane crash up there in the woods," the man panted to Ruby as he pointed back toward the road and bare trees of Sawmill Run.

So stiff and confused about the now trembling man standing in front of her, Ruby heard only the word crash. Her first thought was that he had been out celebrating early on New Year's Eve and wrecked his car up the hollow. The stranger persisted with an explanation that went something like this: "I'm George Albert. I've just walked out of the woods to get help for all those people up there at the plane crash." George then told Ruby how their plane was flying to Buffalo when it went down in the woods, that the pilots were crushed in the cockpit, that many others were dead in the wreckage, and that several survivors were still sitting in the woods waiting for rescue. He explained how they spent two nights shivering around a small fire waiting for help, and when it didn't arrive, he walked out to find it. He briefly described his walk down through the woods, past the locked hunting camps, and down the valley road pockmarked with deep, water-filled potholes, until he found her. Then, George got right to the point with a question similar to this: "You got a telephone so I can call the police?" Ruby hesitated with her answer only because she was stunned with disbelief.

At that moment, on New Year's Eve, Ruby was trying to comprehend George Albert's incredible story. It was puzzling that she had not heard the sound of a crash. Ruby, Charlie and the boys had not heard any news about a plane crash either. Wasn't that a plane she heard flying low over their house a few nights ago as she was lying in bed, trying to go to sleep? It sounded like one but now, with her mind so confused, she couldn't be sure. Still in doubt about his story, Ruby looked directly at George with the suspicious glare of a mother questioning her lying son. Was this strange man standing in front of her making up such a wild story, she wondered? With dead batteries in the farm radio, the Bryant's had not been listening to the news from Buffalo as they usually did in the morning, and no one had been to town for a newspaper. They simply knew nothing about a missing airplane. Could a plane full of passengers really have gone down in the woods near their farm? Several questions about George's story raced through Ruby's mind all at once. She hesitated.

George persisted. "There's been a wreck and I'd like to use your phone. You do have a phone, don't you?"

Ruby replied immediately. "Yes, yes, right away," and she began showing George into the house.

Although the Bryant's telephone was in the dining room, just inside the front door and nearest the road, Ruby led George to the small porch on the backside of the house and the door that led into the kitchen. The front porch didn't have steps.

"*I didn't smell any alcohol so I had decided that he was OK,*" Ruby wrote in her diary. She still thought that maybe George was referring to a car wreck. George later told his family that he believed Ruby's initial hesitation was a response to his dark Syrian complexion. He didn't realize that Ruby would never display bias over the color of a man's skin. The only transgression among men that would ever cause Ruby to hesitate was drinking booze. George never discovered that she simply suspected that he might be drunk.

As they headed inside to make a telephone call for help, George continued his explanation. "I've got to get help for those people. It's awful," he said. When George told Ruby there were about 20 people dead and 14 had been injured, she knew it couldn't have been a car accident. Memories of hearing the airplane and the thumping noise two nights earlier flooded into her mind. The mysterious sounds that she had removed from her consciousness and had not mentioned to her family were now beginning to make sense.

From inside the Bryant's farmhouse, Ruby's older sons noticed the commotion at the door. They rushed to their mother's side. Rodney and Stuart Bryant were 20, and 17, and lived at home with their mother, father, and younger brothers, John, 15, and little Otis. The boys were naturally protective of their mother, especially when their father was at work. They stood their ground to the stranger and maintained a cautious but friendly stance while listening to the details of his story. George's explanation soon began to put their mistrust at ease. Later, Ruby wrote in the margins of her 1951 calendar diary that George told them that his mother had been on the plane and that she was dead. He also described the death of a little baby. With those revelations, the Bryant's felt sympathetic and immediately trusted George. *"He spoke so quietly and was so calm,"* Ruby wrote. *"I could scarcely believe that he had told me his mother was killed. He couldn't help his mother but he could help others and he did. He is a brave young man. He was so thoughtful and considerate and he told us of how wonderful everyone was, thinking of each other and not of themselves."*

In utter amazement, they determined from George's description that he had come out of the woods below Bucktooth Ridge near a hunting camp and wooded plot of land owned by Salamanca railroad worker Earl Plough. Rounding each curve in the road along the creek and seeing nothing but more woods and road in front of him, they figured he eventually passed the Myers' camp, another hunting cabin owned by Plough's brother, Henry "Pete" Plough, and his wife, Leona, and the Johnson family house. All of the buildings were up the hollow from the Bryant farm. George didn't mention that he tried to find a way to the camps and found no one home at the Johnson house. Ruby and the boys led George through the kitchen and into the dining room to their telephone. It was on the same party line as several other telephones along Sawmill Run, including the Myers' empty camp that George had passed over, and to activate it you had to click the handset rocker several times to get the Operator's attention. With the boys' help, George placed the call but when he began talking to the New York Telephone Company Operator in Salamanca and told her why he wanted the police, she thought it was a joke or some kind of prank. At first, the Operator wouldn't put the call through. Ruby grabbed the handset from George and demanded she put the call through. There must have been something in Ruby's authoritative voice because the Operator responded immediately. She sent George's call through her switchboard to the Salamanca Police Department. If she was like most other Operators of the era, she listened in. This dramatic story was too good to ignore. The telephone Operator had no inkling that after she routed George's call for help, the rest of her day on the telephone switchboard would be the busiest ever.

From the Bryant's farmhouse on Sawmill Run, at 2:44 pm on New Year's Eve, 1951, it was Ruby Bryant and George Albert who first relayed the news to the world. Flight 44-2 had crashed and that it was sitting in the snow nearly atop Bucktooth Ridge in Cattaraugus County, one of the most remote regions in all of New York State. The emotional and alarming details as George repeated his story spurred the Bryant boys into action.

Listening to George explain over the telephone how the others were still stuck on the "mountain" as he described it, and desperately needed help, the Bryant boys scrambled, gathering up their winter boots, warm coats, hats and gloves, and ran off to the top of the ridge. Teenage John begged to tag along, but Ruby ruled it out. She knew what her older boys would find on the ridge. From George's description, it was littered with bloodied and mangled bodies and that would be too gruesome for her younger son, she decided. John and little Otis stayed home. Otis was simply too young to have gone but for John; Ruby made an excuse that someone had to stay and complete the chores because Charlie and

Uncle Rollin wouldn't be home until after dark. Even in this time of an emergency, Ruby was adamant about completing the chores. Through the windows, John and Otis watched their brothers heading off for the ridge. The Bryant boys went straight into the woods, then cutting off George's tracks in the snow and following them uphill in the same staggering path he had just walked down to find help, they dug in with their boots toward the most gruesome sight they would ever see.

Still inside the Bryant's farmhouse, Ruby offered George some coffee, food and dry clothing. George replied with a nod toward his bag and said, "No, the folks pooled their food and gave it to me so I could find my way out for help, so I'm not hungry." George and Ruby then discussed how police would start their rescue. He believed that the survivors still trapped at the scene of the crash would best be helped if rescuers dropped food and supplies from an airplane. He discussed with Ruby the idea of placing another telephone call to police to advise them of his plan. "Did police have two-way radios in their cars," he asked? Ruby didn't know the answer. George did not make a second call, however, realizing that it was still so foggy that rescue crews in an airplane would not be able to see the wreckage. He accepted only the coffee, took a few drinks, and then did what was just astonishing to her, John and little Otis.

George promptly went out the back door, carrying his cup of hot coffee, walked out to Sawmill Run Road and, crossing to the other side, he stood alone in his wet coat, and muddied shoes and suit, next to the Bryant's mailbox, waiting for the police. Whether it was out of respect for the Bryant's privacy in their home or fear that he would be missed by the police, George stayed on the road, determined to deliver rescuers to the 13 other survivors still huddling in the snow atop the ridge. Ruby could not convince him to come back into the house where he would be warm.

George Albert's telephone call was taken by Salamanca Police desk officer John Kowalski. When George told Kowalski that he was a survivor of a plane crash, he got the officer's attention right away. Kowalski was well aware of the missing plane because all police departments in the county had been put on alert via New York State Police teletype.[109]

---

[109] Part of a police desk officer's job was to insert a telephone receiver into a

Kowalski turned the phone over to his chief, Milford L. Perrigo. While the chief took down George's information and the location of the crash, Kowalski got on the department's new short-wave radio and called the Cattaraugus County sheriff's office in Little Valley. Coordinating emergency responses was the sheriff's specialty.

A pilot veteran of World War I, Cattaraugus County Sheriff Morgan Sigel was the head of the county's Office of Civil Defense, organized by President Roosevelt in early 1941. Sigel kept it activated beyond World War II because of the Korean War, the threat of Communism, and the Atomic Bomb. Recently installing their first radio communications system as part of the civil defense, it proved to be a boon to get help to Sawmill Run by immediately spreading the word all over the county that the missing plane had crashed on Bucktooth Ridge. It was, perhaps, the first large rapid response alert ever for Cattaraugus County's recently interconnected law enforcement and rescue agencies.

The crackly radio messages bounced around the hills and valleys of the Alleghenies and set the stage for absolute pandemonium along Sawmill Run. Sheriff's Deputy Russell E. Benson intercepted the call in his squad car and made a beeline for Sawmill Run from Napoli. The radio call from Salamanca to Little Valley also interfered with the VHF signal of the first TV recently installed at the Salamanca Fire Department. The new TV set was being sampled for the first time by the firefighters in their ready-room. Hearing the message of a plane crash in their woods at the same time as the most popular western New York State TV program, *Meet the Millers*, from two-thirty to three pm on Buffalo's WBEN-TV, the Salamanca firefighters quickly loaded 15 folding wooden stretchers, blankets, and boxes of first aid equipment onto a trailer, hitched it to the fire chief's squad car, and sped off for Sawmill Run.[110]

---

teletype machine daily to receive special fugitive bulletins or warnings about criminal activity or special investigations. New York State Police updated their teletype warnings several times a day while the C-46 plane was missing. The warnings printed out in large blue letters on rolls of paper. They were pinned to a bulletin board for departmental officers to read.

[110] *Meet the Millers* featured Bill and Mildred Miller, turkey farmers from Colden, New York, north of Salamanca. Begun in January 1950, their TV variety show of interviews, cooking advice, and comedy was a popular hit on

With geographical guidance from the Bryant boys, George told Chief Perrigo that the crash occurred in the woods above the Herrick family farm. Nearly at the top of Sawmill Run, the Kenneth, and Margaret Herrick farm consisted of about 20 acres of hay and corn fields behind a red barn that gave way to about 100 additional acres of forest that swept up the west side of Bucktooth Ridge. The police and firefighters knew exactly where to go.[111]

Telephone calls were immediately placed to the local funeral homes in Salamanca, Randolph, Little Valley, and Cattaraugus, not so much for morticians who could handle the dead, but because it was funeral homes, in 1951, which ran ambulance service in rural areas. Many of them detailed the same hearses they used for bodies to carry injured and sick patients to hospitals. Only minutes behind them, because they had intercepted the county-wide radio call, were reporters and photographers from newspapers and radio stations from the surrounding communities and soon after, from Buffalo, Pittsburgh, and New York. Even though it emanated from the wild forest lands of rural Cattaraugus County, within minutes, word spread across the nation about the location of the mysteriously missing Continental Charters plane.

Before he left the others at the crash wreckage, George double-checked the list of survivors on his pink napkin for accuracy with Pearl because she knew they must provide the survivors' names to Continental Charters, as soon as possible. Within minutes of George dictating the names over the Bryant's telephone, they were sent to search organizers who relayed them to distraught families in Florida, Pennsylvania, West Virginia, and New York. In the process, some of the names were misspelled, contained only first initials, and the message even portrayed the wrong pilot in command of the plane.

Arriving fast from opposite ends of Sawmill Run, Salamanca firefighters, Deputy Benson, and Chief Perrigo all reached George at the Bryant's roadside mailbox at about the same time. Deputy Benson assumed

---

Buffalo's WBEN-TV for many years.
[111] The crash actually occurred on forest land owned by Ernest and Emily Waite, adjacent to the Herrick farm. Most people, however, described the scene as the Herrick farm.

command of the investigation as the officer from the lead agency. He took George into his squad car, and together they drove back up Sawmill Run Road with George pointing out where he came out of the woods. Deputy Benson knew the terrain in the hollow well, and he continued on up to the Herrick farm where he knew access to the top of the woods on the ridge from across the Herrick's large hay field was easiest. First, though, he dropped George at the Herrick's farmhouse. Chief Perrigo also drove farther up the hollow nearly to the Herrick farm where he ditched his car, crossed the hayfield, and went into the woods leading up to the crash scene described to him over the telephone by George. Within minutes of each other, Chief Perrigo, the Bryant boys, Deputy Benson, several Salamanca firefighters, Little Valley Police Chief Bernard Young, and a handful of local residents were all tracking separately through the woods toward the top of Bucktooth Ridge. The Bryant boys got a head start but because they walked a mostly wooded trail from their farm on the lower section of the hollow, it was a longer hike. As he got closer to where he believed the crash scene to be, Chief Perrigo heard gunshots. With the noise guiding him into the approximate location of the survivors, Perrigo first came to Chief Young. He had spent valuable time crisscrossing the wooded hillside trying to find the wreck. Just ahead of them and already at the scene of the mangled airliner were Salamanca firefighter Clemence Myers, and Robert Lilienthal, a 23-year-old co-owner of the Randolph Seed Company with his brother, Donald. Lilienthal had heard the police radio call and raced to the woods from the Napoli side of the ridge following the sheriff's squad car. Entering the woods even before Deputy Benson stopped to pick up George, Lilienthal achieved a tremendous hard start on everyone. Lilienthal's family hunting camp was along Sawmill Run, and he was familiar with the woods from tracking deer while hunting, and flying over the mountains in his small single-engine airplane.[112] A tall, lanky young man who excelled in four years on the Randolph High School

---

[112] Lilienthal crashed his Aeronca airplane in 1945, into a pasture east of Randolph, while a senior in high school but he wasn't hurt. He was a member of the Randolph Civilian Air Patrol and took a keen interest in anything about airplanes.

basketball team and who had been a member of the school's Forensics Club, Lilienthal was fast through the snow and filled with curiosity about the dead and survivors up on the ridge. Additionally, in an unusual twist of fate, Lilienthal's wife, Kentucky Kilburn Lilienthal, had planned to catch the same Continental Charters plane in Buffalo on December 29 to visit her mother in Florida. Illness forced her to cancel her plans at the last minute.[113]

Soon after entering the woods, Lilienthal said he picked up George Albert's wobbly path and followed it up the ridge. With his youth and speed, Lilienthal was the first person on the scene. Coming upon the wreckage, there appeared to be no signs of life. Poking around the large pieces of the plane, he found survivors Mary Messerlos, Ana Piso, and Ava Woodward inside the wreckage. They pointed him toward the campsite where he found the others sitting closely together in the snow. They welcomed him with shouts of relief said a reporter who dictated Lilienthal's story. "We thought we would never be rescued," they told him. "This is a heck of a New Year, but, even though we're battered and broken, we don't care as long as we're alive," Lilienthal said he was told by the survivors.

Stewardess Dolores Beshears showed Lilienthal around the campsite and the plane wreckage. Together, they rifled through some baggage and found a few more pieces of damp clothing that they wrapped around the survivors still trapped in the wreck. They also gave more clothing to Robert Geyer, who had crawled to a small piece of broken fuselage that offered just a little protection from the rain. Almost as an afterthought and because the light was fading and he didn't have a flash, Lilienthal pulled a camera from his pocket and snapped a picture.

Following the agreed upon signal for finding the wreckage, Chief Young fired two shots from his service revolver for other rescue crews, by now scattered across the ridge searching for the plane so they would know where to go. Within minutes, the other police officers and firefighters carrying stretchers tracked in. The rescue was on. However, there was at least one report from the first people on the scene that

---

[113] Lilienthal's story was reported in first-person narratives in two newspapers. He was a classmate of the author's parents at Randolph High School in 1946.

some volunteers who raced into the woods at the top of the ridge were so aghast and sickened by the sight of mutilated and bloodied bodies that they immediately turned around and hiked back out.

Nearly four hours had passed since Pearl wrapped George's feet and since he tucked the passengers' survivor list in his coat pocket and slipped off through the woods toward the train whistle. The small group of survivors had waited for what seemed like an eternity when they first heard sirens in the valley below. Only then did they realize that George found the help they so desperately needed. With each new arrival of rescuers they hollered, "Over here, over here," almost not believing that someone had finally come to help them. The gunshots startled the women, but Myers quickly explained that the gunfire was to draw the others to the scene. "They were huddled around the fire when we got there," Chief Young said. "Some of the women were crying."

Arriving at about the same time, Myers, Chief Perrigo, Chief Young, Deputy Benson, and the Bryant boys found the survivors altogether beneath the parachute that Lt. Bischof had pried from the wreckage. The survivors were shoulder-to-shoulder stretching their hands toward the fire for warmth, but it gave off more smoke than heat. The rescuers quickly built up the fire until it was roaring. The survivors later recounted how they felt when they realized George had done it. Relieved and proud, they said. They were finally saved!

CHAPTER 13

RIDE DOWN THE MOUNTAIN

WHEN CATTARAUGUS COUNTY SHERIFF'S Deputy Russell Benson fishtailed through the snow and ice down the long hill to the bottom of Sawmill Run Road in his cruiser to pick up George, he had to turn around and spin back up the hollow to the Herrick's farm and the closest access to the top of Bucktooth Ridge. In his patrol car, it was a struggle. He immediately called the sheriff's department for plows to clear the road for rescuers.

It was customary for the Napoli and Cold Spring road crews to plow only the section of road that was needed on a daily basis and wait to plow the rest of the road later. By the time he got to the Herrick's farm with George, Deputy Benson had passed several cars ditched along the unplowed section of the road from drivers, such as Bob Lilienthal, who had already entered the woods searching for the crash. Initial reports said George walked back up the ridge to the crash scene with Deputy Benson, but they turned out to be false. George never returned to the scene. He was delivered to the warmth of the Herrick's farmhouse until he was taken to the hospital.

For snow plows, Sheriff Sigel called recently elected Napoli highway superintendent David Shenefiel at home on his farm along Hoxie Hill

Road. David drove over Hoxie Hill to the Napoli highway equipment shed, but his view of Bucktooth Ridge in the lifting fog showed nothing out of the ordinary. The crash was hidden deep in the woods. By the time David and his men arrived with the big butterfly-winged plow trucks and the town's new front-end loader, however, Sawmill Run was so plugged with cars and trucks that no one else could get in. They managed to plow a path to a point just below the Herrick farm where it was easiest to access the ridge. Then, using the loader, a small steel track tractor from the Herrick's farm known as "the crawler," and a Willys-Overland Jeep CJ-2 four-wheel drive vehicle equipped with a cable winch, the Napoli town crews, and local firefighters managed to get a path up the side of the ridge for about a half a mile across the Herrick's hayfield to the edge of the woods. After that, the rescuers had to walk.[114]

Sheriff Sigel placed another call to David's brother, Edwin Shenefiel, at his farm in the valley below Bucktooth Ridge. It was only about a mile away on a map. Edwin and his wife, Edith Hoxie Shenefiel, also had a crawler-tractor on their farm and the sheriff was desperate to have it brought to the ridge. When the sheriff's call came in Edwin was preparing for his overnight job as a machinist grinding stainless steel ball bearings for the aviation industry at the Marlin Rockwell Corporation factory in Jamestown. He was not able to respond to the emergency. Edith took the call and immediately dispatched her brother, Hugh Hoxie, with his flatbed hay truck, to pick up their crawler-tractor and haul it to Bucktooth Ridge. Among Edith and Edwin's sons, Donald, Robert, and Kern, who worked on the farm and were capable of driving the tractor, only 16-year-old Donald was able to help load the heavy machine because 12-year-old Robert had recently broken his leg while playing football at school in Randolph. Kern was too young. Despite the attraction of excitement and adventure at the plane crash scene, Edith ordered the younger boys to stay home.

---

[114] The Town of Napoli road crews eventually got a smooth path open all the way down Sawmill Run Road for the ambulances hearses but only after several cars were dragged out of the way. The Herrick's "crawler" was an Oliver HG *Cletrac*, a small tractor-like vehicle with steel tracks. It resembled a small bulldozer.

By the time Hugh and Donald, along with Donald's cousin, Milton Marvin, arrived at the Herrick farm with the Shenefiel's crawler-tractor, however, the plane crash survivors were already being brought down the mountain trail. The road was so packed with rescuers and plane crash tourists that the men had a difficult time getting their crawler-tractor to the scene. Once unloaded, however, they immediately hitched it to a small trailer and throttled the motor and biting steel tracks across the snow-covered fields toward the woods trail created by the rescuers with the Herrick's crawler-tractor. They knew exactly where to go because they had used the same method to haul freshly cut logs from the ridge just a few years earlier. Two 1940s-era Oliver-Cletrac tractors proved to be lifesavers that night. Few other vehicles could have made it up the steep ridge so quickly under such snow, ice, and mud conditions.

From several different paths created by the first rescuers on the scene, they settled on one which began at the Herrick's old red barn. The first several hundred feet were open fields. With a strong wind blowing across the ridge, rescuers bent forward and plugged along through the knee-deep snow in their leather boots, mackinaws, and bear-skin fur hats, until they reached the wind-breaking woods.[115] There they were forced to jump over or wade through fast-rushing streams of water in several gullies generated by the recent thaw and rain. One by one, the rescuers trekked to the top of the ridge with each step of their boots eroding away snow and mud to create a trail. *Pittsburgh Press* writer John Place described what the rescuers found when they got to the crash scene. *"A girl's thin hand, a pearl ring on her finger, held a strip of green paper, which fluttered shyly. There was a Christmas box still neatly ribboned in red, leaning against a tree. Blue seat from the plane- undamaged but empty – far in the thickets, bathing suit, rag-doll, a man's black shoe, on its heel in some wet leaves – the foot inside, but nothing else. And in the trees, there were bits of clothing and flesh. There was no escape in looking up."*

---

[115] The weather was changing at this time with cooler air moving in with stronger wind that pushed away the fog that had plagued the region for several days and nights.

The dead girl described in Place's article was little Judy Frankel. Her Raggedy Ann doll with orange hair and a blue and white polka dot dress lay scattered among splintered branches, metal wiring and tubing, and Christmas wrapping paper. The coroner later determined that while many of the victims died from broken necks, they also had their legs and feet broken off when the passengers were thrust under the seats in front of them, as indicated by the description of a man's severed foot still in its shoe. A press photograph taken with a bright flash showed a man's foot and a woman's foot sticking out of the wreckage, still in their shoes but no longer connected to legs. Police had difficulty helping the coroner match appendages with bodies. Wooden and wire bushel baskets normally used to pick apples on the Herrick farm were used to gather body parts from the crushed fuselage. Severed feet, fingers, and hands were thrown into the bushel baskets together to be identified later. Place couldn't escape seeing the dead when he looked up because some of the bodies were hanging in the trees. One was a stewardess.

Arriving at the Herrick farm, Sheriff Sigel set up a crash rescue base headquarters at the back of the Herrick's farmhouse. It was a crude but sturdy old farmhouse that had been passed down to Kenneth Herrick from his parents, Marion and Blanche Stoughton Herrick, and it soon became overrun with people. Earlier in 1951, Sheriff Sigel gained approval to purchase and install the county's first two-way radio system. It ushered in all new and rapid voice communications with his deputies in the field and with local police and fire departments throughout the far-flung communities of Cattaraugus County's mountains and valleys. Sigel also appointed his wife, Irene, to run the county-wide radio system at the sheriff's office in Little Valley. It was convenient because the county provided a home for the sheriff that was attached to the jail and the courthouse. It allowed the sheriff to remain at his makeshift headquarters and coordinate the rescue from the Herrick's barnyard. It turned the Herrick's home into a mob scene.

For the first time in the county's history, each sheriff's deputy squad car was equipped with a mobile radio and a long floppy antenna attached to the trunk, and a few portable units were available for deputies to carry in the field during investigations.[116] The expenditure foresight by Sigel would prove to be beneficial after the crash of Flight 44-2 as the sheriff talked over the radio with his men from his field headquarters near the bottom of Bucktooth Ridge in Napoli. His chief deputy was positioned at the crash scene while Mrs. Sigel commanded the base radio at the Sheriff's office. By all accounts, Sigel did an exemplary job except for how he handled the macabre and despicable crime committed at the scene of the crash. As more of his deputies, New York State Police, Allegany State Park Rangers, firefighters, local farmers, and sightseers arrived in mass confusion among the central question, "where's the crash," it wasn't long before Deputy Benson was calling out on his waist-mounted portable radio. He needed reinforcements; doctors, stretchers, blankets, blood plasma, splints, portable lights and generators, and the coroner.

After two days of checking out several false leads sent by New York State Police teletype to his outpost barracks in Allegany, State Police Corporal Eugene Redden also arrived at the scene representing the agency's Bureau of Criminal Investigation (BCI). Already a veteran state trooper, Cpl. Redden previously had some dramatic rescues in his state police career but nothing like this. He had found and rescued a newborn baby from a gas station trash can and saved a Buffalo woman's life by lifting her crushed car so she could breathe until help arrived. At the crash scene, Redden became the investigator who transcribed Pearl's account of how little Judy Frankel died in her arms on the first night. Cpl. Redden was also in charge of making the official list of survivors, and once other troopers arrived, another list of the dead.[117]

At about the same time that George arrived at the Bryant's farmhouse to find help, the skies over Cattaraugus County cleared from the intense fog and low hanging clouds that shrouded the crashed plane on the ridge. And, as the first rescuers arrived on foot at the wreckage, the search planes made their first visual sighting from the air. The crash

---

[116] These portable radios were rather large, about the size of a backpack, and were carried with shoulder straps.

[117] Cpl. Redden recalled these incidents for his family, and they were written up in newspapers from 1947-1951.

scene had been below them all the time, but none of the pilots or crew aboard the dozens of search planes had seen it because of the poor visibility. Relaying the wreckage coordinates to airports in Niagara Falls and Pittsburgh, the Air Force planes from Westover and Cleveland dropped food, blankets and stretchers into the woods. An Air Force Grumman Albatross from Michigan via Buffalo Airport dropped a small crate of blood plasma, but it missed its mark and was never recovered for use on the injured victims.[118] The stretchers were put to immediate use. Four young men from the Salamanca American Legion rescue squad were the first to load injured passenger Anna Piso. Each man grabbed a corner of her stretcher and carried her down the ridge to the Herrick farm. Asking their names, she became fast friends with PFC. Wendell Reed, home from Army training at Fort Dix; Allen Davis; Don Levinski; and Gary Rhodes. As they carried Piso down the ridge wrapped in a warm blanket, they were met by a constant stream of rescuers walking up. Salamanca District Hospital doctors James Fleming and Leland Stoll hiked to the top of the ridge where they administered first aid to Mary Messerlos, stabilized her condition and then, with help from other rescuers, finally got her unpinned from the plane's wreckage. Reporters witnessed the whole thing and then were able to question Messerlos before she too was loaded on a stretcher and carried off the ridge. All she requested was a drink of water.

One by one, between 4:30 and 5:40 pm, each survivor was carried off Bucktooth Ridge. Rescuer George Short arrived early, and upon meeting a police officer at the crash scene with two stretchers, he and companions Richard Benson, Richard Bird, and Richard Hartson, took over one of the stretchers and carried out a stewardess. They never figured out if it

---

[118] Ordered to prepare for airlifting survivors, the twin-engine Grumman Albatross from Selfridge Air Force Base in Michigan landed on the 1,200-foot grass field of Salamanca Airport at dusk on New Year's Eve. However, the field was too short to take off, so the plane was useless. While the six-man crew bunked in local homes and in the women's section of the Salamanca City Jail, special jet propulsion tanks were shipped in, attached to the plane, and with the extra thrust it eventually took off on Wednesday afternoon, January 2. The airport was located in an area used in 2015 for a trash and recycling station and sewer treatment plant along the Allegheny River.

was Pearl Moon or Dolores Beshears. Walking down the already worn path, they intercepted a man carrying blankets to the top. One of them was a dark blue wool blanket, and another was a hand sewn wool patchwork quilt with yarn tassels. They came from the Herrick's farmhouse. Wrapping the stewardess with the quilt, the six men carrying the wooden stretcher hoisted it high because the quilt hung nearly to the ground. Burrowed into the stretcher for warmth, Dolores Beshears said she finally realized that three of the men were named Dick.[119] A photograph of these "men" shows what appear to be just boys with close-cropped hair above their ears and still wearing their high school varsity jackets and cuffed slacks wet to their knees. One of them, a baby-faced boy with pimples is stripped to his shirt. He may have given up his winter coat to a survivor. All the way down, Short said many years later, he kept thinking about the other stewardess he saw at the crash scene, hanging dead in the trees, doubled over in her seat belt.[120]

Robert Geyer and Eva Woodward were removed from the wreckage and carefully placed on the stretchers for the jarring and painful ride down the ridge. Each man on a corner of their stretchers had to lift his legs up high to step into the deep snow. It was difficult and exhausting. A safety walked on each side to catch the stretchers in the event a man stumbled and fell and to take turns carrying the load. As Napoli farmers, area firefighters, and teenage boys waded up and down the ridge, they reported to Sheriff Sigel of their difficulty in the snow. Rudy Mirwald and his brother-in-law, Marion Van Slyke, knew the ridge well from their many years hunting deer. Listening to reports from trusted local men such as these, and his deputies at the scene describing the bodies, the sheriff determined there was no way to cut a path all the way up the ridge for motor vehicles promptly. With darkness falling and realizing the task may last all night, Sheriff Sigel called for toboggans and ropes. They appeared almost instantly from neighboring farms. They were for the bodies.

Sheriff Sigel also requisitioned a small two-wheeled wooden trailer,

---

[119] The stewardess carried down by these men was Dolores Beshears, a tiny woman who was easily hidden beneath the quilt.
[120] This stewardess victim was Delores Harvey.

more like a cart, from the Herrick farm and with rescue crews hitching it to "the crawler" it was used to carry the injured survivors on the last part of their journey down the ridge.[121] By the time rescuers carried the survivors to the head of the cart path, it was dark. With a man driving the crawler-tractor, other rescuers stood in the trailer and even walked along on the slow-rolling steel tracks pointing flashlights so they could see the final half mile to Herrick's barn.[122]

There was no order for who came down off the ridge first — it was the most seriously injured. The men survivors all insisted the women go first, and their early arrival at the Herrick farm made it appear as if all the survivors were women. As each one was carried away, survivor Joseph Wozniak said to his rescuers, "the sheer courage exhibited in that terrible mess was the most wonderful thing, in my experience." Reporters followed them down the ridge, asking questions and listening to the conversations between the rescuers and the survivors. "Where were you sitting on the plane," asked the rescuers. To which each of the survivors, except for Robert Geyer, replied that they were sitting in the back. This remarkable revelation spread down the ridge to the farmhouse and among the reporters. They were all sitting in the back of the plane, the newspaper men repeated, over and over, as they took turns calling their offices in Jamestown, Buffalo, Pittsburgh, and Salamanca on the Herrick's single telephone. Then, survivor Mary Battista started the heroism praise for George. "If it weren't for George Albert setting out again the second day we probably all would have died," she declared to the rescuers and reporters. "He saved our lives." The newspapermen jumped all over this comment from Battista, and it grew into a major part of the story. George Albert alone became the hero of Bucktooth Ridge. Lt. Bischof and Pearl were relegated to a second-class hero and just a stewardess.

---

[121] The Herrick's Oliver "crawler" was often used for skidding logs through heavy snow and plowing fields on steep slopes. The crawler tractor was especially useful during the rescue because of the snow, ice, and mud. On repeated trips, vehicles with wheels would have gotten stuck.

[122] Two of the operators of the crawler-tractor were teenage boys, Robert Herrick, 17, and Marion Herrick, 19, who were most proficient at driving the "crawler." The *Cletrac* used in the rescue was still owned by the Herrick family in 2015.

Sixty years later, Pearl told me it still "galled" her that the reporters virtually ignored her life-saving actions on the ridge for George's and Lt. Bischof's. She blamed it on the fact that all the reporters who hiked up the ridge, except for one, were men.

Those who could walk and were not seriously injured hopped onto the stretchers by themselves. Mary Battista, Marie Norcia, Joseph Wozniak, Albert Dichak, and Ed Wessel were taken out early only because it took extra time to free Eva Woodward, Mary Messerlos, and Robert Geyer from the wreckage.[123] It also took a few minutes for the doctors to stabilize and administer their hand-carried blood plasma to Thomas Patterson. A press photo taken at the campsite shows the 21-year-old Navy man from New Castle, Pennsylvania lying on his back, strapped onto a stretcher, receiving a transfusion, and his bloody, bandaged head resting on a duffle bag for a pillow. His face is gaunt and partially hidden by the wool collar of a coat pulled up around his neck and chin. Two men, tending to his needs, are squatting beside him.

As the only surviving on-duty crew member of the flight, Pearl initially demanded that all others be taken down the ridge first. However, she was outranked by Lt. Bischof. An admittedly stubborn woman, Pearl finally gave in much as she did when George insisted she accept his plan to walk out for help. She was the next-to-last survivor to be carried out. Just before 5 pm, six hours after George walked away from their campsite, Pearl was loaded onto a stretcher and carried by hand down the side of the ridge to where the forest ended at the Herrick's hay field. She was placed in the cart hitched up to the crawler-tractor where she nestled in some bales of hay thrown in for the survivors' comfort. As an old woman living in a nursing home many years later, Pearl still fondly recalled the kindness of the men who put her in the cart. She remembered standing at first and then sitting down on the bales of hay as she was carried to the safety of the Herrick's barn as if she were a

---

[123] Albert Dichak and Joseph Wozniak were both from Canonsburg, Pennsylvania and were flying to Miami to watch the Orange Bowl football game between Georgia Tech and Baylor University on January 1, 1952. In contrast to the weather that caused the crash that nearly killed them, Miami was described as hot and muggy on New Year's Day.

queen. It was the last of Pearl's special attention except for a moment at Salamanca Hospital when nurses teased the rescued heroine about cutting off her clothing for souvenirs.

By the time Pearl emerged from the woods and was transferred to a hearse-ambulance, George was already at the hospital being checked out. Bundled in a heavy coat and covered by wool blankets with her head resting on a tuft of hay atop the canvas tacked to wooden slats of her stretcher, Pearl was photographed lying across two seats in the back of the large black and bulky hearse. Peeking out from beneath her blanket was the head of a small black dog with floppy ears. It may have been passenger Eva Woodward's dog that survived the wreck, was found on a nearby farm, and was returned to the Herrick farm just in time. It may have been a six-week-old puppy described by Lt. Bischof as belonging to a male passenger who was killed, or they may have been the same dog. Whose pet it was remained a mystery. In the photograph it appears the little dog is hitching a ride to the hospital. As Pearl was driven down Sawmill Run to Salamanca, Lt. Bischof was the only survivor who remained on Bucktooth Ridge. Matching his status as a Navy officer, he was the last to leave the crashed ship.[124]

When Lt. Bischof's crew of stretcher-bearers emerged from the woods, they loaded him onto an antique bob-sleigh appropriated from the Herrick's barn. With iron runners for snow and ice, the low, flat bed of the sleigh was ideal for holding the portable stretcher. With a man on each corner, one in front for steering, and another behind holding a rope for braking, Lt. Bischof, in his long dark woolen coat and tan baseball cap, laid on his stiff and sore back for the last half mile ride down the ridge. Some witnesses reported a small cheer when the crowd around Herrick's barn learned the sleigh was holding the last survivor to come down. Their spirit didn't last long, though. There were still 26 bodies at the top.

At 6:30 pm, Mary Messerlos, so severely injured she was carried all the way down the ridge on a stretcher while being attended by Doctors Fleming and Stoll, was loaded into a hearse that departed immediately

---

[124] In 1951 a large airplane was often called a ship or airship.

for the hospital. Minutes later, Lt. Bischof was loaded into another, hearse for the short drive to Salamanca Hospital. All of the survivors were carried off the ridge in two hours and two minutes. When Lt. Bischof was checked into the hospital at 7:07 pm, New Year's Eve, it marked four hours and 21 minutes from the time George Albert called for help on the Bryant's farmhouse telephone. Removing all the bodies wouldn't be completed until many hours later, on New Year's Day.

IN THE NEARBY VILLAGE of Randolph, home from college during the Christmas season, Gilbert Myers was at his family's Myers and Myers Funeral Home planning a New Year's Eve celebration with friends, including his high school pal Frank Vaughn. Ironically, Gilbert and his girlfriend, Barbara Shenefiel, intended to drive into Sawmill Run early that evening to start a warming fire in the wood stove and prepare for the New Year's Eve party at the Myers' camp. It was the same camp George circled that afternoon when he was looking for help.[125] Instead, because his father, Fred Myers, was out of town, Gilbert took an emergency telephone call for the funeral home's big black hearse to report to Sawmill Run for transporting injured survivors, or the dead.

The Myers' Funeral Home was on the ground floor of the family's stately old house on Church Street. It had a third story mansard-style roof with widow's walk, columned front entrance porch flanked by classic six over six paned windows, and a deep side sitting porch. It had been in the Myers family for many years and was a fixture in Randolph. A circular driveway and tasteful landscaping completed one of the most attractive homes in town. The Myers meticulously maintained the old house, painting the white clapboard siding nearly every year to keep up appearances out of respect for the many bereaved families who called upon the business in times of need. The funeral home also included an ambulance service because few small towns had a regular ambulance or rescue squad in the 1940s and 50s. For this, the Myers' simply ran their big black hearse to accident scenes or to people in medical distress for trips

---

[125] Barbara Shenefiel was David and Rosa Shenefiel's daughter and was later married to Gilbert Myers.

to the nearest hospital or doctor in Randolph, Jamestown or Salamanca. If the patient died, it was all the more convenient.

While at college in Alfred, New York, Gilbert, who was named after his great-grandfather and founder of the mortuary, was deciding if he wanted to take over the family funeral home business. His parents were also operating an insurance agency and were ready to pass the mortician business onto the next generation in the family. Gilbert thought long and hard on the proposition. He had a difficult decision because he had his heart set on becoming an attorney and practicing law. As a high school and college student who inherited his father's and grandfather's short legs and slender physique, Gilbert appeared to be too young as he would drive off to pick up bodies in the Myers' big, imposing black and chrome Sayers and Scovill (S & S) Coach Company hearse. His undersized frame would be swallowed up by the red patent leather front bench seat of the customized car body. It had a high rounded hood and roof, rear fender skirts, red flashing lights, white driver's side spotlight, gray ruffled window curtains, Landau bars, red carpeted and chrome hardware casket vault, and a powerful V-8 Chevrolet engine on a stretch Cadillac frame. It was the closest thing to a limousine in Randolph. Gilbert had this beautiful new 1950 Cadillac funeral coach for tooling around town on body pick-up jobs only because his beloved grandfather, Frederick C. Myers, had been severely injured in a 1936 crash with a long, black hearse. Since then, the family made it a practice to purchase new and progressively safer models on a regular basis.

Funerals in 1951 typically took three days and while up to 50 funerals a year doesn't seem to be many, it kept the Myers family busy in small-town Randolph. They did have competition: Hoitink Undertaking Company in Randolph; the Hunt, O'Rourke and O'Rourke, McKenna, and Middleton Funeral Homes, all in Salamanca; and Briggs Funeral Home in Cattaraugus. What little time they could find to get away from two successful businesses, the Myers' spent at their small camp in the woods along Sawmill Run at the Napoli-Cold Spring town line. The woods from their camp reached up the west side of Bucktooth Ridge. It was located about a mile up the hollow from Charlie and Ruby Bryant's family farm.

During winter months in the late 1940s when many back roads in the area were infrequently plowed or not plowed at all, Fred and Gilbert drove the funeral home's Plymouth paneled truck to their camp and entered the hollow from the Napoli side, on the northern section of Sawmill Run Road. They carried bushel baskets of fireplace ashes in the back of the truck because even with chains on the tires and backing the Plymouth up a steep hill (for better traction) at the Herrick farm they needed the ashes for grit on the ice. Sometimes it took three runs up Herrick's Hill to make it but once over the top it was all downhill for more than a mile to their camp. From there they passed only a few hunting cabins in the woods on the way to their secluded getaway. It was a crude camp, built by Fred Myers, but it was equipped with an old hand-crank telephone. Myers, after all, was a mortician and would receive calls at all hours of the day and night. Life in the family mortuary for Gilbert Myers was all the more fascinating when Grandfather Myers would clean up the embalming fluids, close the lid to the casket of the latest client, strike a match to his Pall Mall cigarette, push back his chair, cross his short, skinny legs, and begin telling stories about the business of death. Many dramatic fatalities had come through the Myers' funeral home or caught the attention of the charming old raconteur of an undertaker. They included a saw mill worker decapitated near Napoli when a boiler overheated and exploded shrapnel into his face; a young Randolph woman who bled to death by shooting her left eye out of its socket on the Blood family farm; and a Ringling Brothers, Barnum and Bailey Circus worker who crawled away from his accidental fall from a Pennsylvania Railroad train near Onoville and bled to death. His severed leg was still on the tracks.

Even in rural Randolph the Myers and other local morticians had seen everything until it came to the 26 mangled bodies missing legs and feet, and decapitations from the plane crash. Called to the scene along the treacherous and muddy Sawmill Run Road as an ambulance driver with the family's big black hearse because his father was out of town, what college sophomore Gilbert Myers witnessed at the scene was the repulsive side of the funeral home and ambulance chasing business. It reinforced his plan to become an attorney, instead.

Myers and Frank Vaughn left for Napoli as soon as they got the telephone call. "It was exciting when we heard about it, and we drove the hearse (fast) to Sawmill Run," he recalled. "The place was a mess. It was jammed up with cars, and about half of them were stuck. There wasn't anybody in charge." Even with the hearse, clearly identifiable as a vehicle that needed to get closer to the scene, Gilbert couldn't get through the rapidly growing crowd of cars, trucks and gawking people. "We just sat there," he said. The two young college sophomores watched car after car squeeze past them, and when the drivers discovered they could not get up Herrick's Hill, they turned into Herrick's driveway in an attempt to bypass all the other cars and trucks that were parked on the narrow road. Gilbert estimated that hundreds of people were already there trying to get a glimpse of the crash scene.[126] They didn't know it was another two-mile walk, at least, through the woods up to the top of the ridge. Still they came. Sightseers drove all the way from Buffalo that night; men dressed in suits and women in dresses with open-toed shoes. None had warm clothing for a hike through the woods. Some walked up the ridge anyway, but most of them simply mingled around the farm waiting for a glimpse of a survivor, or a body. Most of them wanted to see the heroes, especially George.

Gilbert never did get to use the hearse for injured passengers or the dead. While the survivors were brought down to Herrick's farmyard, all the bodies were taken out on the path cut by the Napoli town highway crew and carried to Salamanca in hearses from other funeral homes. While waiting, Gilbert witnessed the vulture-like hovering of competing hearse drivers trying to get a payday with a body or two from the crash. Some residents later reported that funeral home responders either coordinated with local police, or hid bodies and body parts in the snow, or laid claim to bodies, and body parts in the bushel baskets until their hearse drivers returned to Sawmill Run with an empty vehicle. The seedy side of the mortuary business further soured any interest Gilbert might have had for taking over his family's funeral home. He and Vaughn managed to turn around in the muddied and rutted, narrow

---

[126] The mob scene grew to the point where police were eventually positioned at key intersections miles away to block traffic from approaching Sawmill Run Road.

road, and they drove the big black hearse back to Randolph, empty. They never made it to lower Sawmill Run or the Myers' camp for their New Year's Eve party. It was canceled. A few days later, when Gilbert and his father returned to Sawmill Run in their Plymouth panel truck, the road was still lined with cars and sightseers. Arriving at their camp, they found one set of footprints that circled the cabin, having paused in front of each window. They belonged to George Albert.

WITH ALL 14 SURVIVORS carried out and on their way to the hospital, the rescuers then began the difficult task of removing the dead from the plane wreckage. Doctors Fleming and Stoll, and the Cattaraugus County Coroner, Dr. James M. Happel, examined the bodies and marked them with paper tags wired to an appendage if they had one. For some of the victims, firefighters used their heavy axes to break away parts of the wreckage to free an arm or a foot. They tried to cut into the cockpit with their crude hand tools but the small space was so compacted, it was impossible. The pilots' bodies could not be moved until late the next day. One of the firefighters found a booklet from the cockpit containing the flight records. It was taken by a Buffalo FBI agent for safe keeping until CAB investigators arrived. It included the terrain charts that did not show mountains along the flight path.

Pearl, George, and Lt. Bischof had carefully placed the three dead children passengers, side-by-side in the snow, and their bodies were carried first down to the cart hitched to the crawler-tractor. A photograph of young men escorting the crawler across the Herrick's hayfield shows the cart, appearing empty. It was filled, in fact, with the tiny, lifeless bodies of Judy and Mark Frankel, and Jeffrey Evans. They were too small to be seen within the bales of hay in the cart.

The body of stewardess Delores Harvey was cut from where it was hanging by her seatbelt, and carried out on a stretcher but not before her lifeless image was captured by a press photographer. Those who were thrown clear of the wreckage were first rolled in blankets and tarps and tied onto the toboggans. Each body was escorted down the ridge by a police officer, sheriff's deputy, state trooper, or park ranger, whose numbers had grown to more than a dozen. The law enforcement officers were easily identifiable from the reflection on their shiny badges caused by the news photographers' flash bulbs.

As the victims' bodies were carefully slid down through the woods, Continental Charters president John Belding, and a public relations official for the Air Transport Association, representing the nonskeds, arrived at the Herrick farm and immediately hiked up the ridge. Belding found his new airplane in three large pieces with the engines and smaller parts of wreckage strewn all over the woods. He found his pilots, whom he knew personally, wedged in the crushed cockpit. A reporter who watched Belding at the scene described it this way: *"inside the wreckage of the middle fuselage of the plane, seats were smashed and strewn about. A baby's bonnet lay on top of one tilted seat. Two playing cards were found, pieces of clothing were hanging from the limbs of trees 50 and 60 feet tall. A man's shoe and a woman's fragile pump lay in the snow. Nearby was the blue-bound Army Manual for Officers' Candidate School."* For the coroner, Belding confirmed the identities of his pilots. It was a sad occasion for the war veteran airline owner. Belding had flown with each of them in the company's C-46 cockpits.

There are only a few records available that describe carrying out the dead. Aside from the images from press photographers who made it early to the scene, little was said about the somber task and, therefore, even less was reported about the bodies that came down from the top of Bucktooth Ridge. One photograph, lit up by a bright flashbulb, showed a woman's hand, just her hand protruding from the crush of the wreckage. It's presumed the woman's body was beyond the hand, hidden from view. Supervised by the coroner, the hand was gently laid in a bushel basket among other body parts. A St. Bonaventure University student, Raymond Gray, home in Salamanca from college when he rushed to the scene, said the crash was an awful mess. "Parts of bodies were scattered around the wreckage and bits of trees littered the ground." He said the head injury to one of the pilots was so severe it was obvious he was dead. Gray joined the victim removal crews and carried down a body on a stretcher with other men whom he didn't even know. He said the only problems the rescuers had was from the growing jam of spectators and their cars blocking Sawmill Run Road and making it difficult for the hearse-ambulances to get through. One rescuer, who walked up the muddy trail as bodies were being slid down, remembers stopping and waiting until a silent body crew swept past him, six, seven or eight times. Not a word was spoken, only a slight nod of the head was made. When asked how many more were up there, one man simply shrugged the reply as in, "We don't know." The photographs of the victims being pulled down the ridge on toboggans were taken with powerful flashes and they made it appear as if it happened in daylight. The reality was a difficult and stumbling trip in darkness, lit only by a few small flashlights, and with toboggans sliding all over the trail, sometimes spilling bodies off to the side. Said one volunteer: "it was not a pleasant experience."

As investigators continued their work at the top of Bucktooth Ridge, the excitement of the story quickly shifted to Salamanca Hospital where all 14 survivors were taken for emergency treatment. Notified that some survivors would be brought to the 52-bed hospital, all doctors and nurses were placed on emergency duty. The nurses' shift change at 3 pm was canceled when every one of them volunteered to remain at work. Nurses scheduled for the evening shift came in early. With only 12 empty beds, a few more were made available from the maternity ward. The seven women survivors were placed in shared rooms in twin metal-framed beds in the more comfortable maternity ward with four beds to a room. With walls painted green, cream-colored ceilings, and a soft glow from bedside table lamps, the warmth, and privacy of thick clean white sheets, blankets, and bed curtains felt like heaven to the women; an irony not lost on them after escaping the jaws of death in their mangled airplane. For the first time in three days, they enjoyed 70-degree temperature as the nurses carefully cut away their dirty and wet clothing and bathed them clean from the mud and dried blood covering their faces and bodies. They were examined and treated by doctors Otis Case, James Taft, and D.J. Meehan. Doctors Fleming and Stoll were still at the scene of the crash helping the coroner with the bodies, and would return later. Broken bones were set and lacerations stitched up by the doctors before each of the women enjoyed a hot meal of steaming vegetable soup. Stewardesses Pearl Moon and Dolores Beshears were placed in beds side by side and later, press photographers were allowed in to snap pictures of the pair with their heads buried in pillows. Whatever they discussed in the shared privacy of their hospital room about their work duties leading up to the plane crash was never revealed. Both were subpoenaed as witnesses for the investigation.

For the men, placed in the main hospital ward, immediate medical attention was given to Thomas Patterson and his badly fractured skull and lacerated forehead. Robert Geyer's broken bones were also a priority, and frostbite suffered by the men was treated immediately too. Of all seven men survivors, George was the only one who didn't go straight to a hospital bed. Since he walked out of the woods on his own, he was perceived to be OK. His heroism and developing celebrity may also have played a role. Instead, George spent the first hours in the hospital giving interviews to the news reporters. Later that evening, apparently after bathing but not shaving his three-day beard, George posed for a press photograph in the hospital while being examined by Dr. Taft. The scene looks as if it was staged. George's handsome hair curls are gleaming in the camera's flash while the doctor is holding a stethoscope to George's muscular and dark hair-covered chest draped only in an open hospital gown. For this photograph, the new American hero of Syrian descent has a slight smile on his perfectly formed and unblemished face. Not a single bruise or abrasion is visible except for tiny scratches on George's right middle finger knuckle and his left ring finger. Except for the tragedy of losing his mother, George appears as the luckiest among the survivors.

In 1951 and '52, press photographers were often allowed into hospital rooms if patients approved and it was common to see photographs of patients lying down or sitting up in their beds along with the story of their calamity or tragedy. On January 1, all the survivors except for the most severely injured women were photographed in their beds. In one close-up photograph, Lt. Bischof s head is so buried in his pillow it's hiding his ears. His boyish face with deeply cleft chin sticking out from a heavy wool blanket pulled up to his neck portrays a pouty 'poor me' appearance. In another, his wife Irene has her arm draped over his head resting on the hospital bed pillow as he gazes up at her with soft blue eyes sandwiched by his chin and bushy eyebrows. Within hours, these Hollywood-beautiful photographs of handsome George and Lt. Bischof, combined with stories of their bravery and sacrifice, would turn them into local celebrities. Within days, they would become national heroes. Pearl and Ruby were nearly forgotten.[127]

By six pm on New Year's Eve, Salamanca District Hospital Superintendent Louise Atkinson was facing a problem she had never experienced before. So many curious spectators were gathering at the emergency room entrance that it became difficult to control the crowd. It seemed like there were hundreds of people. She had to call the police, most who had gone to the crash site, the Herrick farm, or the Bryant farm, to help. Moving the crowd back from the hospital entrance somewhat, the few police officers still available were able to keep the crowd calm. The people who flooded into Salamanca, from all over western New York and Pennsylvania that night waited because they wanted a look at the survivors they had heard about on radio news broadcasts, mostly their new hero, George.

At the Herrick farm by six pm, it appeared as if a thousand people had gathered, many of them attempting to walk up the ridge for a look at the crash scene. Fewer, but still a large crowd of people, gathered at the Bryant farm too, all enticed by the live radio interviews with George, and reports of how he found Ruby to get help. Ruby was disappointed that many people who showed up at their farm and to gawk at the crash scene caused problems for the rescuers and police. *"The way cars flocked in and people started walking up only to be in the way didn't look so good,"* she wrote to herself in her diary.

She also recalled the personal toll. Her son, Rodney, had been sick all day Sunday but was feeling better when George arrived at their house on Monday. At the crash scene Rodney saw the most gruesomely mutilated figures that the 20-year-old man never imagined he would witness on the mountain above his quiet, rural home. It only added to his illness. *"When he came back from the wreck he was very white and he went back to bed,"* Ruby said.

---

[127] Newspapers around the world also portrayed George and Lt. Bischof as heroes for saving the other survivors from the plane crash.

John Bryant, at 15, and forced to stay home with his mother when his older brothers raced up the ridge to the crash site, said their house turned into chaos.[128] "There were rescue personnel, newsmen, thrill seekers, and traffic," he recounted many years later. "All the reporters wanted to use our telephone." The only places there were not mobs of people trying to get a glimpse of or hear more news about the crash and the survivors were the funeral homes, which collected the dead. There, it was quiet and civilized, even when somber family members, after exhausting all their telephone calls and personal trips to the Herrick farm, the top of the ridge, the sheriff's department, and the hospital, gave in to the inevitable and plodded in to identify their loved ones.

By morning, on New Year's Day, 19 of the 26 victims had been identified and were in preparation rooms at funeral homes in Salamanca. Roy Hemphill was identified by his 1951 Coraopolis, Pennsylvania driver's license in his wallet. Anne Frankel's body was taken to one funeral home in Salamanca, but her two children, little Judy, and Mark ended up at a different funeral home. They were all identified by relatives. Jeffrey Evans, the only baby on the flight, was easily confirmed by a friend of his dead grandparents because of his tiny body. Reserve pilots, C.J. Webber, and Gus Athas were identified by their uniforms and by Belding. Pilot Victor Harris and co-pilot Hans Rutzebeck were also identified, still in the cockpit, by their uniforms and by Belding. Stewardess Delores Harvey was identified by her Continental Charters service apron. Navy Seaman Richard Wilson and Air Force Sgt. Dave Arnold were identified by their military dog tags. Family members also helped identify Phyllis Paluzzi, Cpl. Richard Martin, Laverne Kroll, Dorothy Berman Bruce, John Jones, and a single victim taken to a small funeral home in Cattaraugus. Initially, this body was labeled by the coroner as simply a woman, *"about 40 to 50, five feet, two inches, short hair, very black and curly, apparently dyed, wearing black gabardine suit, white sheer blouse, wore diamond wedding ring and another diamond ring."* George's mother, Elizabeth Albert, was the only victim taken to the

---

[128] John later made it to the top of the ridge and the crash scene when his father returned home.

Cattaraugus funeral home. It was never revealed if it was George who went to confirm her identity, but it's presumed he did and that he also made the arrangements for her body to be transported home for services. For the other victims, identification took longer. Some were described by the coroner as, *"so badly mutilated, doubt if relatives can identify."*

Because the only two hotels in Salamanca were sold out, several local residents took in families of the victims and shuttled them around to search the funeral homes. It was a tender display of genuine hospitality by Salamanca residents who were shaken by this once-in-a-lifetime tragedy in their community. One survivor's family was observed celebrating loudly over a steak dinner in a Salamanca restaurant until they realized the somber group at a table nearby was the family of a victim. The celebrants were reported to have quickly quieted. Eventually, the identities of the remaining victims, Roy and Gertrude McLain, Margaret Jones, Audrey Malcom, Margaret Myers, John Opar, Agnes Penman, and Benjamin Siegal were made by relatives. One of the funeral home directors confirmed the coroner's initial report and revealed to a reporter that many of the victims died from deeply fractured skulls, broken necks, and multiple lacerations that caused extensive bleeding. Some of them lost arms, legs, and feet, and two of them lost their heads.

For the many families who had waited the agonizing three days, chased around Pennsylvania and New York not knowing where the plane was or if their loved ones were dead or alive, it was the saddest of New Year's Days. It may have been little consolation, but the bodies of the dead were lying in professional preparation rooms in tastefully decorated funeral homes where they could be visited in quiet and privacy. In the narrow rural valleys of Cattaraugus County, it was a sharp contrast to the Miami Airlines plane crash victims just a few weeks earlier whose bodies were lined up on straw scattered on the cold concrete garage floor of coroner Alfred Haines' funeral home in Elizabeth, New Jersey.

CHAPTER 14

BIG STORY

ALTHOUGH IT WAS NEW Year's Eve, newspaper photographer Dick Hallberg milled around his city editor's desk at the *Jamestown Post-Journal* waiting to run to his car. Hallberg was young for a news photographer, but he was fast becoming a veteran after four years at Jamestown's only daily, and its largest newspaper. He had recently outfitted his 1949 Buick Super Eight sedan with special license plates, *NYP 793*, for New York Press. The very noticeable yellow plates emblazoned with official-looking *NYP* got him past most police barricades in the newspaper's vast coverage area quite easily. The *Post-Journal's* readers were spread out from Jamestown in Chautauqua County, throughout all of southwestern New York State and a sizeable portion of northwestern Pennsylvania. Along with several weekly newspapers, the *Post-Journal* covered everything in neighboring Cattaraugus County too. With a large passenger plane reported missing on a flight track near Jamestown, Hallberg and the reporters and editors at the newspaper smelled a big story that would last for weeks. They just had to find it.

As quickly as Sheriff Sigel installed his first county-wide two-way radio system, the *Post-Journal* newsroom installed its own receivers and began monitoring the sheriff's broadcasts for a fast news tip that would pay off in a good story. At 2:44 pm on New Year's Eve Hallberg and City Editor Charles Stuart were anticipating and listening to the sheriff's radio. Suddenly there it was, loud, clear, and filled with excitement; the shortwave radio message of a plane crash on Sawmill Run. Hallberg ejected from the newspaper office like a hot flashbulb from his camera.

Normally a desk man for the newspaper, Stuart went with him. The story was too big for him to remain behind in the newsroom. Hallberg had fresh batteries and he packed a large supply of negative plates and flash bulbs for his big press camera that he carried around with its long silver battery tube. Pushing his Super Eight east out of the city of Jamestown into Cattaraugus County on Route 17, Hallberg took full advantage of his new press license plates and sped the entire 20 miles, through the village of Randolph to Napoli, before turning off onto Sawmill Run. Within another minute, he and Stuart saw the cars and people flooding into the Herrick's barnyard. Hallberg parked his Buick in a haphazard position, just like the other cars, grabbed his camera, film plates, and extra batteries, and ran up a steep hill to the Herrick's farmhouse. Stuart was right behind him, careful to stay just outside the range of Hallberg's camera lens so he wouldn't obstruct any photographs. "Where's the crash," was the first question from everyone arriving on the scene. Hallberg and Stuart made a quick survey and determined that the crash scene would have to wait a few minutes because the hero they heard about on the sheriff's radio broadcast was sitting in the Herrick's farmhouse. Prominently displaying his camera and large chrome flash reflector so there was no doubt about his intentions, Hallberg entered the house and found George relaxing in an overstuffed chair in front of a tall console TV. There was no picture in the oblong TV tube and everyone packed into the room was watching George. Stuart set in right away engaging George in all kinds of questions about the crash and how he got down off the ridge. *"Sitting in the lonely farmhouse, haggard and weak from his 42-hour ordeal on the snow-covered, fog-bound slope where the ill-fated C-46 crashed...,"* is how Stuart visualized George in those first few moments. He wrote and then dictated a description to the *Post-Journal.*

Hallberg saw George's penetrating eyes, dark curly hair and stubble beard staring directly into his viewfinder. The loud puff from his camera's brilliant flash flooded the room for an instant, casting a shadow from George's hair curls onto the wall behind him. It washed out the color in George's button-down collared shirt, with sleeves rolled up to reveal scratched fingers and dark, hairy arms. The photograph portrayed George's left eyebrow cocked high in a suspicious arch and his lips puffy and chapped. There was no expression, just a long stare sideways toward the camera. The strong flash left nothing hidden. It penetrated his sheer shirt like X-Ray vision. George was wearing a white T-shirt beneath his collared button-down and a hand-knitted sweater vest tucked into his outer pair of pants. The photograph even revealed the twine through the belt loops on these outer pants, indicating they may not have been his own pants at all, but rather, a pair scavenged from luggage in the wreckage or given to him by one of the other survivors. At some point, at the Herrick's farmhouse, George must have removed the string holding up the pants because it is missing from a second photograph – the outer pants open at the waist button and fly. Stuart continued his questioning. *"The stocky-built, dark-complexioned Albert spoke with a tired voice,"* Stuart later narrated over the Herrick's telephone for a writer at the Associated Press (AP).[129] "I had a premonition about this trip," George told Stuart from his first soft, warm seat in three days. "We had some trouble getting transportation in Pittsburgh and we were about to take some other means when this plane came along," he said.[130] "We" indicated himself and his mother. Her mangled and nearly unidentifiable body was still in the wreckage as he spoke. Other reporters gathered around, scribbling down every word and noting the handsome features of this brave man they would portray as a national hero. Pittsburgh *Sun-Telegraph* reporter Ed Bell was also early on the scene from his holding position parked in his car along the Pennsylvania-New York

---

[129] Stuart's dictation first appeared on the *Associated Press* newswire because the afternoon *Post-Journal* had already gone to print.
[130] It is unclear what George meant by "other means" of transportation. It may have been another plane or a train because the Continental Charters Flight was more than five hours late arriving in Pittsburgh.

border. He likely heard the bulletin news while listening to his car radio. Like Hallberg and Stuart, Bell raced to the scene along Sawmill Run until he saw the cars clustered around the Herrick's farm and he determined it was the crash location. Reporters for WJTN radio were also fast on the scene with portable recording equipment. News Director Jesse Price and Chief Engineer Harold Kratzert recorded interviews with George, Lt. Bischof, and the other survivors at the Herrick's farm and raced the recordings to the WJTN newsroom in Jamestown. From there the interviews were sent to New York and aired around the world.

Pressed on by the reporters, including Stuart and Bell, and joined by the only woman reporter on the scene, *Post-Journal* society reporter Millie Hall, George continued with his story. "No one slept Saturday night right after the crash," he said. "We had a few die on us that night, but I don't want to talk about that." With this revelation, even the hardened reporters gave George a silent moment to recover his thoughts. Then, one of them burst in by asking if George would do a live radio interview over the telephone.[131] George readily agreed, with an expression described by Stuart as a *"wan smile."* Stuart wrote a first-person account of covering the story for the *Post-Journal* and it appeared in great detail a few days later. George continued to immerse his rapt audience in the tale of how him and Lt. Bischof tried to "tramp" out of the woods on Sunday but turned back because of the deep snow and their cold feet. It appeared to Stuart that George was enjoying this moment and with his reporter instincts he recognized that a celebrity was emerging right in front of them. "Today, I knew I had to make it outside. I don't know whether some of us could have spent another night out there. I'm glad I made it. I guess I'm one of the lucky ones," George professed to Stuart and the other reporters.

Hallberg cracked open the back of his camera, removed the light-proof negative case, and installed a new one. He was sizing up George for another photograph when word came into the house from the sheriff's

---

[131] George was also interviewed in a live broadcast by Lloyd Gordon of WESB Radio, Bradford, Pennsylvania while he was in Salamanca Hospital. Who performed this first live broadcast from the Herrick's farmhouse could not be determined.

department portable radio that the wreck had been found and that the first of the rescued survivors was being carried down the ridge. They all jumped. George insisted on going outside for the greeting. Muddy boots traipsed across the living room and kitchen but Margaret Herrick proclaimed that she didn't care, she was just happy the crash survivors were finally coming down off the ridge.

Stuart watched George carefully and recorded every detail. *"Too weak to walk by himself, he had to be supported by two men who helped him down to the road from the farmhouse where the ambulances were waiting. It was just about dark by then. Flashbulbs and auto headlights lighted the night as the first of the survivors were lifted into the ambulances."*

It was Anna Piso. "It's good to be warm again," she murmured toward George. Then, both of them were ferried down Sawmill Run toward Salamanca Hospital. On the way, they passed by the hunting lands where George first walked out of the woods. They passed the Myers' camp where George circled the cabin looking for a way in, and they passed the Bryant farmhouse, all lit up and crowded with more reporters and spectators eager to hear Ruby's story as well. Stuart narrated over the telephone to his AP copywriter that George's first task at the hospital was to call his sister, still at their family home in Josephine, Pennsylvania. He wanted to break the news about their mother *"gently"*.

At the Herrick farm, all hell was breaking loose. With George gone to the hospital where another *Post-Journal* reporter, Robert Kilpatrick, would pick up his story, Hallberg and Stuart, reporter Ed Fay, Bell, and Millie Hall, started out for the top of the ridge.[132] AP photographer Walter Stein joined them and after he and Hallberg had taken several more photographs of a survivor being carried down on a stretcher, they surrendered their film cases to another reporter. Larry Hale was disappointed he couldn't go to the top of the ridge, but he left immediately in a car for Buffalo so the photographs could be placed on the AP's wire transmitter and sent around the world.

---

[132] The *Post-Journal* played up the fact that this was society reporter Millie Hall's first time on such a hard news story. The all-male editors of 1951 may have wanted her along possibly thinking that only another woman could gain special access to the women passengers.

As the news crews hiked up the mountain, the story was slowly coming down to them. Each time they spied flashlight beams along the trail the photographers aimed their cameras and lit up at the survivor being carried out on a portable stretcher. Hall wrote about the difficulty of the hike up the ridge, *"The first mile was the worst. I didn't know for a while whether I would make it not. Then we were trudging through the woods, snow, and occasionally stumbling into water up to our knees."* Hallberg and Stein also took dozens of photographs of the scene. They portray the three large pieces of the plane crawling with farmers and firefighters searching for bodies and body parts, even perched in the trees tying off ropes used for stabilizing the wreckage so they could safely search beneath it. *"There were bodies strewn all over the place, many of them still strapped in their seats which had been thrown from the plane by the impact. One was careful where one stepped,"* Hall wrote for her newspaper. The images also showed police scouring the woods for body parts, flashlights aimed carefully downward into the brush-strewn wreckage. When the *Post-Journal* crew later hiked back down the ridge to get their stories and photographs to the newspaper office in Jamestown, Hall recalled, *"the wind blew so hard that it actually knocked me down. Luckily one of the men in our party had a flare – it was pitch-black by that time. I can honestly say this was the most horrible experience that one could ever witness – and to think that the survivors were helpless for nearly 48 hours. I was thankful that the weather wasn't down below zero as it has been in the past month.*[133]

When crash investigators reviewed the photographs a few days later at the *Post-Journal* newsroom to analyze the wreckage as it was first found, they explained that the parachute removed from the plane and used by the survivors as a rain umbrella was originally attached to a high-intensity magnesium flare for war pilots in the event of an emergency. The flare, they explained, floating downward beneath a parachute, could light up the ground over a drop target or a dark landing site. Stored in the plane with a

---

[133] The survivors had been stranded on the ridge for 41 hours. Temperatures through much of December 1951 were well below freezing as western New York State was whipped with several Lake Effect snowstorms off Lake Erie.

quick-release latch, it had taken Lt. Bischof, who was unfamiliar with the device and searching for emergency flares, some three hours to force the parachute out of its damaged compartment.

Crow as they did about getting the first interview with George Albert, the *Post-Journal* reporters were likely chagrined to find that at least two competing reporters beat them to the top of Bucktooth Ridge. Latham Weber and T. Lea Smith, from the *Salamanca Republican-Press*, had gone straight to the top of the ridge where they got interviews with a few of the survivors. Additionally, both of these newspapers were beaten to the presses. The only local newspaper running the story in its main edition on New Year's Eve was *The Post* from nearby Ellicottville. However, the paper was datelined January 2 because of the holiday. Regardless, The Post was distributed on Monday afternoon, December 31, 1951, with a bulletin headline that the plane had been found. *The Post* editors bragged about their scoop a few days later but in reality a few other newspapers ran the same bulletin headlines on New Year's Eve too. *The Buffalo Evening News* broke the story that evening with the headline, *Airliner is Found Near Salamanca; Between 14 and 20 Reported Alive*. The *Syracuse Herald-Journal* ran a late final edition on December 31 with a four column-inch bulletin headlined, *C-46 Found; 14 of 40 Alive*.

All the local press, waiting around for what they were certain would be the biggest story in their backyard, were beaten at their own game by a local resident who happened to be near Napoli. He heard the sheriff's radio call, knew the woods, and literally ran up the snow-covered ridge carrying his compact (for 1951) camera. It was Randolph businessman and small plane pilot Bob Lilienthal.[134] He captured the first and only photograph of the survivors, except for George, huddled around the campfire, beneath the parachute, wrapped in clothing from the dead, heads bandaged to cover bloody injuries, protecting broken bones, hands clasped with numb fingers, even hugging each other for body warmth, and with sheer desperation on their faces.

Lilienthal's single image would tell the whole world about the horrifying

---

[134] Lilienthal, who later changed his last name to Lily, died October 2, 2010, in South Dakota.

story of crash and death, anticipation and heartache, resilience and determination among the survivors, and it was the only picture from the tragedy portrayed in the granddaddy of all media. The only place this single dramatic photograph appeared was in the January 14, 1952's issue of LIFE.[135]

---

[135] Because this photograph appeared nowhere else, it's presumed that it took a few days for Lilienthal to get the film processed. He sold a one-time use of the image to *LIFE* magazine. Lilienthal's family and several other sources have confirmed that he took the photograph.

Top left, clockwise, Sawmill Run extends upstream from bottom right. Bucktooth Ridge is on the right; Bucktooth Ridge and crash scene, right center; Salamanca, 1950s, as "the greatest railroad town you've never heard of"; Erie Limited E8 engine #830 and passenger cars at Salamanca in the winter of 1950. The 1909 terminal burned in 2014; Leslie A200 "blat" train horn similar to the one that saved the survivors of Continental Charters Flight 44-2.

Top left, clockwise, the Charles and Ruby Bryant farmhouse along Sawmill Run Road with Otis Bryant, left, and neighbor, John Schultz, as George Albert first saw it while walking down the road; with deep blue eyes and long auburn hair, Ruby Bryant is hugging her little Otis who turned five on December 21, 1951; Ruby and Otis Bryant at Letchworth State Park, NY; Ruby as a tall, thin, blue-eyed young girl growing up without her mother in West Virginia; Rodney and Benton Bryant playing music at home at Sawmill Run on the night before Benton returned to his Army post; Ruby's sad caricature and signature in her diary on the day she wrote her will.

Top, first picture of the survivors taken by Randolph, NY resident Robert Lilienthal, bottom right, as the first person to arrive on the scene of the crash of Flight 44-2. Left to right, Lt. William Bischof (standing); Albert Dichak, Marie Norcia, Mary Battista, Thomas Patterson, Dolores Beshears, Ed Wessel, and Joseph Wozniak. Pearl Moon, Eva Woodward, Mary Messerlos, Anna Piso, and Robert Geyer were elsewhere or still trapped in the wreckage when the photograph was taken in the four o'clock hour on December 31, 1951. George Albert had already left the scene of the crash and was first photographed (below) in front of a TV at the Herrick farm with oversized pants tied with string.

The *Buffalo Evening News* was one of few newspapers to report on New Year's Eve that rescuers had found the plane crash. When dawn (and the fog) broke on New Year's Day, the tragedy became clear. From the air over Bucktooth Ridge the path through the woods from the Herrick farm by a steady stream of rescuers was visible, left, along with a path created by the survivors walking to and from their campsite, bottom center.

When rescuers of the crash of Flight 44-2 tried to find the pilots, they discovered only their arms stretched out into the snow, top left and right. Their bodies were crushed in the cockpit. One of them, top right, displayed co-pilot stripes on the sleeve of his uniform.

The mid-section of the fuselage, which held most of the victims, is pictured below. Bushel baskets, foreground, from the Herrick farm were used to collect body parts and personal items.

Farmers from Cattaraugus County roam freely through the wreckage of Continental Charters Flight 44-2 late at night on December 31, 1951. This is one of the last times that private citizens were allowed unfettered access to commercial passenger plane crash wreckage as federal investigators began taking a more secure and exclusive role at crash scenes following this tragic event.

The mid-section of the Continental Charters smashed C-46 is pictured, top center. Hole in the fuselage on the right is the area where passenger Robert Geyer spent most of his time, unable to move farther away. At left is a crushed cabin seat with its rounded top handles. Among the luggage here is George Albert's duffle bag, center, on which was written his name and, in large letters, "*Penna*" for Pennsylvania.

Top right, clockwise, Cattaraugus County Sheriff's Deputies Russell Benson, left, and Jack Tillow use their new portable radio system to coordinate the rescue and body count with Sheriff Sigel at the Herrick farm crash headquarters. Passenger luggage is piled beneath the parachute umbrella behind them; two volunteers prepare to carry survivor Thomas Patterson down the ridge; Stewardess Pearl Ruth Moon in a hearse-ambulance for the ride to Salamanca Hospital along with a dog that was on the plane. Tufts of hay provide her pillow; a police official inspects a body prior to a toboggan ride down Bucktooth Ridge; the Herrick's crawler-tractor and cart used to carry survivors and bodies on the final half-mile to the farm.

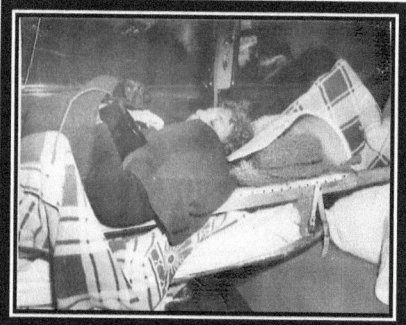

The Kenneth and Margaret Herrick farm on Sawmill Run Road in the Town of Napoli, New York under a deep blanket of snow in the 1950s. Fog-shrouded and iced-over Bucktooth Ridge is in the background. The upper section of Sawmill Run Road is at the bottom right. The simple and secluded Herrick farmhouse, with its wood-fired stoves for heating in the long cold winters, was the scene of one of the most spectacular airplane crash rescues in North American passenger aviation history.

Top, clockwise, there were many quiet, somber treks down Bucktooth Ridge pulling bodies on toboggans from the crash of Continental Charters Flight 44-2. A New York State Trooper and an Allegany State Park Ranger escort this body along with two local volunteers; the Herrick boys drove a crawler-tractor with a trailer hauling both survivors and bodies down the ridge to their farmyard packed with volunteers, the press, and spectators; photo from beyond the plane's tail section shows the long swath cut through the trees. This is the cartwheeled aft section where survivors were sitting. It caused some observers to incorrectly believe the plane was flying in the wrong direction.

Top left, clockwise, Cpl. Eugene Redden in his New York State Trooper winter uniform, wool coat, and fur cap. Cpl. Redden was among the police officials who collected purses and wallets, right, for identification of the crash victims of Flight 44-2. Sheriff's deputies, with a portable radio, and farmers searching for body parts in the wreckage, find a woman's leg; the tail of the Continental Charters C-46 with its newly printed N-number covering the previous registration numbers and letters issued in South America.

Top, the Nylon parachute tent erected by the survivors of Flight 44-2 covers luggage gathered from the wreckage on Bucktooth Ridge. One of George Albert's duffle bags is at the bottom, right. Bottom, teenage boys in varsity jackets help carry stewardess, Dolores Beshears, with her head swaddled in a blanket, to the Herrick's farmyard. It marked one of the last times that untrained volunteers could readily participate in a crash rescue and recovery in North America.

The hero of Continental Charters Flight 44-2, George Albert, is being questioned inside the Herrick's farmhouse by *Jamestown Post-Journal* editor, Charles Stuart, on New Year's Eve, 1951. George is wearing two pairs of pants that had been held up with a string prior to this photograph being taken by *Post-Journal* photographer Dick Hallberg. The other survivors said that if not for George bravely hiking off Bucktooth Ridge after the crash, they may have died on the mountain.

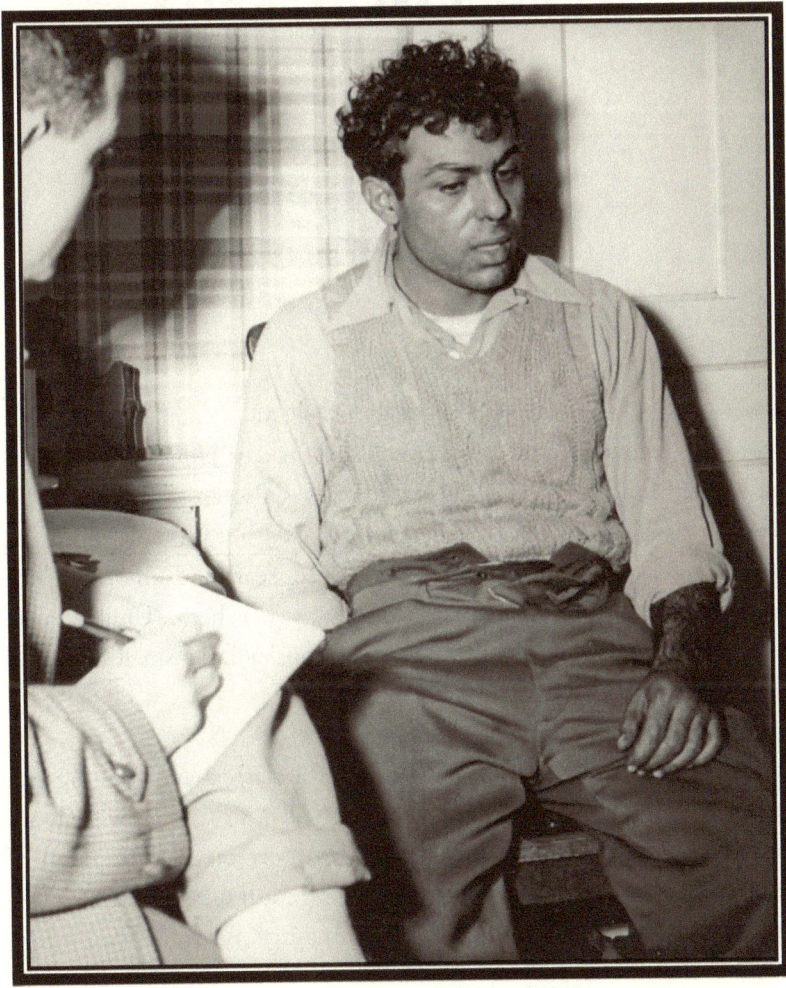

CHAPTER 15

DEADLY NONSKEDS

CONTINENTAL CHARTERS STEWARDESS PEARL Moon often thought about fellow airlines stewardess Mary Frances Housley every time she worked for a flight in 1951. Housley was also based in Florida for her airline which was not considered a nonsked but was still an upstart to the larger, major airlines in America. To Pearl and among all the stewardesses working that year Housley was a hero. Unlike Pearl, George, Lt. Bischof, and Ruby, however, Housley has a small memorial for her heroics during a 1951 crash.

"MY BABY, MY BABY," is what passengers of a crashed and burning National Airlines DC-4 heard as they were led to safety by a brave stewardess at Philadelphia International Airport on the afternoon of January 14, 1951. It was the second airplane crash disaster whose investigation reports piled up at the Civil Aeronautics Board in Washington by the end of this tragic year.

On a routine stopover in Philadelphia while flying from Newark to Norfolk, the pilots of the four-engine DC-4 overshot the 5,240 foot-long runway because of confusion over a construction project to make it longer. It was cloudy in Philadelphia that day and runway 9-27 was covered with about an inch of snow and slush, but planes were making normal instrument landings at the airfield along the Delaware River. When the National Airlines flight failed to stop before the end of the runway, it clipped some light poles, crashed into a ditch, and burst into flames. The pilots were able to jump out of a cockpit window and a cargo door but a stewardess, 24-year-old Mary Frances "Frankie" Housley, bravely kept her wits and personally rescued ten passengers, saving their lives. "She was very calm, and tried to quiet those passengers who were yelling," a soldier passenger was quoted by the *Philadelphia Inquirer*.

"Take your time, don't panic," commanded Housley to the passengers as she pushed open the cabin door and ordered them to jump from the plane, all within 90 seconds. When it appeared everyone was out, Housley jumped too. Then, along came the screams of "my baby, my baby." Housley hoisted her athletic five-foot, three-inch frame back into the plane and disappeared into the smoke and flames.[136] Later, when firefighters found her body in the burned fuselage, she was clutching an infant in a sheltering position. The baby also died.

Housley, who grew up in Fountain City, Tennessee but lived in Jacksonville, Florida while working for National Airlines, was lauded as a national heroine. She was among the seven who perished in the crash as 21 others, including the pilots, escaped. The story of Housley's bravery continued through most of 1951 culminating with a *Heroic Comics* cover image of an expertly coifed and smartly dressed stewardess hauling an ailing male passenger to safety. The message that this tiny brunette stewardess sacrificed her life to save passengers when the pilots fled resonated among Americans and the CAB.[137] Investigators determined that the pilot of the DC-4 was at fault for landing too far down the snow and ice-slicked runway and for not attempting a go-around when he realized

---

[136] National Airlines became renowned for hiring only stewardesses whose sex appeal would help them win businessmen travelers from rivals, Eastern, and United.

[137] A plaque, embedded in stone, memorializes Housley in front of Engine 78, the fire station at Philadelphia International Airport.

there was not enough runway left to stop. The CAB also cited insufficient training of the pilot as a contributing factor in the crash.

The National Airlines disaster in Philadelphia was one of the most dramatic crashes of tragic 1951 for the airlines. The year was only four days old when nonsked airplanes and some scheduled airliners too, began dropping from the sky. Pilot error due to poor training, inadequate maintenance of airplanes, indifference to federal rules and regulations, and overloading were the primary problems associated with the multitude of crashes that made 1951 the year that would forever change the passenger airline industry.

Even before 1951, however, the CAB was focused on new safety regulations for the nonskeds. From the first deadly crash of a nonsked in 1945 involving an Army surplus Lockheed Lodestar from Page Airways flying with a condemned engine part, the number of crashes among the cheap upstarts steadily grew to nearly half the crashes among all passenger planes by 1951. A few of them were so flagrant they caught the attention of the CAB investigators. One early crash would have been comical had it not been so deadly. It was the 1948 crash of a DC-3 for nonsked Burke Air Transport of Galveston, Texas. Burke moved from Galveston to Miami without informing the CAB and sent a passenger flight on a round-trip from Miami to San Juan and Newark. The pilots never stopped to rest for three days. The plane was two thousand pounds overweight and last observed cruising at three to five hundred feet over Melbourne, Florida on a heading back to Miami. No warning was given to the passengers to fasten seat belts. The pilots didn't even have their own seat belts and shoulder harnesses fastened, and they did not call for a landing attempt at the local airport. The DC-3 simply crashed in level flight four miles southwest of Melbourne, killing 12 passengers and both pilots. The CAB investigators were stymied by the mysterious crash because they could find no significant mechanical problems with the plane, other than minor issues with spark plugs and the carburetor on the left engine. Even with a faulty engine, the pilots should have been able to call for a safe landing in Melbourne. Instead, the CAB found that both pilots fell asleep! *"Little imagination is required to visualize the pilots sitting in the semidarkness of the cockpit, actually asleep as the aircraft cruised on automatic pilot, gradually losing altitude,"* said the final report. Burke Air Transport became one of the first in a long line of large nonskeds to be cited by the CAB for numerous safety and economic regulation violations including overloading, extended crew schedules, poor maintenance, and shoddy record keeping. And there were many other airlines soon to follow as the nonsked business took off, reaching its zenith in 1951.

BY THE END OF the 1940s, the CAB had recognized the multitude of problems among the nonskeds, held hearings and proposed changes to the rules that allowed the upstart budget airlines to operate under the regulation radar. Passenger fatality ratios had climbed to a whopping 25.4 deaths per 100-million passenger miles (1948) in contrast to 1.6 for the majors. During the numerous deaths from nonsked crashes certainly grabbed the attention of the CAB before 1950, many other issues, long overlooked by regulators, were also up for strict enforcement.

The 2000 book *Airline Executives and Federal Regulations* recounts how many of the nonskeds resorted to advertising or arranging news items in local newspapers stating their schedules, which were supposed to remain unpublished. Hotel clerks, the book, revealed, were paid by the nonskeds or ticket agencies to solicit passengers by showing them a list of these supposedly unpublished schedules. The independent ticket agencies, with airline-sounding names such as *SkyCoach,* boasted of luxurious passenger cabins, flights on four-engine planes, accident-free miles, and they advertised tickets for as cheap as $13, the cost of tax while the full ticket price was buried in fine print. When passengers took the bait, they arrived at the airports to find planes stripped of every luxury in the passenger cabin to save weight, planes with only two engines because they were cheaper, and *"plane full"* notations until passengers ponied up more money for a seat, with or without a seat belt. Nervous passengers who purchased life insurance from a ticket agent or from a vending machine often didn't read the fine print. It specified coverage only if the flight was on a scheduled carrier, the majors.

Once aboard the nonsked planes, the financial horror stories continued for the hapless passengers. *Airline Executives and Federal Regulation* explains how some of these trips embarrassingly required the passengers to *"pass the hat to pay for refueling at intermediate stops."* Another flight, traveling from Burbank to Newark, never arrived. After three days, it finally made Philadelphia where the passengers had to find their own way to Newark. And a U.S. Congressman complained that it took his secretary three days to fly from Burbank to Washington on a nonsked. Pilot and flight regulations varied greatly between the nonskeds and the majors too. For example, the nonskeds could perform their own dispatching duties without a federally certified dispatcher approving or disapproving flight methods, route, fuel supply, weight and passenger manifests, altitude, and alternate airports in the event of an emergency. Additionally, a nonsked pilot did not have to qualify for license certification for the make and model of his airplane nor the route and airports to which he was flying. The major airlines and their pilots had to follow all of these regulations. Nonsked pilots often flew to new cities on unfamiliar routes for the first time while carrying passengers.

In 1947, the CAB amended its rules under economic regulations and required the nonskeds to secure letters of registration, effectively placing them under the same requirements as the majors. Of the 142 large nonsked companies (those who used big planes and carried a lot of passengers) issued registrations, only 109 were still active by the end of the year. Finally enforcing its rules against the most flagrant violators, (as much as it was able because of understaffing) the CAB revoked registrations of 33 companies or the airlines voluntarily surrendered their registrations to go out of business. Some then reorganized under a different name and climbed right back in the air. In 1948, the CAB closed the door on new registrations for nonskeds applying for exemptions to the rules as a group. And in 1949 it further attempted stricter regulations by changing to individual exemption review of the nonskeds still holding registrations.

The CAB also attempted to impose a mathematical formula for a specific number of flights per month to and from specific airports for the nonskeds. Named *The Investigation of Air Service by Large Irregular Carriers and Irregular Transport Carriers,* the CAB imposed a *"three and eight"* limitation for nonsked flights. This new rule was imposed only on the nonskeds not already under individual exemptions, *"restricting the number of flights between any given pair of cities to not more than three in the same direction in any four successive weeks between a specified list of given pairs of points where substantial amounts of air service are provided and to not more than eight flights in the same direction in any four successive weeks between any other given pair of points."* Not surprisingly, this utterly confusing imposition of new rules was challenged in court by the nonskeds and subsequently suspended by the CAB. By then, American aviation had entered the 1950s.

NONSKED AIRLINES NEEDED TWO key elements to get started: cheap airplanes and efficient pilots to fly them. CJ Webber took advantage of the flying skill he accrued during and after World War II and joined nonsked, Continental Charters, sometime before 1950. With many hours as a pilot ferrying military airplanes to the war zones and weary of the instability of flying for cargo haulers, CJ was looking for a regular paycheck and the prestige of a passenger airline. He became an expert at flying the company's C-46s on passenger runs throughout the Caribbean and along the east coast. Finally, he found stability as a pilot. In 1950, his family at home in Miami was growing. Familiar with the busy Miami to San Juan and Newark triangle route, soon after joining Continental Charters, CJ was likely just one of many South Florida pilots who took notice of a spectacular nonsked crash into the Atlantic Ocean just six months into the new decade. Everyone else did too. Some of the passengers in the crash were eaten by sharks.

ON JUNE 5, 1950, A CONVERTED C-46 Commando war plane operated by Aviation Corporation of Seattle, doing business as Westair Transport, took off from San Juan for Wilmington, North Carolina with 62 passengers and three crew members. The Puerto Rican migrant workers crammed on board were traveling to summer jobs on large sugar beet farms near Saginaw, Michigan. Their transportation on the Westair nonsked was part of a contract arranged by the Puerto Rican government and a sugar beet corporation, according to Luis Asencio Camacho, a University of Puerto Rico researcher and writer. This was during a period of mass migration of Puerto Ricans to the United States for seasonal farm labor and for whom cheap air fares were especially attractive. One way ticket prices for these passengers on the nonskeds averaged about $85 in contrast to $133 for the majors. The migrant workers were required to pay this airfare through deductions in their already meager earnings. It's obvious that not all of the passengers on this San Juan departure flight had proper seats because they far exceeded the C-46 maximum capacity. The Westair plane was also 258 pounds over its 48,000-pound weight limit. Because of the nature of the crash and the manner in which at least one of the passengers perished, this event especially captivated the attention of the press and fueled fear among Americans over flying, no matter if it was on a nonsked or a major.

The Westair C-46 flight took a route over the Atlantic Ocean some 400 miles east of the mainland of Florida and north of the Bahamas. Because most of the Puerto Rican passengers spoke only Spanish, Westair hired a replacement cabin steward, Hector Medina Berrios, on the morning of the flight but gave him scant training on what to do in the event of an emergency. The plane was so overcrowded that there was no place for the new bilingual steward to sit so he occupied the jump seat in the cockpit during takeoff with the pilot, Joseph M. Halsey, and co-pilot, William Holleran. About four hours into the six-hour and 50-minute flight, the C-46 pilots noticed a major oil leak from their right engine. Within a short time, the left engine backfired and lost power. Unable to restart the left engine, the pilots feathered the prop and turned their attention to the right engine and a retreat toward the nearest airport at Nassau in the Bahamas. With such a dramatic loss of oil in the right engine, it began overheating so the pilots decided to do a controlled ditch into the ocean before they lost power in the right engine too. Radio messages were sent from the cockpit to shore stations near Jacksonville, Florida, 390 miles west, as the plane dropped "into the drink," the pilot said, at about 10:03 pm.

Because he was given little training in the event of an emergency, Medina Berrios was clueless about what to do. There was little crash preparation advice given to the passengers seated on wooden benches with short ropes for seat belts. Some of the survivors said they thought, at first, they were landing at an airport. Passenger Juan Velez Marti, 38, said he believed the plane had been hit by lightning. "We heard an explosion, and the plane started to shake. When I looked out the window…it was pitch-black. It rained and there was lightning in the distance; that's how we saw what was happening. I'm convinced we were hit by lightning," said Velez Marti.[138]

The violations for this flight were already numerous before the pilots ditched in the ocean and they continued as the crew entered the main cabin and opened the emergency doors only after going down.[139] Panicking passengers, unable to understand the English-speaking pilots, and with a bi-lingual steward who didn't know what to do, climbed out onto the wings without life jackets while others jumped into the sea. All seven of the plane's emergency 10-man life rafts were thrown into the water, but five floated away in the darkness because no one was instructed or they didn't understand to hold on to the raft retaining lines. That left only two inflated life rafts into which 34 of the 65 occupants of the plane climbed before it sank into waters more than 12,000 feet deep. Survivors believed that about 15 passengers went down with the plane. Adding to their problems, the pilots failed to take the "Gibson Girl," an emergency location transmitter, with them and it too, sank with the plane. Survivor Fortunato Cintron Fiallo, 27, described a pathetic scene of men punching, biting, and crawling over each other to get out of the plane and into the rafts. One survivor denied aboard an already overcrowded raft while treading water in the ocean, reportedly threatened to stab the occupants or the rubber raft with a switchblade knife until he was allowed to climb aboard.

Another C-46 from Westair, flying from Wilmington to San Juan to pick up another load of migrant workers, obtained a fix on the rafts

---

[138] Velez Marti gave his account of the crash many years later to University of Puerto Rico researcher and writer, Luis Asencio Camacho. Another passenger, Fortunato Cintron Fiallo, also believed the plane had been hit by lightning. The pilots did not report a lightning strike to the CAB.

[139] Westair regulations required that the emergency exits be opened before ditching into the water.

from the downed plane during the night through a flashlight pointed skyward by pilot Halsey. The location was relayed to the Coast Guard in Elizabeth City, North Carolina, which located the survivors from a search plane at daybreak. A U.S. Navy Destroyer then cruised in and rescued the passengers and crew who had managed to climb onto several rafts dropped by the Coast Guard plane. The Navy crew also found a passenger, Chabolo Guzman, clinging to an uninflated life raft as sharks swirled beneath him.[140] Navy Boatswain's Mate J.B. Taylor threw a line, but Guzman was too weak to grab it. The seaman jumped into the water just as a shark bit into and wrenched off Guzman's arm. Guzman had died aboard the USS Saufley before it arrived at the Navy Base in Charleston, South Carolina with the survivors. Twenty-eight passengers died and only nine bodies were recovered from the ocean. Several of them were picked up by the United Fruit Company ship *Cape Ann*.[141] Press photographs showed the sullen Puerto Rican migrants aboard the Saufley in Charleston just before they walked down the gangway and kissed the ground. Americans reading about the horrifying story in newspapers surmised the missing passengers were consumed by sharks.

Writing in *Centro Journal* 2013, Asencio Camacho said that the surviving Puerto Rican migrant workers were so terrified that most opted to continue on to their Michigan farm jobs by bus. Four of them chose to go back home. The Puerto Rican government temporarily halted all nonsked flights on the island and negotiated new contracts, with major airlines, Pan Am, and Eastern, to deliver the rest of 5,000 migrant workers to Michigan. It felt that the majors were safer. The unintended message of this tragedy was clear: ride the nonskeds and get eaten by sharks!

THROUGHOUT 1950, '51, AND even into '52 the sensational headlines continued. *"Death Rides the Bargain Airlines,"* screamed *Coronet, a* popular *Reader's Digest* imitator. *"Death Edict?"* questioned *TIME* magazine. *"Murder*

---

[140] The name Chabolo is from Asencio Camacho's research and interviews with survivors. Press reports in 1950 gave Guzman's first surname as Pedro.

[141] The *Cape Ann* also participated in the rescue of passengers from the sinking of the *Andrea Doria* in 1956 off the coast of Nantucket.

by Air Must Stop!" bannered the *Long Island Star-Journal* after equally devastating crashes caused by overweight planes, malfunctioning engines, or questionable piloting.

Between March and November 1950, Northwest Airlines, another of the majors, suffered five crashes among its fleet with 98 of 116 people on the planes killed. The worst of these crashes, which saddled the company with a tarnished safety reputation, was still making headlines 65 years later.

On June 23, 1950, a Northwest Airlines Douglas DC-4, a big, beautiful four-engine plane, crashed into Lake Michigan with such force there was virtually nothing left. The flight originated in New York and, with intended stops in Minneapolis and Spokane, was scheduled to end in Seattle. The CAB ruled that all 55 passengers and the three crew members on board were killed when the plane smashed into the water during a storm and was destroyed. Pieces of the fuselage and some body parts washed up on the Lake Michigan shoreline, but the plane and the occupants were never found. It was the worst commercial aviation disaster in American history and has been chronicled in a thoroughly researched 2013 book by author Valerie Van Heest, titled *Fatal Crossing*. It's what made the Miami Airline C-46 crash in Elizabeth, New Jersey in December 1951, second-worst with only two fewer fatalities.

In May 1950, a Regina Cargo Airlines C-46 flying to Fort Wayne, Indiana and Detroit crashed on takeoff from New Jersey's Teterboro Airport, killing the pilot and seriously injuring the co-pilot. Incredibly, the plane was more than 5,000 pounds overweight, lost its left engine on takeoff, crashed into some trees near the airport, and threw both pilots from the cockpit. It was a classic example of the problems with the C-46, overloaded and unable to fly when losing an engine on takeoff. Regina Cargo was censured by the CAB for a series of violations including overloading, poor maintenance, poor record keeping, and for both a pilot and the plane flying beyond time and inspection limits. Regina's timing was unfortunate. The CAB hearings for the crash occurred when government regulators had decided to further crack down on the most flagrant violators of safety regulations. Regina's air carrier operating certificate was revoked in April 1951 just as the nonskeds were entering their best year for income and profits and their worst year for accidents and fatalities.

The first crash of 1951 occurred on January 4 when a nonsked C-46 from Monarch Air Service took off at only 85 miles per hour, clipped other airplanes on the ground with its wing, then crashed and burned while departing Chicago's Midway Airport on a flight to Newark.[142] Fortunately, all 45 passengers and the crew of three escaped the crash and burn without serious injuries. The CAB concluded that the co-pilot hadn't completed his latest license check, the crew overloaded the plane by 1,100 pounds, and the pilot didn't apply enough power at take-off.

Two days after the Philadelphia crash that killed stewardess Mary Frances Housley and made her a national heroine, on January 16, a Northwest Airlines Martin 202 twin-engine passenger plane, flying from Minneapolis to Seattle, crashed near Reardon, Washington killing seven passengers and three crew members. The pilots sent an emergency radio message which was interpreted as "We are in trouble. The wheel has gone nuts, right engine haywire, going down fast." The impact of the nose-in crash disintegrated the plane to such an extent that investigators determined it may have been traveling at more than 340 miles per hour, an impossible speed for a Martin 202 under normal engine power.

IN MARCH 1951, CONTINENTAL Charters mechanic Victor Harris fulfilled his long-time dream to become a pilot for a passenger airline. Having worked for Continental Charters since 1948, Harris flew its planes but did not achieve his rating to command a passenger plane until this time. Harris flew his company's C-46s all through the summer of 1951. He could not have failed to notice that similar airplanes for several other nonsked airlines and majors were dropping from the sky, more than a few times a month. Like most every other pilot in the sky, Harris surely wondered if his time would ever come.

AS 1951 PROGRESSED, THE crashes got worse. On April 6, a DC-3, operated by the small California carrier, Southwest Airways with 19

---

[142] At least 110 mph was required for take-off in a C-46.

passengers and three crew members on board, crashed into a mountain ridge near Santa Barbara.[143] Everyone on board was killed. The CAB found that the pilot, with more than 1,300 trips on this same route between San Francisco and Los Angeles, failed to stay above the required nighttime elevation of 4,000 feet. They surmised that he was flying low on a visual flight in an attempt to make up for lost time, a scenario similar to the crash of Flight 44-2 in Napoli.

On April 25, a mid-air collision over Key West, Florida shocked travelers in the Caribbean and throughout the United States because it involved a Cuban DC-4, flying from Miami to Havana and a U.S. Navy Beechcraft SNB-5 doing instrument training at 4,000 feet. The Twin-Beech plummeted into the water 548 yards off the Key West Naval Air Station while the Cuban DC-4 continued flying for another 17 miles, losing altitude, until it crashed nose first into the Straits of Florida. All 34 passengers and crew of five on the Compania Cubana De Aviacion DC-4, as well as the four Navy crew members aboard the Twin-Beech, were killed. Both planes were found to be in compliance with all rules and regulations of the CAB and CAA. All the bodies from the Cubana plane were recovered, but only two were found from the Twin-Beech. Although the Navy trainer was equipped with a special orange-colored Plexiglas front windshield that obstructed the vision of the instrument-training pilot, wearing special goggles, the other occupants of the Twin-Beech should have been able to see the DC-4 in the clear skies. What was so shocking to American and Cuban travelers was that both planes were performing as they should have been. It was simply a one in a million chance that the pilots failed to see one another before the Twin-Beech propellers tore into the DC-4's left wing.

On May 21, another scheduled flight in a DC-6 for National Airlines made a miraculous recovery after it plowed into the marsh between Elizabeth, New Jersey and the Newark Airport and then, under full power, jumped back into the air for a somewhat normal landing alongside Runway 6 at Newark. Imagine being a passenger on that plane? Twenty-two passengers were on board the DC-6 when it departed Richmond for

---

[143] Southwest Airways was no relation to Southwest Airlines.

Newark with two pilots, a flight engineer and a stewardess. Approaching Newark Airport with instruments because of poor weather generated by a tropical storm near Cape Hatteras, the plane came in too low over Linden and Elizabeth and actually dragged its landing gear 12 inches into the mud of the large marsh near Runway 6. It made a hard landing and clipped sign markers on the side of the runway. The pilot's poor judgment was found to be the cause of this near disaster which contributed to the nervousness steadily building over Newark Airport among residents of Elizabeth in 1951.

IN EARLY JUNE, 1951, pilot Hans Rutzebeck abandoned his wife and two little children in Fairbanks, Alaska and drove with his girlfriend to Miami. Already a successful bush pilot and co-owner of a small charter freight airline with a partner in Alaska, Rutz said he planned to earn his multi-engine pilot's license in Florida and return to Fairbanks to fly larger planes to Alaska's North Slope. He apparently grew to enjoy the warm and exciting lifestyle in Miami. By the end of July Rutz had signed on with Continental Charters. He began flying as co-pilot on its C-46 passenger planes. With a new job for the high-flying nonskeds in the summer of '51, Rutz put Alaska and his family in his past.

DURING THE SUMMER OF 1951, most of the crash activity involved scheduled airlines. A United Airlines DC-6 from San Francisco to Chicago smashed into Crystal Mountain near Estes Park, Colorado because the pilot flipped off the wrong radio switch and didn't hear controller commands. The plane hit the mountain at 8,500 feet. Forty-four passengers including a San Francisco family of five and all five crew members were killed.

On July 19, an Eastern Airlines Lockheed Constellation flying from Newark to Miami with 48 passengers made an emergency landing in a cornfield and pasture on the 5,513 acre Curles Neck Farm plantation along eastern Virginia's James River. Encountering severe thunderstorms and squalls, the pilots radioed controllers that buffeting of the airplane was so severe they thought it would break up in the air. After the emergency crash-landing that began in seven-foot-tall corn stalks and ended in an open field, investigators learned that a hydraulic reservoir access door on the top side of the left wing had opened during flight causing the buffeting to be worse in the storm squalls. No one was seriously hurt when the plane was set down on the historic plantation but what a ride it must have been. The plane was rocking and rolling so severely that the pilots warned controllers at Richmond that they thought the huge Constellation might disintegrate. These kinds of stories further frightened American passengers with the reality that danger from flying wasn't isolated to the nonskeds.

On August 24, a United Airlines flight in a DC-6 from Boston to San Francisco crashed into a hill while approaching the Oakland Municipal Airport. It killed all 44 passengers and six crew members on board. The impact at an estimated ground speed of 225-240 miles per hour thrust the wreckage over the top of the hill and scattered it, burning, down the opposite slope. The pilot apparently did not follow the proper instrument landing procedures and was too low on final approach, causing the plane to crash into the hillside.

As 1951 flew on, September resulted in four major air crashes, three of them in consecutive days. But first, *Heroic Comics* printed its cover story on September 1 about the audaciousness of National Airlines stewardess "Frankie" Housley. The dramatic comic book cover artwork depicted a brunette, and blue-eyed stewardess in a slim-cut, figure-conforming blue uniform grappling a green-uniformed and red-headed man with a pained expression, presumed to be a soldier, in her arms while a crashed passenger plane burns in the background, shooting yellow and red flames into the air. *"The name Mary Frances Housley is destined for immortality,"* the embellished story proclaimed. It portrayed the shapely but professional appearing Housley, surrounded by shrieking passengers, proclaiming, *"Take it easy! You'll all get out safely if you don't lose your heads."* Then, as Housley escorts passengers from the cabin door, a woman declares, *"my baby is in there. They pushed me out before I could get my baby."* The illustration depicts Housley returning to the plane and shielding herself from shoulder-high flames as she searches for the infant. In the end, comic readers learn that Mary Frances Housley *"died with a baby in her arms. She tried to save not ten, but everyone—and sacrificed her own life in the attempt."* The *Famous Funnies* publication was a powerful message for airline passengers and the CAB but it was somewhat of a departure from its typical comic book covers showing GIs, police officers or firefighters making dramatic rescues. It was a sign of the times for 1951 with a lowly stewardess depicted as the life-saving hero. It was a role that matched Continental Charters stewardess Pearl Moon's heroics perfectly.

ON SEPTEMBER 15, A spectacular and tragic air show crash in Flagler, Colorado killed a pilot and 19 air show spectators! This horrible event alone caused the CAB to immediately issue new rules for what it termed crazy flying at air shows and demonstrations. Waivers for the traditional flight rules at the Flagler Airport had been issued by the CAB to the operator of Rocky Mountain Air Shows. The waivers specified that all aerial demonstrations were to be performed more than a half-mile away from the crowd of spectators and their cars in the airport parking lot. Because the Timm experimental plane scheduled to do the aerial stunts for the air show was late arriving, the pilot, with no prior experience in this airplane other than the 110-mile flight to Flagler from Denver, was ordered to begin his stunts immediately upon arrival at the packed air show.[144] He did, and within 100 feet of the roped-off spectators, his plane's wing hit the ground during a roll, causing the plane to crash into the crowd and the parking lot, killing the 19 spectators. The CAB ruled that had the pilot landed upon arrival and been briefed on the agreed upon safety rules of the air show, the disaster could have been avoided. Once again, it was an example of a small, poorly managed flying company violating the rules either to save time and money or through indifference to the CAB regulations designed to protect everyone. The CAB immediately imposed new safety regulations on air shows with parachute jumping, dog-fighting airplanes, *"crazy"* flying, intentional crashes, and those which did not plan for direct radio communications with the pilots.

Then, on September 16, on the day newspaper headlines bannered the tragedy at the Colorado air show, a jam-packed nonsked C-46, flying

---

[144] The stunt plane was late because of an oil leak.

for Peninsular Air Transport between Chicago and Miami, lost an engine on take-off and crashed-landed in a field near Chicago's Midway Airport. Thirty-six passengers and four crew members were hurt, but another 13 passengers escaped injury. After losing power in his left engine while taking off, the C-46 pilot made a wide left turn and, unable to make it back to Midway, set the C-46 down near 63rd Street and Harlem Avenue in Chicago. The rough crash-landing ripped off both engines and bounced the powerless fuselage to a gradual stop where everyone tumbled out of the plane. The CAB investigation found that improper maintenance with the lack of a necessary spare part for the plane on a Sunday, inadequate take-off speed, and overloading of the plane by 1,860 pounds contributed to the crash-landing.[145] It was Midway's second major crash involving a nonsked in 1951 after the Monarch Air Service C-46 crash and burn in January. It was only by sheer luck that the September 16 accident did not become the second worst commercial plane crash in American history. However, it would come later in the year.

On November 17, a mid-air collision in northern California near the Oakland Municipal Airport between a DC-4 from nonsked California Eastern Airways and another DC-4 from Overseas National Airways killed three pilots in the Overseas National plane. There were no passengers on either plane because the pilots were undergoing instrument check flights using hoods to obstruct their vision. The planes collided while in straight and level flight at about 3,000 feet over Oakland Bay, not far from the approach to the airport. The Overseas National DC-4 spiraled out of control and crashed onto Doolittle Drive on the north side of the Oakland Airport. Several people driving their cars were burned when the wreckage and fire rained down on the vehicles. The pilots of the California Eastern DC-4 immediately removed their vision-blocking hood and requested permission for an emergency landing at Oakland. However, because all the firefighting apparatus had gone to the crash scene of the Overseas National plane, the damaged California DC-4 was diverted to San Francisco International Airport where it managed to land safely. The

---

[145] The necessary spare part, a spark plug bushing, could not be obtained on that Sunday because the supplier was closed.

CAB investigation ruled that the hoods used for the check flights met the regulations in place at the time but that a spotter in the Overseas National plane failed to watch for oncoming traffic while the California plane didn't even carry a spotter.[146] After the crash, California changed the style of hood used for safety check flights to one that allows the check pilot a wider field of vision from the cockpit window. The safety check pilots from both planes were charged by the CAB with the spotter violations.[147] It was later determined that three additional nonsked pilots who were supposed to be on the California DC-4 for their regular check flights, didn't show up that day and the training flight took off without them. Had they been on the plane, they could have served as spotters.

Another mid-air collision occurred later that month, on November 27, between an Eastern Airlines DC-3 with seventeen passengers and a crew of three, and a U.S. Air Force Piper L4-J, a single-engine plane typically used for observation and light patrol. It was on loan to the Civil Air Patrol in Ocala, Florida. No one was hurt on board the Eastern DC-3, but the L4-J pilot was killed when his small plane clipped the landing DC-3's wing, and crashed to the ground at the Ocala Airport. The Eastern pilots were on a midpoint stop between Atlanta and St. Petersburg and were on final approach to Taylor Field when they were hit. They landed safely. The airport didn't have a tower or controllers so the pilots were on their own watching for other planes in the vicinity. Compounding the unusual circumstances in this crash, the pilot of the L4-J, John H. Macy, 33, a former gunner in the Army Air Forces, had limited vision after losing his left eye in a 1946 car accident. While pilot Macy had no medical waiver from Civil Air Regulations, he was approved for flying in the L4-J by the Ocala Civil Air Patrol Squadron Proficiency Board only a few weeks earlier. He apparently did not reveal the fact that he had an artificial eye when he took his final check flight. As a result of the crash, the CAA altered its rules so pilots could no longer hide certain medical conditions during their local check flights. But, that didn't stop them from trying.

---

[146] The hood was a fabric shield hung across the top of the windshield in front of the pilot-in-command.
[147] Even those who died were issued violations.

On November 14, 1951, the CAA regional medical officer in California re-issued a license to pilot Lewis R. Powell, 45, with a strict condition that he fly only for check pilot duties and not to fly passengers. Powell, a veteran pilot with nearly 8,000 hours of flight, had suffered such a severe heart attack on March 30 that he was carried to a hospital in an ambulance and under oxygen. By October, he had recovered and applied for renewal of his pilot's license. It was initially denied by CAA officials in Washington and then, reconsidering, the California regional CAA medical officer issued a license to Powell as a check pilot only. You might be able to guess what happened next. On December 22, Captain Powell applied for a job as a pilot with nonsked Robin Airlines at its home field in Burbank, California. He was given flight checks on a C-46 with Robin's chief pilot, Charles Rector. Powell didn't tell Rector of his license restriction and, apparently, Rector didn't check very thoroughly because Powell was hired to fly passengers in Robin Airlines' C-46 passenger planes. The decision would haunt the airline within weeks.

AFTER THE PILOT WITH the artificial eye crash incident in Florida, things were quiet in the skies over America in 1951 but only for a few weeks. When December came around, the CAB and the fledgling American flying public faced the worst air disasters in an already deadly year. On December 4, a United Airlines DC-3 on a training flight crashed near Denver's Stapleton Airport when the plane was inadvertently put into a spin. The crash obliterated the cockpit, killing the flight instructor and two first officer trainees. The CAB ruled that United did not provide sufficient information about the spin and stall characteristics of the DC-3 to the trainees.

Then, in rapid succession, came the crash of the Miami Airlines C-46 in Elizabeth, the crash-landing of the Robin Airlines C-46 along Lake Ontario, and the crash of the Continental Charters C-46 in Napoli. Three major headline producing crashes got the attention of federal regulators and even the White House. New safety rules and a move to abolish the nonskeds were coming.

CHAPTER 16

FIRST CAB CHIEF ON THE SCENE

AT 10:30 ON THE MORNING of January 1, 1952, a DC-3 VIP flight landed at the recently dedicated Bradford-McKean Airport near Mt. Alton, Pennsylvania and taxied up to the small terminal serving United Airlines and All-American Airways. Two large sedans met the plane on the tarmac, but the passengers on the plane didn't immediately get out. Huddled together in their customized cabin, the occupants exchanged some last minute details of the purpose for their trip and what they had just seen from the air. Airport officials were there to greet the Washington dignitaries. They curiously and proudly surveyed the government plane with its large painted lettering spelling out Civil Aeronautics Board, United States of America, in a circle along a wide red stripe on the side of the fuselage. This was a historic event beginning at the small and remote Pennsylvania airport. For the first time, the chairman of the CAB was making a personal visit to the scene of a commercial airlines passenger plane crash. It would set a precedent for the CAB and its successor, the NTSB, for most large passenger plane crashes decades into the future.

Bradford-McKean Airport was chosen for the CAB chairman's plane because of its location and modern facilities to handle the DC-3. The close proximity to the crash of Continental Charters Flight 44-2 allowed for a few circles around the scene just over the state line in Cattaraugus County, New York. Climbing down the ladder-stairs from the plane, whose well-appointed and warm interior was drastically unlike any of the planes of the nonskeds, and greeting the small airport staff, CAB Chairman Donald W. Nyrop had only a few moments to glance around the airfield and meet the airport executives before climbing into his car.[148] The driver had no difficulty recognizing the 39-year-old Nyrop, even with his gray felt fedora sporting a wide black band. The energetic young chairman of the CAB already had a distinctive swatch of wavy white hair flowing back from his forehead among the rest of his dark hair. Nyrop and the CAB's Executive Director, James M. Verner, got into one car while Chief of the Investigative Division, James N. Peyton, and Director of Safety Investigations, William K. Andrews, rode in the second car. The CAB men came prepared with warm flannel shirts or sweaters, and boots, overcoats, and gloves. Having just surveyed the crash scene from the air, they all knew it would not be an easy trip to reach the wreckage of Flight 44-2 for the chairman's first close-up inspection of a passenger plane crash in America.

Built by the Army Air Corps as an emergency military airfield during World War II, the hilltop Bradford-McKean Airport had only recently been dedicated on a warm August weekend with a large ceremony and air show attended by some 25,000 spectators. It was the largest crowd ever in tiny Mt. Alton, and in McKean County's history. Having grown to handle just under 10,000 passengers per year in 1951, the new airport's 4,500 foot-long main runway could easily handle the CAB plane as it did the DC-4s from United and All-American flying to and from Chicago, Cleveland, Pittsburgh, Philadelphia, and Buffalo. Some of them flew right over Bucktooth Ridge in Napoli. However, from Mt. Alton it was a winding 35-mile drive by car on Route 219, the Buffalo-Pittsburgh Highway, through Brad-

---

[148] Ladders or combination ladder-stairs were often used to board and disembark passenger planes in this era, especially at small airports like Bradford-McKean, which didn't have gates.

ford, across the New York State line to Salamanca and the site of the crash of Flight 44-2 in Napoli. The route was nearly the same terrain that Flight 44-2 had flown over before crashing into Bucktooth Ridge. It gave Nyrop another opportunity to see the forested peaks and valleys of the Allegheny Plateau that both the CAB office in Miami and Continental Charters did not consider to be mountainous.

Packing his warm winter snow boots and a heavy green hooded parka to wear over his gray business suit and a sweater, for warmth, Nyrop and his CAB crew arrived at the Herrick farm and crash scene headquarters along Sawmill Run Road at about noon. After a short meeting with Sheriff Sigel, Nyrop jumped into a Willys-Overland Jeep and hung on tightly for the muddy and bumpy ride up the west side of Bucktooth Ridge. After only a half mile, however, the CAB chairman was forced to get out and walk the rest of the way up the steep ridge. Following closely behind Nyrop and his three-man crew from Washington on the well-worn mud and rocky trail that had been trampled only hours earlier by rescuers, were CAB investigators from Pittsburgh and Buffalo, local police and firefighters, the sheriff and his deputies carrying their bulky, boxy two-way radios, New York State troopers, park rangers, FBI agents, and a handful of press reporters and photographers. The reporters recorded every moment of this first and historic event by a CAB chairman.

Before his appointment as leader of the CAB, Donald William Nyrop was a CAA career attorney who joined the newly created federal agency in 1939. Born in Elgin, Nebraska, Nyrop earned his law degree from George Washington University and then worked for the Army ATC during World War II. After the war, Nyrop returned to the CAA and rose up to become administrator during the early years of airline industry regulations. He was appointed the chairman of the CAB by President Truman in 1950 and already had major crash investigations underway when he was re-appointed to the chairmanship on December 27, just two days before the crash of Flight 44-2.[149]

---

[149] The two most recent C-46 crash investigations begun by the CAB were the Miami Airlines fatal crash in Elizabeth, New Jersey on December 16 and the crash-landing of the Robin Airlines plane in Cobourg, Ontario, Canada on December 20th.

Climbing uphill through the heavy wet snow to the scene of the crash on Bucktooth Ridge, Nyrop arrived amid the wreckage early in the afternoon on New Year's Day before all the bodies had been removed. Still trapped within the remains of the cockpit were the bodies of pilot Victor Harris and co-pilot Hans Rutzebeck, and passengers Margaret Jones and Audrey Malcolm. Recovery crews were rigging a block-and-tackle device to nearby tree branches to lift the crushed cockpit from Rutz's body. Here, photographers respectfully complied with the chairman's request not to take his picture. Nyrop then surveyed the campfire scene built by the survivor passengers with their crude parachute rain screen. Again, he requested no pictures and the photographers, who had been given access to a now secured scene, complied.[150]

Walking over to one of the C-46's Pratt and Whitney R-2800 engines, the CAB chairman could easily see the scrape marks on the blades that indicated it was producing power during impact. Here is where, at the urging of the press photographers, Nyrop placed his heavily booted left foot with wet pants leg atop the smashed four-bladed propeller, and with his parka unzipped for cooling his overheated body, his eyes gazing downward at the engine, posed for a photograph. His right boot rested in the snow as his legs straddled a large sheered tree on the ground. The professional press photograph by Dick Hallberg of the *Jamestown Post-Journal*, lit up by a flash bulb, was of such high quality the manufacturer's part identification lettering and numbering on the propeller blades were clearly visible. 'HUB No. 37667' was stamped on the device holding the four blades in place. Behind it the engine cooling fins so meticulously machine-cut together from the solid metal of the cylinder head forging were easily recognizable as was a sticker from the propeller service company of Miami, including its CAA license number. All along the prop blades were the tell-tale scraping marks of high revolution twirling as they sliced through the hardwood trees of Bucktooth Ridge. The engine na-

---

[150] Only two photographs of Nyrop at the crash site could be found, a carefully staged scene of him looking at a crushed engine from the C-46 and another of him examining the remains of a wing.

celle and cowling were so ripped apart with sharp jagged edges that it was barely distinguishable as a form-fitting cover for the power plant. In all likelihood, Nyrop agreed to this photograph at the engine only because it was a considerable distance away from the fuselage, which still held bodies and the survivors' campfire. For a man of Nyrop's prominent stature, a photograph at the other locations might have been perceived as a public imposition on the privacy of the victims and the survivors. The single photograph so close to the wreckage he did allow, however, published all across America served a valuable public relations purpose for Nyrop, the CAB, The White House, and American passenger aviation. It also signified a defining moment in commercial passenger plane crash investigations. It was the first time in American history that such a high-level government official made a personal trip to the scene and poked among the wreckage of a major passenger plane crash. Nyrop apparently did it by inference of the President.[151] The CAB chief hoped that his trip and his comments about what he believed to be the cause of the crash would help alleviate fears among Americans flying on airplanes, considered to be so critical to the rapid post-war development of modern American business, industry, and tourism. The circumstances and location presented an ideal opportunity for this first visit; it was in a remote area, and on January 1 it was the start of a new year and a new focus on abolishing the problems with nonskeds. At this scene, Nyrop was not mobbed by gawking spectators as he surely would have been at the urban plane crash scenes earlier in the year, and it allowed his team to closely portray the administration's message via the select reporters who went along. Additionally, Nyrop found a highly cooperative, professional and sympathetic figure in Sheriff Sigel, who personally delivered him up the hill to the wreckage where they remained together until after sundown.

At the scene, within hours of the survivors' rescue, Nyrop boldly pronounced the CAB's theory for the cause of the crash of flight 44-2. Standing in the snow in the back barnyard of the Herrick farm, Nyrop

---

[151] President Truman was already seeking advice from prominent aviation experts on how to proceed with handling the many crash events of 1951 when Nyrop made this first visit to a crash scene.

gathered the reporters around for a short impromptu press conference. Some reporters covered every detail; others stuck to the business of the visit. He thanked them first, for their cooperation during his laborious hike up the ridge. Cupping their pocket-sized notebooks in their hands and scribbling with their pencils, one of them came directly to the point with the question on everyone's mind. What caused the crash? "It does not appear to have been caused by either mechanical or structural failure of the airplane," Nyrop replied. There it was, a declaration from the top airplane crash investigator in the United States pointing the blame toward the pilots. After spending three hours on Bucktooth Ridge and in discussions with his CAB investigators who had spent the night at the crash scene, Nyrop calmly informed the small group of reporters that "both engines were developing power at the time of the crash and there was no fire in the plane when it was in the air." His carefully chosen words came from his investigators who had examined the crushed airplane through the night. Both scenarios were causes of several recent fatal crashes involving C-46s. The chairman was here to make a point. The many crashes of 1951 were not so much caused by problems with the C-46 as they were with the pilots and managers behind the nonskeds. Nyrop said the location of the crash led to the determination that the flight was off course and that the pilot was flying too low.[152] His next statement further pointed everyone straight to the focus of the CAB investigation. "If we knew why the pilot was flying low, we probably would know the cause of the accident," he said. Such a statement would have produced a few seconds of silence from the reporters as they wrote each word in their notebooks for a quotation. Nyrop's conjecture was printed verbatim in several newspapers the next day. These critical declarations so early in the investigation, when bodies were still trapped in the wreckage, went a long way toward explaining that the plane did not run out of fuel or have mechanical problems, but more than likely, the crash was caused by pilot error. Nyrop also said his

---

[152] A typical visual flight lane on a direct course was about 10 miles wide. At 11 miles east of direct course, Flight 44-2 was about six miles out of the Buffalo flight lane.

investigators had already determined that an instrument flight plan had not been filed in Pittsburgh when the poor weather required it.

These were risky early statements by the top American aviation crash investigator on a CAB chairman's first visit to a crash scene. However, given the heightened sense of fear among Americans about flying on airplanes, especially among the nonskeds, Nyrop felt it was necessary to immediately announce what was believed to be the cause of the crash. "Although the CAB accident investigators were on the scene as fast as they could fly in from Pittsburgh and Buffalo I decided to visit the scene of the accident and to work with them personally to find out if these three accidents formed a pattern that would require immediate corrective action by the board," Nyrop said.[153] "Formed a pattern" is a strong phrase and, so far, an unsupported indictment of the nonsked airlines but, it fit. Many of them were operating their airlines in the same manner, skimping on everything to save money at the expense of passengers' lives. Two of the crashes among C-46s earlier in December were caused by poor maintenance on engines and a pilot's inattention to navigation and fuel management.

Another concern Nyrop and his CAB investigators had been with overloading C-46s. He declared that there was "not much question" that the weight of Flight 44-2 was under the maximum load limit of 48,000 pounds long used for C-46s. It was below the maximum of 45,000 pounds assigned to this particular plane because it had only days earlier been certified to fly passengers. Even as he spoke the CAB was in the process of reducing the C-46 weight limit to 45,000 pounds and eventually 43,000 pounds for all C-46s. Also, without visiting the hospital where the 14 survivors spent the night, Nyrop commended George and Lt. Bischof. "Their heroic action and leadership saved the lives of many people," Nyrop declared. He did not mention Pearl. The reporters, so fixed on the two war veteran heroes of the crash, apparently didn't ask him about her, either. She was not included in their lengthy reports about Nyrop's visit.

---

[153] The three crash events were: Miami Airlines C-46 crash in Elizabeth, New Jersey on December 16; Robin Airlines C-46 crash-landing in Cobourg, Ontario, Canada on December 20; Continental Charters C-46 crash in Napoli.

Upon leaving the Herrick farm, Nyrop was driven to Little Valley and the Cattaraugus County Courthouse for a meeting with Sheriff Sigel and the CAB investigators. He announced that a public hearing into the crash would be held in the courthouse later in January. Speaking a second time to reporters from Buffalo, Pittsburgh, *Associated Press*, *United Press*, and local newspapers and radio stations, Nyrop again emphasized his interest in airline passenger safety. "The CAB is very concerned about accidents of C-46s, of which we have had three in the past 15 days," he said. "We are going to do our best to find the cause of these accidents and take the appropriate remedial action." He would be true to his word.

Nyrop then left the courthouse in Little Valley for the hour-long drive back to Bradford-McKean Airport in Pennsylvania where the CAB's plane waited to fly him back to Washington. In his office, Nyrop was receiving several reports a day from CAB crash investigators working scenes in Elizabeth, New Jersey, Cobourg, Ontario, Canada, and in the mountains of Arizona. They were also trying to figure out how to get to the scene of a crash at the top of Alaska's Chena Dome. Three of these four crashes involved C-46s.

Nyrop appeared to be the busiest man in America. At about the same time his DC-3 lifted off from the Pennsylvania airfield late on New Year's Day, another Continental Charters C-46 lifted off from the Buffalo Airport for Miami with 25 passengers. Fifteen of them boarded the plane in Pittsburgh and then flew on to Buffalo to pick up another ten passengers for the long overnight flight to Florida.[154] A newspaper reporter who questioned the passengers in Buffalo said none of them appeared to be concerned. A passenger from Niagara Falls said, "I could be just as easily killed falling down the stairs at home as I could on a C-46."

---

[154] This apparently was the same plane in which company president John Belding arrived in Pittsburgh on December 30.

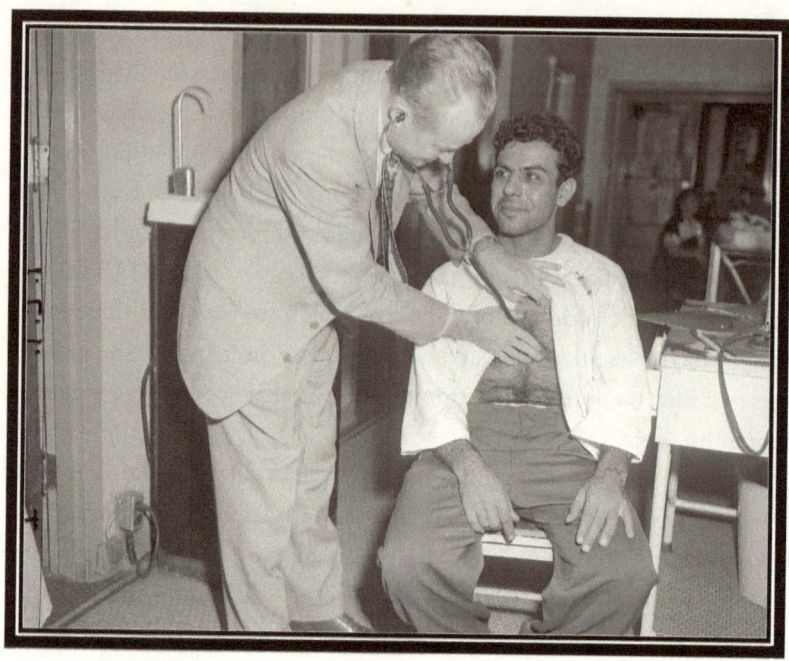

Top, Dr. James W. Taft, Salamanca Hospital, examines the hero of Bucktooth Ridge, George Albert. By George's clean, fresh but unshaven appearance, the photograph was probably arranged for *Jamestown Post-Journal* photographer Dick Hallberg after George was able to bath and dress in clean pants. He has only a small scratch on one of his fingers from the crash; below, survivor Joseph Woziniak is comforted by a nurse at the hospital.

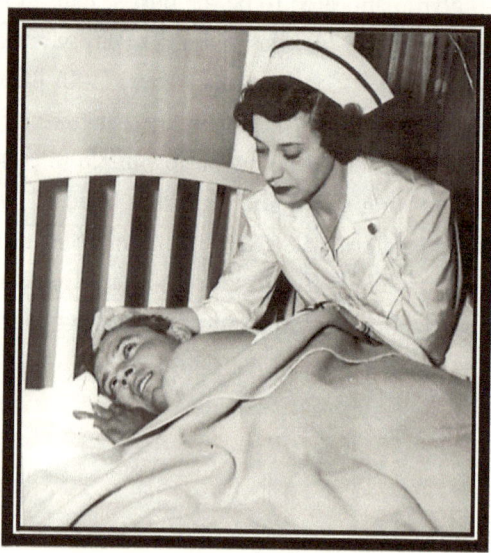

Photo collage from *The Pittsburgh Press* shows survivors and family, left, in the hospital after the crash of Flight 44-2 and scenes from the wreckage and recovery of bodies. Press photographers gained access everywhere except the funeral homes.

Top right, clockwise, Destroyer USS Saufley in the Atlantic after rescuing Puerto Rican migrant workers from the crash of a Westair C-46 on June 5, 1950; USS Saufley commander with the Westair pilot, co-pilot, and steward, aboard ship on June 8, 1950; newspaper headline uses "*Murder*" in connection with C-46 and nonsked crashes of the early 1950s; Coronet magazine article about the deadly nonskeds, reached millions of people in the *Reader's Digest* imitator.

Top to bottom, Bradford-McKean Airport in the early 1950s where Donald Nyrop landed in a DC-3 as the first CAB chairman to visit the scene of a major passenger plane crash, setting a precedent for all future CAB and NTSB leaders; crash-landing of Eastern Airlines Constellation on Curles Neck Farm, Virginia shows that not all the dramatic or deadly crashes of 1951 were from nonskeds; Nyrop is photographed while examining one of the engines of the crashed Continental Charters C-46 on Bucktooth Ridge. Nyrop imposed a multitude of safety regulations on the nonsked airlines of the early 50's partly as a result of what he saw on his first crash scene visit.

Top right, clockwise, CAB Chairman Donald Nyrop, center with sweater, meets with Cattaraugus County Sheriff Morgan Sigel, with glasses, at the old courthouse in Little Valley, NY on January 1, 1952. Traveling with Nyrop from Washington were CAB investigators James Peyton, left, and William Andrews, right; firefighters and a pilot (holding a shovel) in Philadelphia find the body of heroine National Airlines stewardess Mary Frances Housley shielding an infant; Housley portrayed on the cover of *Heroic Comics* in September 1951 as fear of flying spread through American pop culture.

CHAPTER 17

ELIZABETH

As a frosty cold front gripped the northeastern United States with temperatures below 16 degrees, 49-year-old Walter J. Burns was pushing a wheelbarrow filled with firewood from the edge of the river toward his house in Elizabeth, New Jersey. He heard kids, who were sledding in the snow and ice along the steep riverbank, screaming and pointing toward the sky. "I looked up and saw this huge flaming mass coming down on me. I dropped my wood and ran toward the kids," he said. Burns was witnessing the second worst passenger plane crash in American history at 3:10 pm on Sunday, December 16, 1951.

Fifty-six people were on board a Miami Airlines C-46 twin-engine plane that had just taken off from the Newark, New Jersey airport for Tampa and Miami when it suddenly crashed into neighboring Elizabeth and exploded into a massive fuel fireball.

Burns' first-person account of the plane that "just fell from the sky" appeared the next day in the *Brooklyn Eagle* newspaper. "The funny thing was that the plane seemed to have been almost a total wreck before it hit the ground. It was just like a big ball of fire as it came down over the roofs of the houses. When the plane hit the brick waterworks, a terrible roar came out. I was looking at the kids, they were screaming, but I couldn't hear them," he said. The kids were corralled by their father while Burns ran to his home nearby to rescue his invalid daughter and his wife. He smelled and felt the spray of gasoline prickling his skin and he was worried the burning plane might catch houses on fire, including his own. The wreckage ended up in the shallow Elizabeth River where it flowed beneath the Jersey Central Railroad tracks toward the Arthur Kill at Newark Bay.

Another witness described the plane as "toppling down, dropping very fast" and then "it blew up as it hit the water." A woman who watched it from the back of her house a block away said, "It was really pulling hard and was just skimming above some trees. It seemed to burst into flames. I kind of think he (the pilot) hit that spot intentionally to save us."

Looking through a window of their wood clapboard two-story house packed tightly among other similar houses along the railroad tracks and bordered by Union and Lowden Streets, West Grand Street, and Westfield Avenue, Burns' wife thought someone had dropped an Atom Bomb on Elizabeth. It certainly wasn't the bomb, so much feared in the early years of the Cold War, but the crash of a huge C-46 military war surplus twin-engine transport plane recently converted for domestic passenger travel. Everyone on board was killed, many of the bodies burned beyond visual recognition.

Just like a bomb, though, it set off an explosion of political events that would forever change the fledgling commercial aviation industry. And, it would thrust Elizabeth into the political arena over the delicate balance between safety expectations in residential neighborhoods and the rapid growth of federally funded American airports.

MIAMI AIRLINES BEGAN FLYING passengers on the lucrative route between Newark, Tampa, and Miami in 1946. The airline was a typical nonsked just like Continental Charters, started on a shoestring budget with three C-46 airplanes and one DC-3 at the time of the crash, purchased or leased at a bargain price from the U.S. military following World War II. Fifty-two passengers paid a cheap fare of $39.74 (about

$355 in 2015) for the Newark to Florida flight. Full enough to take off on the morning of December 16, the departure time was announced for ten am. Passengers began arriving at Newark Airport before nine.

In 1951, there were no security delays or baggage screening in America's rather dismal airports, little used by passengers and forsaken during World War II. Tickets were hand-written on paper and the passengers were directed to the main terminal door for departures.[155] There were no gates. They walked onto the tarmac and approached their planes from the tail to either climb an aluminum ladder or, in larger airports, mount a few steps on a portable stairway.

Among the passengers was dancer Doris Ruby, 22, from Sunnyside, New Jersey. Ruby appeared in New York stage and television shows during her brief dancing career and had just finished an engagement at a Manhattan nightclub the evening before the flight to Florida, where she was scheduled for another dancing job. Also arriving for the flight were Kay and Rita Mendelsohn of Brooklyn. At 29 and 36, the nurse and dietitian sisters lived together and were embarking on a two-week warm weather vacation in Florida. Several couples, families and mothers with infants from the New York metropolitan area, Connecticut, Massachusetts, Florida, and even Buffalo also arrived for the mid-morning flight. Mr. and Mrs. Benjamin Reh, diamond brokers from the Elmhurst section of Queens, arrived with their 5-year-old son, Eugene, and Mrs. Reh's father.[156] A Brooklyn mother, 39-year-old Marion Bloomfield, arrived with her two daughters, Esther, 9, and Naomi, 4, for the trip to visit her husband and the girls' father, 45-year-old Burton Bloomfield, who had recently moved to Florida to find work. The Bloomfield's sons, Leo, 16, and Kenneth, 13, remained at home in their Bath Beach neighborhood. Inside the terminal, minutes before boarding the plane, passenger Sadie Bernstein, of the Bronx, walked up to a vending machine and purchased a $25,000 life insurance policy for the flight. She

---

[155] Many airports in 1951 didn't have gates. Passengers walked from main terminal doors to a line of planes parked on the tarmac.

[156] That the Rehs drove all the way from Elmhurst, adjacent to New York's LaGuardia Airport, with its regular service by the more expensive major airlines is indicative of how far people went to save money on the nonskeds.

apparently didn't read the fine print before inserting her money. Nonskeds weren't covered.

The crew included the pilot, Albert C. Lyons, 30, a boyish-looking man with a mustache, and reddish hair pushed back off his forehead, co-pilot, John R. Mason, 36, and stewardess, Doris P. Helms, all from Hialeah, Florida, a new and fashionable community near the Miami International Airport. Another Miami Airlines pilot, Edward R. Lily, occupied a third cockpit seat for a complimentary flight home to Florida. They all met the plane that morning in Newark after it arrived from Fort Smith, Arkansas at about 11:30 pm the previous night, December 15. During the flight from Arkansas, two other passenger pilots said the plane had no problems except for the malfunction of two gasoline-fueled heaters in the main cabin. Heater problems were common on the C-46. At Newark, instructions were issued to repair the heaters before the Florida flight. Mechanics from the Babb Company worked overnight and up to departure time on December 16 trying to repair the heaters. They failed to meet the deadline and this caused a five-hour delay for the flight. The only way to determine if the heaters had been successfully repaired would have been with a test flight of the plane. They didn't do it because dispatchers for the nonsked were employed by the airline and, not bound by the same rules as major airlines which would not have been able to take off without a testing the repairs. The company dispatchers wanted to get the plane off to Florida as soon as possible, without taking the time to test the heaters.

As the passengers waited in the 1935 Newark Airport terminal, mechanics also serviced the C-46 former cargo plane with fuel and oil. Manufactured in September 1945 by the Curtiss-Wright Company at its Buffalo plant a week before the end of the Japanese battles in World War II, the former U.S. Air Forces plane was leased to Miami Airlines in December 1948 with only 23 hours of flight. By the time the plane arrived in Newark that morning displaying tail number *N1678M*, it had more than 4,100 hours of flight.

During routine servicing, the left engine required five gallons of oil and the right engine took ten gallons. Seven hundred sixty-seven gallons of fuel were added to the front and center tanks in both wings. At about

2:30 pm, the 52 passengers, including two mothers carrying infants, were finally loaded by walking them out of the Art Deco terminal with its half-round control tower on the second floor and festooned with megaphone-type loudspeakers.[157] The plane was backed up to the terminal at an angle so passengers could mount the ladder-stairs and step into the tail of the plane where they had to dig in their toes and pull themselves up the inclined aisle to find their seats. The cabin was illuminated with natural light from 12 small square windows on each side of the plane and while seated, the passengers were tilted at about 30 degrees where they could easily look through the windows at the baggage loading crew on the tarmac.[158]

Passengers in the front rows were nearly 20 feet off the ground and only the pilots, at 22 feet up, were higher. After all the passengers were on board and the luggage loaded into the belly of the plane, the gross weight of the C-46 aircraft was 117 pounds over the regulated maximum of 48,000 pounds. Despite new weight limits for C-46 passenger planes that had only recently been proposed, there were no adjustments made to reduce the overage. It's believed this extra weight was from the company pilot, Lily, in the cockpit jump-seat. He was getting a free ride home.

As was standard practice in preparation for flight, both Pratt and Whitney R-2800 engines with Hamilton Standard Hydromatic propellers were run up to high RPMs by the pilots for testing and warming. The right engine was run up longer than the left engine and at this time several people saw smoke continuously flowing from this engine. It was *"white, gray or light"* in color. Additionally, baggage handler William J. Barner spotted oil leaking from the right engine during the run-up. He didn't report the leak because he believed it often happened to planes on which he worked. He saw fluid coming down the right engine cowl and it appeared to be fresh oil. Leaking oil was not normal.

---

[157] The 1935 Newark Airport Terminal dedication was led by famous aviatrix Amelia Earhart. Used until 1953, it was virtually abandoned until it was moved in 2002 for runway expansion. It is now the public entrance to the offices of the Port Authority of New York and New Jersey.

[158] This C-46 had been reconfigured with many more windows than the original Army design of four on each side.

Controllers advised pilot Lyons that he was cleared for takeoff on either Runway 24-6, which ran northeast and southwest or Runway 28-10, which ran east and west.[159] Lyons chose his lift off from Runway 28 which would propel the plane west over the Pennsylvania Railroad tracks, Weequahic Park, the Lehigh Valley Railroad tracks, toward Hillside and Union, New Jersey, and then require a left turn to the south for the first leg of the flight, to Tampa. Releasing the parking brake, Lyons revved the 2,000 horsepower engines, taxied off the apron, and with the giant round C-46 nose aimed toward the sky, bounced along the taxiway to the head of Runway 28. Oil was still dripping from the nacelle around the right engine.

NORTHERN NEW JERSEY HAD only recently got its first significant snowfall of the 1951-52 winter season and with temperatures well below freezing, kids in Elizabeth were outside on Sunday, December 16 taking advantage of the new snow for sledding. With few natural hills in the city, the banks of the Elizabeth River and the built up tracks of the Jersey Central provided a slick and fast slope. By afternoon on that Sunday, it had warmed to only 16 degrees but the kids were having a ball.

Where the tracks crossed over the river was also one of the few open areas of densely populated Elizabeth. It's where the city maintained a large brick-sided water pumping station, including a 100-foot-tall brick smokestack for the water station's coal-fired boilers. As Lyons and Mason taxied the Miami Airlines C-46 toward Runway 28 at three pm, several kids were pushing off with their runner sleds and speeding down the train track embankment nearly into the shallow waters of the river.

Having already given her preflight safety instructions, Stewardess Helms was buckled in a second jump seat next to passenger-pilot, Lily. At 3:02 pm the twin-prop airplane was cleared for takeoff. Gaining speed down the runway, the right engine continued dripping oil which burned on the hot engine and was blown away as thick gray smoke by the steadily increasing force of air around the nacelle and the plane's right wing. As the plane picked up speed to full throttle, the smoke was

---

[159] Runway names are numerical abbreviations of their headings, in degrees.

less visible but it certainly didn't stop. A minute later as the C-46 was airborne to the west, Newark controllers observed from their newly-built 65-foot-tall glass-lined tower on the east side of the field, the landing gear retracting into the underbelly of the plane. They were watching what appeared to be a normal takeoff.

Within seconds, however, controllers for the first time observed a trail of white smoke from the right side of the plane. They grabbed binoculars from a shelf in front of their circular windows for a closer look. The tower supervisor, fearing a fire, pressed the airport crash alarm button. Immediately, all other departures and arrivals were delayed. Emergency crews were ordered onto the airfield but told to stay off the runways, especially Runway 6 where the tower instructed the smoking Miami Airlines C-46 to land if it could.

Runway 24-6 was one of three constructed by the U.S. Army when it controlled Newark Airport for military planes during World War II. The longest at 7,900 feet, Runway 6 gave Lyons and Mason a straight line approach from the southwest side of the field directly over the City of Elizabeth. But, they had to turn around and get there first.[160]

During the war, every pilot who flew a C-46 was given a classified Handbook, *Pilot's Flight Operating Instructions for Army Model C-46 Series and Navy Model R5C-1 Airplane*. Large warning notices are posted in the handbook which explains what will happen to the plane when an engine loses power. Pilots were warned that it was impossible, even with a light load, to take off in a C-46 with only one engine operating. Since Lyons had taken off, he obviously had the power to both engines as he left the ground. If an engine was lost after takeoff and before a safe speed of 95-100 miles per hour is reached, the pilot's handbook said the airplane would become uncontrollable. *"Close throttles, turn ignition off and land straight ahead with landing gear up,"* pilots were advised. If the plane loses an engine during takeoff but after a safe speed has been reached, *"the airplane will turn toward the faulty engine."* Pilots were advised to apply opposite rudder controls immediately and bank the

---

[160] A single number designation for a runway indicates only half of the full length of the runway, and its head, whether taking off or landing.

airplane with the running engine down until they could maintain a reasonably straight course. It sounded like good advice in the handbook but actually doing it was another matter.

Saving the smoking and crippled airplane centered on the radio communications from the tower controllers to the cockpit using its tail number. "1678M you can land any way possible, any way you wish. You are cleared back to the field," radioed the controllers. There was no response from the plane.

The takeoff appeared normal, but the airplane's climb through its farthest distance from the field of four miles was extremely slow. Watching his company's plane take off, another Miami Airlines pilot believed the smoke was coming from an overheated right brake on the C-46. He called the tower from an airport telephone and suggested controllers advise the pilot not to raise the landing gear and to extend it if they had already raised it. Controllers passed along the message by radio and, still watching the plane through their binoculars, they observed the raised landing gear extend from the plane until all three wheels were down. Pilot Lyons also replied with the briefest acknowledgment, "N1678M." Controllers then advised pilots Lyons and Mason that winds were from the west at 20 mph and that they were cleared to land anywhere, but to attempt Runway 6. "The airport is yours," they announced. There was no response.

There is no way of knowing exactly what was happening inside the cockpit or the cabin as the C-46 sluggishly climbed into the sky on a westerly and then southerly track over Newark and Union, New Jersey. It's generally understood that Captain Lyons acknowledged an emergency and instructions from the tower when he lowered the landing gear after taking off. With one engine on fire and producing insufficient power, and substantial drag from the extended landing gear, Lyons was fighting a fierce battle just trying to get the plane into the air high enough so he could turn around and line up for Runway 6. In the cabin, veteran stewardess Helms was equally busy making sure the passengers were positioned for the emergency turn and a quick landing at Newark. At this stage, her responsibilities included advising the passengers to tighten their seat belts and lean forward in a cushioning position in the event of a crash. She didn't have to tell them to pray, they were most likely already doing it.

Passengers on the right side of the plane and in the first six window seats would have easily seen the right engine smoking as it shot down the runway. Once in the air, they would have been the first to see the smoke turn into a large ball of fire just as the landing gear was lowered. This move, recommended by the Miami Airlines pilot on the ground, provided a rush of air that further fueled the fire.

A few miles downrange from the end of Runway 28 and when the plane was at about 800-1000 feet in the air, Union, New Jersey engineer William E. Sparrow heard the telltale sound of a struggling plane above his neighborhood. He was accustomed to hearing twin and four engine planes take off at Newark Airport from his Morris Avenue apartment home, and he immediately determined that this plane was in trouble. Grabbing his camera, Sparrow managed to get two photographs of the plane flying overhead while it was turning in a wide arc to line up for an approach to Runway 6.

The first photograph shows the plane directly overhead of Sparrow's apartment with landing gear down and a long trail of thick white smoke flowing from the right engine for several hundred feet. It looks like a thin white sheet trailing behind the long narrow outstretched wings with nothing but sky in the background. The second photograph shows some perspective. Taken while the plane was downrange of Sparrow's home, it shows a few houses and a wire-laden utility pole in the bottom of the photograph. In black and white, (few people used color film in 1951) there is a white blob around the right engine (flames) and thick black smoke trailing for several hundred feet before it turns to white smoke. The smoke flows with a crooked trail indicating shakiness or instability of the plane. Both photographs depict the plane in near level flight, several hundred feet from the ground, and with the right engine obviously burning at a rapid rate.[161]

---

[161] William E. Sparrow's photographs were obtained by federal crash investigators, labeled as investigation exhibits, and released to the public in the final crash investigation report.

Elizabeth police officer Nicholas Bilsky was on patrol along Westfield Avenue when he saw the plane coming in over the city, lower and lower. To him, it appeared as if the pilot was looking for a clear place for a crash landing. Witnesses reported seeing the flames in the right engine nacelle go out for a short period of time as the plane's forward speed grew slower. This was possibly caused by the automatic fire extinguisher, known as a one-shot.

Captain Lyons was in the fight of his life and for the lives of 55 others aboard his plane. A seasoned war pilot, he had only worked as a captain for Miami Airlines since September 21, 1951. However, he had served as a flight instructor for four years during World War II and had more than 8,679 hours in his flight log, 2,600 as a C-46 pilot-in-command. Co-pilot John Mason had worked for Miami Airlines since October 17, 1951, and of his 1,224 flight hours, 234 were in C-46s.

Both pilots would have known that the Curtiss C-46 Commando, originally designed as a civilian passenger plane but redesigned as a troop transport and cargo plane for the war, was extremely difficult to fly with one engine. Some C-46 pilots who flew over the Himalaya Mountains during the war declared that it was nearly impossible to fly when one engine conked out. Making flight even more difficult for Lyons and Mason, by the time the plane passed over Union Township at Route 22 and Morris Avenue it was already dropping parts into the residential neighborhoods below. Landing gear braces and door, nacelle cone fairings, spring clamps, cowl flap brackets, hydraulic tubing, oil tank chafing straps, and numerous other parts all dropped from the plane as it turned southeast toward the communities of Roselle Park and Elizabeth. It's doubtful the plane could ever have made a safe landing even if it succeeded in reaching the airport. Some 30 pieces of the landing gear and right engine had already peeled away and fallen to the ground.

Struggling to stay aloft in a southeasterly direction over the tightly packed homes along Magie Avenue, the plane was too low and lacked enough power to make it to Runway 6 more than two miles away. Passengers, already aware of the life-threatening emergency from the burning engine would have seen the Empire State Building in midtown

Manhattan some ten miles away. The flight to Florida was off. Their lives were in the hands of two pilots trying to make it alive back to Newark Airport.

Suddenly, at about 200 feet in the air, the already low left wing dropped almost vertically downward while the right wing shot upward. Some thought they saw a wing fall off. The plane simply fell from the sky with little forward speed. Hundreds of people watched it. From the Newark tower, controllers held binoculars to their eyes and helplessly watched the Miami Airlines C-46 steadily falling. Their calls on the radio went unanswered as the pilots fought a losing battle trying to fly at such low altitude, at bare minimum speed, and with only one engine. "The plane suddenly dipped and zoomed to the ground shearing off the roof of a house and hitting the water works," recalled Officer Bilsky.

When the airport emergency crews, waiting alongside Runway 6, realized the plane wouldn't make it back to the field, the first rescue truck crashed through a locked gate to clear the way for all the rescue vehicles to rush out of the confines of the airport and to the crash scene. It took them a few minutes to arrive. They had to drive around the marshlands that separated the airport from Elizabeth.

Fortunately, the building clipped by the left wing of the plane was not occupied. However, the plane slammed into a large brick building used by the City of Elizabeth to store water department equipment. It was also empty. Miraculously, the plane narrowly missed the waterworks' tall brick smokestack that was visible all around the city. The plane plunged into the shallow water of the Elizabeth River.

The Elizabeth station for the Jersey Central was just a few feet away but, on a Sunday, it was not nearly as busy as it would have been on a weekday. The aircraft, heavily laden with its full tanks of gasoline, burst into an explosion catching the brick storage building on fire. One man from Union City, who was early on the scene told reporters he heard cries from inside the plane, but there was nothing anyone could do to help the passengers.

Incredibly, the massive fire that sent a column of thick black smoke into the air was extinguished by the airport and community firefighters in just seventeen minutes. It's believed that nearly everyone inside the plane was killed instantly by the impact or within a very short period of time by the gasoline explosion and fire.

Firefighters immediately dug into the task of removing the bodies. They were hampered by the icy creek, extreme cold, and the massive crowd of cars and people who crammed into the area for a look. Elizabeth police did their best to hold people back, but it was useless. There were so many vantage points that bystanders encroached upon the scene in such confusion that police couldn't determine who was supposed to be there and who wasn't. Embedded in the recesses of the creek, the wreckage and burned bodies, illuminated by massive lights and being swept by investigators, were on full display for spectators lining the Westfield Avenue Bridge and the raised railroad tracks as if they were watching a performance at New York's Winter Garden Theater.

Some who rushed to the scene were passenger relatives who had to be held back and consoled by Elizabeth police, of whom nearly all were called in to work all night. Priests and rabbis muddied their shoes sliding down the riverbank to administer last rites and prayers of atonement. Passengers from the Jersey Central peered at the grisly scene from the windows of trains clicking on the tracks above.

New York City and northern New Jersey news media swarmed the scene within minutes. Reporters and photographers with their bulky cameras and popping flashbulbs fired the bulletin news back to their editors who rapidly composed new copy for updates to the evening edition newspapers. A few papers hired small planes at New Jersey's Teterboro and Linden Airports and flew their photographers in circles around Elizabeth while they pushed their camera lenses through the planes' windows to snap pictures. The photos were splashed on front pages the next morning with banner headlines around the world. *All 56 on Airliner Die in Crash* screamed the *Buffalo Courier-Express* above a smaller headline for a massive blizzard that struck western New York State and southern Ontario, Canada with 18 inches of wind-driven snow the same day. *Probe Air Crash Killing 56* blared the *Brooklyn Eagle* above a photograph of firefighters spraying the iced over wreckage as a swarm of rescuers and gawkers bent over the charred remains searching for bodies or parts of bodies. Film cameras whirled away capturing footage that displayed the smoking wreckage, and bodies being carried up the creek bank, on TV news programs and in movie theater newsreels within days.

Universal International News narrator Ed Herlihy, already famous for his voice depictions of World War II battles, intoned with melodramatic inflection over nighttime footage of the crash, "Here is the stark reality of the second worst air crash in America's commercial aviation history. A scant seven minutes after taking off from Newark Airport, a twin-engine C-46 Army surplus plane bound for Miami plummets into the Elizabeth River in the center of Elizabeth, New Jersey snuffing out all 56 lives aboard."

The nation's worst plane crash had occurred the previous year on June 23, 1950 when Northwest Airlines Flight 2501 from New York's LaGuardia Airport to Minneapolis disappeared over Lake Michigan and all 58 on board the Douglas DC-4 were lost in the lake.

In the newsreel, as the filmed scenery changed to daylight, Herlihy continued his narration as the orchestral music reached a crescendo, "Daylight reveals a scene of horror which is made only less horrible by a heroic pilot who fought his plane to the river area after a motor had failed and a wing shorn off.[162] The crippled plane, roaring at low altitude over a densely populated section of the city miraculously missed countless residences and ironically only tore the roof off one unoccupied house. The crash brought a five-pronged investigation by county, state and federal officials into the possibility that overloading of the nonscheduled airplane may have contributed to the crash." In his closing, with deeper and quieter tones from an organ and cello that prophetically described the next several weeks, Herlihy growled, "a tragedy that may well bring about a closer scrutiny of the nation's skyways."

As spectators gathered on the bridge to watch the grisly scene, those who looked up could see a man in a coat sitting quietly in the bedroom of a three story house with the top corner neatly sliced off by the airplane. Nine-year-old Jack Rescoe looked inside the exposed bedroom and

---

[162] The investigation later found that a wing did not break off the plane before impact with the ground.

thought how odd it was that the bed was still neatly made, a lamp still stood on the nightstand, and clothes still hung on hangars inside the door of the room. Just like exposing the many problems among the nonskeds, the crash exposed the privacy of that man's bedroom to Jack and the world. Jack had rushed to the scene with his father, an electrician at the Bayway Standard Oil refinery nearby in Elizabeth and Linden, in their 1949 Chevrolet sedan from their apartment home at Magie Avenue and Edgewood Parkway in adjacent Union Township. The man sitting alone in the bedroom captured his attention only temporarily, however, because down in the creek at the crash scene, stone-faced firemen were quietly gathering incinerated bodies and body parts under bright lights and slipping them into zippered bags for the coroner. A curious boy whose father had taken him to witness the catastrophic and gruesome wreck scene of "*The Broker*," the Pennsylvania Railroad commuter train that collapsed a temporary bridge over the New Jersey Turnpike while it was under construction in Woodbridge in February 1951, young Jack had already seen his share of mangled bodies. This was unlike the train wreck, however, where 85 people were crushed. What he could see in the plane crash wreckage from the bridge in Elizabeth was that everything and everyone were burned nearly to ashes. Growing up on the edge of Elizabeth, young Jack would also rush to the scene of two more plane crashes, within weeks, and listen to the incessant chatter among Elizabeth residents repeating their "I told you so," refrain that airplanes from Newark would crash into their neighborhoods.

Within hours of the Miami Airlines plane crash all but one of the badly burned bodies were removed to a makeshift morgue and laid in double rows in soft straw lining the floor of a garage behind Haines Funeral Home mortuary in Elizabeth. To identify the bodies, Union County Coroner Alfred C. Haines asked family members to first look at the victims' clothing. As a last resort, he would remove the white sheets to reveal the charred and mangled bodies, some far beyond any visual recognition.

For many hours afterward, people from Elizabeth and nearby communities crowded around the crash scene and continued to praise pilot Lyons for how, they believed, he guided the plane to an open area of the city along the river bank. If the aircraft had continued a bit farther on its course, it would have slammed into the Union County Courthouse just a few blocks away. The crash was an absolute tragedy but on December 16 it was just another crash in a long list of crashes in a devastating year. The CAB was already planning new safety guidelines for the nonskeds, but the magnitude of the problem had not yet been realized by the traveling public. The panic would set in over the next two weeks.

CHAPTER 18

WHITECAPS ON THE WATER

NO SOONER HAD CAB investigators gotten knee-deep into the Miami Airlines wreckage in the Elizabeth River, then another C-46 passenger plane, flying to Newark, went down. This one was a controlled crash-landing in Canada that even produced nervous chuckles among passengers, stewardesses, and pilots. Continental Charters pilots read in the newspapers about this flight fiasco in the same kind of planes they flew, with great interest. They wondered how the pilot could have gotten himself so lost he thought Lake Ontario was the Atlantic Ocean.

It happened on December 20, only four days after the deadly disaster in Elizabeth. The pilot of a Robin Airlines flight from Los Angeles got lost in a snowstorm while flying the final leg of the flight, between Chicago and Newark. The plane was loaded with military and civilian passengers flying home to the New York region for Christmas. One of them had an over-the-wing seat looking through the plane's windows as the engines quit one after the other. They ran out of gas.

JERRY LAUFGRABEN READ A newspaper advertisement for an unbelievably cheap $88 airplane ticket from Sacramento, California home to Newark,

New Jersey for the 1951 Christmas holiday. He thought it was too good to be true. It was. He never made it all the way in the airplane.

Jerry was 21, a first-year airman in the United States Air Force in December of 1951, and he was stationed at Mather Field ATC in Sacramento.[163] Born and raised in Manhattan and Brooklyn, New York, his degree from Long Island Agricultural and Technical College got him into the food inspection and sanitation programs of the Air Force where he made sure that meat and dairy products delivered to the military were safe to eat.[164] Eager to get home to visit his parents in Brooklyn for the holidays, Jerry jumped at the chance to save $175 off a regular-priced airplane ticket. There was one catch, however. The plane was from a nonsked airline. It would not leave California for New Jersey until it was full of passengers, all paying the same cheap $88 fare.

Within days, though, Jerry and several other airmen from Mather got a telephone call that the plane was filling up fast and would leave Sacramento for Burbank where the eastbound flight would originate and where most of the passengers would board the plane early in the morning on December 19. In Sacramento, they settled on the first leg of their flight aboard a Curtiss C-46 military cargo plane recently converted for passengers.

There was confusion about who was in charge of the flight. The plane had *99ers* on the tail, not for the *Ninety-Nines*, the all-women pilot club organized by Amelia Earhart, but for the *Route of the 99ers*, a moniker given to nonsked, North American Air Coach, for its one-way fare from coast-to-coast. In this case, however, the plane was utilized by Robin Airlines, which capitalized on the popularly advertised fare, but reduced the gimmicky price even lower to who-could-pass-up $88. No other markings or even a flight number identified the airline to the passengers, a common problem for the CAB when dealing with the nonskeds of the late 1940s and early 1950s. Airport radio communications identified the plane as *N59487*, its tail number.[165]

---

[163] Mather Field later became Sacramento Mather Airport.
[164] Many years later, Laufgraben changed his last name to Lawrence.
[165] This plane was a later-model C-46 and one of only 17 produced that differentiated it from the cigar-shaped C-46. It had a stepped windshield that made its nose appear similar to the popular DC-3 airplane.

The plane took off from Sacramento and flew south to Burbank where Jerry and the other airmen waited while more passengers boarded. The plane then took off on its long eastward trek with stops for refueling or crew changes planned for Albuquerque, Kansas City and Chicago before their final destination, Newark.

Thirty-one minutes after take-off from Burbank, Jerry sensed that something was wrong because the cabin remained cold. The pilots announced they were landing in Palmdale because the cabin heating system wasn't working. The passengers were told to remain on board at Palmdale while mechanics drove from Burbank, to repair the heaters.

In 1951, Jerry and the other passengers were aware that problems and delays often plagued cross-country flights, especially among the nonskeds. They had no clue that their scheduled 12-hour trip would turn into a five-day adventure and a near-death experience before they finally arrived in New Jersey.[166]

Upon leaving Palmdale, the C-46, with repaired heaters (they would soon malfunction again), flew across the southern desert to its refueling stop in Albuquerque. Topped off with gasoline in New Mexico, the C-46 then made an uneventful hop to Kansas City, Missouri. This was cross-country flying for passengers in 1951, short hops from city to city because planes like the C-46 consumed so much fuel. This surplus Army nonsked plane had another problem. It simply couldn't hold much fuel. The reason would be revealed only after the near disastrous crash-landing. Jerry remembers that this leg of the flight was normal with good weather, quality service from the crew and proper behavior from the adults and children passengers on board. Most of them slept because the plane departed Burbank at 3:29 am, arrived in Palmdale at 4:39 am, and arrived in Kansas City at 9:08 pm where they were finally allowed to get off, stretch their legs and get something to eat. In Kansas City, the plane also got a new crew consisting of two new pilots and a new stewardess.

---

[166] Nonskeds were born through a loophole in the Aeronautics Act of 1938 designed to help small cargo airplane operators in the Alaskan bush and the Caribbean survive by relaxing the strict regulations imposed on large carriers. They were organized by cunning businessmen who took advantage of cheap war surplus cargo airplanes and jobless pilots returning home from WW II.

In Kansas City, the *99ers*-labeled C-46 flight full of passengers, and without a designated flight number, owned by International Airports, Inc., leased to Robin Airlines, doing business as North Continent Airlines, and with cut-rate fare sold by ticket agency, Major AirCoach, was effectively turned over to rent-a-pilots who the CAB later determined had little or no training or experience with their C-46, the flight companies or each other. It set up a chain of events that would lead to near disaster within hours!

FORMER U.S. ARMY AIR Forces pilot, Lt. Col. Bruce Smelser was home in Marion, Indiana on December 18, 1951, when he got a telephone call from Robin Airlines to meet the plane in Kansas City. Smelser, 35, had flown for several of the nonsked airlines since 1948 and his discharge from the Army. Despite being listed as a chief pilot for Robin Airlines, Smelser was not an airline employee at all. He was a pilot-for-hire, on call for whenever he was needed, and paid only for mileage he flew, plus expenses. He made the 551-mile, 12-hour drive in his car from Marion to Kansas City and met the plane when it landed late at night on December 19. How much he slept before climbing into the cockpit could not be determined by the CAB during its investigation.

Smelser's assignment was to fly the C-46 to Chicago and Newark to complete the 2,900-mile cross-country trip. His co-pilot, Edgar T. O'Leary was already on the plane, having ridden as a passenger from Burbank. This was O'Leary's first flight with Robin Airlines and his first with Captain Smelser. In fact, it was his first on-the-job flight in a C-46. Stewardess Sandy Daine also boarded the plane in Kansas City.

Before re-loading all 45 passengers, Smelser had the C-46 refueled. He then called the U.S. Weather Bureau for the forecast along the route to Chicago and Newark. Based on the weather forecast, Smelser said he planned to fly to Chicago under visual flight rules. However, after taking off from Kansas City at 10:36 pm, Smelser ran into a snowstorm over Burlington, Iowa and he was forced to change his visual flight plan to instruments. Still snowing when they approached Chicago, Jerry said he remembers the plane landing in almost zero visibility and "using a lot of braking and sliding" on the runway at Midway Airport. Jerry reset his watch to one am Eastern Time, December 20. Their adventure was just beginning.

AT ONE O'CLOCK IN the morning on December 20, 1951, 15-year-old Lawrence "Larry" Wilson was snug in his warm bed on the second floor of his family's farmhouse about two miles west of Cobourg, Ontario, Canada. Situated on the northern shore of Lake Ontario, east of Toronto, Cobourg often got hammered with snow from the notorious Lake Effect storms of November and December. Heavy snow and strong winds blew onto his family's small farm through the night blanketing the wide open pastures and fields around them, just a mile from the lake. Larry's parents, Charles and Ruby Wilson, had purchased the farm only recently and they moved in on April 1, 1949.[167] The Wilson's operated the dairy farm with help from a hired man and they sent their milk to the Cobourg City Dairy. Charles Wilson also raised purebred calves and exported them to other countries for extra cash income. Ruby managed the farmhouse and raised their five boys. Their long driveway, off King's Highway 2, was lined with Maple trees inspiring Charles to name their property, *Maple Lane Farms*.[168]

On December 20, 1951, the driveway was plugged with about two feet of freshly fallen snow. The first one up that cold morning was Charles Wilson, who met his hired man, Harold Drinkwater, in the barn for the morning milking. At about 7:30 am, Ruby Wilson left the family's breakfast simmering on the kitchen stove to holler up the stairs for her only boys left at home, Larry and Bob, to get out of bed and ready for school. Larry sleepily sat up in bed and tried to look through the window facing the barn, but he couldn't see anything because the single pane of glass was frosted over from the snowstorm, freezing cold, and the moisture-laden air from Lake Ontario. Larry hurried to get dressed because he had a few farm chores to do before leaving for school.

---

[167] Charles and Ruby Wilson should not be confused with Charles and Ruby Bryant of Sawmill Run.
[168] The Wilson's farm is long gone, replaced by a shopping mall and homes. In 2015, a Canadian Tire store was situated about where the Wilson's house and barn stood. The Wilson's driveway was later named Rogers Road.

JERRY LAUFGRABEN WAS ALREADY dead-tired when the Robin Airlines C-46 prepared for departure from Chicago. He and the 44 other passengers hadn't any quality sleep since the plane left Burbank 24 hours earlier. The snowstorm that gave them such a frightening landing settled over Chicago as their plane was topped off with 413 gallons of gasoline for a total of 775 gallons in three useable fuel tanks. Two of the original six tanks on the plane had been removed and a third was sealed because of a leak, restricting their long-range flying capabilities.[169]

In Chicago, Captain Smelser filed a flight plan for Newark, with LaGuardia Airport in New York City as an alternate, for a 9,000-foot cruising altitude and a proposed lift off at 2:15 am. However, it wasn't until 2:56 am that Smelser radioed the Chicago Midway tower for airways clearance and taxi instructions. He was told to taxi to Runway 13-R for take off five minutes after the departure of Capital Airlines Flight 804. Then, the Robin flight hit another snag. Midway controllers lost the position of a C-46 in their coverage range near Toledo, Ohio and temporarily stopped outbound traffic and then delayed all traffic. During the delay, Smelser held his plane at the head of Runway 13-R for nearly an hour with engines running and fuel burning. He finally was able to release the brakes and lift off at 3:54 am.

Jerry remembers a "miserable snowstorm" during takeoff. "I was 21 and fearless and wanted to get home to Newark so I went along," he said many years later. In forecaster's parlance, the weather report at four am on December 20, 1951, over Chicago was for a 600-foot ceiling (of clouds), visibility 1 1/2 miles, and variable, light snow. Jerry settled into a window seat on the left side of the plane with a close view of the port engine, a powerful Pratt and Whitney R-2800 with a three-blade Hamilton Standard Hydromatic propeller. He watched it spin.

Smelser and O'Leary guided the Robin flight eastward at 9,000 feet over South Bend and Goshen, Indiana on a heading for Toledo along the southern edge of Lake Erie. At 4:47 am, Smelser responded to a

---

[169] Nonskeds sometimes removed fuel tanks when planes were used for short hops to save weight. It allowed for more passengers and baggage within the mandated weight restrictions.

request from the lost C-46 reported by Chicago to relay messages for a heading fix to Toledo air traffic controllers. Three minutes later he advised Toledo controllers that he was encountering 60 mph winds from the East and that his arrival over Toledo would be delayed. For the next 11 minutes after that transmission, Smelser used his properly functioning radio to relay messages between the lost C-46 and Toledo three times. His relays helped the lost plane get a fix on Toledo and land safely at the airport.

Within minutes, however, of the Toledo C-46 getting out of a jam and landing safely, Smelser and O'Leary ran into trouble with their C-46 and got lost themselves. Whatever happened has long been in dispute. Smelser reported that soon after passing Toledo they ran into a severe snowstorm with a mixture of rime (opaque and granular) ice, clear ice, frozen snow, and rain. He said they lost the plane's automatic direction finder (ADF) antenna and that static made it impossible to get a readable signal on the range receiver, ADF receiver, or their manual direction finder receiver.[170] Smelser said he flew by dead reckoning at their assigned altitude of 9,000 feet at a magnetic heading of 120 degrees. This meant that he flew on his assigned path for about two hours just guessing where he might be based on his airspeed, heading, and elapsed time. During this time, at about 5:36 am, Smelser was able, however, to receive and transmit a message with Cleveland controllers requesting his location and estimated arrival time over Youngstown, Ohio. His response, "(we're) having a little trouble getting orientated; will give check as soon as can get a check on it." It's unclear what that meant.

Then, at 5:44 am, Cleveland controllers made an unusual request. They asked Smelser via the VHF radio if he had reversed course at any time and if he was still on an eastward heading. Smelser or O'Leary replied, "Only workable equipment is manual loop. I am southeast of

---

[170] ADF is a radio receiver with antennae used to find the source of a broadcast signal, such as a radio station. Range Receiver is a short-wave navigation system used to receive signals transmitted by aviation beacons placed along a standard flight route. Manual Direction Finder or Radio Direction Finder or Manual Loop is a receiver with a loop antenna used to find the location of an unknown radio signal when one or more known signals are obtainable.

Cleveland along Lake Shore." Their response continued, "Unable to give Cleveland estimate due to head winds which threw us off course, unable to determine estimate." At 5:53 am, Cleveland further requested Smelser's altitude and position. They made several similar calls to the lost C-46 before getting Smelser's reply that the Cleveland radio signal was very weak. Cleveland then sent out a message for all airports along the plane's scheduled route to Newark to contact the lost C-46. Numerous radio calls were leap-frogged from airports in Pittsburgh, Buffalo, Rochester, Harrisburg, Scranton, and Allentown, but there was no response.

From 5:53 am until 7:26 am, for one hour and 33 minutes, Smelser and O'Leary were lost, with no radio contact, somewhere in a large region east of Cleveland, south of Toronto, west of the Finger Lakes and north of Pittsburgh. What they were doing or thinking in the cockpit at the time is unimaginable.

For the 45 passengers, who would not have known they were lost, staying warm was their main concern. About two hours into their flight from Chicago the heaters on board the C-46 failed again and all of the passengers were bundling against the extreme cold inside the cabin.

Sometime after 7 am, Smelser and O'Leary apparently became concerned about a shortage of fuel placing them in a critical situation. Their Pratt and Whitney engines, consuming more than 150 gallons of fuel per hour, had been running for more than four hours. Enveloped with icing at 9,000 feet, the C-46 was still flying in instrument conditions just ahead of a strong pressure gradient with precipitation being pushed into the Great Lakes by a low-pressure trough and cold front extending from northeastern Missouri, Iowa, and Wisconsin. However, the weather forecast available to them in Chicago stated that while flying by instruments would be necessary eastward to Youngstown, they would encounter "contact weather", or sufficient visibility to fly without instruments, east of Youngstown. They should have had mostly clear skies if they had stayed on course. The forecast also indicated that weather conditions well north of their intended route required continued use of instruments with low cloud ceilings and icing expected. Based on the weather they encountered, they should have presumed they were well north of their intended flight route. They didn't.

At 7:26 am, Rochester air traffic controllers, having been asked to repeatedly broadcast calls for the missing plane, finally got a reply. "N-59487 over waters, 2,500 feet, one engine out, low on fuel, position unknown, heading 63 degrees," Smelser told the Rochester controllers. There was no Mayday or call for an emergency, just a simple radio broadcast to controllers in a tower that was not along their planned route. In fact, they didn't question why they were hearing from Rochester when they believed at the time they were close to Newark.

Heard in the Rochester airport control center, Smelser's short clipped sentences and tone indicated his concern and, perhaps fear, over his now critical fuel shortage. He later said he thought at the time he was over the Atlantic Ocean when he descended and saw whitecaps on the water. He was actually over Lake Ontario. During his descent from 9,000 feet in an attempt to find clear skies and his location, Smelser said he transmitted security broadcasts by VHF radio but got no reply. He said that within minutes of spotting the water he thought was the Atlantic, his left engine became rough and surged to such an extent he had to feather the propeller. An experienced military pilot, Smelser should have known immediately that his left engine problem meant that he was running out of fuel! Losing his left engine also meant that Smelser and O'Leary lost their hydraulic-assist for the already heavy controls on the C-46.[171] Without power from the left engine, both pilots would have had to use brute muscle strength to push the pedals and yoke controlling the elevators and ailerons for control and steering of the airplane. Despite the cold cockpit from no heat, sweat beaded on their skin as they squeezed back in their seats, wrestling with controls that were suddenly many pounds heavier.

Sitting in his window seat with a view of the left engine, Jerry Laufgraben's version of when the engine quit is slightly different than Smelser's. "During the night there was a big flash on the left side of the plane, but it kept flying," he said. "I must have dozed off because at daybreak when I woke up, I looked out and saw the propeller feathered. I

---

[171] The C-46's yoke and pedals were even more difficult to push and pull when the left engine, which provided a hydraulic assist, was lost.

figured that was the flash during the night that I saw, but we were still flying on one engine," Jerry said.[172] He also believed they were over the Atlantic. "I looked down and recognized whitecaps on the water and I thought sure we were over the Atlantic Ocean and headed to Newark Airport. We kept flying and I saw more whitecaps, more whitecaps. I began to become a little anxious. Then, off in the distance I see just white."

FROM HIS BEDROOM, LARRY Wilson heard the distinctive sound of the family's 1951 red Studebaker farm truck, with its split screen windshield and rounded fender wells. His father was revving the engine to make a plunge through the deep snow in the driveway and head to the milk processing plant in Cobourg. Larry also recognized the familiar sound of the heavily loaded milk cans clanging in the back of the truck. Just as the Studebaker cleared the driveway and was turning east on Highway 2, Drinkwater, as was his routine at 7:30 am pushed open the large wooden sliding door of the barn to head for the house where he would wait for Charles to return from the dairy before they would eat breakfast together.

AT 7:32 AM, ROCHESTER CONTROLLERS radioed again to the crippled C-46 to turn 180 degrees for a heading to Rochester-Monroe County Airport on the south side of Lake Ontario. The pilots quickly answered, "Not enough fuel, heading zero degrees over land." Unknown to the crew in the C-46, there were several other radio messages crackling over the airwaves at those very moments. Toronto Air Route Traffic Control Center at Malton Airport tracked the plane on radar and attempted to make contact by radio.[173] CF-100 fighter jets from the Royal Canadian Air Force (RCAF) Base at Trenton, Ontario were being readied for takeoff to intercept the intruding plane as Canadian officials tried to identify the mystery aircraft approaching from such a low altitude off the lake. And officers from the Royal Canadian Mounted Police (RCMP)

---

[172] The term "night" was relative because it was December 20th in the northern hemisphere and they took off just after 4 am Central Time.
[173] Malton Airport later became Toronto Pearson International Airport.

were speeding along Highway 2 trying to see in person what kind of plane had invaded their airspace.

At 7:35 am, the right engine quit, most likely from fuel starvation, but there was no time for Smelser and O'Leary to feather the prop. In contrast to the roar of the engine(s), passengers were now enclosed in absolute silence. Stewardess Sandy Daine gave instructions to the passengers to lock arms, lean forward and bury their heads in the crook of their free arm to blunt the impact. She also told them to pray.

Jerry said the passengers never heard from the pilot on the cabin intercom. He looked across the aisle and saw the unfeathered propeller on the right engine still spinning from the force of the air, a condition called wind-milling. It led him to believe the engine was still running. Smelser and O'Leary, busy at the controls, managed to make their last radio transmission to Rochester at 7:38 am. In it, they said, "Sighted (a) small town. Both engines (are) out. Landing wheels up." They were about to put tiny Cobourg, Ontario on the international map.

In the next two minutes, the C-46, acting like a glider, crossed over Carr's Marsh in a northeasterly heading along the shore of the lake between Cobourg and Port Hope. When the plane passed over the Cobourg Dye Works and was approaching the Golden Plow Lodge, Smelser picked the Wilson's farm for his landing. He turned northwest, crossed over Burnham's Farm and Ontario Orchards and, dropping now below 500 feet, he turned back south and easterly with the large plane and its 108-foot wingspan carrying the precious 45 passengers. He was aiming for a large open field covered with what appeared to be a fluffy white blanket. Miraculously, Smelser did a complete circle with both engines out.

AS HAROLD DRINKWATER CLOSED the Wilson's barn door and began walking through a narrow path in the snow toward the farmhouse, he looked off toward the fields. It was 7:40 am. Drinkwater didn't hear much of anything, but he witnessed a most unbelievable sight. One of the largest airplanes in the world simply floated out of the sky just a few feet over the barbed wire fence at the end of the pasture and, with a barely audible puff, scattered snow in all directions while settling into the pasture. Like a giant surfer riding a spraying wave, the plane finally came to a stop within a few dozen yards of the long driveway's large maple trees. Drinkwater stood there for a few moments in disbelief. When he saw the plane's door open and people jumping out into the waist-deep snow, he rushed into the house bursting to spread the news that a huge plane had just landed on the farm.

CAPTAIN SMELSER LEFT THE wheels of the C-46 retracted during the belly landing as he had advised controllers. One report suggested that he lowered the tail gear only to serve as a rudder in the deep snow, but this would not have been possible. The tail gear on a C-46 could only be lowered independently of the main gear by hand cranking it down from a position in the tail of the plane. Both pilots remained in the cockpit and Smelser told the Rochester controllers he was landing with gear up. From the appearance of tracks in the snow, however, he apparently dipped the tail into the snow first for some rudder-like steering ability. It captured the Wilson's barbed wire fence like the arresting gear on an aircraft carrier, but it didn't slow the plane at all. Smelser's piloting was a brilliant display of a crash landing and it worked! The plane made an almost perfectly straight line path through the pasture.[174] It was so smooth that Smelser's coffee never spilled and a passenger couple's sleeping baby never woke up. Upon landing Smelser's primary concerns were the line of maple trees along the Wilson's driveway and the possibility of a fire, despite the loss of power in both engines from empty fuel tanks. He immediately ordered everyone to evacuate the plane.

Jerry and two other airmen were the first to grab the main exit door's handle and open the hatch to escape the plane. Smelser appeared in the cockpit door and screamed, Jerry said, for everyone to get out. They jumped from the open door into the snow several feet below them. It was so deep it cushioned their fall. "I remember jumping into snow up to our butts," Jerry said. "The Wilson boys were running through the snow toward us and we had a long line of people (passengers) marching to the

---

[174] On a present day map the landing would have occurred in the area between New Amherst Blvd., King's Highway 2, Carlisle Street, and Rogers Road.

farmhouse." Within minutes, their near-death crash landing had become a spectacle.

The Wilson's neighboring farmer, Robert Staples, was also hauling milk when he saw the plane come in for the crash landing. When he arrived at the Cobourg Dairy, he told Charles Wilson of the spectacular event but Wilson, knowing that Staples was always joking, didn't believe him. Why Staples continued on to the dairy instead of going to help the passengers is a mystery except that he had his precious milk on board his truck and, seeing that everyone was OK, in typical farmers' fashion he must have considered his milk first.

Drinkwater ran into the Wilson farmhouse to report that "nearly 100 people" were heading toward them from the crash landing. Ruby Wilson confirmed Drinkwater's account with a quick look out the farmhouse door, and then, she scampered upstairs and ordered Larry and Bob to quickly get dressed so they could help.

Excitement pierced the air as Larry rushed out the back door of the house and ran smack into an RCMP officer (Mountie) who got his cruiser stuck in the snow in the Wilson's driveway, blocking the entrance. The Mountie commanded Larry to round up the passengers so he could talk to them. Larry galloped through the deep snow to open a gate between the barn and the house as passengers streamed into the barnyard. One of the women, trying to step into the snow with her open-toed, high-heeled shoes was obviously in pain with red, swollen feet so 15-year-old Larry picked her up in a cradle lift and carried her to the house. He felt like a hero.

Inside the Wilson's 150-year-old farmhouse, the passengers were spread out through all the various rooms. Ruby first helped the women passengers tend to the four children who had been on board by warming milk for them to drink. She then gathered all the socks she could find and handed them out to passengers who had freezing, wet feet. As Ruby tossed more firewood into the kitchen warming stove, Larry dipped into the cellar and threw several scoops of coal into the furnace for more heat throughout the rest of the house. It was fast becoming a chaotic scene with excited passengers chattering away with introductions to the Wilsons.

Smelser went first to the Wilson's telephone and at 7:55 am called Rochester controllers to report their forced landing. Charles Wilson arrived home, leaving the Studebaker truck in the driveway blocked by the Mountie's cruiser, and together the family played host to the passengers and crew. The whole house was buzzing with excitement as each passenger recounted how they braced for the crash and then scampered out of the plane. Everyone kept repeating to one another that it was a miracle no one was hurt and because they didn't yet know what caused the crash landing, they kept congratulating and thanking Smelser for saving their lives. He and O'Leary rejoiced over their fortunate landing but remained quiet about and coyly kept the details of what happened in the cockpit of themselves.

The Mounties called off the emergency at the Trenton Air Base as news that it was an American plane quickly flashed to Cobourg over the provincial police radio. Neighbors arrived with baskets of bread and meat for sandwiches, and with Christmas fruit cakes and cookies. Ruby Wilson made tea, as a British-Canadian tradition, but someone sent for the coffee on the plane and soon she was refilling empty English tea cups with American coffee. Passengers lined up at the Wilson's only large, heavy black dial telephone and began calling family and friends to further spread the news of the crash and assure their relatives that they were OK. One airman asked Ruby for permission to call long-distance to his fiancé who had already postponed one wedding date and now had to cancel another scheduled for the next day, December 21.

When the excitement waned a bit, Larry and Bob Wilson took some of the passengers to the barn where they helped the boys muck out the stalls, throw down feed grain for the cows, slop the pigs, and scatter seed for the chickens. It was a laughable sight for these city slickers from New York and California squishing in the manure on the floor of the Wilson's cow barn in their wingtip Oxfords and two-tone Saddle shoes.

At the farmhouse, Cobourg Police and the RCMP questioned and took statements from passengers who had new details to add to the chain of events. By 11:30 am Ontario Provincial Police were able to send official notification to the U.S. Civil Aeronautics Board, which launched an immediate investigation in conjunction with the Canadian government. It was decided the passengers should be taken to the Trenton Air Base because it was the only facility nearby that could handle such a large group who, because of Canadian Customs regulations, had to remain together. Police sent for Burley Bus Lines in Cobourg and it was the Wilson's good friend, Keith Burley, who showed up at the farm driving a bus, himself. However, because the driveway was still covered with two feet of snow and blocked by the Mountie's cruiser, Burley had to park the bus along Highway 2, a major route between Toronto and Montreal. This caused the passengers, with suitcases, some wearing fur coats and the Wilson boys' wool socks, to walk single file again through the deep snow to get on the bus. Newspaper photographers had arrived by this time and they swarmed the farm snapping pictures of the line of passengers stomping through the snow.[175] The miraculous story was front page news that evening, December 20, 1951, in the Toronto Star and hundreds of other newspapers around the world.

The passengers were taken to makeshift barracks at the air base for a hot dinner. They each got folding cots to sleep on for the night. Jerry said that he and some of the other airmen passengers spent the evening in the air base club calming their nerves with strong Canadian beer.

After breakfast on December 21, Burley loaded the passengers back onto his bus for the trip to Malton Airport for an official head count by Canada Customs and then he drove the passengers to Fort Erie and the International Peace Bridge at the Niagara River on the border with Buffalo. Burley said the border crossing officer declared the "lost souls" from the crash landing could pass through without inspection. It took another 12 hours before Jerry and the other passengers finally arrived at the newly-built Port Authority Bus Terminal in New York's Times Square.[176] He said it was so late it might have been the next day. It's not known how the pilots and stewardess returned to their homes. They were about to undergo an intense investigation. A U.S. Air Force officer-pilot who was sent to the scene in Cobourg to assist the

---

[175] For many years, these photographs of passengers tramping through the snow to the bus were mistaken for passengers getting out of the airplane.

[176] This was before the construction of the New York State Thruway, in 1954.

Canadian investigators said he witnessed both Smelser and O'Leary in the Cobourg police station a few hours after the crash-landing busily attempting to complete a flight plan and fill out other papers in the flight log. They were required to surrender the documents to the investigating authorities. The heroes who landed their C-46 safely in the snow-filled farm field without so much as a scratch among the passengers were trying to cover their tracks.

CHAPTER 19

TRUMAN AND SAFER PLANES

WHEN CAB CHAIRMAN DONALD Nyrop visited Little Valley on January 1 with Sheriff Sigel, he kept a secret. When it was finally revealed, it created a small sensation among the reporters covering the crash event and would lead to dramatic changes in the commercial passenger airlines industry.

Nyrop announced that investigative hearings into the crash of Continental Charters Flight 44-2 would be held in Little Valley on January 17 and 18. When what appeared to be a fast track hearing schedule was confirmed from Washington just days later, the small community began buzzing with excitement. Sheriff Sigel reserved the only courtroom in the old Cattaraugus County Courthouse for the CAB officials to conduct the hearing. The CAB initially believed it would be the first of several hearings to be held in Little Valley, Pittsburgh, Washington, and Miami, but Nyrop was so eager to complete the investigation and release a report that the hearings began and ended in Little Valley. Some suggested a rush directive came from the White House, but there is no record of any such order or even suggestion that it be conducted this way, only a narrative from President Truman to Nyrop that he wanted something done soon about the safety of passengers in airplanes. That the crash investigation of Continental Charters Flight 44-2 was placed on some kind of fast track among the three big ones that month became certain when the investigation report came out. It was first, on March 13, 1952, before the report on the Miami Airlines crash in Elizabeth, which came out on April 13, and the Robin Airlines crash landing in Cobourg, which came out on July 16.[177] Politics was trying to influence Americans' feelings about safety on airplanes.

On January 15, two days before the hearing for Flight 44-2, President Truman sent a letter to Nyrop in which he wrote, *"I've been very much worried about the nonscheduled airlines situation. We are faced with a serious situation and I'd like very much to have some concrete action on it more for the safety and saving of lives than for any other reason."* Earlier in January, Truman asked his aviation aide, Air Force General Robert B. Landry, to look into the problems surrounding the nonsked crashes of 1951, especially those in December, and to issue a report. General Landry was in charge of the President's airplane, *The Independence*.[178] He also advised the President on issues relating to the Air Force and general aviation. Landry kept tabs on the plethora of crashes in 1951, and from his many contacts in commercial aviation and at American airports he realized there was growing hysteria over the crashes and Americans' concern for safety while flying. He correctly sensed the absurdity of a highly publicized plan by residents of Elizabeth to form a human chain across Runway 6 at Newark Airport to stop airplanes from flying over their city. He referred to the advice he prepared for President Truman as "the hysteria report."

Presenting his quickly prepared recommendations to Truman in the first few days of January 1952, Landry's advice was that the nonsked crash and airport problems of 1951 could not be solved by the large and bureaucratic agencies such as the CAA and the CAB. "The airlines

---

[177] The crash report on Flight 44-2 took just 52 days for the completion of the hearing on January 18. It was approved on March 10 and released on March 13. In contrast, crash reports in 2015 typically took more than a year to complete.

[178] This was before the Presidents' airplanes were named Air Force One.

couldn't do it (either). It involved the whole country, not just one state. I think, from what I read in the papers, that maybe the President ought to ask somebody to look into this thing, maybe a survey," Landry said.[179] Landry told Truman that the airport and crash problem among the airlines, especially the nonskeds, needed a reputable expert to study the problem and issue recommendations for the President to fix it. With Nyrop's report to Truman about the carnage he witnessed at the top of Bucktooth Ridge in Napoli still fresh in his mind, the President, who as a Missouri Senator helped craft the Civil Aeronautics Act of 1938, and who took an interest in all things about aviation, readily agreed. Landry suggested national war and aviation hero Jimmy Doolittle for the job. Nyrop agreed that Doolittle would be a good choice. Doolittle's report, *The Airport, and its Neighbors* was issued 90 days later. Landry said in an interview many years later for the Truman Library and Museum that all of the report's recommendations may not have been followed, but it went a long way toward reducing the hysteria over flying after the catastrophes of 1951, especially those in December.

ON JANUARY 17 THE CAB hearing into the cause of the crash of Flight 44-2 began in the courtroom on the second floor of the old courthouse in Little Valley. Built in 1868 and later joined with a jail for 38 prisoners, and the sheriff's residence, the old Cattaraugus County Courthouse was a tall two-story brick and figured-slate building anchored by an imposing 100-foot-tall bell tower on which was mounted a large figurine of an American eagle. Large, heavy double wooden doors opened into the main offices on the first floor of the four-columned front veranda. The second-floor courtroom was cavernous, taking up the entire 56-foot width of the building but leaving enough room in the 82-foot-length for offices for the judges, attorneys, and other court officers. The CAB officials positioned large wooden tables and chairs in the center of the courtroom with its 20-foot-tall ceiling. They left the long bench seats open for the anticipated large crowd of spectators and press. By 1951, the stately old building was already outdated and had

---

[179] General Landry later explained his role during an interview for the Harry S. Truman Library and Museum.

suffered a devastating fire in 1946 which severely damaged the bell tower.[180] The hearing was, perhaps, the most spectacular and widely reported event to take place in the old courthouse aside from the farcical trial of Buffalo mobster and bank robber, 'Baby Face' Palmisano more than a decade earlier. The gangster flashed a toothy grin during his trial. The bank teller remembered it from the day of the robbery and shootout at the State Bank of Randolph. Baby Face went straight to New York's Auburn Prison for years.

EARLY ON THE MORNING of the 17th, Nyrop revealed his secret, one that he hadn't mentioned for strategic reasons. In another first for a CAB chairman and a complete surprise to everyone at the hearing, Nyrop appeared in person, and although not officially on the docket of CAB questioners, he participated in the hearing, playing a key role. He even led the questioning of Continental Charters president John Belding. Nyrop then surprised people again by canceling plans to fly back to his office in Washington after the first day, to stay for the entire two-day hearing. Nyrop's assistants described it as "very unusual" for the CAB chairman to participate in an accident investigation hearing and to stay for the entire proceeding. It demonstrated the importance of this issue to President Truman, Nyrop, the CAB, and American passengers.

It was also part of Nyrop's strategy for dispatching the many problems among the nonskeds without the customary public hearings in Washington which could be influenced by politicians and airlines lobbyists. Unknown to operators in the airlines industry, Nyrop was about to put the nonskeds out of business. It was not just the incessant crashing; during the Robin Airlines investigation, Nyrop's men determined that most, if not all of the nonskeds, were not paying their transportation taxes and "were not subject to a uniform system of accounts and reports." Both the CAB and the Congressional Interstate and Foreign Commerce Committee were investigating the nonskeds' abysmal crash record in early January 1952. They planned to hold the delinquency tax issue to fend off any of the pesky nonsked owners who wished to complain about the crashing probe.

---

[180] The old Cattaraugus County Courthouse was replaced in 1965.

A CAB investigation hearing is not a trial but a method of installing sworn and official accounts from witnesses and those involved in a crash into the investigation record. From this information, the CAB investigators issue a finding for the cause of a crash. In Little Valley on January 17, first up on the witness stand was the assistant director of the CAB's investigation division, Gordon Matthews. He explained how Flight 44-2 was five hours and 40 minutes late arriving in Pittsburgh due to mechanical problems with the newly refitted C-46 in Miami. Another federal agent testified that the plane had been installed in the Continental Airlines fleet only five days before the crash but that it had been "properly modified for civilian use" and that an inspection on December 24 showed the plane to be airworthy. Then, the courtroom spectators heard testimony from the CAA official on duty the night of December 29 at Allegheny County Airport near Pittsburgh. Lester H. Bowman testified that a man he understood to be Captain Victor Harris called him by telephone to file a visual flight plan from Pittsburgh to Buffalo. Bowman said that he replied, "The weather is pretty bad up there," and he suggested that Harris file an instrument flight plan instead. Harris flew the Miami to Pittsburgh leg of the trip under an instrument plan and it could not be determined why he changed to a visual flight plan for the second leg of the trip except for the theory that he was trying to make up for lost time. Then, despite their willingness and eagerness to testify in person, statements taken from Cattaraugus County witnesses who either saw or heard the low-flying plane on the night of December 29 were entered into the record by a CAB official. CAB investigator Richard Hughes went to the homes of John and Florence Jackson and Monty Conklin of Steamburg; Eli Jimerson of Quaker Bridge; Lillian Pierce and Luther Dickson of Onoville; William Fargo of Cold Spring; and several other residents, to gather their sworn statements.[181] Each described the plane flying anywhere from 250 to 550 feet through clouds and heavy fog over their farms and houses that

---

[181] Quaker Bridge was a hamlet on the Seneca Indian Reservation that was flooded with the construction of the Allegheny Reservoir. William Fargo lived in the Town of Cold Spring, but his mailing address was Randolph.

night. Florence Jackson told Hughes the plane was moving in and out of the low hanging clouds surrounding her Steamburg Valley home about six miles south of Bucktooth Ridge. *"It was so low I watched to see if it would hit a hill nearby,"* she said in her statement.

In the courtroom that day in 1951, few knew that this was not the first spectacular airplane crash event in the area. On September 24, 1911, the first airplane ever to fly over Cattaraugus County, the *Vin Fiz Flyer*, made a crash landing on the Willard Jimerson farm at Red House, along the Allegheny River. It was a nationally infamous event with the crude kite-like airplane, built by the Wright Brothers and licensed to the famous daredevil pilot, Calbraith Perry Rodgers. The grandson of Navy Commodore Oliver Hazard Perry was trying to win a $50,000 prize put up by newspaper magnate, William Randolph Hearst, to become the first pilot to fly across the country in 30 days. *Vin Fiz* grape soda was his advertising sponsor, hence the name of the plane. As his crash and three-day delay in Cattaraugus County is a testament, Rodgers failed miserably. He did make it across the country after many more crashes, but 19 days too late to win the cash prize. However, like the Napoli crash it was a national spectacle, and after Rodgers had repaired the plane, thousands of people crammed the Allegheny River valley to watch him take off and fly westward.

Jump ahead 40 years and once again, rural and little-known Cattaraugus County was taking part in an infamous aviation event as scores of spectators packed into the spacious courtroom in Little Valley to hear about who was to blame for the plane crash. Sworn statements from the crash survivors, including George Albert, Lt. Bischof, and Marie Norcia, who boarded the plane in Pittsburgh, were entered into the investigation record. All the survivors said their plane tickets were for a direct, non-stop flight from Pittsburgh to Miami. Norcia said she and other passengers didn't hear about the plan to fly first to Buffalo until they were strapped into their seats. When Norcia asked to be let off the plane, she was told it was too late. The survivors also said they could feel that the flight from Pittsburgh was at low altitude and they experienced turbulence strong enough to make them nauseous. However, they said, aside from the blinking seat belt warning light and the horn that sounded, and admonishments from the stewardesses just before the crash, they were given no verbal warning of any serious danger.

The ticket booking agent for SkyCoach Air Travel Agency in Pittsburgh, William S. Herr, testified that it was Captain Harris who made the decision to load all the Miami passengers for the trip to Buffalo, skip the return stop in Pittsburgh and fly directly from Buffalo to Miami with the new crew. However, it's difficult to believe that reserve pilots CJ Webber and Gus Athas were not part of this decision process or at least informed of the decision since they were to take over as flight crew in Buffalo. Reporters covering the hearing described testimony from the two surviving stewardesses, Dolores Beshears, and Pearl Moon, as *"at odds with the witnesses."* Described in one article as *"pretty,"* Beshears said the cabin announcement to the passengers that they would fly to Buffalo first, *"brought no surprise,"* and, she and Pearl said, *"The passengers taken aboard in Pittsburgh knew all about the change."* When pressed about exactly who made the announcement, though, neither stewardess could remember. It typically would have been the senior stewardess's job to make such an announcement. Moon earlier told reporters that she informed all the passengers of the schedule change but at the hearing she couldn't remember who told them. Both Beshears and Moon described the flight to Buffalo as normal until the crash. They said they couldn't remember much because the crash happened so fast. Their limited sworn statements were a substantial departure from the many recollections they had when questioned earlier by members of the press and from first-person written statements published in newspapers. The result of their testimony came as no surprise, however, because they had plenty of time to consult with company lawyers. At the hearing, Moon and Beshears sat next to their boss, Continental Charters president John Belding, and his attorney. Questioning Belding at the CAB hearing in Little Valley became Nyrop's role on the first day of the hearing and it became clear that this was the reason Nyrop attended and kept his participation a secret until the last minute. Belding spent two and a half hours in the wooden witness chair where he was grilled by Nyrop about the amount of fuel in the plane, pilot training procedures, maintenance programs, record keeping, and weight regulations for the C-46, of which Continental Charters owned or leased four for their cargo and passenger flight operations. Nyrop's inquisition was conducted as if Belding represented all the nonskeds of America. As one of the three key nonsked legislative affairs leaders, he essentially did represent the entire group. It was as if the nonskeds caused the crash, not the pilots, not the plane, not the airline, not the CAB's lax regulations. Whatever his motive, observers in the courtroom that day noted that Nyrop displayed brilliance for placing all the problems of the nonskeds into the public record where he would soon dispose of them in the CAB's new regulations. Belding, a war veteran, and pilot handled Nyrop's questioning with professionalism and grace. He was sympathetic to the families who lost loved ones in the crash, attending the pilots' funerals where he and his wife, Margaret, signed their names in condolence books. He also appeared at Salamanca Hospital visiting the bedsides of the survivors. One press photograph shows Belding holding hands with Pearl as she was propped up in her hospital bed displaying bruised eyes and a very sad face. Before flying himself to Buffalo with his lawyer, Beshears, and Moon to attend the hearing in Little Valley, Belding visited with Captain Harris' wife, Evelyn, at her home near the Miami airport. He offered condolences for the loss of her husband, Vic. However, Belding was also a businessman who claimed his attendance at the crash investigation hearing was voluntary when trying to escape a subpoena for a civil suit thrust into his hands at the Cattaraugus County Courthouse. A judge later ruled Belding had to accept the subpoena because his attendance at the hearing was compulsory. The legal papers thrust into Belding's hands were also the beginning of the end for Continental Charters.

In the first stage of the hearing, Belding withheld some important new details about Continental Charters that he had set upon a path toward expansion just before the devastating crash. Perhaps he understood the reason for the CAB chairman being there in person and the nature of the probing questions about his airline, whose name had become synonymous with all that was wrong with the nonskeds. Seven times since 1948 Continental Charters had been cited for violations of CAB regulations, mostly for overloading their C-46 planes. For these,

Belding paid fines totaling $1,150 without admitting guilt. Belding knew that even a relatively small takeoff weight reduction for the C-46 would further trim the slight profit margin under which the nonskeds operated. Regardless of the weight issue, Flight 44-2, like a C-46 installed in passenger service only days before the crash, was governed by the proposed new weight regulations of 45,000 pounds. Continental Charters' three other C-46s, slightly different models and in service much longer, fell under the old weight limits of 48,000 pounds but were subject to the proposed reduced weight guidelines for all C-46s. Both Nyrop and Belding knew that weight was not the cause of the crash of Flight 44-2 and that the plane was not overloaded for the trip. However, the weight issue, with Nyrop as the first CAB chief to personally attend and participate in a crash investigation hearing, took center stage in the Cattaraugus County Courthouse. It was the beginning of a CAB-charted course to break up the nonsked concept. Stay below 45,000 pounds or don't take off.

The other issue Nyrop focused upon in the Little Valley hearing was fuel. When pilots file an instrument flight plan, they must follow certain pathways at specific elevations set by federal regulations and check in with radio signals along the predetermined route. These are often not the most direct routes to a flight's destination and require more time, fuel and expertise. For example, if Flight 44-2 had chosen to fly an instrument plan to Buffalo, Captain Harris would have had to fly almost due north to Erie, Pennsylvania and then northeast along the shore of Lake Erie into Buffalo, all the while checking in at certain markers and at predetermined elevations. This type of trip requires more fuel for the extra distance, climb and descent, and greater fuel reserve for alternate airports. In contrast, a visual or contact low elevation direct flight consumes less fuel for the flight and requires less to be held in reserve for alternate airports. Both Nyrop and Belding agreed that Harris miscalculated his fuel consumption on the flight from Miami to Pittsburgh. The plane burned a considerable amount of fuel during the Miami delay. What they could not agree on was how much fuel remained in the C-46 at Pittsburgh when Harris filed his visual flight plan for Buffalo. Nyrop knew that micro-managing fuel was another method of padding the slim profit margins of the nonskeds. Fuel mismanagement had been the primary reason the Robin Airlines C-46 crash-landed in Canada a month earlier. Hammering Belding and his chief pilot, Captain Paul Satterfield, about fuel management, down to what may have been the plane's last 250 gallons, was part of the CAB's crackdown on what it called failure by the nonskeds to ensure plane and engine maintenance and operational procedures at a high level. Belding's response: "That plane had plenty of fuel." And he stuck to it.

However many gallons of fuel were left when the plane crashed, it's certain it did not run out. Both engines were developing power at the time of the crash and the survivors said they could hear, smell and feel the fuel dripping from the wreckage immediately after the impact. Nyrop's insistent questioning about fuel, however, focused on the small amount of reserve fuel that would have been left over if the plane had made it to Buffalo. Some estimates were as low as 150 gallons; not enough to make it safely to an alternate airport if required, and certainly an example of poor operating procedure.[182] By questioning the CAA aviation safety agent from Miami, Nyrop also focused on the nonskeds' failures to maintain pilot training and proficiency. Many times in recent years the CAB crash investigations found that nonsked pilots had skipped, skimped, or failed to take their required training courses on schedule or at all and that the airline companies had sometimes disregarded the importance of the training requirements. Miami agent Jasper Rafferty testified that when he gave Captain Harris his most recent instrument test on a C-46 in September 1951, he failed some of the maneuvers. Allowed an immediate retest, however, Harris passed the exam and was approved to continue flying with his instrument rating on multi-engine planes.

The CAB officials testifying at the hearing confirmed that poor weather conditions on the night of the crash were not conducive to flying a plane visually. Forecaster Herbert D. Crawford said the rain and

---

[182] The nearest airport to Buffalo was about 20 miles away in Niagara Falls but commercial flights typically used Rochester, 70 miles away, for an alternate airport because the weather was the most frequent cause of diversions.

fog along nearly the entire Pittsburgh to Buffalo route made it impossible to fly the plane contact.[183] Another federal government weather forecaster, Philip J. Lucid, working at Pittsburgh's Allegheny County Airport, said he was "relatively sure" that neither Captain Harris nor co-pilot Hans Rutzebeck called the airport weather station or appeared in person for a report on weather conditions along the route. A Detroit CAB investigator who handled accident reconstruction told the hearing there was no structural or mechanical failure of the airplane that might have caused the crash. The engines of the C-46 were developing power at the time of the crash, he said.

One revelation that came from the hearing appeared to support some other cause of the crash. The survivors stated, and the wreckage showed, that the plane did not fall from the sky or plunge into the ground at an angle but that it simply flew into the trees atop Bucktooth Ridge in nearly level flight. U.S. Weather Bureau aviation forecaster Crawford told the hearing that when he tested the two altimeters recovered from the wreckage of Flight 44-2 they showed discrepancies in measuring altitude. Altimeter readings are based on barometric pressure and, according to Crawford, the pressure on Bucktooth Ridge at the time of the crash was 29.79 millibars. When Crawford tested the altimeters, they showed the pressure of 29.88 millibars. CAB safety unit expert Matthews translated this to mean that the plane's altimeters were 90 feet off at the time of the crash. This meant the plane was actually flying 90 feet lower than the elevation displayed on the altimeters at the time of the crash. Would this have made a difference? Probably not, since Continental Charters did not even consider this area to be mountainous. Additionally, Captain Harris did not have specific information about exact elevations of the ridges and hills below him, and he may not have realized he was 11 miles off direct course. However, it should be noted that the plane crashed less than 100 feet below the top of Bucktooth Ridge. Another 90 feet higher and it may have cleared the

---

[183] Contact is a term for flying a plane visually in contrast to flying by instruments. Flying contact meant that a pilot would always have visual contact with the ground. As soon as he lost visual contact, he was required to change to instrument rules and notify controllers of such.

ridge (barely). After that, there were no more similar-sized peaks on a straight flight path into Buffalo.

When Nyrop was completing his grilling of Continental Charters' managers on the second day of the Little Valley hearing, he calmly asked Satterfield, and then Belding, if they considered Flight 44-2 to be a "good operation." Satterfield replied, "No flight(s) which fail(s) to reach their destinations are good operations." Then, Satterfield and Belding were coaxed by Nyrop into revealing company information they had kept secret until now. Within days after the crash, Belding and Satterfield instituted new rules for Continental Charters' pilots. They could no longer perform any portion of a night flight under visual flight rules. And, they could no longer use automatic pilot when flying below 3,000 feet. Perhaps these concessions were part of an arranged agreement with the CAB because Belding and Satterfield also announced at the hearing that they imposed on their company pilots that all future night flights must follow the CAA charted airways. Within weeks, the CAB followed suit and instituted the emergency weight limits. Then, it imposed new or stricter regulations on aircraft and engine maintenance, pilot training programs, use of itinerant pilots, record keeping, fire protection, certification of repair stations, and imposed what became known as the Continental Charters rule; *"all nonsked flights at night, especially along routes not equipped with adequate navigation and communications facilities, are to use civil airways unless specific approval has been obtained from the CAA to operate off-airways."* Items not addressed during the hearing were the theft of cash from a dead passenger and the theory that everyone who survived was fortunate to be riding on the back of the plane. These were not critical components to the CAB probe but if they had been discussed at the hearing, they would have provided more details of how the survivors made it out alive and how they handled themselves afterward. The fact that each survivor had been in the back of the plane was repeated over and over in the hundreds of newspaper reports in the first few months of 1952. The theory that passengers are always safest in the back of a plane appears to have originated with this crash, especially from the many reports that two survivor passengers, George Albert, and Eva Woodward changed seats with victims, Elizabeth Albert, and Gus Athas, at the last minute. Fear of being killed in a crash was so prevalent among new airplane passengers that booking agents reported that for many years after 1951, nervous ticket buyers would often request a seat in the back of the plane hoping to improve their chance of survival in the event of a crash.[184]

The suppression of prosecution of the corpse pickpocket theft involving more than $700 cash pinned inside a dead passenger's clothing by an unnamed survivor was absent from the hearing. The quiet handling of the crime was apparently orchestrated by Sheriff Sigel, with help from the dead passenger next of kin. In 2015, values, the cash amounted to about $6,400. While there is no official record of the resolution of the theft, Cattaraugus County residents have surmised for years that Sheriff Sigel quietly went to Salamanca Hospital and discreetly confronted the culprit who carried out the macabre body rifling theft, whoever it was.[185] A guess of survivor's names could easily be whittled down to a few. Of all survivors, four were still trapped in the wreckage on December 30 and couldn't have done it. Several others, who were able to gather at the campfire, had injuries so severe they couldn't have done it either. That left just a few who would have been physically able to steal the cash. They were the mobile survivors who regularly returned to the plane to search for food and dry clothing. The cash was prudently handed over to Sheriff Sigel when he confronted the thief in the hospital, and the crime was never prosecuted because the victim's family declined to press charges. Nor was it revealed from which passenger's body the bills were stolen; only that it was a woman. In contrast to the stories of bravery and heroism, it was the only despicable act during the tragic event.

---

[184] This perception was only a theory, however, and was not supported by statistics until 2007 when *Popular Mechanics* analyzed 36 years of plane crash data and determined that passengers have a 69 percent survival rate in the back of a plane versus 49 percent in the front.

[185] This revelation, however, wasn't made until a year later when newspaper reporters who covered the crash questioned Sheriff Sigel about it for anniversary stories on the big event.

AT THE CLOSE OF the hearing, Belding returned to the stand to testify that he still believed the C-46 was "rugged, well-constructed, and capable of handling the gross weights assigned. We have found the aircraft eminently satisfactory in every respect," Belding said. Despite the many deaths and the families in financial and psychological ruins as a result of the crash, it was clear the C-46's takeoff weight issue was the main event at the Little Valley hearing.

With that, Nyrop added the final words thanking Sheriff Sigel and the residents of Cattaraugus County, who performed such a rapid search and rescue for the survivors and the dead. He then turned his attention toward Belding and Continental Charters, "You and your company are to be commended for this very constructive action to improve your operations, Nyrop said." It was too little too late, however. The first of several lawsuits filed against Continental Charters was entered in Circuit Court in Miami by Irma Wessel Link of Pittsburgh, mother of the 19-year-old survivor, Edward Wessel, on January 7, 1952. It claimed that Wessel's feet were frozen and that he suffered permanent injuries to his head and body. It asked for more than $250,000 in damages. Along with several other lawsuits, demanding more than a million dollars, filed in early 1952 by other survivors, including Mary Battista, Anna Piso, and Eva Woodward, and victims, such as Benjamin Siegel, Roy Hemphill, and Albert Dichak, they worked concurrently with the new C-46 regulations to drive Continental Charters into bankruptcy and eventually out of business.

CHAPTER 20

ELIZABETH II

WHEN CAB CHAIRMAN DONALD Nyrop departed Little Valley on January 18, his second time, to return to Washington, he had both the Flight 44-2 crash investigation and his plan to transform America's abysmal nonsked airlines at an accelerated pace. He quickly ran out of time. Even before the reams of legal paperwork from the two-day hearing were unboxed, another plane from Newark Airport crashed into Elizabeth. With his memo to Nyrop to fix the crashing problem only seven days old, President Truman was saddened when he heard about the second Elizabeth crash. It claimed the life of a prominent American, the President's friend.

ON THE AFTERNOON OF January 22, 1952, an American Airlines Convair 240 passenger plane with twin Pratt and Whitney R-2800 engines was turned away from its scheduled flight from Buffalo to Chicago because of severe winter weather conditions over Lake Erie, southern Ontario, and Michigan.[186] Instead, the 1948 Convair plane was renamed Flight 6780 for

---

[186] The Convair, both name, and company, was the result of a merger of the Consolidated Aircraft Corporation and the Vultee Aircraft Company. Briefly named Consolidated-Vultee, it eventually became simply Convair and was

Rochester, Syracuse, and Newark where the upstate New York, eastern Pennsylvania, and New Jersey snowy weather, while poor enough to require instrument flight, was somewhat better than to the west of Buffalo. The pilot was a highly-seasoned veteran. Captain Thomas John Reid, 33, who lived in Elizabeth with his wife and children, had learned to fly while a student at Georgia Tech in Atlanta. He was an ATC pilot during World War II and had flown for American Airlines since the end of the war. His family treasured a photograph of Captain Reid as part of a crew that flew Saudi Arabian Prince Faisal bin Abd Al-Aziz in the late 1940s. Of Reid's 7,062 hours piloting planes, 2,483 had been in Convairs and many of them over the Buffalo to Newark route. He was extremely familiar with landing at Newark and had performed six instrument landings at the airport since October 1951, all of them on the longest strip, Runway 24-6. Reid was the kind of pilot that passengers wanted in the cockpit when something went wrong.

The Convair's instrument flights to Rochester and Syracuse were uneventful that day although somewhat late arriving in the snow. In Syracuse, Reid and his co-pilot, Lawrence (Bud) S. Iudicello, 29, of Easton, Pennsylvania, again checked the weather at the American Airlines office. They reported that they saw no problem with instrument flight to Newark. They expected to encounter light snow, sleet, and freezing rain. The plane was topped off with 340 gallons of fuel for a total of 900 gallons in the Convair's tanks, more than enough to return to Syracuse or alternate airports, Albany, and Windsor Locks, Connecticut. In Syracuse, the final passenger count by Stewardess Marilyn Ruth Siegle, 21, of Darby, Pennsylvania, was 20, including a few VIPs whose deaths grabbed the attention of policy makers in Washington. John F. Chester, 45, was a former *Associated Press* editor and war correspondent, who was the public relations director for Carrier Air Conditioning Corporation of Syracuse. He and two Carrier executives boarded the flight in Syracuse for a business trip to New York. Also on board were executives from the Wilkening Manufacturing Company, Philadelphia; Fiber Tex Fabric Company, New York City; Oxford Button Company,

---

later absorbed by larger aircraft companies.

New York City; Detrex Corporation, Detroit, Michigan and Maplewood, New Jersey; Hernon-Pearsall Company, New York City; Farm Bureau Insurance Companies, Columbus, Ohio; four Syracuse University students, two employees of the CAA working on future airport radar and navigational systems for airports, and two employees of American Airlines. Also on board the plane that day because of a last-minute decision to change from his scheduled nine-hour train ride from Buffalo on the New York Central was former Secretary of War and President Truman's former nominee to the U.S. Supreme Court, Judge Robert P. Patterson, 60, of Philipstown, New York and New York City.[187] President Truman was already on alert because of the many crashes among passenger airlines in 1951 and the death of a close friend in Judge Patterson showed how the crashes were impacting all Americans, not just budget travelers.

ROBERT PORTER PATTERSON WAS a decorated U.S. Army hero from World War I. After the war, a distinguished law career led him to the highest levels of government. During the war, Captain Patterson, along with two corporals, performed a daring daylight reconnaissance mission into German enemy lines on August 14, 1918, near the Vesle River in Bazoches, France. He wrote about his wartime near-death experience many years later. *"Suddenly we came upon a nest of Germans in a shell crater, killed two, and I got caught there for the rest of the day. The German fire got so heavy, I suddenly decided to crumple up and play dead. For hours, I had to lie on my stomach in no man's land, surrounded by bodies, in full view of two German machine-gun nests. I was still alive by nightfall, unwounded, and able to make a run for safety,"* Patterson explained. Realizing their captain was trapped, five other soldiers of lesser rank crawled

---

[187] Secretary Patterson's country home was described by national media as being in West Point but his family farm was across the Hudson River from the U.S. Military Academy, in the Town of Philipstown. Judge Patterson and his wife, Margaret, lived on the farm with their son, Robert, Jr., daughters Aileen, Susan, and Virginia, and two servants. They also maintained an apartment in Manhattan. A biographical profile of Sec. Patterson was published by his law firm, Patterson, Belknap, Webb & Tyler, New York City.

to him on their bellies. When the German's opened fire pinning all of them in the mud, other American soldiers tossed hand grenades until each of the stranded men returned. They had saved Patterson's life. For his bravery and *"extraordinary heroism,"* Patterson was awarded the Distinguished Service Cross. He was later wounded in battle, awarded the Purple Heart and promoted to Major. Born in Glens Falls, New York on February 12, 1891, Patterson was graduated from Schenectady's Union College and Harvard Law School. From a law practice in New York City, he was named U.S. District Court Judge for the Southern District of New York but his stint on the bench was interrupted when he volunteered for the Army as America entered the war. Returning to his law practice for several years after the war, Patterson was appointed to the U.S. Circuit Court of Appeals in 1939, and in 1940 he was named Assistant Secretary of War under Secretary Henry L. Stimson.[188] Patterson's office organized procurement and delivery and supplies for the war. Because he was in charge of America's war mobilization, Patterson would have been involved in or at least aware of the decision for the Army to take over Newark Airport and expand Runway 6 nearly into Elizabeth.[189]

After World War II, Democratic President Truman tagged Republican Judge Patterson to be on the Supreme Court to fill the vacancy of retired Pennsylvania Justice Owen J. Roberts. However, the two leaders determined Patterson would be more valuable to the war department. Truman appointed Patterson Secretary of War on September 27, 1945, and he served in that post until July 18, 1947, a period when the military branches were consolidated into the Department of Defense. Years

---

[188] Assistant Secretary was later retitled Under Secretary.
[189] Judge Patterson's son, Robert, Jr., served in the Air Force during World War II, assigned to a B-24 bomber crew known as *The Available Jones*. He broke his elbow and was shipped home just before his crew flying on the renowned raid on the oil fields of Ploesti, Romania, temporarily destroying them from the Germans on August 1, 1943. Their B-24 Liberator was hit, and they ditched in the Ionian Sea. Crew members were captured by a German U-Boat and imprisoned. Patterson recovered from his broken elbow, returned to the war and flew on a total of 45 bombing missions. Robert Patterson, Jr., also became a federal judge in New York.

later it was revealed that Patterson was a decision maker in the development and use of the atomic bomb to end World War II. Interred at Arlington National Cemetery, the cemetery website reports that one of Secretary Patterson's proudest achievements was his responsibility for desegregation of the U.S. Army.

AS THE AMERICAN AIRLINES Convair made its final approach to Newark Airport on January 22, Patterson had been in private law practice for four years and was returning home from a client meeting in Buffalo with Thomas J. Watson, Sr., chairman of IBM. Patterson was a seasoned traveler and in 1951, for those who could afford it, canceling a train reservation when a flight suddenly became available was growing more common. With its Midwestern flight canceled because of poor weather, the Buffalo to Newark flight became available and Patterson grabbed it. Despite stops in Rochester and Syracuse, he was saving considerable travel time by avoiding several hours on the train. Because it was the longest, Runway 6 (24-6) was the instrument landing strip at Newark and, depending upon winds, it often required planes to come in from the southeast, directly over Elizabeth. In fact, the glide path for an approach from the southeast was slightly more than three blocks away from Captain Reid's home at 611 South Broad Street in Elizabeth. He could easily look down on his house as he came in for landings.

In January 1952, controllers working the Newark Airport Ground Control Approach Radar were housed in a rudimentary trailer with ten-mile and three-mile dual precision scope radar screens showing vertical elevation and lateral deviation from the prescribed glide path for airplanes. Other controllers were positioned in the airport's new glass tower from where they could use binoculars to easily see across the vast marshland on the south side of the airport into Elizabeth.[190]

As Captain Reid radioed his required position report to controllers while flying over Linden, south of Elizabeth, the weather ceiling at the

---

[190] In 1951-52 there were several square miles of marshland separating Newark Airport from the City of Elizabeth. It has since been filled in and is now part of the airport runway system, a massive fuel farm, and aviation shipping facilities surrounded by Amelia Earhart Drive.

airport was 400 feet with visibility of three-quarters of a mile, and with light rain and fog. However, minutes earlier, Reid had flown through icing conditions as he descended through 4,000 feet which, by company regulations, required the use of carburetor heat to prevent icing in his engines. The pilot of another American Airlines Convair, which landed just five minutes before Reid's approach, reported that he used carburetor heat on his plane. It's a simple process whereby the pilot trips a switch that diverts hot engine exhaust into the carburetor to prevent or melt ice. However, it causes a momentary reduction in power from the engine, and under extreme conditions can lead to engine detonation, a sudden burst of burning gasses in piston chambers under intense heat and pressure. In some circumstances, detonation can lead to engine failure.

As he approached the glide path at about five miles out, Reid was given clearance to land, immediately following the previous American Airlines Convair, on Runway 6. At that moment, the only issue between Reid and the controllers was his lateral position. Initially, the Convair was running 300-900 feet left of its glide path. Then, at just a half-mile from the tall tower of the Union County Courthouse in Elizabeth, and near the scene of the crash of the Miami Airlines C-46 just 37 days earlier, controllers advised Reid he was 900 feet to the right of the glide path. Within seconds, the Convair disappeared from the controllers' radar.

Witnesses reported to the CAB investigators that Reid's plane came in over Elizabeth extremely low and with one engine backfiring while the other engine roared with intensity. If carburetor icing had occurred during the approach and Reid had applied more power to his suddenly weaker engine, it could have caused backfiring or surging of either engine. Among 26 witnesses interviewed by the CAB, most agreed that the plane appeared over Elizabeth at about 100-150 feet and traveling east. Noises were described as "loud bangs with a roar, rumbling as it passed over, (like the) sound of a car when all spark plugs are not working," and, "the noise stopped, the pilot speeded up motors as loud as he could."

Vincent J. O'Connell said he was standing in his Fay Avenue yard at 3:43 pm when he heard one engine backfire three times and then one motor seemed to stop. He said the plane seemed to veer sharply to the right. Narrowly missing St. Mary of the Assumption Catholic School and Battin High School for Girls on South Broad Street, across from St. Elizabeth Hospital, was fortunate. Most, but not all of the students had gone home 45 minutes earlier.[191] The fuel-laden Convair crashed into two large wood frame homes at 306 and 310 Williamson Street, which had been converted into apartments. Captain Reid's wife, Henrietta Paczkoski Reid, 30, and expecting a baby amid their plans to move into a new house in Point Pleasant Beach, New Jersey, had been preparing for a birthday party for her mother. She heard sirens and fire trucks pass by their home, just three blocks south and one block west of the crash scene. On the phone within minutes, she was told it was, in fact, an American Airlines plane. She said her heart sank as she just knew it was her husband.

The Convair smashed into the ground at 3:43 pm, January 22, 1952, while generally flying east-southeast over South Broad Street, and into the homes along Williamson Street between South and Montgomery Streets. Elizabeth police said a hero, Carmen Venezia, 21, "dashed into 310 Williamson Street and came out with a woman, her daughter, and a grandchild." Two Elizabeth police officers tore away some wreckage and rescued Rose Caruso from her flaming kitchen at 306 Williamson Street. Teachers who were finishing up work for the day at Battin High School across the street witnessed the only survivors from the homes. "People came running out into the street. One woman was screaming, "my baby is in there." Another witness, foundry worker Peter Lesniak, told reporters at the scene, "I'll never forget the screams of the dying. I was there in a minute, but I couldn't do anything…the flames. It was a miracle any of the people got out of those houses. I knew many of them and I couldn't help them," he said.

One of the children who didn't get out was seven-year-old Donna Mandel, who lived with her parents, Albert and Florence Mandel, and her toddler sister, Linda, in a small house in the neighborhood. Donna Mandel was killed and Linda was severely burned from the crash. In

---

[191] St. Elizabeth later became Trinitas Hospital.

HANG ON AND FLY 291

1954, the Mandel's produced a third daughter, Judy Mandel, who in 2009 wrote a book about the family's difficulty coping with their loss. Its title is *Replacement Child*.[192]

Rescue crews in Elizabeth jumped into action. It was just over a month from the last big plane crash in their city and they knew too well what they had to do. The Convair had crashed almost vertically into the ground, catching the two large houses on fire and killing seven occupants in the homes, including children. All 23 on board the plane were killed instantly. The two engines were found just feet apart and the main fuselage was found destroyed but within a small area around the homes. Witnesses counted three explosions followed by screams from women and children running or being rescued from the homes by neighbors. As it grew dark within the hour, rain only added to the dismal scene.

CURIOSITY AGAIN GOT THE best of nine-year-old Jack Rescoe, who had only recently gone to see the aftermath of the Miami Airlines crash in Elizabeth. He rode his bicycle along South Broad Street, following the sound of the sirens and the odor from the burning wreckage. He was familiar with the neighborhood because he and his brothers were born at St. Elizabeth Hospital and his great aunt lived at 412 South Broad Street. Jack's entrance to the scene was blocked, however, and seeing little, he simply turned around on his bike and rode home in the drizzling rain. Within weeks, young Jack would wake up in the morning to hear his father report that it had happened again. He would curiously make his way to the scene of a third fatal plane crash in Elizabeth and witness still more carnage on the streets.

ONCE AGAIN, ELIZABETH POLICE, firefighters, and volunteers passed bodies and body parts hand over hand from the American Airlines wreckage to stretchers illuminated by lights. The bodies were then lined up with planks laid across the mud in an empty lot. A priest from a

---

[192] Author Judy Mandel, who worked as an editor on this book, said it was probably her mother, Florence, who was the woman running from the house shouting that her baby was still inside.

nearby church performed last rites as the bodies were removed to the straw-lined garage floor at Haines Funeral Home for identification.

At the White House that night, President Truman issued a statement with kind words for his friend, Secretary Patterson, as *"a great American and a great public servant,"* and condolences to his family. Despite being members of opposing political parties, Truman and Patterson were friends from when Patterson was named Assistant Secretary of War and when then-Senator Truman was chairman of a special Senate Committee to investigate graft among recipients of the National Defense Program and its $10 billion buildups for the war. The publicity and notoriety the Missouri Senator gained from chairing this prominent committee thrust him forward to become President Roosevelt's choice for Vice President. Truman called Patterson one of the true heroes of World War I and one of the eminent figures in the buildup and victory of World War II. Condolences and tributes also poured in from war Generals Omar Bradley and George Marshall. Patterson's funeral at the Washington National Cathedral was attended by President and Mrs. Truman, Secretary of State Dean Acheson, Generals Bradley and Marshall, and Generals James "Jimmy" Doolittle and Maxwell Taylor, among many other Washington dignitaries. In Patterson's will, he left $200 to each of the five soldiers who saved his life in World War I. As the White House condolences for Secretary Patterson were transmitted around the nation, a period of mourning set in. Around Newark Airport, and especially in Elizabeth, shock turned to anger, again.

Whether it was a nonsked or a major involved in the Elizabeth crash, Americans didn't know the difference or care. It was simply another large passenger plane crash. They did, however, want something done about it. On January 31, just one month after the devastating crashes of December 1951 and nine days after the second Elizabeth crash, the CAB imposed its special regulation on all C-46s, reducing their maximum take-off weight to 45,000 pounds. It spelled the beginning of the end for the nonskeds, many of which used Newark Airport. In Elizabeth, the anger and demands to close the airport were revving louder than the hundreds of airplanes that took off and landed there daily.

WHEN THE ARMY RELINQUISHED Newark Airport after the war, there were eight airlines operating 78 daily flights to cities all over the world. The planes were using the Army's three long intersecting runways, including Runway 24-6. As air travel grew, airport management was taken over by the Port of New York Authority, which instituted a master plan for expansion. Along with a new passenger terminal to replace the old administration building, the Authority developed a new concept for parallel runways. It purchased more than 880 acres of land and marsh, some within the City of Elizabeth. The cost for the massive expansion project was estimated at more than $50 million, but it was scheduled to take more than seven years. That didn't sit well with residents of Elizabeth.

By the time of the American Airlines crash, the outcry to close Newark Airport had been long and bitter. Mayor James T. Kirk had guided the City of Elizabeth since 1939 and had led a public demand since 1946 to remove the airport. He called it a "continuous umbrella of danger" even as he personally led the rescue and fire-fighting in the American Airlines crash. "Planes landing and taking off from Newark Airport are a constant threat. The airport is mislocated," he said. After the American Airlines crash, the mayor's charges were amplified because, for the first time it appeared, people in Washington were listening. CAB chairman Donald Nyrop made his second on-scene visit to a major airlines crash when he personally toured Elizabeth to survey the wreckage of the American Airlines plane. Nyrop vowed that the federal government would make a "full and careful examination of citizen demands to stop the planes using Newark Airport from skimming rooftops (in Elizabeth)."

Before the violent and fatal crashes in December and January, most complaints from Elizabeth residents about the airport dealt with the noise of the planes. With the end of Runway 6 just two miles from the city limits and pointed directly at them, the roaring planes taking off and landing at all hours of the day and night kept people awake. Many prophesied there would continue to be catastrophic crashes in their heavily populated neighborhoods. They were correct.

On January 24, two days after the American Airlines tragedy, more than 500 Elizabeth residents crammed into City Hall for what was described on widely distributed fliers as an *"indignation meeting"* called by the Elizabeth City Council. After a moment of silence to remember the victims of the American Airlines crash, council members approved a resolution demanding a full investigation of Newark Airport's operations and any future expansion plans *"to remedy intolerable and unbearable"* conditions. Residents and council members further pressed their demands to move the airport to another location. Elizabeth City Councilman Thomas Dunn made a prophetic statement to the fired up crowd. "The first tragedy, we looked for excuses," he said. "The second, we will try to explain. But a third would be murder!" For a few seconds, there was silence among the people gathered at Elizabeth City Hall. The word murder stunned the crowd but only briefly. Someone started clapping and then everyone else joined in. Elizabethans were united.

SOMETIME AFTER THE AMERICAN Airlines crash and all the funerals there was another gathering to mourn the victims. Mrs. Margaret Tarleton Winchester Patterson, the widow of Secretary Patterson, respectfully hosted Captain Reid's wife and her two young daughters at the Patterson farm just across the Hudson River from West Point. Mrs. Patterson had been a dignified supportive spouse during her husband's long legal and political career. She was a former director of the Army-Navy Relief Society and founder of the Junior Army-Navy Guild Organization. Her only son, Robert Porter Patterson, Jr., who would later become a federal judge, had flown 45 bombing missions during World War II in B-17s and B-24s. A year after the crash that claimed her husband's life, Mrs. Patterson filed a $2.6 million lawsuit against American Airlines in what would be, at the time, one of the largest damage claims against a commercial passenger airline.[193] Henrietta Reid had suffered a grief-induced miscarriage before attending the sad and informal gathering at the Patterson farm. Reid's daughter was too young to remember the occasion but said she much later learned from someone who was in the Newark Airport radar trailer at the time of the crash that "something (in the plane) did the opposite of what it should have." Captain Reid's daughter received her father's wedding band as a family keepsake.

---

[193] In 2015 dollars, the amount would be $22.9 million.

He so valiantly fought the controls of the stricken airliner that it forever bent his ring. Both his wrists were broken in the crash.[194]

THE CAB RELEASED ITS theory for the cause of the crash on April 28, 1952. It too may have been fast-tracked because it came out well before the report on the Robin Airlines crash in Canada and soon after the report on the Miami Airlines crash in Elizabeth. Because of the lack of physical evidence, however, it was forced to *"advance conjecture as to cause of the aircraft's rapid descent. Whatever happened during the very short period of time before impact was of such nature that it was beyond the capabilities of both pilots to (make) a complete recovery."* Despite Captain Reid's long training, expertise and experience as a Convair pilot and company rules that required the use of carburetor heat during icing, the CAB ruled there was *"insufficient evidence to predict a probable cause... but there was some evidence of carburetor icing, followed by severe surging."*

ON JANUARY 25, 1952, AS A 19-gun salute honored Secretary Patterson during his burial service at Arlington National Cemetery, and the American flag draped over his coffin was presented to Mrs. Patterson, President Truman was already contemplating what to do about the hysteria over crashes among the nation's airlines.[195] A decision, however, wouldn't come soon enough. Within 18 days of Patterson's funeral and before Truman could appoint a famous national hero to investigate and offer solutions to the nation's airport and airlines safety problems, it happened again. Incredibly, a third large plane filled with passengers crashed into Elizabeth. It advanced a long-held theory about the safety of passengers in a plane and shut down Newark Airport for four months.

"A THIRD WOULD BE murder," Elizabeth City Councilman Thomas Dunn had said to his constituents on January 24, 1952. That was two days after the American Airlines crash and 39 days after the Miami Airlines

---

[194] Captain Reid's daughter made these comments for researchers at Arlington Cemetery.net.
[195] A 19-gun salute honors someone at the position of a cabinet secretary. Twenty-one gun salutes are for the national flag and Presidents.

crash in their city. Dunn wouldn't have long to wait for his admonishment to come true.

IN WASHINGTON ON FEBRUARY 11, a congressional subcommittee was scheduled to begin hearings into the fatal crash of the American Airlines plane that killed Judge Patterson on January 22. For the hearing, the Port Authority of New York issued a press release calling Newark Airport one of the safest in America. Early that morning, the hearing was quickly postponed and the press release was asked to be withdrawn. The night before, at 10:33 pm, February 10, a National Airlines DC-6 arrived at New York International Airport in Idlewild from Washington, West Palm Beach, and Miami.[196] After unloading passengers, the tanks of the large plane, with four Pratt and Whitney R-2800 engines, were filled with fuel and a new crew was assigned for a short hop to Newark to pick up passengers and then a return trip to Florida. The plane arrived at Newark at 11:35 pm. There, mail, baggage, air freight and 59 passengers, including an infant, were loaded for the overnight non-stop flight to Miami. The weather forecast called for clear skies with ceilings of 30,000 feet all the way down the east coast. Stars would be visible. It was a perfect night for flying.

The Douglas DC-6 was ideal for this kind of flight. Luxurious and spacious for 1952, some DC-6s were equipped with fold out seats and fold-down overhead luggage bins where extra paying passengers could sleep in a berth similar to those found on overnight trains. It also had a reversible pitch or reverse thrust Hamilton Standard Hydromatic propellers, developed during the war, to help slow down a plane during a landing on a short runway or when a pilot overshot the head of a runway. This did not mean the propellers would spin backward. Rather, it meant that through an electrically charged switch controlled by the pilot, the air cutting edge of the props would pivot while they were spinning, pushing air forward and providing reverse thrust. Pilots sometimes used the reverse pitch to back up their DC-6s from terminals and turn them around while on the tarmac. The sleek style, design, and

---

[196] New York International Airport was later renamed JFK.

configuration of the DC-6 were well known to Americans because President Truman's plane, a Douglas VC-118, named *The Independence*, was the military version of the DC-6.

At 13 minutes after midnight on February 11, Flight 101 was given instrument clearance to take off from Newark's Runway 24-6. Tower controllers observed the plane becoming airborne at 12:18 am. The climb-out appeared to be normal until the aircraft passed by the Newark Range Station at the edge of the field and on the border with Elizabeth. Here, the controllers observed the plane losing altitude and veer toward the right in a westerly direction. Controllers radioed the pilot, Captain Wayne G. Foster, 46, a veteran of 11,901 hours, of which 1,059 were in the DC-6, and asked if everything was OK. Foster replied, "I lost an engine and (I) am returning to the field." Controllers first told Foster he could land on Runway 6 and then told him he could land on any runway. His last clipped message was, "can't make it." Within another minute, at 12:20 am, Foster's DC-6 disappeared from radar and controllers saw a large fireball over Elizabeth. It had happened again.

DESPITE THEIR EXTENSIVE TRAINING for composure and calm under the intense pressure of directing scores of planes at the same time, the Newark controllers who were perched high aloft in their three-legged metal and glass-lined tower, grabbed their binoculars and zeroed in on the dreadful scene just two miles away. With few other planes to control at that early hour of the morning, they had a few moments to reflect on the frustration of three catastrophic crashes from their busy field in the past several weeks. The impact was immediate. By daybreak, Newark Airport would be described as *"ghostly."*

The southwesterly track of Runway 24-6 took the National Airlines plane into airspace over Elizabeth on a diagonal crossing of U.S. Route 1 at the intersection of North Avenue. Then, with a hard right over the Pennsylvania Railroad tracks just north of Fairmount Avenue, the pilots pulled the fuel dump handles in an attempt to lighten their weight for an emergency landing, and sprayed fuel over Elizabeth neighborhoods. Crossing over North Broad Street, The DC-6 slammed into a four-story brick apartment building at 652-58 Salem Avenue and smashed nose first into a playground for the Janet Memorial Home orphanage along Westminster Avenue, southeast of Scotland Road. It happened when most residents of Elizabeth were sleeping. There were 48 boys nestled in their beds of the large mansion-style orphanage when the crashing plane rained death nearly on top of them.

Moments after takeoff, the CAB determined, the propeller on the DC-6's number three engine reversed pitch in flight, probably because of an electrical malfunction in the circuit that fed electricity to both the pitch reversal switch in the cockpit and the engine's governor solenoid valve.[197] Investigators believe the pilots didn't realize that engine three's propeller had reversed but, rather, they believed they had lost power in the number four engine. Therefore, they feathered the prop on engine four to avoid a severe yaw and lost all forward thrust on the right side of the plane.[198] This caused the high rate of descent and the crash within seconds. The DC-6 was not equipped with propeller reverse pitch warning lights which would have identified the problem engine and may have prevented the pilots from feathering the wrong prop.

The first impact of the plane was light contact with the top of a tree on the west side of Salem Avenue. That was immediately followed by the belly of the plane grazing the roof of the large U-shaped 52-family apartment building. A rooftop parapet on the northwest corner sheared off the right wing of the plane just outside the engine nacelle and flipped it into the building's courtyard. Gasoline from the wing tanks spewed over the roof of the building and ignited into a fireball. The plane rolled to the right with the number four engine smashing to the ground. As the nose of the plane plunged into a playground behind the orphanage, the rear of the cabin jackknifed and broke off from the main fuselage, cartwheeled, and rolled into a tree along Westminster Avenue. It broke into two pieces and wrapped around the tree, 465 feet from the apartment building. The center, or main cabin, broke into several pieces

---

[197] These two critical functions receiving power from the same electrical circuit on the DC-6 were later isolated to individual circuits.

[198] A yaw is a sudden turn, as if on an axis. In this case, it was to the right.

along with the left wing. The fuel from the left wing splashed into the hot engines and burst into another fire. From the top floor of the apartment building, the three-member Zahler family, and a second-floor resident, 65-year-old Alexander Prentiss died in the fire. Irving and Marilyn Zahler were 29 and 27, and their son, Monte, was only four. The deaths of these innocent Elizabeth residents were what Councilman Dunn had warned about in his "murder" speech only two weeks earlier. In the plane, Rosemary Stafford, 27, of Glens Falls, New York and her two children, Craig, 5, and 15-month-old Kathleen, were killed. Her husband, Harold Stafford, 27, was critically injured. They were traveling to Hollywood, Florida to visit Stafford's parents. Captain Foster and his co-pilot, C.E. St. Claire, and flight engineer, I. R. Shea, were all killed instantly in the crash. Stewardess Nancy J. Taylor, 22, of Coral Gables, Florida, survived without any injuries. She was found hanging upside down, still strapped into her jump seat, reportedly by 18-year-old Elizabeth resident James Aker, who opened a door, reached up into the rear of the mangled cabin along Westminster Avenue, snapped open the seat belt and caught Taylor as she fell into his arms. "I was sitting in the jump seat. That's in the back, right beside the door. I think that saved me," Taylor said in a first person narration compiled by reporters at the scene. In fact, most of the survivors were in the rear of the plane and they made it well known that they believed they lived only because they were sitting in the back. Their stories of miracle survival because they were sitting in the back of the plane were combined with the stories from survivors of Continental Charters Flight 44-2 in Napoli just weeks earlier to continue the new hypotheses that passengers are safest in the back of a plane. With press reports from the third Elizabeth crash, the concept became more widely accepted by American travelers and continues today.

Stewardess Taylor said they had flown up to about a thousand feet when "one of the engines conked out." She said the engine made a terrible rumbling noise and the plane fell more than 250 feet. The pilot, she reported, applied a burst of power as they leveled off and then they began falling again. "As the plane fell I could hear screams and yells. All the passengers had their straps around their waists." Taylor's press photographs, with her slender body, stylish hair and attractive appearance, were attention-grabbers in the nation's newspapers. She was hounded by the press even after returning to her home near Miami for a long hug with her family. She became a minor celebrity for a few days after the crash and again at the crash investigation hearing. Of the 63 people on board the DC-6, 29 perished. Forty people, mostly from the plane, were injured. One of them, Joseph Lease of Walden, New York was one of the heroes of the disaster. While hurt he dragged four people out of the wreckage.

AT FIVE AM ON FEBRUARY 11, the alarm on John Rescoe's small white FADA Radio on his bed stand went off and, tuned to 710 WOR-AM from its tower in nearby Newark, he was startled awake by news of still another airplane crash in Elizabeth. Passing along the news to his young son, Jack, and his wife, Anna Mae, John hustled off to catch a bus for work at the Bayway Standard Oil Refinery along the Arthur Kill in Linden. Jack and his mother were soon in the family's Chevy headed to the scene of their third plane crash within the past two months. They arrived by six am and joined hundreds of others milling about. "We got to stand right up close to the scene, actually so close that we were at the entrance to the courtyard of the apartment building," Jack recalled. A woman with a few small kids was trying to lug a large, shiny all-aluminum suitcase covered with soot from the fire, so Jack carried it for her out to the curb along the street. It was warm for February and although the fires from the fuel and the apartment building had been put out by Elizabeth firefighters, Jack could still smell the stench of burned wood, clothing, electrical wiring, fuel, gear oil, and, he believed, human flesh. After an hour, he left with his mother, off to St. Genevieve's Catholic school. Witnessing the gruesome scenes of three large passenger plane crashes in the span of several weeks in his small working class neighborhoods would leave indelible memories in the mind of the fifth grader from Elizabeth and Union, New Jersey.[199]

---

[199] In 2013, Rescoe was temporarily relocated from his Portland, Oregon apartment building during renovations. Discovering that his new digs were in a suite hotel at the end of a runway at Portland International Airport, Rescoe was seized with fear from his Elizabeth crash memories. He found new temporary quarters.

INTERNATIONAL HEADLINES OF THE crash, combined with the two other tragedies in Elizabeth, the near disastrous crash-landing in Cobourg, Canada, and the spectacular crash in Napoli, in December, made banner headlines in all newspapers. They pushed aside the other big world news of King George VI's death, funeral and return to Windsor Castle for burial. Two Elizabeth's captured world attention that day, the 25-year-old mourning, black-veiled and newly ascended Queen Elizabeth II, and Elizabeth, New Jersey.

For the third time in just 58 days, Elizabeth firefighters and police officers fought an aviation fuel fire and then combed through the wreckage for bodies. Victims were carried on stretchers, laid on straw and covered by blankets and sheets in the garage at the rear of Haines Funeral Home where Union County Coroner Alfred Haines and victims' family members would identify them in the morning, one by one. The Elizabeth radicals who had threatened to lay themselves across the runways at Newark Airport didn't have to deliver their menace. By 4 am on February 11 the Port of New York Authority closed the airport with no advance notice or public announcement. Planes on the ground at Newark were stuck. All incoming traffic from 11 major airlines and 12 nonskeds, with 265 daily flights, was diverted to New York's LaGuardia and International Airports, New Jersey's Teterboro, and even Philadelphia International Airport. The fear of death from the low-flying planes had so intensified, Queens, New York officials demanded that all Newark-diverted planes using LaGuardia and International should land and take off over water and when visibility dropped, the "death planes," as the Queens officials called them, should be sent elsewhere.[200] However, the immediate closing of the once busiest airport in the world was premature. Airlines with planes stranded at Newark complained they would lose revenue from aircraft parked on the ground. At 9 am the runways were reopened for a brief period as every plane that could fly vacated the field. Sixty-five empty airliners took off for other airports

---

It's evidence of how the Elizabeth crashes continue to impact people more than 60 years later.

[200] New York International Airport was also referred to as Idlewild Airport from its former use as Idlewild Golf Course in Jamaica, Queens.

and when they were gone, Newark Airport was shut down for four long months. An aerial photograph from later that day shows the entire field empty. The *"ghostly"* description appeared in several newspapers. Finally, it was quiet in the skies over Elizabeth.

NINE DAYS AFTER THE National Airlines crash, on February 20, 1952, President Truman sent a letter to a long-time friend and American hero. On Presidential stationery labeled *The White House* it began, *"Dear Jim, For some time now, I have been seriously concerned about airplane accidents, both commercial and military, that have occurred in the take-off and landing of aircraft, especially in heavily populated areas. I have been concerned about the loss of life and I have been concerned about the anxiety in some of our cities. I have decided to set up a temporary President's Airport Commission to look into the problem of airport location and use. I am delighted that you are willing to serve as Chairman of the Commission."* The letter was addressed to Mr. James H. Doolittle, Vice President, Shell Union Oil Corporation, New York. Jimmy Doolittle, Medal of Honor recipient for leading the first bomber raid on mainland Japan at the end of World War II, would get just 90 days to study and report back to the President on how to make the nation's airports safer. One of Doolittle's primary recommendations in the May 16, 1952, report titled, *The Airport and its Neighbors*, was to get rid of intersecting runways such as Runway 24-6 at Newark that carried the death planes into Elizabeth. Doolittle suggested parallel runways instead, which were already under construction at Newark when his report was released.

DOOLITTLE'S REPORT WAS BASED on crash investigations and examinations of airports all over the country, but there was no question that the incidents from Newark Airport that so devastated Elizabeth played a major role in its formulation. The report on the December 16, 1951, Miami Airlines crash in Elizabeth had come out on April 13 and it wasn't kind to the shortcomings of the nonsked business model. The CAB New York office chief, Joseph Fluet, headed up the investigation. He secured the communications records that included only two brief radio messages from the cockpit of the Miami Airlines plane. When the

Newark tower controllers suggested Captain Lyons lower the landing gear immediately after he took off, he simply replied, "N1678M." Just before the plane crashed, the tower also heard from the cockpit, "Newark Airport, this is 78." Neither scant communication helped identify a cause of the crash.

Not many of the C-46s were equipped with throat microphones and push-to-talk radio buttons on the yoke. Most had bulky hand-held L-shaped microphones hanging on the window frame on each side of the pilots. Investigators surmised the pilots were so busy trying to control their plane they either forgot to call out on the radio or simply didn't have the time to grasp the mics with their hands and flip the switches to talk.

Sixty-four people on the ground were determined to be substantial witnesses to the burning engine on the flying Miami Airlines plane or the crash in Elizabeth. Some witnesses, including airport tower controllers viewing everything through their binoculars, claimed the right wing folded upward and separated from the plane. Other witnesses reported the plane lost its forward motion, indicating a stall, not where the engines stop running, but where the wings of a plane lose a steady flow of air and their ability to create lift. Investigators found that while the plane did stall, causing the crash, it did not lose its right wing. The controllers' report of the wing dropping off was likely an optical illusion. The right wing was found embedded among the wreckage indicating it was still attached when the plane hit the bedrock in the Elizabeth River.[201]

Almost immediately, and because Miami Airlines president Robert W. Duff floated the theory, speculation focused on the defective cabin heaters that caused the five-hour delay in departure. "It may have been that the fuel line of the heater became disconnected and sprayed raw gasoline into the engine nacelle," Duff recklessly guessed to reporters. Other speculation focused on the excessive weight on the plane, over its limit of 48,000 pounds. The CAB had determined that at 48,000

---

[201] Even in 2015, a heavily dramatized fictional account of Elizabeth residents impacted by the Miami Airlines crash repeated the inaccurate press reports from 1951 that the right wing of the Miami Airlines plane fell off before the crash.

pounds the C-46 *"takeoff performance (was) insufficient for the airplane to continue flight if one of the engines should fail during the critical phase of take-off."* The CAB also found what many C-46 pilots already knew; that at 48,000 pounds, the C-46 was nearly impossible to fly safely on one engine.

Instead of speculating over the malfunctioning heaters on the Miami Airlines plane, the CAB investigators focused on the right engine from which the smoke and flames flowed through the seven-minute flight. They also examined the excessive weight of the aircraft. They found that the pitch of the right propeller had been altered from its standard takeoff position in a measure called feathering, but it was only partially feathered to 57 degrees.[202]

While the wings and fuselage of the crashed plane were removed from the creek bed and taken to Building 50 at Newark Airport for reconstruction, the engines were taken to the engine overhaul shop of the Pacific Airmotive Corporation at the small Linden Airport just a few miles away. At Newark, the wings, fuselage, and nacelles were laid out on the floor in their constructed positions. From this reconstruction, investigators could carefully study the fire patterns on the plane while it was in flight. Because the plane crashed into a river and was partially submerged in water, they could determine what parts of the plane burned during flight and what parts burned after impact. The damage caused by the fire in flight *"left its own highly descriptive pattern of destruction, localized, sharply defined and obviously of a nature that could have been produced only under extreme forced draft,"* the CAB reported. All three cabin and cockpit heaters were recovered and it was determined there was no fire in or near them before impact. That quieted the Miami Airlines owner's wild speculation. The plane's landing gear was examined and it revealed no evidence of overheating or burning in the right brake assembly, as suspected by the Miami Airlines pilot who called the tower controllers to report his theory of the origin of the fire.

---

[202] Feathering a prop is a procedure used by pilots to stop a non-functioning propeller from windmilling and causing drag so the functioning engine(s) can operate more efficiently.

Instead, the in-flight burn patterns revealed that the fire in the right engine originated at or near the base of the number 10 cylinder which was located at the extreme bottom of the front row of the engine cylinders. The right engine had been recently overhauled by the Opa-Locka Engine Overhaul Base in Opa-Locka, Florida and installed on the plane 41 days before the crash, on November 5, 1951. Maintenance records indicated that the required inspections of the engine had been completed but with the most recent inspection being done by a copilot-mechanic before and after its flight from Fort Smith to Newark. Because this copilot-mechanic started the required inspection in Fort Smith and finished it and signed off on it in Newark, it must have been the third pilot on board the plane, Ed Lilly, who performed the duties. By then, the engine had 103 ½ hours since the overhaul. The CAB reported that using a combination copilot-mechanic to accomplish periodic inspections was not a violation of CAB rules *"but is not considered good and accepted practice and is not conducive to either good maintenance or piloting efficiency."*[203]

Lilly's name was originally on the passenger manifest as a fourth company employee, but it was stricken from the document in Newark. Although Lilly was on the plane, he was not listed on the flight plan as a working crew member either. He was simply hitching a ride home to Miami. The CAB did not blame Lilly for the crash, but it did suggest that his and the company's method of engine inspection caused a failure to notice a problem with leaking oil from the right engine. In Newark, it was noted by service mechanics that the right engine required nearly twice the amount of oil as the left engine, despite the fact that it was the engine most recently overhauled and had far fewer hours in flight. *"It is reasonable to assume that there was oil seepage somewhere in the right engine which could well account for this increased oil consumption,"* the CAB scolded. Additionally, there was evidence that the number 10 cylinder was not properly secured because it showed signs of movement such as galling of the crankcase pad, fretting, and polishing. While Lilly's visual

---

[203] In 1951-52 using combination pilot-mechanics was a common practice among the nonskeds.

inspection of the right engine was performed in Fort Smith, per regulations, and he did not report any leaks or oil seepage at that time, the CAB still issued a reprimand. *"The fact remains that had the engine cowling been removed it's quite possible that any oil seepage from the number 10 cylinder pad would have been observed."*

With Lilly off the hook for blame only because he was dead, the CAB turned next to the aircraft mechanics, those who performed the right engine's most recent overhaul. It determined that the number 10 cylinder in the right engine separated completely from the crankcase during or shortly after takeoff. This was caused by the improper installation of nuts on the cylinder's hold-down studs which then broke and caused the cylinder to separate from the crankcase pad. Because of the smoke observed and the smeared oil noticed by the baggage handler, it's likely that oil continued seeping from the damaged number 10 cylinder as the right engine was run up just before takeoff. Then, as pilot Lyons pushed to full throttle down Runway 10-28, all the factors necessary for the severe fire were in place.

A high draft of air through the engine nacelle, liquid and atomized lubricating oil went from dripping to shooting out of the cylinder hole, a broken connecting rod began flailing, and exhaust and inlet ducts were opened. The exhaust duct emitted flame from the engine's high RPMs. The intake duct emitted inflammable and even explosive fuel mixture. Therefore, a high-intensity fire developed and continued to be fed with a mixture of fuel, atomized oil, exhaust and fast flowing air. The high-temperature fire quickly burned through fire resistant lines carrying inflammable liquids to the front of the firewall. Once behind the firewall, the red hot fire rapidly burned through the other lines that were not fire resistant. All this happened while the passengers and crew sat in the airplane, watching in horror as the impending disaster blew through the right engine. They were helpless.

Emergency procedures for an engine fire were displayed on a placard in the cockpit of the C-46. The first item listed is to shut off fuel, oil, and hydraulics to the burning engine. Then, feather the prop, turn off the ignition, close the cowl flaps and the oil cooling flaps, retract the landing gear, pull the fire extinguisher switch, and then land as soon as possible. Lyons and Mason failed to perform the first and most important item of this critical emergency procedure possibly because of lax training by the company, declared the CAB investigators. The shut-off valves to the fuel, oil and hydraulic systems to the right engine were found in the open position. The CAB declined to blame the pilots, however, for lowering the landing gear upon the tower controllers' advice *"because they probably did not have knowledge at that time that the right engine was on fire."* There was some evidence that the fire extinguisher had been activated, but it could not be determined if the pilots pulled the pin or if the fire's intense heat burned through the spray nozzles and activated the carbon dioxide.

Lax training and overloading of aircraft had dogged Miami Airlines since at least February 18, 1947, as it did many of the struggling nonskeds. Miami Airlines was cited for 16 violations of civil flight regulations back to September 10, 1950. They paid settlements of $1,800 for the infractions. Fourteen of the violations involved overloading of their airplanes.

In the case of the Elizabeth crash, 117 pounds over the approved weight of 48,000 pounds seems insignificant, but one must consider that these maximums were set by the Army where risk in the C-46 was common and accepted. And they were set during the war when air transport of heavy payloads was absolutely necessary. Additionally, the military had a large contingent of aircraft mechanics, hundreds of C-46s at their disposal instead of three operated by Miami Airlines, and they were not flying fare-paying passengers. In simple terms, the Army could afford the risk, Miami Airlines could not.

As the CAB had determined, a takeoff weight of 43,000 to 45,000 pounds was much safer for the notorious C-46 when flying civilian passengers. The CAB declared that when Miami Airlines willfully overloaded its aircraft it created a grave public danger. *"This overload and the numerous previous cases of overloading are plainly indicative of the carrier's attitude toward sound and accepted practices pertinent to safe operation."* This statement could have applied to most all of the nonskeds of the late 1940s and early 1950s, and especially in 1951.

One other factor could have played a role in why the crash occurred where it did, over Elizabeth and not sooner or later as Lyons attempted to get back to Runway 6. As the crippled C-46 came in over Elizabeth at 200 feet, Lyons still had the plane pointed in a generally southeast direction and he was some 60 degrees off course for his intended runway at the airport.

If Lyons was attempting a sharp left turn into his live engine over Elizabeth to line up to Runway 6 as it appeared, his degree of the bank would have increased his stall speed anywhere from .5 to 25 percent, according to the 1945 U.S. Army Air Forces *C-46 Pilot Training Manual.* Stall speeds of a C-46 with 40,000 pounds of weight and the R-2800 engines are listed at between 67 and 88 mph among a variety of flaps, landing gear and power configurations. With a single engine and normal loads, however, the pilot must always maintain a speed above 105 mph to avoid a stall in the C-46, the flight manual warns. Flying on one engine, excessive drag from the landing gear, and attempting a sharp left turn would have dramatically increased the C-46s stall speed. It's possible that Lyons was so intent upon his one shot at lining up his plane with Runway 6 that he failed to maintain adequate speed to avoid the catastrophic stall. This is conjecture but it may explain why the witnesses reported hearing the engine roar louder – it was an attempt at more speed, just as the plane fell from the sky.

The final CAB report on the cause of the crash of the Miami Airlines flight in Elizabeth determined that the aircraft was loaded above its maximum allowable takeoff weight. The oil leaks in the right engine were not properly inspected, and the hold down studs of the number 10 cylinder failed because the nuts were improperly installed by maintenance workers. It caused the cylinder to separate from the crankcase during or shortly after takeoff. The report confirmed that a fire started at the base of the number 10 cylinder, rapidly becoming uncontrollable. It confirmed that while trying to return to the Newark Airport with a fierce fire in the right engine, the plane stalled at 200 feet and fell into the Elizabeth River. It ruled that Miami Airlines' pilot training program on emergency procedures was *"informal, irregular, and, therefore, inadequate."*

ON APRIL 9, 1952 THE CAB imposed additional regulations designed to curb the out-of-control safety problems, especially among the nonskeds. Stricter enforcement of minor violations, such as poor record-keeping, would be imposed, clarity would be required in records of ownership and control of aircraft, improvements in fire protection systems of the C-46 were imposed, maintenance facilities came under stricter control with enhanced qualification checks on mechanics, and the nonskeds must designate chief pilots and check pilots. They would also have to increase flight training and safety inspections, and as a result of the Continental Charters, Miami Airlines, and Robin Airlines crashes, nonskeds pilots must fly only on designated civil airways at night and not go off on their own for the fastest and lowest route to the next airport. The nonskeds' use of itinerant or "rent-a-pilots" was greatly restricted, and stronger enforcement of adequate rest between flights for pilots was prescribed.[204] The feds were reigning in what some considered the wide open rules of the airways for the nonskeds.

IT TOOK LONGER FOR the CAB investigation report to come out on the crash-landing of the Robin Airlines C-46 in Canada. The delay could have been caused by interaction with a foreign government or it could have been the multitude of problems that Robin was displaying with its poorly operated and utterly unsafe airline in 1951 and '52. Its first crash was comical. The second was deadly.

Just after 3:30 on the morning of April 18, 1952, the thunderous and vibrating noise from the piston-driven engines of a large airplane rolled a farmer and his wife out of their bed in the Puente Hills, near Whittier, California, 20 miles east of Los Angeles. Looking through a window of their farmhouse over their cattle pastureland on a 500-foot-tall hill, they saw the flashing lights of a low-flying plane heading west into a thick fog. Within moments, the plane was out of their sight, but they could still hear it. It very soon returned and, without seeing it this time, the bewildered couple

---

[204] Ironically, regulations for crew rest between flights would be revisited following the crash of Colgan Air Flight 3407 operating as Continental Connection from Newark to Buffalo on February 12, 2009. All 49 people on board and one person on the ground in Buffalo were killed when the fatigued pilots didn't know how to respond to the loss of speed and a stall caused by icing on their wings. The pilots had commuted to Newark from South Florida and Seattle without adequate rest. As a result, passenger transport pilots are now required to have 10 hours rest before flights.

heard the plane roar low again over their farmhouse heading east until it became quiet again. They went back to bed.

Later that morning, about 10 am, La Puente rancher Hayden Jones was driving around his pasture searching for farm animals lost in the fog when he smelled burning wreckage. It was the charred hull of a C-46 on a grassy hillside about two miles east of Whittier, in the Puente Hills between Colima Road and Turnbull Canyon. The number on the tail was easily recognizable, *N8404C*. The plane was a half-full nonsked flight from New York, flying to the Lockheed Air Terminal in Burbank. It had been diverted to Los Angeles International Airport because of poor weather. It was owned by Air Charters, Inc. but leased to Robin Airlines, doing business, without the CAB's knowledge or authorization, as North Continent Airlines, companies owned by businessman Norman D. Kessler. Robin was the same airline whose pilot got lost, ran out of fuel, and ditched a loaded C-46 in the snow in Cobourg, Ontario, Canada on December 20. The pilot on this Robin flight was none other than Lewis R. Powell, the heart diseased aviator who had been hired by Robin after flight checks in December. He was placed as a co-pilot for Robin's C-46 passenger planes on February 20. By April 1st, Powell still held a pilot's license restricting him from flying passengers but he had flown nine passenger flights for Robin when he was elevated to pilot-in-command. He then made nine more flights for the nonsked before his last ended in tragedy on April 18 in the Puente Hills. All 29 people on board the plane were killed. It was determined that Captain Powell had suffered a hemorrhage of his heart within a few hours of or immediately preceding the crash. Now, in April of 1952, the CAB had two major crash events involving Robin Airlines in its investigation chain. The crash-landing in Cobourg, Canada still produced laughter and insults toward the small nonsked, especially after the press reported the results of the investigation hearing.

THROUGH CHRISTMAS OF 1951 and all through the final week of the year, the Robin Airlines C-46 sat crippled in the Wilson family's farm pasture along the shore of Lake Ontario in Cobourg, Canada. For a few days, military police from the RCAF guarded the plane. At least one

Trans-Canada Airlines flight from Montreal to Toronto circled low around the marooned plane, apparently so the pilots and passengers could get a better look. It was still that much of a spectacle. However, despite the apparent miracle and heroics, this story faded rapidly on December 30th, replaced by the disappearance of Continental Charters Flight 44-2 just 100 miles south in Napoli. It may have been out of the public eye for several weeks, but it was still on the CAB's radar.

As CAB investigators gathered evidence from the Robin Airlines crash landing, and even as the same investigators responded to the Continental Charters crash in Napoli, the effort to recover the C-46 from the Wilson farm got underway. The job went to Cobourg heavy machinery contractors Ron Gagne and Fred Ito. The men used A D-7 Caterpillar bulldozer, an old military truck with a backhoe, and a large dump truck. They first dug ramps in the ground beneath the plane and then hand-cranked the landing gear down so the plane was sitting on its wheels. Using the bulldozer, they pulled the plane up the ramps and turned it around to face northwest into the strongest Ontario winter winds. Using the arm of the backhoe, they lifted off the damaged propellers and installed new props. The batteries were recharged and just enough fuel for a short flight was pumped by hand into the tanks. Gagne then ran the bulldozer over the Wilson's pasture to smooth out about 2,000 feet of the runway from south to north with a lift off point just south of Highway 2. Throughout the job bitter cold with temperatures of six degrees below zero nipped at the men and their equipment. Finally, by January 10, 1952, the crude Wilson Farm airport was ready for an attempt by one of the largest passenger planes in the world to take off from a cow pasture and farm field that had been plowed under in preparation for spring planting.

Charles A. Rector was the chief pilot and director of flight operations for Robin Airlines in 1951. He was also some kind of a daring C-46 pilot who could get a plane out of a tight spot. He had just returned from Africa where he and mechanic Gordon McBride shot a C-46 out of a short jungle airstrip. Arriving in Cobourg on January 9, Rector and McBride walked and drove Ito's truck along the crude field looking for bumps that might trip up the C-46 wheels as it gathered speed for takeoff. They found only one.

When farmer's such as Charles Wilson plowed a field for planting crops they typically plowed around the perimeter a few times to open up the field and then plowed back and forth in parallel lines. This method alleviated constant lifting of the plow and was useful during harvest season to better access the rows of corn, a typical crop for a Canadian dairy farmer. At the end of Ito's runway, Charles' perimeter plow mound could not be flattened without several more time-consuming passes with the bulldozer. Rector decided that because it was nearly at the end of the makeshift runway he'd take a chance with the mound in place so they could take off the next morning.

At dawn on the 10th, McBride checked over all the repairs. The props were tested by revving the engines for several minutes until they whirled smoothly. The landing gear checked out, the new tail rudder pivoted freely and the nylon glued to the damaged underbelly of the giant plane remained intact. Spectators who had lined the farm runway jumped with excitement as Rector pushed the throttle of the 2,000 horsepower engines several times. Some covered their ears. Electricity was cut off from the power lines along the highway where police stopped traffic. No one drove anyway because they all wanted to see the plane take off. News media from Ontario and the United States lined up with film cameras to record the event. And all the Wilson's neighbors were given front row seats to watch the take-off phenomenon. Everyone questioned, would it fly?

On a typical long-runway takeoff, a large passenger plane pilot will gradually apply full throttle so passengers won't be jolted back to their seats from the sudden full thrust. Rector didn't have the luxury of a long, smooth runway and he and McBride were the only people on board. At the edge of Wilson's field, with less than 2,000 useable feet of crude bulldozed snow and earth in front of them, Rector held his brakes with the wheels behind wooden blocks and shoved the throttles all the way forward. Pushing the plane's two Pratt and Whitney engines to full power, Rector released the brakes so quickly the front wheels actually jumped the blocks. Gathering speed along the field, Rector knew he had to clear the plow mound to avoid disaster. Witnesses say that just as Rector lifted off the wheels rubbed along the top of the plow mound and the plane nosed up into the sky, clearing the highway electrical wires with several feet to spare. At 2:30 pm, January 10, 1952, 21 days after the miraculous crash landing that made heroes out of the simple and previously unknown Canadian Wilson farm family, the C-46 was back in the air on the first leg of its journey home to California. With only enough fuel for a short flight to the Trenton Airbase, (a weight reduction measure), Rector circled the field and dipped his wing as the crowd of the Wilson's, their neighbors, half of Cobourg, Ontario, sightseers from Toronto, and the hustling press all cheered, clapped and hollered after the plane. On January 11, refueled in Trenton, the C-46 took off again on a real runway for Malton Airport to clear customs and then on to Chicago for more fuel and the long flight home to Burbank. In a signal of what was to come for Robin Airlines, the flight home was empty.

Leading up to the official crash investigation for the Robin Airlines emergency landing in the snow, Smelser, O'Leary and Daine laid low, probably at the advice of Robin executives and, except for one national radio interview by Smelser, they didn't say anything about the crash-landing that was reported by the news media. Because there were no fatalities, the public reacted differently to this crash event than they did to crashes which killed everyone on board. The Robin Airlines crash was something to joke about and it quickly became an embarrassment to the company and the nonsked industry.

As the crash investigation hearing approached, many people wondered what Bruce Smelser would say about his terrible flight. An otherwise proficient pilot, it can only be surmised that he flew blindly through the snow from Chicago eastward attempting to complete his flight because he feared being crossed off the list of pilot's for- hire by Robin Airlines, and he needed the work.

Bruce Lamar Smelser was a highly experienced pilot with extensive training before he joined the U.S. Army Air Forces in World War II. He was the oldest of six children, born and raised in Marion, Indiana on June 14, 1916, to bakery truck driver, Bion Smelser, and his wife, Helen. After dropping out of high school before his senior year, Smelser was married in 1935 at the age of 19 to Evelyn Osburne, living in a rented house on Washington Street in Marion and working as a driver and restaurant waiter on meager wages.

By 1941, Smelser had his pilot's license and was working as a flight instructor at the Roscoe Turner Aviation Institute at Weir Cook Airport (Indianapolis International Airport in 2015). Turner was a flamboyant aerial showman, Hollywood stunt pilot, and friend of famous actors, who set land speed and aviation racing records among contemporaries Eddie Rickenbacker and Amelia Earhart. His newly organized Roscoe Turner Aeronautical Corporation at Weir Cook needed pilot trainers so Smelser eagerly joined. It didn't last long, however, because after America had entered the war in December 1941, the military needed pilots more than Turner. Smelser joined the U.S. Army Air Forces in July 1942. Among his pilot duties was flying American-made Lockheed P-38 Lightnings across the Atlantic. He attained the rank of major during the war and when the Army Air Forces were being dissolved to form the United States Air Force, Smelser was transferred to regular Army duty for the Nuremberg Trials of Nazi war criminals. He left the Army as a Lt. Colonel in October 1947 and returned home to Marion still eager to fly.

Smelser told investigators about the Robin Airlines crash-landing at the January 24 and 25 hearing that he had flown C-46 aircraft for nonskeds for three years before his "forced landing," as he described it, in Cobourg. There was no doubt that Smelser was an experienced pilot, but he simply failed to demonstrate any proficiency what-so-ever on the Chicago to Newark flight and for that, the CAB blamed both him and Robin Airlines. Co-pilot O'Leary attempted to convince the investigators of his C-46 experience but in the end they determined it was *"extremely doubtful that he ever had any C-46 flying time as a pilot."* While the CAB investigation blamed the pilots for the flight fiasco, they reserved most of the criticism for Robin Airlines and the CAA.

Soon after passage of the Civil Aeronautics Act of 1938, commercial aviation regulation in the United States was split into two agencies. The CAA was responsible for overseeing all safety programs and standards, route development, and traffic control. The CAB was responsible for accident investigation, safety rulemaking, and economic regulations. In the case of the Robin Airlines accident, it was one agency heavily criticizing the other.

The CAB investigators determined that the problems encountered by Smelser and O'Leary in the cockpit began with serious deficiencies on the part of Robin Airlines. Robin began operations in January 1949 as a nonsked and, therefore, did not have to follow all the regulations of the major airlines. An example involved its pilots. With three C-46's and a DC-3 in its fleet, Robin had only one full-time pilot, Charles Rector. All others, including Smelser and O'Leary, were pilots-for-hire who were paid as they flew. As a result, training and certification of these pilots were shoddy at best. Between February 1949 and February 1951, Robin racked up nine CAA violations or reprimands for everything from improper flight plans, failure to keep proper airmen or pilot records, multiple citations for overloading planes, improper take-off, excess crew time, and for the simple safety infraction of not having seat belts for every passenger. One violation notice alone listed 12 counts of safety issues on ten individual flights.

On March 5, 1951, the safety violations were so numerous and egregious the CAA asked the CAB to revoke Robin's Air Carrier Operating Certificate. However, before the CAB could act on the complaint, Robin's certificate expired, on June 30. The complaint was then withdrawn. Concurrently, during the spring and summer of 1951, Robin had a re-certification application on file with the CAA but apparently stalled the required hearings for several months until it could reorganize with a new corporate name. From April until August 1951, several CAB hearings for Robin were postponed when neither lawyers nor the owner of the company, Norman D. Kessler, showed up. Finally, on the last no-show by Robin both American and United Airlines successfully lobbied the CAB to get rid of this pesky, upstart nonsked that was stealing their business. The application was denied.

The owner of Robin then apparently reorganized the company and began doing business as North Continent Airlines, but without authorization by the CAA or CAB. In a crafty procedure of either legal trickery or obfuscation, on December 18, two days before the Cobourg crash landing, Robin's certificate was reissued by the CAA. For that, the CAB openly criticized its regulatory partner. *"Considering the past operating history of this carrier, which has been involved in continuous violations since the beginning of its operations, it is difficult to reconcile this action taken by the CAA,"* the CAB chastised in its crash investigation report.

The March 5 violations had never been resolved, and before recertification, Robin did not properly train its pilots to get back in the air. In fact, it appears that by the timing of the newspaper advertisement for $88 airfares on Robin Airlines from Lockheed Air Terminal in Burbank to Newark read by Jerry Laufgraben and other passengers, Robin managers anticipated their recertification before the Christmas holidays of 1951. Regardless, the CAB found that Robin never properly checked its pilots on the C-46. O'Leary was supposed to have had an extensive instrument flight check with a hood blocking his vision in the cockpit. Instead, his check flight on the C-46 included simple maneuvers such as straight and level flight, turns, three landings and take-offs, and a very brief instrument check with the check pilot holding a map in front of his face. He did not receive any training in emergency flight procedures. Six days later, when O'Leary got into the co-pilot's seat, it was his first flight for Robin and his first working flight in a C-46. Smelser never got a flight check before Robin resuming flight operations, as required by CAA regulations. Rector, as director of flight operations for Robin, said he didn't think it was necessary because Smelser had flown C-46's before and had an Airline Transport Rating on his commercial pilot's license. Even though Smelser was listed as Robin's "chief pilot," he hadn't been involved with the airline for months. On December 18, Rector called Smelser at his home in Indiana to join and take over the flight in Kansas City. It was a recipe for disaster. Smelser was coming off a long non-flying hiatus with no training or check flight in the recently overhauled C-46 by a safety-lax airline just recently recertified (under the guise of another company) to fly. O'Leary was a dead-head rookie pilot, with poor training and only a brief check flight on the C-46, climbing into the cockpit as a beginner. Jerry Laufgraben and the other passengers had no idea what kind of danger they were facing. They just wanted to get home for the holidays.

At Kansas City, Smelser and O'Leary did at least one thing correctly. They checked the weather forecast for the route to Chicago and Newark. Based on a forecast of the clear weather for four hours between Kansas City and Chicago, Smelser filed a Visual Flight Rule (VFR) plan for Chicago but changed to an Instrument Flight Rule (IFR) when they encountered snow and poor visibility near Burlington, Iowa. After this, the CAB found, the list of errors made by the pilots caused by poor training and lack of oversight by Robin, began multiplying, and they ended with the crash-landing in Cobourg.

The final conclusion by the CAB for the cause of the crash was difficult to obtain because the flight plan and log record were so poorly kept (filled out after the crash landing) that the CAB was forced to make conclusions based on incorrect or insufficient data. Estimated arrival times, fuel consumption, speed, elapsed time reports, and radio frequencies were all absent from the flight log. The passenger manifest was prepared in such a way that it was not possible for the CAB to determine exactly how many passengers were on board when departing Chicago. The accurate number ended up being 45, including a baby and required a head count because the flight manifest had been altered so much it was illegible. Fuel consumption data were critical to the flight and the pilots failed to reconcile three missing or useless fuel tanks and nearly an hour of burning fuel while sitting on the taxiway at Midway Airport waiting for takeoff clearance. As a result, they took off with less fuel than required for an ILR flight which mandated a backup airport and a substantial fuel reserve. Smelser and O'Leary's flight log estimated burning 99 gallons of fuel per hour on the flight when the C-46 required about 150 gallons per hour. The lost flight ended up burning fuel at a rate of 164 gallons per hour. If the pilots had properly prepared for their flight from Chicago to Newark and if they were familiar with the C-46 they should have known that they would not have enough fuel for an instrument flight and barely enough for a visual flight.

The CAB also discovered the crew's failed attempts to conceal their poor flight planning. In the flight log, filled in at the Cobourg police station after the crash landing, Smelser listed his Goshen, Indiana arrival time four minutes before his arrival time at South Bend even though South Bend came first on the eastward trek. It was a glaring error for any pilot but especially for one born and raised in Indiana. It also showed that Smelser obviously scribbled his flight plan after the crash landing by stating he flew the 150 miles from South Bend to Toledo in four minutes. The CAB investigators sarcastically declared that this flight segment would have required the C-46 to fly at 2,280 miles per hour! They wrote, "*it was apparent that they* (Smelser and O'Leary) *were attempting to conceal such inadequate flight planning.*"

Passengers continued to praise Smelser and O'Leary for getting them on the ground safely, but this was in the weeks leading up to the CAB's final report on what caused the debacle. Many news reports portrayed Smelser as the hero for landing the plane safely without any injuries to the passengers. A report in *The New York Times*, however, was more cautious. It did not place blame but neither did it commend the pilots. Critics of *The Times* pounced. *CBS Radio* talk show host Arthur Godfrey invited Smelser to speak by telephone on his national program a few days after the crash landing where Godfrey praised the Indiana pilot as a national hero. Godfrey, an accomplished pilot himself who advocated flight safety on his program and who often promoted conservative views on his entertainment show, lambasted the liberal *Times* for not praising Smelser as a hero. He contrasted Smelser with pilot Albert Lyons, who crashed the Miami Airlines C-46 just two weeks earlier in Elizabeth, killing all 56 people on board. Back home in Indiana, Smelser's family gathered around to listen to the radio broadcast from New York. Godfrey's heaping praise for Smelser turned out to be premature.

THE FINAL CAB INVESTIGATION report was released on July 16, 1952, and while it was not kind to the pilots, it placed most of the blame on Robin Airlines. The flying public, still embracing the pilots as heroes, was stunned with the conclusion. "*The chain of events preceding the forced landing of this aircraft was of an operational nature and clearly shows the company's lack of safety consciousness, as well as its substandard operating practices. (It's) not limited to this particular accident but has prevailed almost continuously from the inception of this carrier's operations.*" For Smelser, the report was especially critical. "*It is apparent that (he) was not proficient in such duties and that there was inadequate crew coordination.*" The CAB declared that Smelser's "*incompetence*" showed the company's "*indifference to the appropriate safety standards.*" As for O'Leary, the CAB determined that he simply didn't know what he was doing and that Robin was negligent for even allowing him in the cockpit.

In a panic, with 45 passengers on board, Smelser and O'Leary made an emergency crash landing 200 miles off their intended course and 300 miles from their final destination. *"The cause of this accident was the crew's incompetence in flight planning and navigation, fostered by failure of the company to check crew competency and provide proper flight training, which resulted in the crew becoming lost and making an off-course landing due to fuel exhaustion."* There was no mention of the failed duties of the CAA in the CAB's final conclusion or of the federal policies which allowed abysmally performing nonskeds like Robin Airlines to take flight in the first place.

Later in 1952, after the CAB completed its second Robin crash investigation report placing blame on the heart diseased Captain Powell (and Robin) for the Whittier, California crash, Robin went out of business forever. Fellow nonskeds Continental Charters and Miami Airlines followed.

The Robin Airlines crash in Southern California caught the attention of residents living in rapidly developing Los Angeles County in 1952. A near disastrous nonsked airplane incident from Hollywood captured the attention of the entire nation.

Top left, clockwise, a Miami Airlines C-46, about 1950; Newark Airport terminal dedicated by Amelia Earhart in 1935; Miami Airlines C-46 with engine fire over northern New Jersey, Dec. 16, 1951; William Sparrow photos obtained and released by the CAB show the doomed plane over Union and Elizabeth, NJ; Miami Airlines crash scene in the Elizabeth River; Captain Albert C. Lyons, pilot of Miami Airlines C-46; crash scene from the ground where young Jack Resco looked up to see a man sitting in the exposed bedroom of a house.

Top left, clockwise, Elizabeth police and firefighters pick through charred debris of wreckage of Miami Airlines plane on Dec. 16, 1951; badly burned body removed from the wreckage; 1945 schematic of Newark Army Air Field shows war-built intersecting Runway 6, top right to bottom left; Elizabeth residents prepare bodies for a priest to administer last rites.

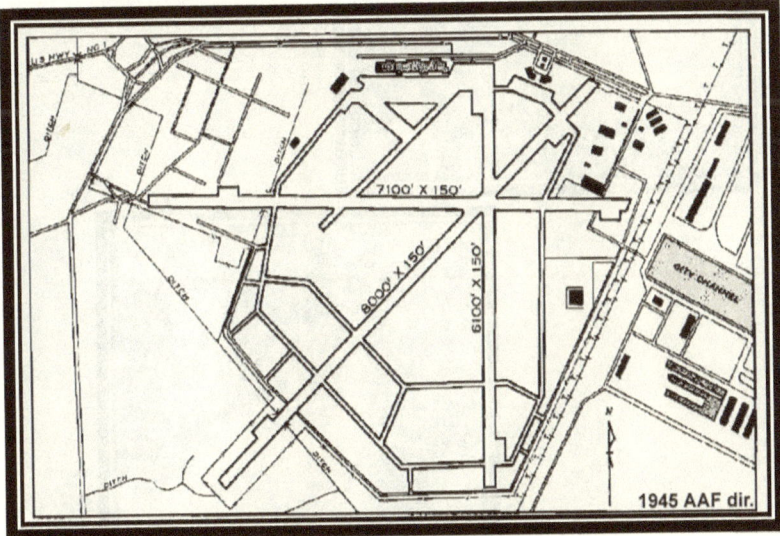

Top right, clockwise, firefighters douse flames in the wreckage of American Airlines Convair 240 which crashed into homes in Elizabeth, NJ on January 22, 1952, killing all 23 on board and seven on the ground; bodies lined up in the rain on a muddy lot for transport to a concrete garage floor at Haines Funeral Home; firefighters douse flames in a storefront, apartments, and houses where seven people on the ground were among the dead; former Secretary of War Robert P. Patterson, a friend of President Truman. His death, among all the others in the horrific crashes of 1951 and early 1952, caused Washington to take notice of the safety problems among the airlines, especially the nonskeds.

Top left, clockwise, *American Airlines* pilot Thomas John "TJ" Reid in his company portrait; co-pilot Reid, left, with his *American Airlines Flagship* flight crew and Prince Faisal, center, later crowned King Faisal bin Abd Al-Aziz of Saudi Arabia; (the plane appears to be a Convair) Reid in the cockpit sporting prestigious transport pilot bars but in the co-pilot's seat; Captain Reid holding his young daughter, Robin Reid, in 1951 in New Jersey.

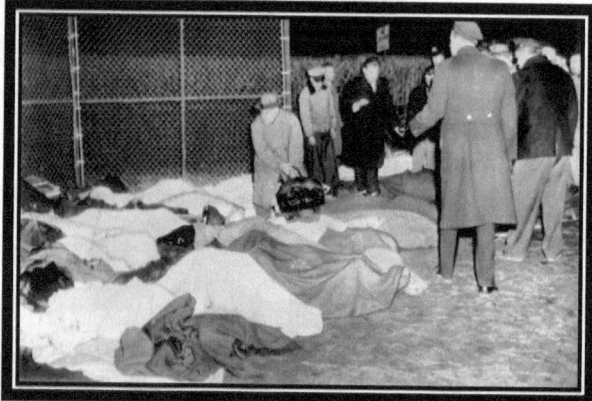

Top left, clockwise, fire from National Airlines crash into Elizabeth, NJ on February 11, 1952; bodies for Haines Funeral Home; apartment building struck by the plane; the National Airlines DC-6 narrowly missed Janet Memorial Home filled with sleeping boys.

Top right, clockwise, Murder! Elizabeth residents gather at the scene of National Airlines DC-6 crash on February 11, 1952, the third passenger plane crash into Elizabeth in weeks. Aft section, top, is where most survivors were sitting; plane hit apartment building from right to left, killing several inside and dropping pieces into the courtyard. Young Jack Rescoe watched this scene from the among bystanders on the sidewalk in front of the apartment building while on his way to school.

Top left, clockwise, Robin Airlines passenger, Jerry Laufgraben, who later changed his name to Jerry Lawrence; Robin Airlines C-46 after crash-landing in snow in Cobourg, Ontario, Canada; Robin Airlines pilot Bruce Smelser; pulling the Robin C-46 up onto its wheels at the Wilson farm in Cobourg, December 1951.

Top left, clockwise, National Airlines DC-6 that crashed into Elizabeth on February 11, 1952 was the same type of plane as President Truman's *The Independence*; Truman departing on his plane in July 1952; Truman at the White House with Air Force and aviation advisors, General James Doolittle, seated left, and Lt. General Hoyt Vandenberg, standing left, Major General Lauris Norstad, standing right, and Assistant Secretary of War, Stuart Symington, seated right, July 1947; Newark Airport on February 12, 1952, the day after it was closed. New Jersey Turnpike and Newark Channel are at top left. Arrows denote notorious Runway 24-6 aiming toward Elizabeth off the top right. This image led to its description as "ghostly."

CHAPTER 21

HOLLYWOOD

FOLLOWING THE MANY AIRPLANE disasters among the nonskeds and the majors in 1951 and '52, Americans were panicky enough that a fictional nonsked near-miss implanted a soothing impression upon flyers. It had the opposite effect of the many tragic crashes. It calmed fears.

Hump pilot Ernest K. Gann, son of a co-founder of Northwest Airlines, and already a best-selling author with his 1944 warplane crash and survival novel, *Island in the Sky*, worked for nonsked, Transocean Airlines after the war as a pilot flying passenger planes between the West Coast and South Pacific islands, including Hawaii. There, he developed the plot for his 1953 best-selling novel, *The High and the Mighty*.[205]

The story is about a DC-4 passenger plane that loses power in two of its four engines during a 12-hour flight from Honolulu to San Francisco with 16 passengers and a crew of five. The pilot loses his nerve and wants to ditch the plane in the Pacific Ocean while the washed-up and older war-veteran co-pilot commandeers the controls and convinces

---

[205] *The High and the Mighty* was published by William Sloane Associates, Inc. in 1953, and Permabooks, Doubleday and Company, Inc. in 1954.

the pilot to risk a low fuel and low elevation attempt to make San Francisco. The novel was a best-seller. It was immediately made into a feature length movie with Gann's old friend, John Wayne, who also starred in *Island in the Sky*, to produce and play the co-pilot. Actor Spencer Tracy passed up the role. The cast also included Robert Stack as the pilot, Doe Avedon as the stewardess, and Claire Trevor as a passenger. The movie plot follows the classic examples of commercial piston-engine airplane mishaps of the late 1940s and early 1950s, many of which were similar to the numerous crashes of 1951.

Nervous passengers check into the newly-named Honolulu International Airport asking the company dispatch agent for fictional TransOrient Pacific Airways about the number of engines on the plane and what happens when one of them conks out over the Pacific.[206] "The plane has four so don't worry," they're told. The dispatcher loudly announces the flight is ready for takeoff with 3,050 gallons of fuel for the 9,000-foot elevation flight across the ocean, mostly at night.

Passenger fears about engine failure, fuel management, and elevation were issues that plagued real 1951 flights and crashes. Inside the cabin, where the double-rows of spacious twin seats appear to be more opulent than present-day first class seats, the nervousness continues and the stewardess asks pilot John Sullivan, Stack, to come back into the cabin to calm a passenger's fears. "Every time you bank right or change a propeller pitch, he goes all white," the stewardess exclaims. "He's the original frightened Freddy." Stack, handsome and elegant in his crisp lemon chiffon-colored uniform with bright gold buttons, epaulets, pocket lids, and captain's four gold stripes on his wrist sleeves, assures the passenger, a famous Broadway producer, that the DC-4 "can fly without an engine, or even two lost. I feel safer than I do in a car," he declares, loud enough for the other passengers to hear.

The movie is an exceptional piece of public relations for the beleaguered nonskeds of the early 1950s. Each mishap is carefully portrayed with a method of solving the problem, safely. The early part of the

---

[206] TransOrient Pacific or TOPAC was simulating the real nonsked, Oakland, California-based Transocean.

flight is portrayed as smooth and casual with the cockpit on autopilot while the passengers, handsome men dressed in suits and ties and attractive women in low-cut dresses displaying ample cleavage for the voyeur audience, are introduced to a variety of personal and cultural issues that would be found on any flight. There is the young newlywed couple shown embracing in a long French kiss and even sexually petting (thinking it would be their last time) in their side-by-side seats which are nearly large enough to be a bed. We see a little boy traveling alone, put on the plane in Hawaii by his father who is divorced from his mother in California, and comfortably sprawled across two seats. We also listen in on a couple from New York City arguing over moving to a mining town in the West, admire a Chinese woman on her first flight, sympathise with a nuclear scientist still angry with his profession over the Atomic Bomb, and laugh at a back-slapping vacationing couple from the Midwest, a thickly-accented Italian fisherman, and a middle-aged spinster with heavy make-up and platinum-blond hair traveling to meet her mail-order groom-to-be, for the first time. Some of the men passengers even break into an argument over a woman, with one man pulling a handgun on the other. This was the 1950s, after all, when weapons could easily be carried on planes. The gun was expertly confiscated by the Italian fisherman.

Soon after the pilot, Robert Stack, makes a routine radio position report announcing, "1,500 gallons of fuel remaining," co-pilot Dan Roman, played by John Wayne, goes into the plane's tail with a flashlight to investigate the cause of minor vibrations that only he, the pilot, and the stewardess seem to notice. When he returns, and soon after the navigator, grappling with his own domestic issues of a drunk and lonely wife at home, loudly announces, "I've got news for you guys, we just passed the point of no return," with dramatic music, the number three engine bursts with a loud explosion and fire, and the prop blows off.

The pilots are shown pulling the levers for the fire extinguisher bottles with spray nozzles inside the engine nacelle. The fire goes out but without the engine, the plane begins losing altitude. Maydays are called and they're intercepted by a ship which transfers them to the Coast

Guard. Then, the plane begins losing fuel from its ruptured wing tank. Each of these unfortunate circumstances had been partly blamed for the myriad crashes of 1950-51.

At this point in the movie, with passengers rotating between tears, panic, anger, and bursts of heavily animated bravado, John Wayne's character, the seasoned and calm veteran pilot with many World War II bombing missions and South American commercial flights (one with a crash that killed his wife and daughter and left him with a limp), gradually takes command from the indecisive pilot, Stack. John Wayne helps the stewardess demonstrate for the passengers the life vests and rafts they will need for ditching in the Pacific. He organizes the passengers to open the non-pressurized cabin door and jettison luggage amid ample footage of the women bent over showing bare shoulders, cleavage (again), runny makeup (from crying) and tousled hair from the strong Pacific winds as depressed men passengers sulk in their seats, unable to do much of anything. The message is that women can survive emergencies on the nonskeds too.

Movie patrons also see long, vivid shots of the plane's emergency flares and flare gun, (which couldn't be found in the Continental Charters crash) and the process by which the Coast Guard scrambles search and rescue planes, "even a plane that can land on the water," the copilot calmly tells the passengers with his distinctive (John Wayne) cadence. Additionally, director William Wellman spends considerable time showing each passenger, especially the buxom women, popping open the carbon dioxide canisters that immediately inflate their personal life vests, something few passengers ever get to experience. It's a reminder that the early aviators' life vests that inflated to large breast-like tubes were nicknamed for Hollywood stage sexpot Mae West. Additionally, it depicts a real life scenario. When the Westair nonsked ditched in the Atlantic Ocean in June 1950, the Puerto Rican passengers had no idea how to put on or inflate their life preservers.

An extensive search by the Coast Guard, until they finally found the plane through the newly installed long-range navigation system (LORAN), nearly replicated the real but unsuccessful two-day search for Continental Charters Flight 44-2 in December 1951. Through it all, the little boy passenger is sleeping, sprawled out in his double seats while his toy airplane has suffered a broken wing.

In the end, with two engines out and after a few scenes of the attractive stewardess ducking into the galley for private moments of tears and hands-in-the-face anguish, the hero co-pilot, John Wayne, despite miscalculations by the navigator, determines they may have enough fuel to make it to the coast. "We'll make an ILS approach," he declares boldly while grasping the throbbing yoke. "Now hang on and fly!"

It's a great film with a lot of suspense and personally introspective scenes.[207] Americans, scared numb by three years of fatal crashes, lapped it up when *The High and the Mighty* was released in 1954. It was a respite of good aviation news because it portrayed survival, not death. The movie was very successful, recouping its $1.47 million production cost rapidly and achieving several Academy Award nominations, for which the original musical score by Dimitri Tiomkin won. The theme song went on to top the music charts because of its whistle-ability and kept the movie and its message of safety on an airplane in the forefront of passengers' minds for many years. The credits show that Transocean cooperated with the production by providing planes and pilots, and it was a beneficiary of the publicity with a positive image among the nonskeds. However, the airline eventually succumbed to financial pressure amid federal regulations which its owner, Orvis Nelson, claimed favored the majors.

The High and the Mighty is portrayed by film critics as the first of the modern airplane crash genre films that eventually led to *Fate is the Hunter*, the *Airport* series, *Alive*, *Airplane*, and, much later, the popular films *Castaway*, and *Flight*. Their origin, therefore, is traced to the dramatic crash events of 1951 and '52.

---

[207] Damaged by water, the original print for *The High and the Mighty* was restored by John Wayne's Batjac Productions, owned in 2015 by his daughter-in-law, Gretchen Wayne. A digital version of the movie is available for viewing.

CHAPTER 22

SOUVENIRS AND BROKEN FAMILIES

ON TUESDAY, JANUARY 1, 1952 Isobel Rutzebeck called her insurance company from her mother's home in Edmonton, Alberta, Canada. She was inquiring about a payment that was due on Rutz's life insurance policy. She was concerned because Rutz's daughter from a previous marriage was the beneficiary and Isobel still hadn't heard from Rutz since he left Alaska with his girlfriend in June of '51. She also thought that if Rutz had made the policy payment, she could find out from the insurance company where he was. "They told me to check the newspaper," Isobel said. Isobel had a sinking feeling when she first learned her husband was missing on a Continental Charters passenger plane over the telephone from a clerk at her insurance company.

"I went downtown in Edmonton to a newsstand and bought a newspaper with the story of the Continental Charters plane crashing on the side of the mountain and it said the co-pilot was Hans C. Rutzebeck," she recalled.[208]

---

[208] Although the newspaper article said his middle initial was C, Isobel knew it

The misspelled name didn't matter. It was a shock, but perhaps not as great as it would have been if she and Rutz had still been together. She had no idea he had been flying passenger planes for Continental Charters. Unable to obtain any information about what caused the crash, and in the absence of a traditional husband-wife relationship with Rutz, she made sensible decisions about her future. She arranged for her brother to fly to Florida to pick up the Studebaker car that Rutz had taken, and he delivered it to Edmonton where Isobel drove it for many years. She consulted a lawyer who discovered that Rutz also had an insurance policy through Continental Charters. The regular monthly disbursements provided a small measure of financial security for Isobel and her children. Through her many telephone calls and letters to settle his estate, she also discovered that his Florida girlfriend had suffered an emotional breakdown. Isobel then turned forward to focus on her new life as a widowed mother.

ON SAWMILL RUN, THE first week in January 1952 was worse than trout fishing and deer hunting seasons together. On Wednesday, January 2, car after car continued streaming into the hollow near Ruby and Charlie Bryant's farmhouse with most of the drivers stopping briefly to holler out the car windows, "Where's the plane crash?" Someone from the Bryant farm would point up the hollow and off would go another car for the top of Sawmill Run, blocking the narrow road while the sightseers went hiking up the ridge for a look at the scene of the crash of Continental Charters Flight 44-2. They ignored the *No Trespassing* signs hastily tacked to the trees along the road. It would go on for days, weeks, months, even years after the crash.[209] It was the last thing Ruby needed during this time of her medical crisis. She was trying to put the crash excitement behind her and prepare for her doctor's appointment at the end of the week.

BEFORE DAWN ON THURSDAY, January 3, a Continental Charters C-46 flown by company president John Belding into Buffalo was loading for

---

had to be Rutz, whose middle name was Edmund.

[209] Even in 2015, people were still driving into Sawmill Run for a hike up the ridge searching for the crash scene, which can no longer be found. The forest has regrown and reclaimed everything.

the return trip to Miami. Along with Belding and a co-pilot, there were only five passengers. Two attractive women wearing long wool coats to ward off the Buffalo winter, one with a fashionable head scarf tied around her chin, expertly climbed into the plane on the few rungs of a short aluminum ladder that hung from the rear cabin door. Stewardess Dolores Beshears was accompanied on the flight by Pearl Moon's sister, Minnie Moon.[210] She was the only Moon family member who came to visit Pearl, who remained in Salamanca Hospital. Three caskets were lifted in through the cargo door, containing the bodies of the pilots, Victor Harris and C.J. Webber, and co-pilot Gus Athas.[211] Since the return flight did not stop in Pittsburgh, Belding flew the plane nearly over the top of Bucktooth Ridge and the remains of his crashed C-46 airplane, during the flight to Florida. Minnie Moon later told her sister Pearl, it was a long, quiet and somber flight home. Pearl also returned home to Florida quietly and without any press coverage, on another Continental Charters flight a few days later, and she resumed her stewardess career.

ON JANUARY 4, RUBY CAUGHT a ride with her brother-in-law, Rollin, to Salamanca Hospital and her appointment with Dr. Fleming, the same doctor who, only days earlier, hiked up Bucktooth Ridge above the Bryant and Herrick farms to administer first aid to the victims of the plane crash. Ruby had procrastinated since mid-November about seeking medical treatment for the pain, redness and swelling in her breast and armpit. While riding to the hospital to see the doctor who, like her, had been so deeply involved in the plane crash and getting help for the survivors, Ruby most likely thought again about how her symptoms were just like cancer. She wrote in her diary how it consumed her private thoughts and fears.

Also on January 4, the CAB investigators finished their examination at the scene of the crash. Pulling out the police officers guarding the

---

[210] Minnie Moon Hunsberger died in 2005, before the beginning of research for this book.
[211] Hans Rutzebeck's body was cremated, and his ashes were buried in Alaska.

wreck, the CAB ordered Continental Charters to post a security guard. It lasted for one day. Unguarded, the crash site became a free-for-all. Within hours, sightseers and thrill seekers who hiked to the top of the ridge pilfered the scene. Margaret Herrick reported seeing teams of men dragging large pieces of the plane down to Sawmill Run Road where they encountered difficulty getting the items into their cars. The Herricks discussed with the CAB, and Continental Charters' insurance company, the possibility of salvaging the plane to help pay for the cost of damage done to their farm by the rescue crews but the looters beat them to it. Even parts of the plane's landing gear, radios, and fire extinguishers were hauled off by souvenir hunters. Word of the mass looting got out quickly and by Sunday, when sheriff's deputies were called back to Sawmill Run to control traffic, again, it was estimated that a thousand people were mobbed along the trail going up and down the ridge carrying off pieces of the plane.[212] In no time at all, the souvenir hunters and looters picked the wreck nearly clean. The only items they left behind were too large and heavy to carry – the engines and fuselage.[213] For weeks, the wreck tourists kept coming. The Herrick's had to lock their doors, even in the barn. They had never been locked before.

IN SALAMANCA HOSPITAL ON January 4, Ruby wrote in her diary that she was treated like a celebrity by the nurses who were also caring for the crash survivors. "Are you the lady from the airplane crash…," they would typically begin their greetings. Several of the crash survivors were still in the hospital just down the hall from where Ruby consulted with her doctor. There were no reports that nurses passed along news of Ruby's hospital visit to the survivors, but in a small town and small hospital buzzing with the big plane crash news, it's likely that some of them were told. And, Ruby never mentioned in her detailed diary if she and Dr. Fleming talked about the plane crash but it's very likely they did. The crash was only days old,

---

[212] This account may have been inflated but the large number did appear in at least one newspaper.
[213] During research for this book, a few Cattaraugus County residents told me of people who kept pieces of the wreckage for souvenirs. However, at the time of publication, none had come forward with evidence.

but it had been well over a month since Ruby first noticed the pain in her breast. Then, just as stewardess Pearl Moon had done with the pilots of Flight 44-2, Ruby placed her confidence in her doctor and turned to him for her examination. Lifting her blouse and removing her brassiere to show Dr. Fleming the lump and the red spot on her breast, Ruby explained how it had been sore and painful almost from the beginning. To her relief, but confusion, she heard the doctor say he thought it was a mastitis condition. While Ruby replaced her clothes with a somewhat refreshed sense of her health, Dr. Fleming suggested she take some medicine and rub camphor oil on her breast twice a day for the next month and then return to see him.[214] Later, Ruby wrote in her diary, *"I wasn't sure if I liked being an old cow so I looked it (mastitis) up in the dictionary and it said 'an inflammation of the breast.' Well, cows have udders so, I thought, at least I'm not an old cow."* What Ruby didn't realize at the moment was that an accurate diagnosis of breast cancer, which she had been suffering from November and all through December and the plane crash events, was delayed another month, further jeopardizing her life. She returned home to Sawmill Run and the daily horde of plane crash sightseers to spend the next four weeks rubbing camphor oil on her breast and nipple to alleviate the pain, redness and swelling from breast cancer. *"I waited about a month to give plenty of time for the treatment to help, but it didn't,"* Ruby wrote in her diary. Through all this time, most of the crash survivors were discharged from Salamanca Hospital, funerals and burials were performed for the dead, lawsuits were filed against Continental Charters, the crash investigation hearings were held in Little Valley, another passenger plane crashed in Elizabeth, and President Truman and the CAB ordered sweeping safety improvements for the nonsked airlines. Ruby, the woman who first helped George Albert tell the world about the downed plane, kept rubbing oil on her chest.[215]

---

[214] There is no way to determine the initial diagnosis except Ruby's diary. Ruby was also given "medicine." Rubbing camphor oil on the breast and nipple was a common home remedy for cystic mastitis. Overall, survival rates for breast cancer were low in 1951 and many women, including Ruby, considered it a death sentence.

[215] This is not to suggest indifference by the doctor or a misdiagnosis, but, rather, the difficulty women of this era had with early detection and treatment of breast cancer. Often, by the time they noticed a lump, it was too late.

ON JANUARY 17, THE SAME day as the investigation hearing began into the cause of the crash of Flight 44-2, Evelyn Harris sat down with a pen at her home in Miami and crafted a poem in her notebook. By this time, it was clear that the CAB was blaming her husband, Victor, for the crash. Her heart ached, despite the marital difficulties between them. Evelyn was left at home with two little children and no insurance for Victor's death through Continental Charters. She wrote in blue ink across the page:

Your First and Last Flight

You went away not long ago and how I've missed you, no one knows.

The memories of years keep flooding back, so fast and furious I soon lose track.

Like the day you made your very first flight and I waited through a cold and anxious night. It was over water and I was so afraid until you were home and the trip was made.

You were so proud and happy when you returned, my worries seemed small and nothing, I learned. I became used to your flights and being alone, of waiting without worry until your were home.

You were on the road that led to the top. You worked and studied, just never stopped. You were made Captain in a very short time and I was so proud and happy that you were mine.

But now you're made your very last flight. Your plane vanished on a cold, dark night. But wherever you are tonight, my own, you'll know that in memories, I'm not alone.

Just as in memories of that first flight the nights are long. But that's alright for wherever you are in heaven above, you will know that I'm sending my eternal love. E.L.H. 1/17/52

ON FEBRUARY 6, A LARGE flatbed tractor-trailer truck parked along Sawmill Run Road just a short distance from the Herrick farm. From the barnyard, the Herrick boys drove their *Cletrac* through the mud on separate trips hauling a trailer loaded with each of the C-46's mighty Pratt and Whitney engines. The boys alone hauled the heavy and mangled power plants down Bucktooth Ridge cutting deep ruts through the woods with the crawler-tractor. Photographs taken with a cheap camera show the boys riding atop the *Cletrac* together, dwarfed by the giant engines on the small trailer behind them. In the photos, as the Herrick boys emerge from a dark tunnel created by the tall, bare trees of Bucktooth Ridge, the engines tower behind them on the same cart that hauled the motionless bodies of the little kids down the ridge. Dressed in grease and manure and mud-stained denim dungarees and jackets, and with their hat bills bent upwards in teenager style, Marion, and Robert Herrick are shown clowning around for the camera, their valuable prize; two R-2800 engines, partially covered with a torn canvas tarpaulin. With chains and hooks, a large crane lifted the engines and dropped them in place on the flatbed truck. Large pieces of fuselage followed; the smashed cockpit, the middle section that claimed so many lives, and the life-sparing aft section that held the survivors. The large rudder with its tail identification number, *N3944C*, was the last piece to be loaded onto trucks. Unable to reach an agreement with its insurance company for payment on the crashed plane, the pieces of the wreckage not hauled off by looters were reclaimed by Continental Charters. Already entering bankruptcy, the airline hired a Florida salvage company to haul the wreckage parts back to Miami. Salvage workers said thousands of dollars of small mechanical parts had already been stolen by the time they arrived. The extended-bed trucks with special escort vehicles pulled out of Napoli that night for the airplane's long, slow trip down the east coast. Finally, the wreckage spectacle was gone from Bucktooth Ridge and Sawmill Run. Its vestige would remain, however, for another 60 years.

A FEW DAYS LATER, in early February, Ruby called Dr. Fleming and told him the pain, redness, and swelling in her breast was getting worse, not better. She wrote in her diary that he suggested over the telephone that she give the oil treatments another two weeks. In 1951, a doctor's advice was treated with great respect, and second opinions were often not obtained, especially by people, like Ruby, with limited funds and education. In fact, doctors and airplane pilots were revered much the same. Theirs were prestigious professions and, all-knowing, with people's lives in their hands, their expertise was seldom questioned. Dutifully, Ruby self-administered the camphor oil treatments to her chest. Twice a day she rubbed the oil over her breast and nipple where the rapid absorption into her skin was supposed to alleviate the pain and swelling. It didn't work. Finally returning to Salamanca Hospital and Dr. Fleming on February 22, nearly 100 days after first noticing the pain and a lump in her breast, Ruby wrote that she was told *"that's getting bigger and the treatment isn't helping. You'd better have it out."* She was given an appointment for surgery on March 7. Ruby stole a glance at her hospital chart and for the first time saw Dr. Fleming's written diagnosis: *"breast tumor."*

When Ruby entered the hospital for surgery by the same two doctors who hiked up Bucktooth Ridge and gave first aid to the plane crash survivors, she was treated again as a celebrity. The nurses asked her if she was the Ruby Bryant to whose home George Albert hiked to find help for the crash survivors. Replying yes, Ruby was quietly informed that one of the survivors, Mary Messerlos, was still a patient in Salamanca Hospital but would probably be discharged soon. Ruby's doctors had been caring for her too. The kind and sympathetic nurses, Ruby learned, were alarmed at the condition of her breast and she heard them questioning in the hallway outside her hospital room why the doctors hadn't already taken a tissue sample and sent it to a laboratory for analysis.

Along with Dr. Fleming, Dr. Leland Stoll, Ruby wrote in her diary, made his preoperative examination *"with a face as grave as an Indian's. He kept feeling under my armpit and asking me how old I was. Then, he looked graver than ever and asked me if I had been pregnant lately."* Both doctors' hands were icy cold, she wrote, but Ruby didn't mind because her breast felt red hot. Whether Ruby initially realized the extent of the surgery is unknown. It was only to remove a tissue sample from the tumor in her breast, not to remove the tumor or her breast. From her description in her diary, it appeared as if Ruby's breast cancer was being treated the same way the CAB had long treated the crash problems among the nonskeds: by procrastinating, analyzing, examining, and picking at the problem, without a clear solution, until it was too late. The last thing Ruby had remembered before surgery was looking up to see Dr. Fleming's green eyes, blending in with his green surgical mask and gown and the green walls of the operating room.[216] It was 9 am on March 7. On the same day, in Washington, the CAB adopted the findings in its Continental Charters crash investigation report. It blamed the pilots.

BEFORE RUBY LEFT THE hospital, and even before her breast tumor tissue sample had been analyzed by pathologists, Dr. Fleming came to see her with the bad news. *"He looked so sorry for me but, I felt sorrier for myself,"* she wrote in her diary. Perhaps Ruby only then clearly understood the result of her procrastination because the doctor's next advice was to tell her husband, Charlie, and then make arrangements to visit Roswell Park Cancer Institute in Buffalo. He told her *"it was a state-owned hospital and free." He said I should have deep radiation treatment."* Her premonition of cancer had come true.

Not long after Ruby went home to recuperate from her surgery, she wrote a diary passage that indicates she long contemplated her inaction which put her in such a predicament. *"I'll never forget it as long as there's any me. And if they can't cure or ever hold in check that 'ole cancer, I at least will do all I can to help the fight against cancer so others may be helped."* Ruby celebrated her 46th birthday on March 18 where her family and friends gave her a birthday cake, chocolate candy, many dollar bills, four pairs of nylon stockings, and even a pound of butter. Afterward, brave and optimistic Ruby, the woman who first got help for the plane crash survivors on Bucktooth Ridge, made another entry in her diary about the night of her birthday party, *"After I went to bed tears slid down my cheeks because it made me so happy...lucky, lucky me,"* she wrote.

WITHIN DAYS OF THE crash, school resumed for local children who returned to classes from the Christmas holiday full of stories they had

---

[216] Ruby's surgery to collect a tissue sample was invasive, under anesthesia, and with probing to snip and remove the tissue. She was hospitalized for six nights for what would be a simple out-patient procedure in 2015.

heard from their parents about the dead and survivors atop Bucktooth Ridge. Some of the children in Randolph played pranks on others with imagined stories about the victims of the crash. "Look in this box," a student would command to another while holding out a small jewelry box. The top would be removed to reveal a finger with red ink around. "What's that," the other student would ask. "A finger from one of the dead passengers," was the reply. And the childish trick would be repeated as long as it offended people, or until the box with a hole in the bottom was confiscated by a teacher. Gossiping about the bickering among the survivors stuck on Bucktooth Ridge was also rampant as Cattaraugus County residents tried to imagine how they would have dealt with the cold, lack of food and bathrooms, and the fear of death. Some residents clipped the gruesome newspaper photographs of the stewardess hanging dead from her seat belt, the pilots' arms sprawled into the snow, the foot still in its shoe, and Judy Frankel's Raggedy Ann doll in the wreckage. Others repeated the story of how two passengers were decapitated. The photographs and articles were glued into scrapbooks, read over a few times, and then filed away. Soon, the crash was forgotten. Ruby couldn't forget. However, she still had the daily parade of crash tourists driving past her farmhouse searching for the crash site. And she still had the pain in her breast.

When April Fools' Day arrived, there was no fooling about Ruby's mood as she eagerly awaited the warmer weather of spring. She sat down at home and wrote two full pages in her diary. She signed and dated them. It was her will. The 14 survivor passengers from Flight 44-2 had all gone home to resume their lives, but Ruby knew that her life was coming to an end. In the will she doled out her wedding ring, watch, and other jewelry (beads), and assigned her photographs to anyone in the family who wanted them. Then, she wrote, *"My red gown is good enough for a burial garment after Roswell Park Memorial Institute gets through with my body (but) leave my feet bare, I like them so."* The homespun girl from West Virginia wore cowboy boots for her breast surgery, but she wanted to be buried in her bare feet. Ruby considered cremation but then decided to leave that up to her family. She offered her cedar chest, RCA Victrola, and 78 RPM records to whoever wanted them, and then she declared that it was *"not much of a will after all."* Ruby realized that she didn't have much except what was most important, *"Most of my treasures are my family and friends."* Ruby then wrote her most intimate thoughts about death after hearing that a friend's teenage daughter was killed in an automobile crash[217] *"I feel depressed hearing about cute little Pee Wee. She was so vibrant with life. And now (she) is forever caught in silence and stillness or, at least, is now motionless, emotionless and stilted by the stillness of death."* Then, perhaps realizing she was really writing about herself, Ruby masked her feelings. *"Oh, I'll stop writing here now and I'll try to remember others and not think so much about myself."* Still sad, Ruby then drew a caricature of herself with dark pigtails and with the corners of her mouth turned down. She labeled it *"Petunia Pig."*[218]

Ruby kept herself busy through the next few weeks of April supervising her family at home on the farm because she couldn't do much work. Little Otis provided brief respites of joy and comedy, but her arm was in such pain from the breast cancer tumor that it was useless. She could barely lift it. She dutifully paid her $50 bill for Doctors Fleming and Stoll, she skipped several Sundays at church, slept and read a book, *The Man from Dakota*. She and Otis took walks up the hollow when the older boys were at school, past the hunting camps, and along the same route George Albert had walked down to find her. On weekdays, it was quiet on Sawmill Run like it used to be before the crash, but weekends were still busy with tourists. On her walks, she took notice of the grass growing, the frogs singing, a dove cooing, and she listened, even while standing on her back porch. These were the sounds of new life in the spring that she had certainly heard before but had not truly appreciated, until now. Even the buzzing sounds of an airplane flying overhead, which she had dismissed that foggy night on December 29 before she fully realized she had breast cancer, caught her attention now. Ruby had heard that officials in Washington somehow

---

[217] The girl was Ann Louise Plough, daughter of "Pete" and Leona Plough, the same couple that owned a hunting cabin on Sawmill Run bypassed by George Albert when he was searching for help.
[218] Petunia Pig was a character in the popular Looney Tunes comic book and film cartoons who wore her black hair in long pigtails.

made them safer but to this development she hadn't paid much attention because of her illness. She watched the brief excitement of the fishermen sweeping into the hollow for the first few days of trout season and then it was quiet again, except for the crash sightseers on weekends. On one Sunday in April that she took a long nap, Uncle Rollin even joined the tourists and hiked up the ridge to see what was left of the crash site. By this time, the wreckage was gone but the chopped off remains of the trees were visible, and the gouges in the earth had turned to mud. Even the galvanized trash can that the survivors used for their campfire had been carried off by looters. It was as if the crash had never happened. Ruby wished her cancer had never happened.

And then, on April 18, Ruby got up early and caught the Edwards Lakes to Seas bus in Salamanca for the trip to Buffalo and Roswell Park. Her mastectomy surgery must have been a traumatic event because Ruby stopped writing in her diary until June when she wrote only about her follow-up visits. They included hormone injections that made her voice deep and hoarse and made soft, fuzzy hair grow around her lips, on her cheeks and chin. The hormone injections also intensified her sexual urges, she wrote. She wished they would go away. Many times, through all the visits for her 18 hormone shots, when a nurse at Roswell Park noticed her home address on Sawmill Run, Ruby was asked again if she was the woman who helped rescue George Albert and the other survivors. Just like the continuous stream of crash tourists that now invaded the quiet hollow of Sawmill Run, Ruby could not escape her new celebrity. She wished that would go away too.

Ruby's final entry in her diary was on June 29 when she wrote that the oldest of her beloved five sons, Benton, got married and returned with his wife, Florence, to his Army post in Washington. Now, there were just four boys at home with Charlie, Ruby, and Uncle Rollin. Strangers passed by almost every weekend asking how to get up the ridge to the scene of the plane crash. Ruby's skin and muscle healed from her mastectomy and left a scar, but the cancer was still in her. Her health worsened. She waited. There was no rescue in sight.

Pearl had returned to her stewardess job with Continental Charters, Lt. Bischof was back at his Navy post commanding a ship, and even

George Albert had returned to Miami and his restaurant, although he still suffered from guilt and regret over the crash and the death of his mother. Ruby may have wondered if the quietness and calm of their lives before the plane crash that she so craved would ever return to Sawmill Run. It would, but not for another six months. Just over a year from George Albert's sudden appearance in their yard turned their lives upside down, it grew quiet again in the Bryant's farmhouse. There were no banner headlines, no bright lights from cameras, no live radio interviews, and no crowds of police, rescuers, reporters, and sightseers. Silence and stillness finally returned to Sawmill Run.

Top left, clockwise, 1954 theater poster for *The High and the Mighty*, starring John Wayne, left; William Wellman, on ladder, directing Wayne in the cockpit of a DC-4 loaned by nonsked Transocean, 1953; John Wayne with passengers and crew in publicity stills released by Warner Brothers to promote the movie in 1954. Many of the scenarios in *The High and the Mighty* resembled real scare and crash events among nonsked airlines of 1951-52.

Top left, clockwise, teenagers Marion and Robert Herrick haul plane crash wreckage from the forest on Bucktooth Ridge with their crawler-tractor; posing for their family's camera in front of one of the C-46 engines in the same cart that hauled survivors and bodies; loading the C-46 engines and the floor of the plane onto flatbed trucks with a crane at the Herrick farm for transport to Florida. Salvage of wreckage not carried off by looters was an attempt to recover the enormous financial cost of the crash.

The Bryant boys and their children in front of Benton's Model T Ford at the family farm on Sawmill Run, about 1969. Front, left to right, John, and Benton holding Stuart's daughter, Sonya. Standing, left to right, John's sons, Charles and Mark; Otis, Rodney, Stuart, and Stuart's daughters, Lorraine and Suzanne. This is one of only a few photographs of Ruby's and Charlie Bryant's boys, together. The world renowned plane crash on Bucktooth Ridge above their farm marked the beginning of dramatic and tragic changes in their lives, leading to the loss of their parents.

EPILOGUE

ON SATURDAY, JANUARY 15, 1953, Ruby Jewel Bowles Bryant died at Salamanca District Hospital from complications caused by her breast cancer. It was a year and 16 days since George walked out of the woods and into her farmyard. Ruby left behind her husband and five boys, including little Otis, who turned six just weeks earlier. As difficult as it was to adjust to a new life without their mother, a year later the Bryant boys were hit with another tragedy. In poor health with stomach ulcers, despondent over the loss of his wife, medical bills, and from recently being laid off from his job, Charlie Bryant took his 12-guage shotgun to go hunting in the woods above Sawmill Run on February 20, 1954. Worried when he didn't return by nightfall, the older boys including John bundled in their winter clothes, just as they had done for the plane crash, and entered the woods to search for him. They heard a shotgun blast. Sheriff Sigel made the official report that Benton, Rodney, and John found their father's body in the snow nearly a mile from the farm. It wasn't far from the plane crash scene. Bucktooth Ridge claimed another life.

ON TUESDAY, FEBRUARY 23, the Bryant boys, Uncle Rollin, and the rest of the family gathered for services at the same funeral home that cared for their mother's body and which handled several victims from the plane crash. Charlie was buried next to Ruby in the family plot at Wildwood Cemetery in Salamanca. His obituary briefly mentioned how the family helped George after the plane crash but Ruby's didn't. It was as if her important role in rescuing the crash survivors was erased and forgotten.

When Charlie Bryant took his own life, only two years had passed since the crash. But, in that short time the family that took in George Albert, and helped spread the news to the world of the tragedy on Bucktooth Ridge, had been torn apart just like the families of the crash victims. The quiet and simple life they so enjoyed for decades had been ripped from them since the day George appeared at their front door. The job of raising little Otis fell to Rodney and Stuart. Much like Ruby had pitched in to raise her little sister in West Virginia when their mother, Belle, died, Rodney became a surrogate father for Otis through his formative years. In the late 1960s, when Otis caught up in size to his much older brothers, they all posed for a photograph in front of Benton's Ford Model T, parked in front of the old family farmhouse. Each adult son of Ruby and Charlie, surrounded by a handful of new children born into their family, is smiling for the camera. From such a happy scene, it's difficult to imagine the tragedies of their past.

The Bryant farm on Sawmill Run is still in the family, but the old frame farmhouse was torn down long ago. New homes line the road and several more camps have been constructed in the woods. In 2009, John Bryant, who lives on the old farm, got a telephone call from a Buffalo newspaper reporter inquiring about a plane crash. A regional commuter turboprop passenger plane operated by Colgan Air and flying as Continental Connection crashed in Buffalo on February 12 of that year killing all 49 people onboard and one person on the ground. For the reporter, John again told the story of the long forgotten crash on Bucktooth Ridge but without many of the private and painful details that had such a great personal impact on his family. The newspaper story revived interest in the crash of Flight 44-2 and soon more strangers were driving into the hollow asking for directions to the scene. Even though the woods have reclaimed the crash site, more than 60 years later people continue making the trek to the top of the ridge looking for signs of the wreckage. Most of them leave disappointed. There is simply nothing left to see.

Pearl Ruth Moon continued in her job as a stewardess for Continental Charters until it was forced into bankruptcy and out of business by the mid-1950s. Pearl was involved in another plane crash after the tragedy on Bucktooth Ridge but it wasn't serious, just a crash landing into the ocean while flying from Miami to the Bahamas in a small plane. Florida state records show that she was married briefly in 1957, but she chose to deny it during her interview. I found her living quietly as a ward of the State of North Carolina at a nursing home near Raleigh. Eager to discuss the crash in 1951 and her struggle to survive in the cold and snow on Bucktooth Ridge, Pearl had her hair styled and makeup applied for an on-camera interview. She emphasized her position that she was not given enough credit for her leadership among the survivors on those three days and two nights stranded on the ridge. She blamed it on the men reporters, suggesting they ignored her story for those told by George and Lt. Bischof. A brief portion of the interview I conducted with Pearl can be found on the internet. Pearl's health declined and on December 27, 2012, she died from old age. As if she were still stubbornly holding out for rescue, Pearl was the last of the survivors of Flight 44-2.

George Albert returned to Miami and married Ava G. Isley in 1952. He was apparently haunted by his mother's death in the plane crash and was wracked with guilt over his decision to exchange seats with her. He kept his bloodied plane crash clothes in a closet for years, according to information from his sister, Dorothy, provided to blogger Jaclyn Hoard-Beals of Salamanca.

George and Ava were divorced in May 1967. George died in Winter Haven, Florida on June 17, 1989, at the age of 67. Except for the hours and days immediately following the tragedy, he never really accepted the accolades as the hero of the crash of Flight 44-2.

Lt. William Bischof returned to his Navy career and rose in rank to become a commander of destroyers and Oilers in the Pacific Ocean. He later joined the faculty of the Naval War College in Norfolk, Virginia. He died at the age of 80 on December 31, 2005, 54 years from the day he was rescued from the plane crash. Newspaper articles about his advancing career often mentioned his heroics among the survivors on Bucktooth Ridge.

Donald Nyrop left the CAB to become president of Northwest Airlines in 1954. He is credited with rescuing the financially ailing airline, with a lackluster safety record, and turning it into one of the giants of the industry as it expanded into Asia, becoming Northwest Orient. Nyrop's son, Bill, became a professional hockey player, winning three Stanley Cup Championships with the Montreal Canadiens. Bill Nyrop died from cancer at his father's home in Edina, Minnesota in 1995 at 43. Donald Nyrop lived to the age of 98. He died at home on November 16, 2010. His precedent-setting visit to the scene of the crash of Flight 44-2 is now standard practice among leaders of the NTSB and his early public relations skills, calming the nerves of American fliers, are practiced today by the NTSB through Twitter.

David and Rosa Shenefiel lived on their farm along Hoxie Hill Road until 1969, when they sold it and moved to East Randolph. Rosa died a short time later, but David lived until 1996 when he died in Randolph at the age of 87. He rarely talked about his connection to the plane crash. His parents' farm, in the valley below Bucktooth Ridge, and their woodlot next to the crash scene, are still in the family, and they appeared in 2015 much the same as they did in 1951. The Hoxie Farm, with its commanding view of Bucktooth Ridge from the top of Hoxie Hill, was sold during the financial crunch on small family farms in the 1970s and '80s and was part of a larger producing farm in 2015. The view from Hoxie Hill to Bucktooth Ridge remains the same as it did in 1951 except for the installation of a tall communications tower on Parker Hill, just below Bucktooth Ridge.

Many of the children of victims and survivors of the crash of Flight 44-2 were still alive in 2015 and contributed to this book. While all of them deserve recognition for contributing documents, photographs, and personal details of their parents, hurt or lost in the crash, one deserves special attention because he lost nearly everyone. Upon hearing news of the crash on New Years' Day, 1952, Manny Frankel left Miami for Pittsburgh in a car with his grandmother and aunts and uncles. When they reached Roanoke, Virginia they got the news that his mother Anne, younger brother, Mark, and little sister, Judy, were dead. They continued on to Pittsburgh for the funerals. Manny eventually returned to Florida where he was raised by his aunt and uncle, became a dentist, and practiced for many years in Miami and Ormond Beach. He said he had a difficult time dealing with his loss. He felt guilty that they died while traveling to see him. He eventually overcame his feelings, however, with help from his father and other relatives. The sad story of how his little sister, Judy, died in Pearl Moon's arms tugged at the heart strings of Americans when it was retold several times in the newspapers of 1952. Dr. Manny Frankel told me many years later that the loss of his mother and siblings has had a positive impact on the love he shares with his own family of "a tremendous wife and three great sons. Who knows what would have happened if this tragedy had not befallen me," he said.

Three of the four wives of the pilots on Flight 44-2 were still alive during the time of my research for this book too. Evelyn Harris Ross had remarried and was living in Florida. She told me that her son, Raymond Victor Harris, who turned one just two days before his father was killed in the crash, grew very excited to help with research about his father's flying career. Evelyn also raised a daughter, Judith Evelyn Harris. After revisiting the painful story one more time including the emotional poem she wrote about her husband, Vic, Evelyn said, "now I'm going to tuck all the memories and put them even deeper in the corner of my heart."

Isobel Rutzebeck was in her 90's and living in California when she participated in a lengthy interview about her husband, Rutz. After his death in the crash, Isobel took night courses for a college degree and became a school teacher. Upon retirement, she traveled the world, teaching English in Thailand and Gambia. She later traveled on the famous Orient Express passenger train into China and Russia before returning home on a freighter. The adventurous woman, who once trapped beavers in Alaska to pay for repairs to Rutz's damaged airplane, lived in a small cabin on Lac St. Anne, Alberta, Canada before old age required that she move to California and into an assisted-living home near her son. Lief Hans Rutzebeck provided many biographical documents about the father he never knew and he was very curious about any new details uncovered during my research. Isobel also raised her daughter, Peggy Rutzebeck, mostly alone. Appropriate for his daring bush pilot past, in March 1952 Isobel arranged for Rutz's ashes to be buried in a nondescript Veterans of Foreign Wars cemetery outside the small town of Nenana, Alaska, about 50 miles from Fairbanks and within the greater Yukon-Koyukuk region of his earlier bush-flying adventures. The cemetery is at the end of a long narrow gravel road hidden by fir and deciduous trees. About a mile away is the short paved runway for the Nenana Municipal Airport. As planes take off toward the west and bank south, they dip their wings over Rutz's grave.

Pearl Quam Webber returned to her teaching career after her husband, CJ, was killed in the plane crash. She lived in Florida while raising her three children. Pearl Webber Thomas died on March 15, 1984, and she was buried next to CJ at Woodlawn Park Cemetery in Miami. Her daughter, Nancy, consulted with siblings Conrad and Barbara, and provided a well-researched family biography of CJ for this book, to which I have added and reconstructed.

Joan Athas continued living in Florida for many years after the death of her husband, Gus, but later moved back to her childhood home in northern New Jersey. She remarried and became Joan Visco. Like the Harris, Rutzebeck, and Webber children, her two sons, Gus (Michael) and James Athas were so young at the time of the crash they don't remember much of anything about their father. Joan described Gus as *"a lovely, sweet young man. I miss him to this day,"* she wrote during her first response to my inquiry. She has visited his grave in Miami many times at Flagler Memorial Park Cemetery. As if they were still in the cockpit, Victor Harris is buried beside him.

Kenneth and Margaret Herrick lived on their farm for many years after the crash, but their quiet, peaceful country life was constantly interrupted by crash plane tourists making their way to the top of the ridge. So many people invaded their farm during the summer of 1952 that they had to tack *Posted* signs on the trees lining the road. Deer hunters that autumn reported that there were still pieces of metal and torn clothing around the crash scene, and it remained that way for several years. Eventually, though, everything disappeared. The Herricks died in 1980 and 1985, respectively, with no mention in their obituaries about their farm being used as the staging area for the plane crash survivors and victims. The old farmhouse and the red barn were still there in 2015, on a knoll overlooking Sawmill Run Road and the steep incline of Herrick's Hill. Members of the Herrick family still owned large plots of woodlands on the west side of Bucktooth Ridge through which George walked to find Ruby but the farmhouse and barn had been sold. I should point out that Kenneth Herrick was related to me although I never met him or any other members of the Herrick family. Kenneth Herrick's mother, Blanche Stoughton Herrick, was the oldest sister of my paternal grandmother, Pearl Stoughton Lake. All have been dead for many years.

Aside from growth of trees, and logging over the years, the landscape along Sawmill Run and the west side of Bucktooth Ridge hasn't changed very much. It is, however, private land and, therefore, off limits to trespassers. On the east side of Bucktooth Ridge, much of the land is owned by the State of New York as part of Bucktooth State Forest. While the state land comes close to the scene, it does not include the crash site, which remains privately-owned. During my years of research, it was suggested to me by an interested party that perhaps the state land would be an appropriate location for a stone memorial to the victims of the crash of Flight 44-2. To my knowledge, a memorial has never been contemplated or erected. There is nothing to memorialize the victims of Flight 44-2 or the survivors and brave heroes, George, Lt. Bischof, Pearl, and Ruby.

All through 1952, relatives of the dead and survivors made their way to the Cattaraugus County Sheriff's Office in Little Valley to collect luggage, clothing and personal items recovered from the wreckage. Clothing items not claimed were sent to a laundry and then distributed among needy families, recalled a reporter. A full year after the crash, Sheriff Sigel's wife, Irene, was still trying to find the rightful owners of a wrist watch, necklace, and a pair of earrings found in the wreckage. Sheriff Morgan L. Sigel continued serving in his elected post until he retired in 1963, setting a record of 23 years in office. Sheriff Sigel died in 1983 at the age of 86 in Olean. His obituary included a long list of accomplishments but did not mention his role in coordinating the plane crash rescue, removal of the bodies, and the two-day hearing. To this day, a few old-timers still wonder who it was that Sheriff Sigel declined to prosecute for the theft of $700 from one of the bodies in the plane crash. Considering all the pain caused by the crash all these years, perhaps it's better to be left a secret.

Robin Airlines passenger Jerry (Laufgraben) Lawrence told me he always got nervous when flying for many years after the crash-landing in the snow in Cobourg, Ontario in December 1951. Jerry changed his last name to Lawrence and moved to Nova Scotia where he operated a marine chemical-cleaner distribution business. In the 1970s while returning from a trip to take his daughter to college, Jerry stopped by the Cobourg police department and asked if anyone remembered the Robin Airlines crash-landing incident. A veteran police officer did and took Jerry to the old Wilson farm where they looked around for a time and talked about their shared memories. The police officer joked with Jerry that he thought at the time that the mysterious plane would have to be shot down by the Canadian Air Force. The Wilson farm, where the plane landed, was developed into a shopping mall, a Canadian Tire store, and residential housing in the late 1980s. Jerry Lawrence was 83 in 2012 when he did an extensive interview with me about his near-death experience as a young man. He died at his retirement home in Florida a short time after that.

The wide array of new safety regulations imposed on airlines operating in the United States since the many crashes of 1951 and '52 have been listed in the previous chapters of this book. One question about safety on an airplane will always remain, however. Where is the safest seat? Turn to the passengers in your aisle the next time you take a trip by airplane and ask them. They will likely tell you it's in the back of the plane, but they probably have no idea how they got this information. While I've never come across a report or professional study stating the origin of this notion, I firmly believe that it began with the crash of Flight 44-2 on Bucktooth Ridge in Napoli. Even the hardened news reporters who hiked to the top of the ridge were amazed to find that 14 people survived such a horrific crash. Asking each one where they were sitting, the reporters found that they all received the same answer: "In the back of the plane." As this phrase was repeated in newspapers across the country at a time when people were frightened to travel on airplanes, passengers began to accept the concept that they were safest in the back of a plane. A few weeks later, when the National Airlines DC-6 crashed into Elizabeth, more surviving passengers told reporters they lived only because they were in the back of the plane. Public perception that passengers are always safest in the back of a plane had taken hold and it spread until it was universally accepted as fact. But, there was still no scientific proof that it was true. In fact, for years many aviation organizations stated that it could not be determined in which seat passengers were safest. It wasn't until 2007 that a professional organization, *Popular Mechanics*, examined every commercial passenger jet plane crash in America since 1971 and found that it was true! *"Passengers near the tail of a plane are about 40 percent more likely to survive a crash than those in the first few rows up front,"* reported the magazine's David Noland. The survivors of the crash of Flight 44-2 in 1951 certainly could have provided testament to his findings.

No longer do we have to *Hang on and Fly* as passengers did in 1951 and '52. Statistically, we're actually very safe in an airplane. But, if you really want to increase your chance of survival, skip paying for first-class and go to the back of the plane. It's closer to the lavatory, and if you do encounter the extremely rare chance of a crash, and survive, you may end up as a long-lasting hero in the headlines like George, Pearl, and Lt. Bischof, or at least, an instantaneous and brief hero portrayed in modern social media.

SURVIVORS OF FLIGHT 44-2

George Albert, 30, Miami, FL
Mary Battista, 28, Weirtown, WV
Dolores Beshears, 21, stewardess, Miami, FL
Lt. William W. Bischof, 26, Johnstown, PA
Albert Dichak, 29, Canonsburg, PA
Robert Geyer, 35, Mt. Lebanon, PA
Mary Messerlos, 45, Pittsburgh, PA
Pearl Ruth Moon, 24, stewardess, Miami, FL
Marie Norcia, 47, East Liberty, PA
Thomas Patterson, 21, New Castle, PA
Anna Piso, 52, Crafton, PA
Edward Wessel, 19, Pittsburgh, PA
Eva Woodward, 62, Miami, FL
Joseph Wozniak, 33, Canonsburg, PA

VICTIMS OF FLIGHT 44-2

Elizabeth Albert, 46, Miami, FL
Sgt. David E. Arnold, 23, Miami, FL
Gus Athas, 25, co-pilot, Miami, FL
Dorothy Berman Bruce, 27, Kingston, Ontario, Canada
Jeffrey Evans, 1, Bridgeville, PA
Anne Frankel, 33, Pittsburgh, PA
Judy Frankel, 2, Pittsburgh, PA
Mark Frankel, 7, Pittsburgh, PA
Victor A. Harris, 28, pilot, Miami, FL
Delores Harvey, 22, stewardess, Miami, FL
Roy C. Hemphill, 19, Coraopolis, PA
John R. Jones, 31, Fairmount, WV
Margaret A. Jones, 30, Fairmount, WV
Laverne Kroll, 23, Bellevue, PA
Audrey Malcom, 24, Lockport, NY
Cpl. Richard J. Martin, 20, Buffalo, NY
Gertrude McLain, 54, Morgantown, WV
Roy McLain, 59, Morgantown, WV
Margaret B. Myers, 36, Hickory, Pa
John Opar, 19, Jeanette, PA
Phylis Paluzzi, 30, Hialeah, FL
Agnes Penman, 61, Opa-Locka, FL
Hans E. Rutzebeck, 33, co-pilot, Miami, FL
Benjamin M. Siegal, 35, Pittsburgh, PA
CJ Webber, 38, pilot, Miami, FL
Richard Wilson, 21, Sharon, PA

NOTES

VERY LITTLE HAS BEEN written collectively about the multitude of plane crashes among the nonskeds in 1951-'52 whose tragedies rippled all the way to the White House. I found that to be unusual because airline passenger travel has become such an integral part of our lives and because the crashes of this period have long shaped our perception of safety while flying. Based on the many interviews I conducted for this book, the research, and the glaring newspaper and magazine headlines of that era, it was one scary time for contemplating a trip on an airplane, especially among the nonskeds. However, flying was so new and exciting for Americans that they ignored the risk and boarded the planes anyway, often to their deaths. Can you imagine that today? There is simply no way the traveling public today would tolerate three or four crashes of commercial passenger airplanes every month. But, it happened in 1951-'52.

Aviation is regulated by the federal government. There is a fine publication that touches on the lax early federal regulations that, in part, caused this chain of crash events. *Airline Executives and Federal Regulation*, edited by W. David Lewis, is a scholarly publication which discusses the obstacles faced by CAB Chairman Donald Nyrop as he tried to reign in the irreverent non-scheduled airlines of the late 1940s and early 1950s. *The Best Transportation System in the World*, by Mark H. Rose, Bruce E. Seely, and Paul F. Barrett is another textbook-like publication which examines the problems associated with the nonskeds. Both books, published by Ohio State University Press, were written more for academia than for the general public. I have utilized a few brief passages from these books with attribution. If you wish to know more about the political and economic issues facing the nonskeds of this era, I encourage you to read these publications.

Additionally, in the final months of preparing this book for publication, I became aware that renowned fiction author Judy Blume had written a young adult fiction book, *In the Unlikely Event*, based upon the series of plane crashes in Elizabeth, New Jersey in 1951 and '52. I wish to emphasize that Blume's book is fiction, and it diverts from the crash events for many passages that are the mainstay of her writing style: coming of age and social interaction among young adults, including sexual activity. That these two titles would be released within months of each other is purely coincidental. I first began researching this story in 2008. In 2011, I wrote articles about the crash events for the *Pittsburgh Post-Gazette*, the *Buffalo News*, and the *Jamestown Post-Journal*. I hope that my deeply researched non-fiction story compliments Blume's fictional tale as her story has complimented mine. Another great book about one of the Elizabeth crashes was written by my editor, Judy Mandel. It's titled *Replacement Child* and is described in the manuscript.

While there aren't many books about the nonskeds, there are several books about the venerable C-46 airplane. The *Curtiss C-46 Commando*, by John M. Davis, Harold G. Martin, and John A. Whittle, lists small details about every C-46 built by the Curtiss-Wright Company. *C-46 Commando in Action* is a wonderfully illustrated booklet by Terry Love and Squadron Signal Publications. The Glenn H. Curtiss Museum in Hammondsport, New York also has a wealth of information about the C-46. Additional information about the construction of the C-46 was obtained from newspaper articles, and documents contained within websites about the history of Buffalo, New York. Old copies of the *Buffalo Evening News* and *Buffalo Courier-Express* contain many column inches about the former Curtiss-Wright factories that flanked the Buffalo Airport until the late 1940s.

Two choice publications about the C-46 flying The Hump were also useful for research on this book. *Born to Fly the Hump*, by Dr. Carl Frey Constein, was supplemented by a personal interview with Constein, at his home near Reading, Pennsylvania, about his many missions as pilot and co-pilot in C-46s flying over the Himalaya Mountains into China.

Flying the Hump, Memories of an Air War, by Otha C. Spencer, Texas A & M University Press, also provided great details about what it was like flying the C-46 in some of the worst weather conditions on earth. Ironically, some of the problems and anomalies associated with the C-46 that were encountered by Constein and Spencer while they flew the planes in 1944 and 1945 were never fixed or addressed before commercial pilots flew C-46s to carry passengers in 1951 and 1952. I've attributed the few citations from these books to their authors and publishers. Additional information about the C-46, the CAB regulations for non-scheduled airlines and crash investigations was obtained through research at the National Archives and Department of Transportation in Washington, DC. Details about the President's involvement in the CAB investigations and the crashes of 1951 and 1952 were provided by the Harry S. Truman Library and Museum in Independence, Missouri.

A complete listing of primary sources for this book is in the Selected Bibliography section.

Preface

The description of CAB chairman Donald Nyrop flying into the Bradford, Pennsylvania airport is taken from newspaper reports in *the Bradford Era* and the *Jamestown Post-Journal* and cross-checked with Nyrop's CAB schedule for the time period. The newspaper reports list who arrived with him on the CAB's DC-3 from Washington after viewing the wreck site from the air. Descriptions of the scene of the crash of Flight 44-2 were provided during a lengthy personal interview with Stewardess Pearl Ruth Moon at her North Carolina nursing home in 2010. The graphic and precise descriptions of Pearl's bruises from the crash are derived from the excellent photographs taken by press photographers, most notably Dick Hallberg of the *Post-Journal.* Hallberg's photographs were so clear and crisp you could count the hairs in his subjects' eyebrows. The newspaper, for which I once worked, has allowed publication of these wonderful photographs.

My hypothesis that the origin of Americans' perception that we're always safest in the back of a plane is gathered from the many, many news reports in numerous newspapers and magazines in the weeks following the crash of Flight 44-2. Before this crash event, in research among many other articles and accounts of plane crash survivors dating back to the infancy of passenger aviation, there appears to be no recurring theme of how a seat choice may have spared such a large number of passengers in a single crash. Each of the three hero survivors, George, Lt. Bischof, and Pearl (George being the first) declared that they were alive only because they were sitting in the back of the plane. Because this was repeated so many times in newspapers all across the country, it caught on with passengers who began requesting seats in the back of planes believing it would increase their chance of survival in a crash.

The accounts of the three plane crash events most relevant to this story that I covered as a news reporter were gleaned from my memory. I also consulted my work notes and videotapes I've saved all these years along with documents from the crash investigations by the Department of Transportation and the National Transportation Safety Board, the successor agency to the CAB.

Chapter 1 – Pearl and Ruby

Retired stewardess Pearl Ruth Moon sat down with me for a long and detailed videotaped interview at her nursing home residence in North Carolina in 2010. She explained every detail, even pouring coffee for all four pilots as their flight was leaving Pittsburgh and checking her watch to determine their exact time of departure. Other details of this chapter are taken from the CAB crash investigation report and cross checked with newspaper accounts, weather reports, first-person newspaper diaries by some of the passengers, and interviews with families of the crash victims and survivors. Unless I'm proved wrong by someone who comes forward and discounts my exhaustive research, I found that Pearl was the longest-living survivor of the crash of Flight 44-2 and the only one still alive when I prepared this story. Her recollections were invaluable. Ruby Bryant's recollection of the night of the crash is taken from a 92-page diary she kept during her breast cancer battle and from statements by her sons. I confirmed her hand written account through newspaper articles and the CAB investigation report. My grandfather, David Shenefiel's, activities on the morning after the crash are a reconstruction of his daily routine as a Napoli farmer and from my personal recollections of his daily life on the family farm. The portrayal of the radio reports is from newspaper articles which told how news of the crash was first distributed to the public.

Chapter 2 – "Get That Plane in the Air"

Events surrounding the Miami departure of Continental Charters Flight 44-2 on December 29, 1951come from personal interviews with Pearl Moon, Evelyn Harris, Isobel Rutzebeck, and Joan Athas, using their 1951 married names for clarity. I also consulted the crash investigation report and many newspaper articles. Details about Continental Charters and its president, John Belding, were taken from CAB reports and legal document filings made during lawsuits against the airline. Historical information about Continental Charters and its planes was gleaned from the CAB crash investigation report, newspaper articles, documents in connection with the company's bankruptcy filings, and the book, *The Curtiss C-46 Commando*. By following the tail number of the C-46 plane that crashed in Napoli, it was possible to trace its cargo-hauling journeys around the world until it was leased for a passenger plane by Continental Charters. Both company records, and Joan Athas, widow of co-pilot Gus Athas, confirm that Athas flew the C-46 to Miami from Dallas after it was refurbished into a passenger plane in late December 1951. Great information about Continental Charters' Stratoliner, traced by its tail and manufacture number through the Aero Transport Data Bank, was uncovered at the Smithsonian National Air and Space Museum's Steven F. Udvar-Hazy Center near Washington in Chantilly, Virginia. The beautiful vintage plane, *Clipper Flying Cloud*, is fully restored and on display inside the large hangar museum near Dulles International Airport. Among all of the vintage planes at the museum, this one gleams in shiny silver and really stands out. The theory that Continental Charters gave up on the expensive and smaller Stratoliner for a cheaper C-46 is mine, alone. The source for the incredible bit of information about the two aborted departures for Continental Charters Flight 44-2 began with a passenger who got off the plane in Pittsburgh and later described the flight to a newspaper reporter. Uncomfortable with only one source, I carefully consulted the crash investigation report which stated that the flight had been long delayed in Miami. Then both Gus Athas' widow and Victor Harris' widow described a second flight delay, or, at least, a second mechanical delay instigated by the pilots before the boarding of the passengers. Two sources for a story element are reliable, but four independent sources confirming similar incidents are rock solid for historical research. While the CAB report declared there was nothing mechanically wrong with the plane that crashed, there certainly was something amiss that caused pilots Victor Harris and Hans Rutzebeck to abort their flight and return the plane to the Continental Charters mechanics in the Miami hanger shop, twice! Since Harris was described as a quality mechanic and Rutz often worked on his own small planes while, in Alaska, I have no doubt that they recognized some kind of problem with the C-46. Whatever it was will always remain a mystery. With Evelyn Harris' recollection of this event, I've chosen not to reveal the name of her Continental Charters pilot source because he has long been dead and was certainly not able to provide additional information or approve the public disclosure of his family name for such condemnatory information. Further descriptions of the flight are drawn from the mechanical operation of the plane, flight manuals, and parts identification booklets, and typical procedures and methods used for a long, cross-country flight in a war surplus C-46.

Chapter 3 – George Albert

Unlike the many newspaper accounts which initially portrayed him as a cosmopolitan businessman from South Florida, George Albert really had his roots in rural western Pennsylvania. For background on the Syrian-immigrant Albert family, I consulted the Virtual Museum of Pennsylvania Iron Furnaces and Iron Works for the history of the small company town of Josephine, Pennsylvania. Cross referencing dates and locations on Ancestry.com, I was able to trace the Albert family back to its homeland in Tripoli, Syria, which today is in Lebanon. Debrah G. (Dee) Albert provided details about the Albert family life in Josephine, Pennsylvania and Paterson, New Jersey. She provided the wonderful photograph showing the whole family together for Christmas a few days before the crash, despite the marital estrangement between Elizabeth and Abe.

Additional information was provided from a weblog researched and written by Salamanca, New York resident, Jacklyn M. Hoard-Beal. In 2010, Ms. Hoard-Beal compiled a blog titled *Unsung Hero* and posted it briefly on the Internet. She described the crash of Continental Charters Flight 44-2 from newspaper articles and from George Albert's former wife, Ava Isley, and his sister, Dorothy Albert Turner. The blog has since been removed from the Internet. Ms. Hoard-Beal presented theories about the cause of the plane crash that were not supported by the CAB investigation report, namely, that the plane may have run out of fuel and that it may have been flying in the opposite direction. Based on the engine and propeller wreckage findings, and debris field, neither was possible. Descriptions of the gathering and departure from Allegheny County Airport in Pittsburgh are from first-person news reports from survivors and flight support personnel who testified at the investigation hearing. For example, Robert Geyer's story was printed in the *Pittsburgh Press* exactly as he said it to a reporter, in first person prose. The Frankel family account of booking the flight was provided by Dr. Manny Frankel, a dentist from Florida. Lt. Bischof's story about taking the plane was provided by a first-person account in newspapers. Details of the airplane's departure, provided by Stewardess Pearl Moon, were cross-referenced with news reports and her testimony for the crash investigation hearing. There were some conflicting descriptions but, for the most part, the various stories complimented one another. Most of the information about decisions made by the pilots that sealed their fate was derived from the official crash investigation report and Continental Charters' rules and regulations for pilots. The gasoline volume and consumption calculation is mine based upon figures provided by the CAB. Weather reports were provided by the Weather Bureau via the CAB report and then cross-checked with daily weather observations printed in newspapers in Pittsburgh, Jamestown, and Buffalo.

Chapter 4 – Cursing at the Cockpit Door

Perhaps the most startling revelation from my extensive interview with Stewardess Pearl Moon was her recollection that the two reserve pilots, CJ Webber, and Gus Athas, jumped from their cabin seats in the final seconds before the crash and were shouting expletives at the cockpit door and in the cockpit. This is revealed here for the first time. It was not reported by any of the newspapers, and it was not found in the CAB investigation report. I asked Pearl three times to revisit her memory of this detail and for each recitation she was adamant that the reserve pilots, scheduled to fly the plane back to Miami from Buffalo, jumped out of their cabin seats and were attempting to make or instigate some sort of flight correction or life-saving maneuver inside the cockpit. Pearl acknowledged that this was a very unusual procedure because, to her, no one was to interfere with the working pilots in the cockpit under any circumstances. The suggestion that this sudden move may have contributed to the confusion already under way inside the cockpit is mine. Pearl also provided details of the sleeping children just as she had done with reporters more than 60 years earlier. Lt. Bischof provided a first-person account of his recollections with his bylined narration printed verbatim in newspapers. Initial confusion in a few newspapers over who was at the controls of the plane became clear when investigators determined that both Webber and Athas were in or very near the cockpit when the plane hit the ridge because of where their bodies were found, unsecured from the plane. Webber's and Athas' bodies were more easily and quickly removed in contrast to the bodies of Harris and Rutzebeck, which were pinned to the cockpit seats. Theirs' were two of the last bodies removed from the wreckage.

The declaration reportedly made by Major General Henry H. 'Hap' Arnold that "I want that airplane," came from Terry Love's colorful and authoritative book, *C-46 Commando in Action*. However, the original quote, the source unknown, is more likely to have come from a newspaper report or biography of General Arnold. Whatever the source, a few derivatives of this quote have been passed around since its origin at the Curtiss-Wright manufacturing plant in Buffalo in September 1940. *The*

Buffalo Evening News and *Courier-Express* both chronicled General Arnold's tour of the plant. History of Curtiss-Wright comes from a variety of sources including the Glenn H. Curtiss Museum, Curtiss-Wright Corporation, Buffalo History, Niagara Aerospace Museum, and Aviation History. Descriptions of the C-46 airplane were made, in part, from the C-46 pilot training manual, and the C-46 flight handbook and parts list compiled by the U.S. Army Air Forces. Both handbooks were declassified many years ago. Further descriptions of flight in the C-46 were provided, in part, from Hump pilots and authors Carl Constein and Otha Spencer. A website, MichaelProphet.com also describes the C-46 airplane in an article about its 70th anniversary in 2010.

Chapter 5 – Silent Night, Silent Crash

The detailed description of the crash of Flight 44-2 would not have been possible without the astounding recollection of stewardess Pearl Moon and the highly technical recitation by investigators for the CAB. Some of the macabre details were not provided by Pearl or the CAB but, rather, by reporters from the large city daily newspapers who arrived on the scene days later. They wrote the morbid articles in their newspapers based upon interviews with unnamed local residents who were among the first on the scene.

Chapter 6 – Searching and Waiting

Information about the CAA waiting for more than an hour to declare Flight 44-2 overdue and lost was obtained from the crash investigation report. Observer witness testimonials were also contained in the report and investigated by reporters. The names of search and rescue teams called to help were also contained in the crash investigation report and in several newspapers. Press photos showed searchers in Pennsylvania. Witness and Continental Charters' president Belding's statements were in the crash report and in newspapers. An unpublished photograph shows Belding arriving in Pittsburgh before the crash site was found. Accounts of how Congressman James Fulton criticized the search was contained in several newspapers, written by different reporters but with similar stories. The tactic used by *Pittsburgh Sun-Telegraph* reporter Ed Bell to remain within striking distance of the crash scene was contained in a first-person account in his newspaper. I was impressed by his forethought. There are two full days of articles from dozens of newspapers about the long, frustrating search in the air, water, and on land for the missing Continental Charters C-46 somewhere over Pennsylvania, New York State, in Lakes Erie and Ontario, and even into southern Ontario, Canada. Weather reports from these two days on December 30 and 31 were all the same in each of the newspapers around the region: raining and foggy with vast disparities in temperatures on the ground and aloft that caused the incessant fog. Most likely, over these two days western New York State, was caught in what is known as advection fog. The snow-covered hills and valleys of the Allegheny Plateau were ice cold from massive amounts of snow through December. A warm, moist air mass moved in from the west (over Lake Erie) with rain that melted snow during the day but formed a crust of ice on the snow at night. Warm air meeting a cold ground produces a fog that travels horizontally. During the final days of 1951 it also led to rapid melting of the snow, hence the rivulets of water flowing down Bucktooth Ridge that caused so many problems for George, Lt. Bischof, and the rescuers. Advection fog is different than radiation fog that valley farmers were used to seeing in the cool autumn months. Instead of sitting deep in the valleys like radiation fog, advection fog covered the entire region to elevations of well above the two thousand-foot-high ridges. Therefore, while the search planes could fly by instruments and the survivors could hear the planes above their wreckage, they couldn't see through the fog. Many stories of the searching were cross-checked with logs kept by the military air squadrons who flew the missions, specifically from Westover Air Force Base. Several press photographs and maps of the ever expanding search area were also consulted to determine who was searching and where. Historical background on the Pennsylvania Railroad was provided by several official histories about the formerly mighty railroad, and the 1951 airline passenger statistics were provided by an Eastern Airlines news release. Projections of future airline passenger statistics were provided by the Federal Aviation Administration, the agency that took over duties of the CAA.

Chapter 7 – "They're Never Going to Find Us"

A few of the details in this chapter are paraphrased from *Airline Executives and Federal Regulations*. Information about the Reconstruction Finance Corporation is taken from CAB documents obtained from the National Archives. Values of leases and sales of C-46 airplanes are from CAB documents. Descriptions from inside the C-46 after it was refitted for passenger travel are from the rare few photographs taken inside a C-46 cabin of this era. Economic and Korean Wartime analysis of the nonskeds flying with C-46 airplanes is from the CAB.

Bucktooth Ridge is an area that I'm somewhat familiar with after traveling through the hills and valleys of Napoli for many years. Compiling historical documents about this area during genealogy research on my family led me to appreciate how rugged this country was in 1951 and still is today. It's the dividing line where the fertile farmland of Randolph and Napoli gives way to the vast hardwood forests of the Allegheny Plateau. Histories of Cattaraugus County, Salamanca, Randolph, and Napoli have been gathered and published long ago and are online or at the Cattaraugus County Historical Museum and Research Center in Machias and at the Randolph Public Library. Frederick Larkin's 1888 report, *Ancient Man in America*, which I recall reading as a boy at my grandparents' farmhouse, is also available on the internet and at these repositories. All of this past research accurately describes the mountainous lands that make up the Allegheny Plateau in Cattaraugus County. A forest ranger who helped carry the plane crash victims off Bucktooth Ridge told a reporter on the scene that the survivors were lucky to find Ruby Bryant. If George Albert had gone in the other direction he could have walked for miles before finding civilization, possibly even dying of exposure before he found help. Today, this combination of publicly and privately-owned land is mostly part of the Bucktooth State Forest and is dotted with hiking trails. Few of them existed in 1951 and most of the present day logging roads and truck trails were not there either. This is the forested area where my great-grandmother's family attempted to hit riches with an oil lease on their wooded farmland on the east side of Bucktooth Ridge. Newspaper reports indicated that drilling rigs were transported by train from Dunkirk on Lake Erie and then carried by horse and oxen-drawn wagons to the John and Anna Snyder farm on Bucktooth Ridge for installation. As it turned out, their effort produced a dry well in the brief but exciting western New York State oil boom of the 1880s. While the crash scene remains on private land and should not be visited without permission, in 2015 the vast region of state-owned forest and ridges was enjoyed for hiking, biking, camping, hunting, and fishing. Since the late 1950s and early 1960s, people have also enjoyed this region for snow skiing at the public Holiday Valley and private HoliMont ski resorts northeast of the crash scene near the quaint and historic Village of Ellicottville. The same massive Lake Effect snowstorms that buried Bucktooth Ridge under several feet of snow in December 1951, still blanket the hills and valleys in winter today for skiers who travel to enjoy the abundant snowfall. The description of George Albert finding his dead mother in the crash wreckage was provided by Robert Geyer, who either wrote or narrated his story to a reporter who printed it verbatim. George's former wife, Ava Isley Albert, also provided information to blogger Jacklyn Hoard-Beal about how George found his mother dead in the plane. Additional information was provided by Pearl Moon during my interview with her. Survivor stewardess Dolores Beshears also did a first-person account for a newspaper, *Daily News-Digest,* and survivor passenger Mary Battista gave a first-person account of her recollection of the crash many years later for a reporter from the *Pittsburgh Post-Gazette.* She explained losing her shoes and finding candy bars in her purse. Ruby Bryant's and David Shenefiel's morning routines were culled from Ruby's diary and from my grandfather's many stories of how he tended his farm for years. The schedule of the Erie Limited is from the railroad's archives. I've concluded, based on the time the survivor's reported hearing the train whistle, and the Limited's schedule through Salamanca that this was the train they heard from the top of Bucktooth Ridge. The whistle saved their lives for it pointed George in the correct direction to walk safely from the ridge to find help. Without it, he might have walked the wrong way, to his death.

Chapter 8 — Thief

This chapter contains subject matter that was difficult to pin down. During my research, I found only a few newspaper articles with references to someone removing items from one of the bodies of a crash victim. The details were sparse, and the suggestion of theft was vague. Expanding my search to include subsequent years, I found articles published in the one year and five year anniversaries of the crash that spelled out the sinister and macabre crime in the *Randolph Register*, *Buffalo Evening News*, and *Buffalo Courier-Express*. They matched a few incomplete stories told to me by older Cattaraugus County residents that Sheriff Sigel stifled a theft investigation. Only the anniversary articles described why: the victim's family declined to press charges. I wish to emphasize that I alone have reconstructed, based on all the details available, the nature of the criminal act. It is my own supposition from studying the injuries among the survivors and the financial means of the passengers that the guilty party and the victim could be found among just a few. As I analyzed each passenger carefully, I finally came to the conclusion that the victim was most likely passenger Dorothy Berman Bruce. She was moving from Nicaragua back to her home in Kingston, Ontario, Canada, by way of Buffalo to visit with her mother. She was the woman most likely to have been carrying such a large amount of cash because she would not have wanted to leave it behind in Nicaragua or risk wiring it from such a third world country. Berman-Bruce was delayed in Florida so she could take a short course of a telephone operator's job. The money could have been part of her savings for Miami living expenses while her engineer husband had gone ahead to their home in Canada. I chose to include this story with the prominence of its own chapter because it was such a contrast to the many other stories of heroism, bravery, and sympathy. One of these able-bodied survivors committed this dastardly crime. When I asked Pearl, as the only living crash survivor in 2010 if she did it and wished to confess, she simply didn't recall anything about it. She didn't appear to be offended by my question which indicated to me that she was truly unaware that it happened. It's important to point out that the crime was never prosecuted and, therefore, could not be properly solved. However, there are more than a few Cattaraugus County residents who occasionally revisit the story of this cold and despicable crime committed on a dead plane crash passenger on Bucktooth Ridge. To my knowledge, except for giving a few details to two reporters who asked him about it years later, Sheriff Sigel took the identities of the corpse thief and the victim to his grave.

Chapter 9 – Trust the Pilots

The background on CJ Webber could not have included so much detail of his incredible aviation career without help from his daughter, Nancy Webber Harrison. Using CJ's pilot log book, Nancy reconstructed much of her father's aviation career with the loving touch of a woman who obviously missed having him as part of her life. Nancy presented many personal family stories and traits which I've tried to reorganize for a mass audience. I've included a lengthy narrative of his highly developed skills to supplement Pearl Moon's supposition that the crash would not have happened if the much more experienced CJ had been flying the plane. Additionally, CJ played a minor role in the early stages of the formation of the State of Israel through his business association with Charlie Winters. C-46 pilot Harold "Hal" Rothstein played an even bigger role; he illegally flew one of the Winters-Webber B-17s from Miami to Europe. The B-17s became the first bombers to form the Israeli Air Force. Rothstein talked with me at length over the telephone and sent documentation of his involvement in these clandestine and illegal flights. Matched with newspaper articles and even government documents for the Presidential pardons of Charlie Winters, Herman Greenspun, and Al Schwimmer, Rothstein's long memory proved accurate except for one item I could not confirm. Rothstein remembered a David Goldberg flying one of the planes while all other reports I've uncovered identified the third pilot as R. Weid Mayer. It's possible that Goldberg was a co-pilot. Rothstein was 91 when he talked to me several times about his flying career, and he kept his thumb-worn documents all those years hoping they would be useful someday to tell his fascinating story. Finally, his recollections of this little-known historical event are in print.

The family of Gus Athas also eagerly provided information about their beloved husband, father, and grandfather for inclusion in the book. My first contact was with Joan Harrison Athas Visco, who replied to an inquiry I placed on a genealogy website. "He was only 25-years-old, a lovely, sweet young man. I was his wife. We had two little boys. I miss him to this day," she wrote. I could almost see tears in her eyes as she thought about that day on December 30, 1951 when she learned her young and handsome husband and father of their two little boys was missing and probably dead in the plane. Meeting Joan Visco and those two boys, now grandfather-age men, was a highlight of my research. They spoke of Gus as if the crash had only just happened. "One of the ladies sitting in the front was very cold, so they switched seats," Joan explained. "He died, she lived." When the initial stage of mourning was over, it was Joan who arranged for two cemetery burial plots at Flagler Memorial Park at 51st Street and Flagler Avenue in North Miami. Although not related, Gus and Vic Harris were laid to rest side by side, just like a pilot and co-pilot flying together forever. The cemetery lots cost $250 each. They were paid for in $10 installments, due on the 15th of every month.

Tracking down the background of co-pilot Hans E. Rutzebeck proved to be challenging and took more twists and turns than the old Al-Can highway which he grew to know so well. I was finally able to find Lief Rutzebeck, Hans' son, who put me in touch with his mother, Isobel. She was 93 when we corresponded by mail and when she did an audiotaped interview about her life on the Canadian and Alaskan frontier with Rutz. As painful as it was for her to be left behind in Fairbanks with two little children when Rutz left her in 1951, Isobel graciously recalled the many details of their adventurous life together in the wild bush country of Alaska as Rutz flew his small planes for hunters and trappers. A Folkways Records biography provided background information on Rutz's colorful father, Hjalmar Rutzebeck, with photographs of his seafaring life, and lyrics to the shanties that he wrote over many years. And for confirmation of Rutz's flying adventures and mishaps in

Alaska, I consulted Sidney Huntington's book, *Shadows on the Koyukuk*, where he described how much Rutz was paid for flying trappers into the bush. I found it ironic that both Isobel Rutzebeck and Evelyn Harris lost their husbands the same way. The dashingly handsome men fit the stereotypical image of a passenger plane pilot of the post-World War II era: itinerant, wandering, unfaithful, adventurous, and daring.

Pilot Vic Harris' exciting life flying gleaming passenger planes around the country had an inauspicious beginning in a tiny crossroads community in the middle of nowhere: Tom, Oklahoma. When you look it up on a map, you still find virtually nothing. I initially tracked Harris' family life on Ancestry.com and then, with the help of a relative, Julie Clark Close, made contact with Harris' son, Raymond Victor Harris. He was just a baby boy when his father was killed in the crash. Ray introduced me to his mother, Evelyn Harris, who provided a long list of details about her husband's life before and during his career as a mechanic and pilot. She implied that she knew in 1951 about his affairs with stewardesses and about his girlfriend (whom I've not named) and Ray acknowledged that his father did, indeed, match the stereotypical image of a pilot who spent many nights away from home in the company of stewardesses and other women. Today, such marital strife would be closely investigated among pilots involved in aviation disasters.

Chapter 10 – "Go Down, Never Up"

During my interview with Pearl in 2010, she still insisted that the survivors should have stayed in place and waited for help to arrive. As it turned out, Pearl was correct. When the skies finally cleared over Bucktooth Ridge late in the afternoon of New Year's Eve, search planes spotted the wreckage from the air at about the same that the first rescuers reached the crash scene on foot. The scenario of Pearl and George getting into arguments over his and Lt. Bischof's plan to walk off the mountain to find help were compiled from several newspaper articles and Pearl's recollections while still smoldering anger 60 years later that George disregarded her insistence on staying put. The failed hike off the ridge was compiled from George's and Lt. Bischof's first-person newspaper articles. Both men professed more concern over failing the others than themselves and, realizing their mistake of not preparing their clothing properly for a hike through the snow, readily returned to their campsite. The segment about the topics they discussed while sitting around the campfire, and while waiting for George to get help, come from first-person articles by the survivors including Mary Messerlos, Mary Battista, George, Lt. Bischof, Pearl, and Dolores Beshears. George's solo walk through the woods was compiled from his first-person articles, from the accounts of Gilbert Myers, who saw George's footprints around the Myers' camp, and Robert Lilienthal, who back-tracked George's wobbly path up the ridge from Sawmill Run Road. He saw the branches broken off from George grasping at them to stay on his feet. Pearl Moon told me that she advised George always to walk downhill, never up. This may account, in part, for him continuing downhill even after he spotted the Herrick farm beyond an open field surrounded by the woods along Sawmill Run Road. It was uphill. The theory about the crash survivors being the largest group stranded for a long period of time in North America is mine. Through many years of research, I could find no other instance of such a large group of plane crash survivors being stranded for an extended period of time without rescue in North America.

Chapter 11 – Diagnosis Interrupted

Details in this chapter about Ruby Bryant are from her diary and from recollections of John and Otis Bryant. Otis also provided many photographs that I've utilized here to describe their farm. Statistics on deer hunting in Cattaraugus County were compiled from New York State game records. Weather observations for December 31, 1951 that were printed in several local newspapers provided evidence of a changing weather pattern. Teenager John Bryant was by his mother's side when they initially spotted George Albert mingling in the road in front of their farmhouse. John described the scene to me as best he could from such a distant memory. The first words George spoke to Ruby were reported by several newspapers, in quotations. It appears George first loudly said hello from the road and then made the comment about Christmas being over as he approached Ruby in her farmyard.

Chapter 12 – "Christmas is over, Huh, Lady"

The description of George's clothing and disheveled appearance were recalled by Otis Bryant from notes written on a calendar by his mother, Ruby, and from the incredibly crisp photographs taken by the Jamestown Post-Journal's Dick Hallberg. Ruby's reaction to George has been somewhat reconstructed from comments in her diary and from newspaper reports that detailed the encounter based on interviews with both Ruby and George. The actions of the Telephone Operator and Salamanca police when George first placed his call for help are reconstructed based on newspaper articles from the *Buffalo Evening News*, *Buffalo Courier-Express*, *Salamanca Republican-Press*, *Jamestown Post-Journal*, and *Randolph Register*. Some of the accounts were first-person reports. There is no doubt that Salamanca firefighters were sampling *Meet the Millers* with their newly installed TV. WBEN-TV was one of only a few channels available in 1951, and everybody in western New York State watched the program.

Robert Lilienthal's trek through the woods and first appearance upon the scene of the crash are reconstructed from a lengthy interview he gave to the *Jamestown Post-Journal* and the *Randolph* Register. He appeared in both newspapers displaying his photographs, only one of which is still available today. Additional information about Lilienthal was confirmed by his widow, from my own family archives, and from *The Hilltop*, Randolph Central School yearbooks from the years 1945-46.

Ruby Bryant's meeting with George Albert is taken from several first-person newspaper reports and from details in her diary. I've reconstructed this first meeting somewhat based upon descriptions presented to me by members of the Bryant family, the CAB report, and the newspaper reports. Cattaraugus County Sheriff's Deputy Russell Benson was quoted by several news reporters as having driven fast to the Bryant farm on Sawmill Run to pick up George and then even faster to the top of Sawmill Run to find the best location to enter the woods. Because the road wasn't plowed all the way and was covered with several inches of snow and ice, I've described his rear-wheel drive squad car as fishtailing. Nearly everyone who had some connection to Sawmill Run in 1951 has stated that the single lane road was seldom plowed all the way through.

Gilbert Myers described many trips into the hollow to their camp when their panel truck was spinning and fishtailing on the slippery Herrick's Hill. The description of the Town of Napoli highway equipment came from my uncle, Randall Shenefiel, confirmed by snippets in the *Randolph Register*. Additionally, I reviewed several color slide photographs from my grandfather's collection showing him driving the town's snowplows with their huge butterfly wing snow blades. These plows were behemoths and were made for the deepest Lake Effect snow common along the shore of Lake Erie. Descriptions of the crash scene and Sheriff Sigel's new two-way county-wide radio system were provided by several newspaper articles that described the modern technology that had only recently arrived in rural Cattaraugus County. Details about Sheriff Morgan Sigel are from county history records, Sigel's obituary, and many newspaper articles that chronicled his career over more than 20 years in office.

Chapter 13 – Ride Down the Mountain

Many details in this chapter have their sources identified within the narrative or came from personal accounts of the people involved, such as Pearl, George, Lt. Bischof, Gilbert Myers, photographs, and the crash investigation report.

Brothers Donald and Robert Shenefiel provided details of how the Shenefiel's Oliver crawler-tractor was hauled to the crash scene by their uncle, Hugh Hoxie. Their farm was in the woods along Whipple Road about a mile from the Herrick farm. "I remember the fog that night (of the crash)," Donald said. "We called it Cattaraugus County pea soup."

Donald and Robert Shenefiel are my first cousins, once removed. Hugh Hoxie is my great uncle. Milton Marvin, another cousin once removed, provided more details about the Shenefiel's crawler-tractor being loaded onto the Hoxie's truck and hauled to the crash scene to help carry the survivors and the dead.

In 1951, the Shenefiel boys knew Bucktooth Ridge well because of a 10-acre woodlot the family owned on the ridge adjacent to the crash scene. In the late 1940's, the boys helped cut timber from their woodlot and they determined that the crash survivors had set up their camp in a clearing created by a road they built to haul logs to a saw mill near the upper portion of Sawmill Run Road, not far from the Herrick farm. They also knew the ridge well by crossing it many times while hunting squirrels, rabbits and deer.

Robert Shenefiel recalled that his mother, Edith, told the boys that she heard an unusual noise at about 10:30 on the night of December 29th, after they had all gone to bed. "I thought I heard a crash last night," Edith told her sons when they gathered in their kitchen for breakfast on the morning of December 30th. They discussed it and determined that the crash must have been from a falling tree in the apple orchard on a hill behind their house. Because the Shenefiels did not have a TV in their home, and because it was a holiday weekend, they did not hear any news about a plane crash until Edith took the telephone call from Sheriff Sigel late in the afternoon on December 31st. Only then did she realize that the crash she heard from the quiet of her bedroom was, in fact, the plane hitting Bucktooth Ridge. Edith Mary Shenefiel lived to the age of 92 and she insisted until the day she died that she heard the plane crash that night.

Milton Marvin also believed that he heard something on the ridge the night of December 29th as he walked in front of the Hoxie farm near the top of Hoxie Hill. Milton had gone to visit the Hoxie farm's tenant house neighbor, Fred Benson, and his invalid wife, Walza, across Hoxie Hill Road from the Hoxie farmhouse, after helping with the evening cow milking chores in the dairy barn. At the age of 15, Milton often went to the Benson's house to sit with Walza and watch television, a novelty in 1951, especially in a rural community like Napoli. Like most other families in the area, his Hoxie grandparents didn't have a television. Upon returning to the Hoxie farmhouse at about 10:25 pm, Milton had a panoramic view across the valley to Bucktooth Ridge but, in 1951, it was completely black without the white dots from outdoor lighting fixtures that would appear in later years. He recalls "hearing a plane rather loudly." Then, he said, the noise suddenly stopped. "I didn't hear a crash or anything, but I thought the plane noise stopping suddenly was funny." He didn't think about it again until two days later when, upon hearing sirens in the valley, the women of the Hoxie farmhouse informed the men working outside that a plane crash with survivors had been found on Bucktooth Ridge. Later that night, Milton recalls, he and the other Hoxies, and the Bensons gazed out across the valley and watched a long line of lights moving up and down Bucktooth Ridge as rescuers worked to remove the bodies.

At the deadly crash scene near the top of the ridge, it appeared from their vantage point on Hoxie Hill as if the soft amber lights were reaching to heaven.

In the fall of 1952 after Donald Shenefiel recovered from his broken knee, Robert Shenefiel recalled that the brothers were hunting squirrels on their Bucktooth Ridge woodlot when they observed small pieces of the plane wreckage still in the woods along with something that scared them terribly. "He kicked a big ol' bear out of there," Robert said about his brother, Donald. The Shenefiels, Hoxies, Bryants, Herricks, and the other farm families of Napoli and Bucktooth Ridge often came across black bears.

Although it was hibernation season, the stranded crash survivors had faced more danger than the freezing weather.

New York State Trooper Eugene Redden's family provided details about the teletypes he kept for many years reporting progress or lack of progress in the two-day search for the missing plane. Pearl Moon expressed her pent up anger more than 60 years later about how her role in the passengers' survival was discounted by the men reporters on the scene. Additionally, the historical narrative for the Myers and Myers Funeral Home and the family's Big Black Hearse that nearly got stuck on Sawmill Run Road on the day the crash was found was provided by the memories of Gilbert Myers. He was destined to become the fourth in a family line of funeral directors but opted for a legal career, instead. Details about Cattaraugus County Sheriff Morgan Sigel are from county history records, Sigel's obituary, and many newspaper articles that chronicled his career over more than 20 years as sheriff. Two newspaper reports portrayed how the crash victims' bodies were found and identified. And a high-quality photograph of George Albert at the hospital gave me the ability to describe his features. Other photographs of the survivors in their hospital beds added to personal descriptions, including injuries.

Chapter 14 – Big Story

Jamestown Post-Journal City Editor Charles Stuart wrote a lengthy column explaining exactly how he and photographer Dick Hallberg heard about the crash on the county's new radio system. He explained how they raced to the scene, conducted interviews, and sent film and descriptions back to their newspaper offices and to Buffalo for distribution to the world via the *Associated Press*. Additionally, there is a great photograph in the *Post-Journal* of a proud Hallberg perched in front of the gleaming chrome grill of his Buick displaying his new press license plates. Hallberg was the first daily newspaper press photographer to reach the scene and by then, the survivors were already being brought down the ridge. Hallberg told me he was wearing only rubber galoshes over his street shoes as he hiked up the ridge in knee-deep snow, ice and slush to witness the crash scene and take photographs. That night he had skipped out on what was supposed to have been the first date with his future wife, Janet Anderson. "She accepted it when I showed up late with water sloshing around in my shoes," Hallberg said of his future wife's understanding of his profession. Dick and Jan Hallberg were married for 63 years until her death in December 2014.

Reporter Millie Hall also wrote a first-person account of hiking up the ridge and witnessing the scene. Some of the actions of the reporters on the scene were reconstructed based on my many years of experience covering similar stories. For example, Hallberg would certainly not have stopped sizing up George Albert for more photographs after taking just one. He would have continuously pointed his camera at George waiting for the right moment for another great image to appear in his viewfinder. Further, I deduced that it was Lilienthal who took the only photographs of the survivors huddled beneath their parachute-umbrella because he was the first person to reach the scene with a camera. Although he took several photos of the survivors at the scene and he appeared in newspapers displaying the paper prints, none appeared as individual photographs in any newspapers. The disposition of these photographs upon Lilienthal's death, if they still existed, could not be determined.

Chapter 15 – Deadly Nonskeds

The *Philadelphia Inquirer* published the story of the National Airlines DC-4 crash-landing in January 1951 as one of the first of many disastrous and deadly plane crashes in this benchmark year for aviation crashes and safety regulation revisions. However, the story was reported via the *Associated Press*. It's difficult to understand why the Inquirer didn't byline such a major story in its own city from one of its own reporters. Most all other details of the crash came from a lengthy crash investigation report filed by the CAB. A few anecdotes were gleaned from the *Heroic Comics* story that appeared later in 1951 and posthumously made a heroine of the stewardess, Mary Frances Housley. Although presented in a comic book format, the story was serious in nature, and correctly portrayed Housley as the hero she was on the day of the crash. The many other crashes of 1951 were compiled from the CAB crash investigation reports and cross-checked with photographs and more reporting and commentary from a variety of newspapers in the respective crash cities. While 1951 appeared to be no worse than previous or succeeding years for crashes among the nonskeds and the major airlines, it was the year of crashes that led to so many changes in safety rules and regulations. Publicity and fear were intensified because of the quick succession of fatal crashes in the month of December, capped off with the crash of Flight 44-2 at a time when Americans were off work and celebrating Christmas and New Year's Eve. There is no question that press fervor over the 1951 crashes also contributed to the panic.

Chapter 16 – First CAB Chief on the Scene

Donald Nyrop's first visit by a CAB chairman to the scene of a passenger plane crash was chronicled at the Bradford, Pennsylvania airport by the *Bradford Era* newspaper and then, by the time he arrived at the crash scene, by nearly every other newspaper that covered the crash. His schedule was further documented in CAB papers now held by the Department of Transportation at the National Archives. History of the development and expansion of the Bradford-McKean airport was taken from documents and photographs on the airport's website and from history compilations from McKean County, Pennsylvania, including photographs contributed by the Bradford Landmark Society. The brief biography of Nyrop is from the CAB chairman's official biography from government records obtained from the Department of Transportation. A wonderful photograph of Nyrop taken at the crash scene by the Post-Journal's Dick Hallberg was useful for describing the CAB chairman's clothing worn on the day of his historic first visit to a crash scene. It's one of only two photographs that I've found of Nyrop at the scene. Nyrop's many quotations used in this chapter were taken from newspapers, including the *Post-Journal, Buffalo Evening News, Buffalo Courier-Express, Bradford Era*, and the *Randolph Register*.

Chapter 17 — Elizabeth

The great description of the scene before and after the Miami Airlines crash in Elizabeth on December 16 is from the now defunct *The Brooklyn Eagle* newspaper. It published first-person reports from people on the scene who witnessed the crash. I painted a picture of Elizabeth in 1951 from historical photographs and descriptions of the area around the city's waterworks plant of that era. Along with the CAB crash investigation report, details of the crashes were provided by articles in newspapers including *The Brooklyn Eagle, The New York Age, The Elizabeth Daily Journal, Long Island Star-Journal, Toronto Star, Schenectady Gazette, Philadelphia Inquirer, Buffalo Courier-Express, Buffalo Evening News,* and *Syracuse Post-Standard*. Press photos helped me describe the gruesome details of the crash scenes and their aftermath, even the many blanket-covered bodies lined up outside the coroner's funeral home. I reviewed many, many press photographs taken of the scene immediately following the crash and watched newsreel footage still available today. Additional information was obtained from Jack Rescoe, of Portland, Oregon, who as a young boy, witnessed the scenes of all three catastrophic plane crashes in Elizabeth and wrote his memories to me for inclusion in the book. Much of the information, however, is from the long CAB crash investigation report. The book *Disaster in the Air*, by Edgar Haine, provided some details, but it incorrectly stated that the airplane's wing fell off, so reference from this book was used primarily to confirm other accounts and for background information. Details about Newark Airport were obtained from the National Park Service's Historic American Engineering Record (HAER). It provided background about the use of the airport before and during World War II and design of the terminal building and runways before reconstruction in the mid-1950s. Photographs from the Newark Airport HAER report were viewable but unusable because of poor quality. A photograph of another Miami Airlines plane (not involved in the crash) was provided by photographer Bill Larkins.

Chapter 18 – Whitecaps on the Water

The Robin Airlines crash investigation report provided much of the detail about what happened to the plane during its flight from Burbank to Chicago and its attempt to make Newark. Jerry Laufgraben gave a description of what it was like inside the cabin and Larry Wilson told the story from his Canadian farm family's point of view. C-46 historian and photographer Bill Larkins solved the mystery of why the Robin Airlines plane had 99ers on the tail. Several Toronto newspapers confirmed each account. Many photographs of the plane were provided by Northumberland County, Ontario. Bruce Smelser's nephew provided details about his uncle's involvement in the incident along with confirmation of the interview Bruce Smelser did on the Arthur Godfrey radio show.

Chapter 19 – Truman and Safer Planes

Many documents from the CAB were reviewed for information about how the airlines' regulatory agency initially hoped to reduce the frequency of crashes among the nonskeds. The documents obtained from the National Archives indicate that the CAB first thought that by reducing the takeoff weight of the C-46 airplane it would prevent many of the crashes caused by engine failure at takeoff. Cracking down on pilot training, use of itinerant pilots, maintenance regulations, and requiring the use of instruments in poor weather came only later, in 1951, especially after the devastating month of December. Details about the flamboyant Amos Heacock came from documents culled from the CAB and the lobbying group, Air Coach Transport Association. Additional details about Heacock's crash in Seattle came from the CAB crash investigation and various newspaper accounts. Copies of Heacock's testimony before Congressional Committees provided details about his ownership of the nonsked, Air Transport Associates, in Seattle. Press photographs of Heacock and his wife and the crash scene enabled me to describe the attractive couple and the scene where their C-46 crashed. Both Amos and Dorothy Heacock gave first-person accounts of the crash to newspapers which published them verbatim.

The details of the American Airlines crash into Elizabeth, New Jersey were compiled from the CAB report and the many newspapers which covered the second major crash event within weeks. The profile of Secretary Robert Porter Patterson was compiled from several sources including a memorial booklet published by his New York City law firm, Patterson, Belknap, Webb & Tyler; *The New York Times,* Arlington Cemetery.net, and the Truman Library and Museum. Patterson's son described his WW II activities in a letter sent to a website devoted to B-24 bomber groups in the raid on Ploesti. John E. "Jack" Rescoe, Jr., further described the scene during interviews with me from his home in Portland, Oregon. Details of Newark Airport operations during and after the war are contained in the HAER report. The information about the National Airlines crash into Newark is from the CAB report and many newspaper articles and photographs taken at the scene. The term "ghostly" was in a few newspapers. Jack Rescoe also provided a description of this crash scene. He went to each of the three crash scenes in Elizabeth in 1951 and '52. President Truman's letter to Jimmy Doolittle was provided by the Truman Library and Museum and the 1952 report, *The Airport and its Neighbors.*

Donald Nyrop's surprise attendance at the Flight 44-2 investigational hearing in Little Valley on January 17 and 18, 1952 was chronicled in the *Jamestown Post-Journal,* the *Buffalo Evening News,* and the *Buffalo Courier-Express.* President Truman's letter to Donald Nyrop calling for new safety regulations on the nonskeds was provided by the Harry S. Truman Library and Museum in Independence, Missouri. Additionally, recollections of Truman's aviation aide, General Robert B.

Landry, were compiled by the Truman Library and Museum from an audio interview with General Landry in the 1970s. Details of the report compiled for President Truman by World War II hero pilot, Jimmy Doolittle, titled *The Airport and Its Neighbors*, were obtained from the report, copies of which are readily available in libraries and from the National Archives. Descriptions of the old Cattaraugus County Courthouse were obtained from newspapers, historical photographs, histories of the county, and from architectural renditions of the building. The narration of the two-day hearing was made from the CAB report and from many newspaper articles written in 1952 about the proceedings. The story of the *Vin Fiz Flyer* is from an early article in the *Randolph Register* and cross checked with historical writings about Calbraith Rodgers. Signatures in funeral condolence books were provided by the pilots' widows. Legal documents provided evidence that Continental Charters president John Belding tried to avoid service of a summons while attending the hearing in Little Valley. Theories about who committed the theft of cash from a dead passenger's pocket are my conclusions only. Legal filings and, in some cases, notices of settlement in newspapers, provided evidence for the many lawsuits against Continental Charters. The exact date in which the beleaguered airline stopped flying passengers could not be determined, but from legal filings, it appears Continental Charters was insolvent before 1956. It ceased operating long before then, but the last known references to the airline as a business are within bankruptcy court cases in April 1955.

Chapter 20 – Elizabeth II

The description of the Robin Airlines C-46 crashing into the Puente Hills east of Los Angeles is derived from the CAB crash investigation and newspaper reports. History of the Aeronautics Act of 1938 comes from an official legal opinion written by CAB attorney George C. Neal and obtained from the National Archives in Washington. History of the nonsked crashes leading up to 1950 are from the official CAB crash investigation reports via the Department of Transportation with additional details culled from newspaper accounts and press photos from these crashes. Terry Love's book, *C-46 Commando* listed early nonsked owners, and photographer Bill Larkins' photographs provided documentation for what many of these airlines looked like as they painted their C-46 airplanes. The compilation of early crashes among the nonskeds is from the CAB accident investigation reports. The "shark" crash of the Westair nonsked was obtained from the crash investigation report, newspaper articles, press photos, and from University of Puerto Rico writer and researcher Luis Asencio Camacho in his essay for *Centro Journal*, Volume XXV, Number 11, 2013. Evidence of sensational headlines from the nonsked crashes was obtained from the former *Coronet* magazine, *TIME,* and the *Long Island Star-Journal,* among many other publications.

Chapter 21 – Hollywood

The narrative about the fictional TransOcean DC-4 near-disaster comes from the John Wayne film, *The High and the Mighty,* based on the bestselling novel of the same title by the late author-pilot Ernest K. Gann. The plot and occasionally silly lines in the film are included to show how the fear of flying on the nonsked passenger planes worked its way through American pop-culture. I found it somewhat amusing that the press photos of shapely stewardesses involved in the real crashes suddenly came alive in the color feature movie. With permission from John Wayne's daughter-in-law, Bridget Wayne, owner of Wayne's Batjac Productions, Inc., the title for this book, was borrowed from a single line shouted by the famous actor in the film. "Now hang on and fly, he commands. A slightly different line was contained in Gann's book for John Wayne's character, "Hang on, chum! We'll make it this way! You can do it, man! Just Hang on. Fly, and let me pray," it says. Additional details about the nonskeds flouting the rules of the CAB are from *Airline Executives and Federal Regulations* and CAB documents obtained from the National Archives.

Chapter 22 – Souvenirs and Broken Families

Isobel Rutzebeck told me in an extensive interview how she first learned of her husband's death in the airplane crash. Ruby Bryant's diary and newspaper articles described the scene around Sawmill Run after the crash with additional first-person accounts provided by Margaret Herrick. A press photograph shows Dolores Beshears and Minnie Moon boarding a C-46 in Buffalo for their return trip to Miami. Pearl Moon told me 60 years later that she also flew on a Continental Charters C-46 back home to Miami but that she did it quietly and without anyone from the press to record it. Evelyn Harris provided the poem she wrote about her husband's death in the C-46. She didn't think it was worthy. It happened to be dated January 17, the same day that the investigation hearing began in Little Valley. The salvage of the remaining pieces of Flight 44-2 was observed and reported by a reporter for the *Randolph Register*. Additional information about the airplane salvage operation is from photographs supplied by Will Herrick. The description of practical jokes by school children after the crash was provided by Randall Shenefiel, who was in grade school at the time and heard the story repeated for many years afterward. Several Cattaraugus County residents reported keeping scrapbooks of the crash, one which I obtained from a contributor from Canada. The scrapbook contained many photographs, newspaper articles, and other documents related to the crash and its investigation. It was invaluable for my research. Whoever prepared it would probably remain a mystery. Ruby Bryant's will is from her diary. It made it clear that she understood her fate so soon after helping the crash survivors find the help they needed to live. Clarification of several points in the diary was provided by her sons, four of whom were still surviving in 2015. Only Rodney Bryant died before completion of the research for this book.

The personal and intimate details of Ruby Bryant's struggle with breast cancer, her home life on the farm, and her story of meeting George Albert would not have been possible for this story without her personal diary. It was entrusted to me by her son, Otis Bryant, on behalf of all the Bryant boys, survivors of their mother's death from breast cancer exactly one year after the plane crash, and their father's suicide a year later on Bucktooth Ridge. Ruby wrote most of her diary after the crash and after she discovered that she did, in fact, have breast cancer. I want you to know that for this story I have reorganized her entries for a chronological order of events and to make it easier to follow her dilemma before, during, and after the plane crash. Ruby was clearly struggling with pain, discomfort and the realization that she had breast cancer long before her much-delayed diagnosis. Why she didn't do something about it earlier, only Ruby knows but her reasons are most likely simple procrastination, fear, a lack of knowledge and information about breast cancer, and concern that her family needed her more than she needed to take the time to go to see the doctor. Ruby didn't even consult her doctor when she suffered a miscarriage sometime in the late 1940s. Like many rural women, she handled it privately by herself. Ruby and the Bryant family background, farm life on Sawmill Run, and a description of the old Bryant homestead were provided by Otis and John Bryant. John and his late wife, Mary, founder of the website, *Painted Hills Genealogy Society*, inherited the old Bryant farm, but the farmhouse that George found in 1951 was long ago torn down and replaced by a new residence.

Stuart and Rodney Bryant both went to the scene of the crash and described what they saw. As the first custodian of the family farm after their parents died, Rodney Bryant worked as a farmer and logger until he was diagnosed with Juvenile Diabetes (Type 1) and retired to Florida and later, California. Otis Bryant said of Rodney, "He was my brother, my best friend, and like a father to me." Rodney Bryant was also an author who wrote and published short stories. After a kidney transplant rejection, Rodney Bryant died from a heart attack on March 3, 1983.

Stuart Bryant understood the details of flight after he and his older brother Benton took pilot training courses in high school. Stuart Bryant served with the 4th Armored Division in the U.S. Army before returning home to work for the Niagara Falls State Park Police and the U.S. Border Patrol, serving along the Canadian and Mexican borders. His daughter, Sonya, died from breast cancer 50 years from the day of the death of her grandmother, Ruby Bryant, also from breast cancer.

Stuart Bryant also retired to Florida. Although I respectfully submitted several requests for him to participate in my research for this story, Stuart politely declined. He was in poor health with pancreatic cancer and perhaps the painful memories were too great at a time when he was fighting a progressive and deadly disease. He died on October 30, 2015, the day before publication of *Hang on and Fly*.

Epilogue

Obituaries for Ruby and Charles Bryant described their lives and deaths in the *Jamestown Post-Journal* and the *Randolph Register*. Confirmation of the details was provided by the Bryant boys. "My father took his own life," explained Otis Bryant, during a telephone interview, confirming that his body was found by the older boys in the woods along Bucktooth Ridge. In 1952 and '53, Charlie Bryant had been sick with stomach ulcers and was being treated at a Buffalo hospital. Laid off from his job at the New York State Conservation Department, he was not called back when many others returned to their jobs. With the medical bills piled up and still mourning the loss of Ruby, Charlie grew more despondent until the final day of his life.

Family members of the victims and survivors further described in this chapter provided details about the later years of their lives and, in some instances, obituaries provided details about their deaths. After I had written newspaper articles for the 60th anniversary of the crash for the *Pittsburgh Post-Gazette*, the *Buffalo News*, and the *Jamestown Post-Journal*, several people contacted me with small bits of information about the crash or the scene today. The topic grew into quite a lengthy discussion on a website devoted to railroad hobbyists because of the item about the survivors hearing the train whistle in the valley when they were deciding to walk out of the woods. One of the discussion board members from Railroad.net flew his airplane over Bucktooth Ridge and provided some excellent photographs of what the scene looks like today from the air. In contrast to an aerial photograph that was taken on January 1, 1952, there is no evidence whatsoever that a large passenger plane crashed on Bucktooth Ridge. All the splintered trees have regrown. I wish to emphasize: there is nothing left of the airplane at the crash scene.

Obituaries for both Donald and Bill Nyrop appeared in *The New York Times* and the *Minneapolis Star-Tribune* and an article about a Northwest Airlines History Centre tribute to Nyrop appeared on the website, Lady Skywriter, by Anne Kerr, in July 2011.

Finally, in July 2007, *Popular Mechanics* put to rest the unproved theories and guesswork involved in deciding where passengers are safest in an airplane. Even Boeing, on its website under aviation safety, insisted that one seat is as safe as another. Meanwhile, a study of airplane crashes by the University of Greenwich, in England, suggests that the safest seat in modern jets is near an exit because of the high risk of fire upon crashing. Wherever you sit, front or back, traveling on a commercial airliner is extremely safe today, in part, because of the accidents in 1951-52 that led to many new safety regulations.

ACKNOWLEDGMENTS

LIKE MOST PEOPLE TODAY I had no idea what happened on that long mountain ridge in December 1951. Nearly everyone is familiar with the incredible story of the tragic crash of Uruguayan rugby players trapped in the Andes Mountains in 1972, but few realize that the first time a large group of plane crash passengers became trapped on a mountain for an extended time happened in the Alleghenies of western New York State. Like the internationally known story from the Andes, it produced heroes who helped save lives. Unlike the story from the Andes, it's been forgotten. And everyone I interviewed for this story said it should not be forgotten.

How many times had I walked or driven over the crest of the hill named for my ancestors and soaked in the magnificent view across the wide Cold Spring Creek Valley toward Bucktooth Ridge? Who knows? It was too many to count. But, I do recall sitting there in the hayfield atop Hoxie Hill on many occasions, where my grandparents and great-grandparents harvested apples from their apple orchard, and scanning the vast forest of the ridge without a clue that it was the site of such tragedy and drama, pain and resilience, heartache and miracle among the crash survivors and those who found them. It is my wish that the story of the 14 survivors, the 26 who lost their lives, and Ruby, whom I've portrayed in *Hang on and Fly*, will never be forgotten.

In 2008, while on a genealogy research trip to my ancestors' farms in western New York State, my uncle, Randall G. Shenefiel, was serving as a companion and tour guide with his minivan as we glided around remote regions of Cattaraugus County that I recalled throughout my boyhood and college years. After touring the old Shenefiel-Hoxie family farms on Hoxie Hill Road where my mother was raised, we climbed to the top of the 1,890 foot high Hoxie Hill to enjoy the view. It felt like I could reach out and touch Bucktooth Ridge. "You should look into the plane crash that happened over there on the mountain," Uncle Randy said, pointing off toward the heavily forested Parker Hill with its modern cell phone tower and flashing lights. "Your grandpa was called to make a path up that hill, and I think he helped bring out some of the victims." Having rooted around four generations in the small farm community of Napoli, New York and finding 1920's vintage artifacts such as my great-grandfather's farm tools, and his name burned into the wall of a wooden horse stall of his old barn, I thought I had discovered just about every significant detail of their rather dull and uneventful lives until I heard this. Of all the years I had spent with my grandfather, David G. Shenefiel, he never mentioned the spectacular and dramatic events of New Year's Eve and New Year's Day in 1951-52 with which he was involved. Not once! But then, the more I thought about it, the more I realized that it was just like my grandfather not to say a word about something so significant that happened so long ago. For example, he never mentioned the devastating and dramatic fire that destroyed his family's farmhouse in Napoli in 1923, for which they had spent the only large sum of money they ever had. A progressive thinker, Grandfather David Shenefiel was more interested in the future than talking about the past. And to him, what he saw and experienced that night at the plane crash scene on the ridge above his parents' farm in Napoli was better left unsaid and forgotten.

So, with my uncle's recommendation, I began researching and gathering everything I could about the tragic passenger plane crash in Napoli on December 29, 1951. I discovered that while the story had been sensationally and widely reported in 1952, by 2008 it was all but buried. Many people had never heard of it. Even those who lived a few miles from the scene had not heard the story. I also discovered that this one tragic event, occurring so recently after two other passenger plane crashes in December 1951, played a major role in shaping public opinion about flying, airline safety regulations, the perception we all have that we're safest in the back of a plane, and the methods used for all future plane crash investigations in the United States. To me, this was too good of a story to be forgotten.

Soon after I began researching this incredible story, I found a scrapbook for sale on eBay. There was some competition to get it but when the auction closed, I had obtained the scrapbook from a seller in Canada. It contains a wonderful array of newspaper articles, photographs and personal notes about the plane crash. The author and maker of the scrapbook remain unknown. It was likely a local resident in Cattaraugus County and to this person I'm grateful for keeping the records. Some of the information in *Hang on and Fly* was gleaned or confirmed by accounts in the scrapbook. It was especially useful to fulfill my personal research rule that every detail needs a second or even a third source or confirmation before it goes into a book. For example, when a source told me that the pilot who landed his C-46 in a snowy field near Lake Ontario appeared on the Arthur Godfrey radio program a few days later, I was able to confirm it through a snippet in a 1951 newspaper article who's author recounted listening to the pilot on *The Arthur Godfrey Show*. Through the many days and nights writing this story, I constantly referred to the articles, photographs, and notes in the scrapbook. But it didn't stop there. Using the Internet, I was able to consult with thousands of newspaper articles written by reporters who plied their profession a generation before me. These men and a few women used pencils and notebooks, boxy press cameras with large flash bulbs, manual typewriters, paper maps, and landline telephones, and their publishers printed their stories with galleys full of hot lead spit out from Linotype machines. To this large group of reporters and photographers, in whose steps I've followed, I'm eternally grateful. They covered the story well.

Hang on and Fly would not have been possible without the assistance of the many family members of plane crash victims, survivors, investigators, rescue teams, police and firefighters, and witnesses and bystanders of the many crash events. Except for a few, who required frequent and friendly persuasion, and who waited months and years to send information, most everyone eagerly participated in my reconstruction of the crash and rescue events, hoping to see the story come to life in a book.

A special thank you is reserved for the sons of Charles and Ruby Bryant of Sawmill Run. Despite the pain, the boys endured for the loss of their mother and father so soon after the trauma of the plane crash, John and Otis Bryant represented the family and sent letters and maps, notes, photographs, and documents. I used them extensively in piecing together the tale of how Ruby Bryant became the first person to help the plane crash survivors stuck on Bucktooth Ridge. Ruby's personal diary was provided, and it gave the emotional details of dealing with her breast cancer illness at a time when she and the family were distracted by the excitement and trauma of the plane crash. Ruby's diary was also a valuable resource for confirming newspaper and investigative accounts of the crash and the rescue. John and Otis Bryant also proofread several chapters in the book and helped reshape the narrative for accuracy and clarity. The family of Kenneth and Margaret Herrick was represented by their grandson, Will Herrick, who shared several photographs and details of the family and their farm on the edge of Bucktooth Ridge. Eagle Free Library in Bliss, New York helped scan some of the Herrick family photographs. Will and his siblings still own much of the old family farm through which George Albert made his staggering hike out of the woods to find the help that the stranded passengers needed to survive. Will and his wife, Louise, still have the old Oliver *Cletrac* crawler tractor which was used to haul survivors, bodies, and plane crash wreckage from Bucktooth Ridge.

Donald and Robert Shenefiel provided information about their mother, Edith, hearing a crash late at night on December 29, 1951. Donald was the only one of the Shenefiel boys who made it to the top of the ridge. Robert stayed at home with a broken knee. Donald remembers about a foot of snow in the woods and more in the fields leading up to the woods on Bucktooth Ridge. Donald Shenefiel also provided a description of the scene when police and volunteers carefully slid toboggans loaded with bodies down the ridge. He was one of the volunteers who held the ropes tied to the toboggans so the bodies wouldn't slide off them.

Salamanca, New York resident Jacklyn Hoard-Beal researched and briefly published a blog about George Albert's heroism after the crash on Bucktooth Ridge. From her blog, since removed from the Internet, I was able to confirm a few details about George's life after the crash. He was troubled by sadness and guilt over the loss of his mother. George's son, George Duane Albert, put me in touch with Phylis Osman, wife of L. Michael Osman, a son of George Albert's sister, Dorothy Albert Osman. The family provided confirmation of many of the details uncovered during research about George's life before and after the crash.

Jack Warf of North Carolina is commended for helping me find survivor stewardess Pearl Ruth Moon at her retirement home near Raleigh. He sent me an email one day explaining that Pearl was living quietly in a small community and that she sometimes told the incredible story of surviving the plane crash, which few believed from a feeble old lady living in a small town nursing home. I am grateful to the staff at Pearl's nursing home and the State of North Carolina for granting me permission for an interview. Pearl was the only crash survivor who was still alive. A son of Lt. William Bischof, Marc Bischof, MD, of Florida, provided me with valuable information and photographs of his father for the book. Lt. Bischof had also saved several press photographs and documents he collected after the crash and Dr. Bischof passed them along to me for research. Some of the photos appear in the book. A special thank you is reserved for the families of pilots, including Joan Athas Visco and her sons, Gus Michael Athas and James Jay Athas. They invited me to Joan's home in New Jersey for a lengthy interview and to share photographs of Gus as a young man and pilot. Also, thanks to the family of CJ Webber, specifically Nancy Webber Harrison for a written biography of her father's life, and Conrad Webber and their sister Barbara for their input and support. Victor Harris' widow, Evelyn Harris Ross contributed many details about her married life with Vic and about his pilot career with Continental Charters, including her intimate January 1952 poem about his last flight. Their son, Raymond Victor Harris, made the arrangements for a written interview with Evelyn and additional correspondence, and he supplied several photographs of his pilot father that he never knew. I also owe a special gratitude to Isobel Rutzebeck, widow of co-pilot Hans Rutzebeck, and their son, Lief Rutzebeck, for sharing some very intimate and adventurous details about Hans. From each of the children of the pilots of Flight 44-2, the shared feelings about their fathers were the same: even though they never got to know their deceased fathers, they all missed them terribly, and they continued to mourn the sad circumstances of the tragedy, 60 years later.

Additionally, for research into the crash of Continental Charters Flight 44-2 I received valuable input from John Redden, who provided photographs and details of his father's involvement in the crash investigation. New York State Police Corporal Eugene Redden was based at the former Allegany, New York police barracks and was heavily involved in the search and rescue. A vintage railroad hobbyist, John Redden also helped identify the trains that ran along the old Erie Railroad tracks in the 1940s and '50s. Frank Vallone of ErieRailroad.org, Railroad.net, and *Trains* magazine, May 1951 also provided assistance with Erie Railroad research. Dan Syrcher is also a rail fan, and he provided aerial photos of Bucktooth Ridge in 2012. Donald Budrejko served as my researcher at the National Archives in Washington, DC. Budrejko known as "Bud" uncovered documents and photographs of the nonsked era that I could never have found in the vast government archives. As a retired Navy aviator, his advice was invaluable. Bud continued working on the research while mourning the loss of his son, Tom, in a helicopter crash. Susan Stahley conducted research at the Cattaraugus County Courthouse and helped uncover parts of the story related to the county's mass mobilization for the rescue and recovery. My aunt and uncle, Barbara and Gilbert Myers helped me portray the rural agrarian lifestyle of Cattaraugus County in the 1940s and 1950s and Gilbert expertly narrated his memories of running the Myers Funeral Home hearse to the crash scene. My mother, Allegra Shenefiel Lake, and my aunt, Margaret Shenefiel Bailey, also provided background information on the rural Cattaraugus County family farm lifestyle that is now long gone from the American scene. George Short provided his memories of walking up Bucktooth Ridge soon after the crash was found, and Bob Lilienthal's wife, Christine Lily, provided confirmation of his role as the first person to reach the scene of the crash. I also wish to thank, in no particular order, Todd Plough of Sawmill Run, Mike Mirwald, Molly Lindahl of Bradford Landmark Society, Art Louderback of the Heinz

History Center, the family of Dawn Brahaney, Courthouse History, Rance Bennett, Mike Schafer, Dorothy Bair, and Julie Close. Also, John Whittaker of the *Jamestown Post-Journal*, and the Painted Hills Genealogy Society, of which John Bryant's wife, Mary, was the founder. Mary Bryant died on May 7, 2015.

I'm also grateful to Dr. Manuel (Manny) Frankel who shared his very emotional and personal story of the loss of his mother and younger brother and sister in the crash. Dr. Frankel sent family photographs and many notes and documents that helped me explain the sad story of the Frankel family. Additional help in researching the Continental Charters plane crash came from Betty Bartok of the Albert Dichak family, and Tom Patterson's widow, Joan Patterson.

For help with research on the crash-landing of the Robin Airlines C-46 in Cobourg, Ontario, Canada, many thanks are reserved for Larry Wilson for sharing his exciting story of that cold, snowy morning in December 1951. Larry sent lengthy notes, and documents and photographs that helped me piece together the comical but dramatic story of the largest passenger plane in the world making a belly landing in the pasture of his family's farm. Some of the Wilson files and photographs are now held in trust by Northumberland County, Ontario, Canada. Emily Cartlidge helped me access the files to compare notes with Larry's highly accurate memory. Additionally, Steven Smelser provided family notes, memories, and photographs, from his uncle, Bruce Smelser. They were compared to official documents and newspaper reports. Jerry (Laufgraben) Lawrence shared his personal memories of riding on the Robin Airlines plane as it made the crash-landing into the snow in Canada. Arrangements for the interview were made by Jerry's wife, Sherri Lawrence. Jerry died before publication of this book. Lee Munsick helped me understand more about Arthur Godfrey during the heyday of his network radio show when Godfrey interviewed Robin Airlines pilot Smelser for a national audience.

Research into the crashes of passenger planes into Elizabeth, New Jersey, began with the CAB's official crash investigation report. I had additional help from Jack Rescoe, who as a young boy, went to the scene of all three crashes. His memories matched the facts gathered by investigators. The New York City law firm of Patterson, Belknap, Webb & Tyler, through the family of Robert P. Patterson, provided background details on the former Secretary of War with its published tribute to the life of Judge Patterson. Thank you to David Clark of the Harry S. Truman Library and Museum for providing documents from the Truman Administration's involvement in the crash investigations. My editor, Judy Mandel provided not only expert advice on grammar, punctuation and style, but she helped with some of the details of her own family's involvement in one of the crashes in Elizabeth. Judy's story is briefly told in this book. She also wrote her own memoir about how her family dealt with the crash. It's titled *Replacement Child* and is available at www.ReplacementChild.com. Robin Reid Sherman confirmed details of the events surrounding the American Airlines crash that killed her father, the pilot. Robin also provided the great photographs of her father, including one taken after he flew a trip for the future King of Saudi Arabia. Gary Haszko, a captain with the Elizabeth Fire Department, provided a photograph of a crash scene, and Robert Sklar provided some background about his family's connection with the crashes. Other sources of information for the Elizabeth crashes are cited in the bibliography section of this book.

Others who provided information for research into crashes profiled in this book include Hal Rothstein with his riveting account of flying B-17s to Europe and Palestine; Luis Asencio Camacho for his account of the Puerto Rican migrant workers crashing in a C-46 into the Atlantic Ocean, and Etan Tal for his father's photographs of the interior of a C-46 passenger plane. Others include Gretchen Wayne, daughter-in-law of actor and producer John Wayne, for her permission to use a description of Wayne's movie, *The High And The Mighty*; the estate of the late Dodie Gann, widow of renowned author Ernest K. Gann, executor attorney Robert S. Mucklestone, and the Gann's daughter, Polly Gann Wrench, for approving use of a derivative of Gann's original phrase, 'hang on, fly' for the book's title. William T. "Bill" Larkins for approving the use of his great original photographs of the nonskeds from the 1940s, and Eddie Coates for helping me understand some of the nonsked business names from this era.

Background information on the C-46 airplane, specifically in World

War II, was provided by Carl Frey Constein, Ph.D. veteran C-46 Hump pilot, educator, and author who sat for me during an interview at his home near Reading, Pennsylvania. Carl also posed for me for a photograph at the cockpit controls of *The Tinker Belle*, one of the few C-46 airplanes still flying today. For Carl's expertise, I'm grateful.

The exceptional cover design was provided by Renee Barratt of *The Cover Counts*. Renee took my general idea and, utilizing great photographs, expertly designed a cover that is factual, compelling and mysterious and portrays the general concept of the story. Maureen Cutajar of *Go Published* designed the book's interior, and Jiban Dahal constructed the map. Proofreaders included Donald Budrejko, Tom and Lisa Rainey, Mike and Mindy King, Tammara Maiden, Jack Rescoe, John Bryant, Otis Bryant, George Duane Albert, and John Redden.

Lastly, I want to emphasize the value of my annual membership in Ancestry.com for conducting historical research. I've subscribed to Ancestry for many years. It allowed me to cross-check dates, names and spellings, occupations, residential locations, military backgrounds, and family members of the many people involved in the crash events of the 1940s and 1950s, including my own. It also helped me find the crash survivors and victim family members living today. I could not have completed this book without it.

BIBLIOGRAPHY

Rutzebeck, Hans Hjalmar Biography, and recordings. Folkways Records, 1980. Smithsonian Folkways.org

Construction of the Alcan Highway in 1942. J. David Rogers, Ph.D. Missouri University of Science and Technology

Shadows on the Koyukuk, Sidney Huntington, Alaska Northwest Books, 1993

Airline Executives and Federal Regulation, Edited by W. David Lewis, Ohio State University Press, 2000

The Best Transportation System in the World. Rose, Seely, Barrett. Ohio State University Press, 2006

A State of War: Florida from 1939 to 1945. Anthony D. Atwood, Florida International University. Sept. 25, 2012

Aviation History.com. Life and Times of Glenn Curtiss

Glenn H. Curtiss Museum, Hammondsport, NY

Curtiss-Wright Corporation, History by decades, company history.

Buffalo History. Aerospace Industry in Buffalo. Glenn Curtiss in Buffalo, NY

Niagara Aerospace Museum. Glenn Curtiss and Curtiss-Wright plants in Buffalo and Western NY

Ghost Squadron/Curtiss C-46 Commando

CAT, Air Asia, Air America – the Company on Taiwan I: Structure and Development. Dr. Joe F. Leeker, March 2013. UT Dallas

Ed Coates Collection.com. Photos of nonsked airplanes

Bill Larkin photos. Used by Permission

Ancestry.com

Tails Through Time

The New York Times

Our Jerusalem.com

Israel Vets.com
Erie Railroad.org
Early Cattaraugus County History, Hope Farm Press
History of Napoli, Ella Sibley, 1920
A History of New York State, Ellis, Frost, Syrett, Carman. Cornell University Press
Gangsters and Organized Crime in Buffalo: History, Hits, and Headquarters. Michael F. Rizzo
Randolph Historical Society, Randolph, New York
Randolph Register, Randolph, New York
EWR Turns 80. A history of Newark Liberty International Airport, Newark Public Library
Civil Aeronautics Board Annual Reports 1946-1954
Civil Aeronautics Board monthly board meetings and memoranda, 1951-1952
Disaster in the Air, Edgar A. Haine. Google Books
Jamestown Post-Journal, Jamestown, New York
News and Courier, Charleston, South Carolina
Philadelphia Inquirer, Philadelphia, Pennsylvania
Pittsburgh Press, Pittsburgh, Pennsylvania
Pittsburgh Post-Gazette, Pittsburgh, Pennsylvania
FAA Aerospace Forecast 1014-2034, Federal Aviation Administration
Heinz History Center, Pittsburgh, Pennsylvania
Syracuse Post-Standard, Syracuse, New York
Schenectady Gazette, Schenectady, New York
Aviation Safety Network, Flight Safety Foundation
Bradford Landmark Society, Bradford, Pennsylvania
Stars and Stripes newspaper, Washington, DC
Daily News-Digest, Springfield, Missouri

ILLUSTRATION CREDITS

Front Cover Images: Randall G. Shenefiel; *Associated Press*.
Back Cover Images: William Sparrow photo courtesy of the Civil Aeronautics Board; *Associated Press*; Continental Charters; Shenefiel-Lake Family Photo Collection
Title Page C-46 Drawing: US Army Air Forces Intelligence Division, 1943- National Archives
Map: Jiban Dihal, Cartographer
Sheet 1: Heinz History Center; Continental Charters; Bryant Family Photo Collection
Sheet 2: US Air Force; Bill Larkins Photo Collection
Sheet 3: Etan J. Tal-Josef Tal Photo Collection; Author's Collection; Randall G. Shenefiel
Sheet 4: Shenefiel-Lake Family Photo Collection; Albert Family Photo Collection
Sheet 5: Bryant Family Photo Collection
Sheet 6: US Army Air Forces-National Archives
Sheet 7: US Army Air Forces-National Archives; Author's Collection
Sheet 8: Shenefiel-Lake Family Photo Collection; Courthouse History; Author's Collection
Sheet 9: Shenefiel-Lake Family Photo Collection; Rance Bennett, Hearse Works
Sheet 10: Bill Larkins Collection; *Pittsburgh Press*; *Pittsburgh Post-Gazette*; Author's Collection; Harris, Rutzebeck, Athas, Webber, Berman-Bruce, Beshears, Martin, and Arnold family photo collections
Sheet 11: Albert, Bischof; Frankel family photo collections
Sheet 12: *Pittsburgh Press*; *Pittsburgh Post-Gazette;* Fairchild Aerial Photos-New York State Archives; *New York Times*; *Bradford Era*; US Air Force, 5th Rescue Squadron

Sheet 13: Geyer, Dichak, Woodward, and Messerlos family collections; US Army-National Archives; Etan J. Tal-Josef Tal Photo Collection

Sheet 14: Nancy Webber Harrison, Webber Family Photo Collection

Sheet 15: Webber, Athas, and Harris family photo collections

Sheet 16: Harris, Athas, and Rutzebeck family photo collections

Sheet 17: Dan Syrcher; Bradford Historical Society; Jack Boucher- Library of Congress HAER collection

Sheet 18: Bryant Family Photo Collection

Sheet 19: Robert C. Lilienthal; Richard Hallberg-*Jamestown Post-Journal*; Randolph Central School-Hilltop

Sheet 20: *Buffalo Evening News; Associated Press*-Walter Stein

Sheet 21: Richard Hallberg-*Jamestown Post-Journal, Associated Press*-Walter Stein

Sheet 22: *Associated Press*-Walter Stein

Sheet 23: *Associated Press*-Walter Stein

Sheet 24: Richard Hallberg-*Jamestown Post-Journal*

Sheet 25: Herrick Family Photo Collection, Will Herrick

Sheet 26: *Pittsburgh Press; Pittsburgh Post-Gazette;* Herrick Family Photo Collection, Will Herrick; Pauline Young-Dawn Brahaney Photo Collection

Sheet 27: John Redden, Redden Family Photo Collection; Richard Hallberg-*Jamestown Post-Journal*

Sheet 28: Richard Hallberg-*Jamestown Post-Journal*

Sheet 29: Richard Hallberg-*Jamestown Post-Journal*

Sheet 30: Richard Hallberg-*Jamestown Post-Journal*

Sheet 31: *Pittsburgh Press; Pittsburgh Post-Gazette*

Sheet 32: US Navy-National Archives; *Long Island Star-Journal; Coronet Magazine-Esquire*

Sheet 33: Bradford Historical Society; Library of Virginia-Adolph B. Rice Studio Collection; Richard Hallberg-*Jamestown Post-Journal*

Sheet 34: Richard Hallberg-*Jamestown Post-Journal; United Press-Corbis; Famous Funnies-Heroic Comics*

Sheet 35: Bill Larkins Collection; Port Authority of NY and NJ; William Sparrow photo courtesy of the Civil Aeronautics Board; *United Press-Corbis*; Lyons Family Photo Collection

Sheet 36: *United Press-Corbis*; US Army Air Forces-National Archives

Sheet 37: Civil Aeronautics Board: Robin Reid Sherman, Reid Family Photos; National Archives
Sheet 38: Robin Reid Sherman, Reid Family Photo Collection
Sheet 39: *United Press-Corbis*; Civil Aeronautics Board-National Archives
Sheet 40: *United Press-Corbis*; Civil Aeronautics Board-National Archives
Sheet 41: Lawrence, Wilson, and Smelser family photo collections
Sheet 42: Harry S. Truman Library; *United Press-Corbis*
Sheet 43: Warner Brothers Pictures; Batjac Productions-Gretchen Wayne
Sheet 44: Will Herrick, Herrick Family Photo Collection
Sheet 45: Bryant Family Photo Collection

www.ingramcontent.com/pod-product-compliance
Lightning Source LLC
Chambersburg PA
CBHW021114300426
44113CB00006B/146